Intro

Welcome to the [P9-DOC-052] *Crossword Book*. You will find herein one hundred puzzles, edited by the legendary Eugene T. Maleska, all of which originally appeared in the pages of *The New York Times* on Mondays.

The *Times* crosswords have traditionally increased in difficulty through the week, with Monday's puzzle meant to get your week started on a confident note, and Saturday's, worked on by most people at home, meant to provide a substantial mental workout. By introducing this new series of *Times* crosswords grouped by the day of the week, it is our hope that puzzlers of every skill will find the book that is just right for them.

This book of Monday crosswords, while no means "easy," is definitely the easiest book of *Times* crosswords available. If you're unsure of your skills or would like to progress to successively more difficult puzzles, this is a good place to start.

Your comments on any aspect of this book are most welcome. Send your comments, queries, or suggestions to me at: Times Crosswords, 201 E. 50th St., New York, NY 10022. If you'd like a reply, please enclose a self-addressed envelope (no stamp needed).

Best wishes for happy puzzling!

Stanley Newman
Managing Director,
Puzzles & Games

Published by Ivy Books:

THE NEW YORK TIMES DAILY CROSSWORD PUZZLES —
MONDAY

THE NEW YORK TIMES DAILY CROSSWORD PUZZLES —
TUESDAY

THE NEW YORK TIMES DAILY CROSSWORD PUZZLES —
WEDNESDAY

THE NEW YORK TIMES DAILY CROSSWORD PUZZLES —
THURSDAY

THE NEW YORK TIMES DAILY CROSSWORD PUZZLES —
FRIDAY

THE NEW YORK TIMES DAILY CROSSWORD PUZZLES —
SATURDAY

THE
NEW YORK TIMES
DAILY CROSSWORD
PUZZLES

MONDAY

VOLUME 1

Edited by
Eugene T. Maleska

IVY/TIMES BOOKS • NEW YORK

Ivy Books
Published by Ballantine Books
Copyright © 1997 by Random House, Inc.

http://www.randomhouse.com

ISBN 0-8041-1579-6

Text design and typography by Mark Frnka

Printed in Canada

First Edition: February 1997

10 9 8 7 6

THE
NEW YORK TIMES
DAILY CROSSWORD
PUZZLES

MONDAY

VOLUME 1

ACROSS

1 Popular TV war sitcom
5 Nose-bag filler
9 Golden Gloves contests
14 Treaty associate
15 Early stringed instrument
16 Golf "army" leader
17 Seated upon
18 Writer Lazarus
19 Mother-of-pearl
20 First U.S.-born saint
23 Showed the way
24 Wing
25 Public outburst
27 Silent-screen star Gloria
31 Found treasure
33 National sports org.
34 Tennyson's Arden
37 Severe
39 Actress Lollobrigida
41 Thin cooked cereal
43 O'Neill's "__ Christie"
44 "Toys in the __," Hellman play
46 Parisian mothers
48 Longing for Japanese money?
49 Farm storage structures
51 Weight added for stability
53 Anglo-Saxon slaves
55 "Life With Father" author
56 Provide weapons
58 G.K. Chesterton's clerical sleuth
64 __ and desist
66 Make over
67 "Dies __"
68 Less exciting
69 Covering for a 13 Down
70 Walking stick
71 Pours forth
72 Go out with
73 Coaster

DOWN

1 Royal form of address
2 Singing voice
3 Coin opening
4 Punctuation mark
5 Too lengthy
6 Intentions
7 Large volume
8 Wood strips
9 Flags
10 "__ pro nobis"
11 Chekhov play: 1899
12 Become fatigued
13 Plant starter
21 Otherwise
22 Nov. preceder
26 Part of N.B.
27 Heroic prose tale
28 Tarries
29 Rosalind Russell title role
30 Standard

2

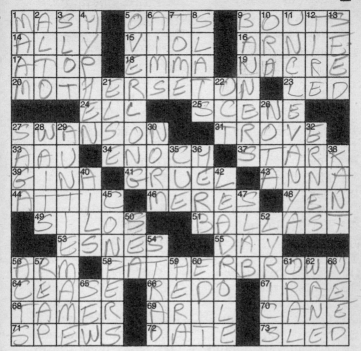

The grid is filled in (handwritten) as follows:

Across:
1. MASH
5. OATS
9. BOUTS
14. ALLY
15. VIOL
16. ARNIE
17. ATOP
18. EMMA
19. NACRE
20. MOTHERSETON
23. LED
24. ELL
25. SCENE
27. SWANSON
30. TROVE
33. AAU
34. ENOCH
37. STARK
39. GINA
41. GRUEL
42. ANNA
44. ATTIC
46. MERES
49. SILOS
51. BALLAST
53. ESNES
54. DAY
55. DAY
56. ORM
58. FATHERBROWN
64. CEASE
66. REDO
67. RAE
68. TAMER
69. ARIL
70. CANE
71. SPEWS
72. DATE
73. SLED

32 Cousins of fish hawks
35 Minnesota Fats implement
36 Marjoram, e.g.
38 "Critique of Pure Reason" author
40 Feels under the weather
42 Starring part
45 Bestows upon
47 House foundation

50 Neptune's home
52 Ira Gershwin forte
54 Fine violin, for short
56 Takes measures
57 Gather in
59 Wife of Zeus
60 Redact
61 Kind of history
62 Slack off
63 Indigence
65 Ply a needle

3

ACROSS

1 Box
5 A Celt
9 Thin coin
13 Scarlett O'Hara's home
14 Old Norse symbols
16 __ of March
17 Collar or jacket
18 Unit or tract follower
19 Melodies
20 Song from "A Chorus Line"
23 Former French coin
24 Public vehicle
25 Sports enthusiast
28 Caustic remark
32 Depot on a RR
35 Greek god of war
37 Saw or hammer
38 A Philippine island
40 Song identified with Ruth Etting
43 Odor
44 British carbine
45 Region
46 Cereal spike
47 Serves
50 Blunder
51 Fruit drink
52 Lubricant
54 First popular song that won an Emmy
63 Assert
64 Stock-exchange memberships
65 Stumble
66 Start of Caesar's message
67 Follow
68 Ireland, to 5 Across
69 Poker stake
70 Despot
71 Rank

DOWN

1 Fret
2 Trail
3 Venezuelan copper center
4 Is in a rage
5 Receive a college degree
6 Gold: Comb. form
7 Wife of Geraint
8 Sheet of paper
9 Tunes in the radio
10 One's own: Comb. form
11 "Jeopardy" creator Griffin
12 To be, to Tiberius
15 Supercilious people
21 Large moths
22 Cuban dance
25 Not true
26 Fragrance
27 At no time
29 Perch
30 Spanish tribunal
31 Ethan or Woody

4

32 Cubic meter
33 One who domesticates
34 Close to, in poesy
36 Parisian's condiment
39 Actress Gardner
41 Rimsky-Korsakov opera
42 One who sanctions
48 Taut
49 Title Churchill had
51 Eagle's nest

53 Metric liquid measure
54 Molten rock
55 Hot spot
56 Air passage
57 Disfigurement on a car
58 Bulk
59 Polynesian spirit
60 Operatic offering
61 Encircled
62 Fencing sword

ACROSS

1 Nile ophidians
5 Hitch
9 Growl
13 Thrash
14 Domesticates
16 Jacob's third son
17 Double negative
18 Former Broadway hit
19 Muscat site
20 "The Color Purple" star
23 Kind of signal
24 Dead duck
25 R.S.V.P. part
26 __ Aviv
27 Genetic letters
29 An abrasive
31 Dandling site
33 Ditty bag's cousin
36 Map detail
37 Fuss
40 Juliet's beloved
43 Wading bird
44 One of the tenses
48 Driving reversals
50 Paddle's next of kin
52 Corp. boss
53 "__ in the bag"
54 Voltaire's religion
57 Jibe
59 Without value
62 Ningpo nanny

63 Ranch in "Giant"
64 Opposite of vive
66 Source of poi
67 "Wait Until Dark" actor
68 Labels
69 Some are tight
70 Like-minded group
71 Seethe

DOWN

1 Grain beard
2 Theatrical producers
3 Tiny opening
4 Frighten
5 Short distance
6 Aircraft crewman
7 Pablo's pal
8 Grow older
9 Rounded lump
10 Bane
11 Cupidity
12 Curl
15 Orchid tubers
21 "__ the ramparts . . ."
22 Celtic priest
23 N.Y.S.E. listing
28 Recent: Prefix
30 L-Q connection
32 Water pitcher
34 __ tree (cornered)

6

35 Peculiar to a
particular group
38 John Wayne
western
39 Guido's high note
40 Fallen into decay
41 Low, cushioned seat
42 Hot-dog spread
45 Circus performer
46 Oozing
47 Kind of dance

49 Junipero __,
Spanish
missionary
51 Stadium cheer
55 Brain passages
56 Quiver
58 Blame bearers
60 "__ Afraid of
Virginia Woolf?"
61 Desire
65 Vienna-to-Graz dir.

ACROSS

1 Caesar or Waldorf
6 Molten rock in the earth
11 Boone or Benatar
14 Opera part
15 Register
16 Ratite bird
17 Film in which Paul Newman played a detective
20 What Othello did to Desdemona
21 Part of ancient Asia Minor
22 Gaelic
23 Actor Cariou
24 Actress Lombard
28 Film with Newman as a lawyer, with "The"
32 Unique persons
33 Lock of hair
35 Neon, for one
36 Slightly open
37 Greenland air base
38 Snug
39 Policeman, to a hood
40 Scent
41 Lone Ranger's aide
42 Film with Newman as a pool shark, with "The"
44 Unfasten
45 Kind
46 Casino token
48 Magna cum __

51 " 'Mid __ and palaces . . .": Payne
56 Film in which Newman gets revenge
58 Digit
59 Large animal
60 Metal mass
61 Newman western
62 Symbols of bondage
63 Bank offerings

DOWN

1 Concordes, e.g.
2 Eight, in Essen
3 Salacious look
4 Forever __ day
5 Weedy rye grasses
6 Whimpers
7 Year, in Annecy
8 Grating
9 "Hiroshima __ Amour"
10 North African port
11 Oaxaca laborer
12 Mine, in Amiens
13 City near Tolstoy's home
18 Folklore monster
19 Walden, e.g.
23 __-majesté
24 Rockne was one
25 Pear type
26 Harvests
27 Hockey great
28 Soft palates
29 Sacred pictures

8

30 Hindu group
31 Test, as a garment
33 Son of Odin
34 Daiquiri base
37 Migration
38 Bill's partner
40 High Commissioner for Egypt: 1919–25
41 Square-rigger feature
43 Companion of time
44 Writer O'Flaherty
46 Near

47 Weighs
48 Lattice part
49 "__ Ben Adhem": Hunt
50 Employed
51 Pikes __
52 Of an armbone: Comb. form
53 Latvian port
54 Coll. course
55 Gels
57 Co. head

ACROSS

1 Lunch, e.g.
5 Indigo
9 Lab animals' milieus
14 "Aeneid" starter
15 Fogy
16 Kind of acid
17 Reporters' subject on February 2
19 Annie's companion
20 Rounded hills
21 "__ Fall in Love," 1933 song
23 Romaine lettuce
24 Floor covering
26 Petroleum
28 Seasonal listlessness
34 Show to be true
38 Draft status
39 Granular snow
40 A son of Leah
41 Swiftly
42 Follow closely
43 Purse stuffers
44 Fulfilled, as a promise
45 Jackassery
46 Shakespeare play, with "The"
49 Fuss
50 Of part of the eye
55 Poke
58 Monogram pt.
61 Isolated mathematical point
62 Skipper's "Halt!"
64 Radio character who "knows"
66 Very, in music
67 Rescue
68 Actress Velez
69 Curse
70 Inspired reverence
71 W.W. II vessels

DOWN

1 Igneous-rock producer
2 Slip
3 Love, in Livorno
4 Author Hobson
5 Makes sense
6 Japanese drama
7 Fan-club hero
8 Theater part
9 Range backbone
10 Drs.' org.
11 Kind of oxide
12 Inner: Comb. form
13 Oriental sauces
18 Vikings
22 Garments for Cato
25 Feels one's way
27 Slow, in music
29 Lacking skill
30 Bees' collection
31 Calf meat
32 Wicked
33 Depend (on)

10

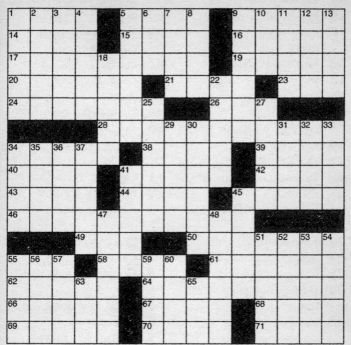

34 Word with man or share
35 Painter Guido __
36 Kitchen feature
37 Outlook
41 City SE of Cleveland
45 "To __ a pail of water"
47 Redactor
48 Rented
51 On the whole

52 Complication
53 Take as one's own
54 George Eliot's mate
55 Toast spreads
56 Admit frankly
57 Cotton bundle
59 "__ boy!"
60 Spell of warm weather
63 RR depot
65 Abel's mother

ACROSS

1 Greek letters
5 More talented
10 Bolshevik's bête noire
14 Marshal Wyatt __
15 Statue covering
16 Lab burner
17 Large dogs
19 Black, to Blake
20 Lithoid
21 Tuckered out
22 Chemical endings
23 Pitcher
24 French secular clergymen
27 Like a spellbinder
31 Job
33 Cuckoopint, e.g.
34 Reverence plus fear
36 Greets the opposing team
37 Latin dance
39 Tomtit
40 From __ Z
41 Blend
42 Like some questions
44 Counselors
47 Methods: Abbr.
48 Handle
49 Like
51 Intact
53 Fár from recalcitrant

58 Tow
59 Small, high-spirited dog
60 "Comus" composer
61 Lazed
62 Best or Ferber
63 Neat
64 Orchestra section
65 Actual

DOWN

1 Cols.' commands
2 Rodgers lyricist
3 Popular sandwich cookie
4 Silky-coated dogs
5 Confound
6 Cook in a tightly closed pot
7 Lean and long
8 Fencing sword
9 Thing, to Darrow
10 Home of a brave
11 Some powerful dogs
12 Soon
13 Rave's partner
18 High-strung
21 What Spitz has done well
23 Peer
24 "Dancing Queen" singers
25 Flora and fauna
26 Tracking dog

28 Debussy composition
29 Sphere; globe
30 Whistle sound
32 Verb on a penny
35 What skimpers hope to make meet
38 Employ
39 Traveler
41 Drum's partner
43 Willow
45 Hollow

46 Like some peanuts
50 What malamutes pull
51 "__ Price Glory?"
52 Mata __
53 Style
54 Shaft on a car
55 Dwell
56 Actress Olin
57 Of an epoch
59 An evergreen

ACROSS

1 Dwindles
5 Fen
10 What to keep from the door
14 Capriole or jeté
15 Where Pocatello is
16 On __ (equivalent)
17 Actress Lanchester
18 Sturdy fabric
19 It goes oom-pah-pah
20 Hangers-on of a sort
23 Dowdy
24 Pinna's organ
25 Burst of activity
29 Casino patron
33 "Love __ Many-Splendored Thing"
36 Begone!
38 Dough
39 Wallflower
43 Magna cum __
44 Soccer great
45 Bandleader Brown
46 Nest robbers
48 Michener best seller
51 "__ Maria"
52 Fling
56 Do-gooder of a sort
61 Surrealist Salvador
63 Maugham's __ Thompson

64 A wife of Esau
65 Cupid
66 Coral island
67 Rudner or Hayworth
68 Bulb unit
69 U.K. part
70 By and by

DOWN

1 Chosen
2 Politician Abzug
3 Elementary
4 Punishes a naughty child
5 French region
6 Mideast gulf
7 Knelled
8 Hood's knife
9 More comfy
10 Where Napoleon was defeated
11 Composition
12 Chem. room
13 __ Filippo Lippi
21 Rip-off
22 Ruth's mother-in-law
26 Invite
27 Steamer, e.g.
28 Painter of water lilies
30 Droop
31 Robert __
32 Snitches
33 Wight, for one

14

34 Catch flies
35 Cut __ (jitterbug)
37 Eye amorously
40 Utopia seeker
41 Audacity
42 Rub the wrong way
47 Fluctuate
49 Blonde shade
50 Stalks of asparagus
53 Active beginner

54 A Muse
55 Patriot Allen
56 A __ on one's escutcheon
57 Computer fare
58 Golden calf, for one
59 Cairo's river
60 Thickens
61 "Into a sea of __": Eugene Field
62 Parseghian

ACROSS

1 Spanish house
5 Sphere of work
9 Cuts of lamb
14 Pindaric works
15 Sitarist Shankar
16 Up's partner
17 Employer of Jane Eyre
19 Trouble
20 __ Nouveau
21 Movie cult figure
22 Modify fittingly
23 Mitigate
25 Cavalry weapon
27 Actor Sharif
29 In the van
33 Ned Buntline hero
37 Civil War veterans' org.
38 Director Kazan
39 Caustic
40 Speck
41 M.I.T. grad.
42 Legendary kidnap victim
46 Hobby
48 Inevitable
49 Musical composition
51 Tantalizes
55 Famous theater couple
57 "Ave atque __"
59 What shad are prized for
60 Edith Cavell, for one
61 Ill-fated English settlement
63 "Ragged Dick" author
64 Mine entrance
65 Small bills
66 Sanctify
67 NL team
68 "Le __ Goriot" Balzac

DOWN

1 Yellowish red
2 Worship
3 Denominations
4 Cigar residue
5 Arms depot
6 Pro __ (in proportion)
7 Ties
8 Make public
9 Unfair treatment
10 Having entrained
11 Business org.
12 Composer Weill
13 Farmyard structure
18 Swelling
22 First murder victim
24 Couch's cousin
26 Outlanders
28 Used wheels
30 Stravinsky
31 Former Haig command
32 Grizzled

16

33 Alert electronically
34 Larger forearm bone
35 Fruit trees
36 By the __ (incidentally)
40 News story
42 Batters like Ruth
43 Kin of ostriches
44 Wall sockets
45 Rids (of)

47 Verb forms
50 Escape by trickery
52 Inclined (to)
53 Babel structure
54 Meaning
55 Letup
56 Yen
58 Surrounded by
60 Collar
61 Sound harshly
62 Go one better

ACROSS

1 Confesses, with "up"
5 Quite distantly
9 Recipe abbr.
13 Antitheses of midnights
15 Restricted area
16 Choirboy's collar
17 "Peanuts," e.g.
19 Threesome
20 Raise
21 Mrs., in Madrid
23 Worldwide labor org.
24 Vote into office
26 Production in general
28 Shiite, for one
31 Uncover
33 Total: Abbr.
34 Coming out
37 Etruscan king __ Porsena
39 Speaks harshly
41 Dirk of yore
42 Doodads
44 Gangster's gun
45 This might be soft
46 Rolls along easily
49 Caught
51 Intelligent
53 Pub drink
54 Potato part
56 Olympics athlete, often
60 Wild try
62 Ecdysiast's specialty
64 Allowance for weight
65 EPA concern
66 Ruhr city
67 Formerly
68 "__ is the forest primeval . . ."
69 Londoner's radial

DOWN

1 Twice halved
2 Type of gatherer
3 Alaskan city
4 Whine pathetically
5 Nahuatl conquered by Cortés
6 In favor of
7 Flavoring for a Cannes cordial
8 Chides
9 Vietnamese New Year
10 Youths
11 French soldier
12 Snobbish one
14 Map feature
18 Watch part
22 Leopold or Mischa
25 Long locks
27 Labels
28 Fountain order

18

29 Persian poet	**48** Swear (to)
30 Shift shiftlessly	**49** Moisten meat
32 Royal one: Abbr.	**50** Where a communion
35 Straight	is given
36 Obtains	**52** Posts
38 Hitch in plans	**55** Engrave with
39 "__, go!"	acid
40 LL.B. holder	**57** This does it
43 Swiss painter	**58** Consumer
Paul	**59** M. Coty
46 David is one	**61** Wager
47 Declaim	**63** Louis XIV, e.g.

ACROSS

1 Gypsy __
5 Driving force
10 Actor Alda
14 Away from the gusts
15 Late, in Siena
16 Pottery
17 Cauterize
18 Church instrument
19 On the briny
20 Gusty-day advice
23 __ Moines
24 Opposite of arr.
25 Astonishes
29 Inter __
31 Possesses
34 Like Silver's rider
35 Patton portrayer
36 Unit
37 Mitchell masterpiece
41 Canton follower
42 Pierre's notions
43 Large land mass
44 Harrison or Reed
45 Retreats
46 Weasel's cousin
48 Lion in the sky
49 Rhine tributary
50 Headed for Sugar Loaf Mountain
59 Thin
60 Type of type

61 Portal
62 Concerning
63 Similar
64 Sicilian volcano
65 Tablets
66 Allotted
67 Genuine

DOWN

1 Series starring 10 Across
2 Margarine
3 Duck or color
4 Group of wildebeests
5 Gems
6 Pastries
7 Hence
8 "Let's call it __"
9 Obelisk, e.g.
10 Not in the dark
11 Part of an eyelid
12 Scope
13 Trim
21 Sappho creation
22 Conserve of grapes
25 Author Horatio
26 Deer's cousin
27 Append
28 American's omega
29 Yearns
30 Parcels of land
31 Raise

20

32 Broadway musical: 1977
33 Type of car
35 British gun
38 Enlarge
39 Graphic symbol
40 Conflict
46 Equipped with crew
47 Actor Carney
48 Queues

49 Not napping
50 Toss
51 Singer Horne
52 Three feet
53 1996 candidate
54 Neglect to include
55 Frankfurt's river
56 Old-school method
57 One of the Hebrides
58 Of the mouth

ACROSS

1 Fisherman's barbed spear
5 Thick slice
9 Ointment
13 __ Range, U.S.S.R.
14 "__ We Dance?": 1951 hit song
15 Jai __
16 Actress Albright
17 Rice dish
18 Promontory
19 Get rich via opportunism
22 Cause to incline
23 Ta-ta
24 Show displeasure
27 Broadway, e.g., in slang
32 Manifest
33 River at Orléans
34 Evangelist's inst. at Tulsa
35 Squarish
36 Steak or table preceder
37 Actor Cooper
38 D.D.E.
39 He wrote "John Brown's Body"
40 Slipped
41 Rainy-day resources
43 "__ Fideles"
44 Above, poetically
45 "M*A*S*H" actor

46 People with common interests
54 Saharan
55 Excessive
56 Bern's river
57 Dickens girl
58 Feigned
59 "Trinity" author
60 __ of Capri
61 Caspian et al.
62 Illustrator Rockwell __

DOWN

1 Chasm
2 Indonesia's __ Islands
3 F.D.R.'s dog
4 Excessive praise
5 Polo, for one
6 "Namouna" composer
7 Comedian King
8 Colorful songster
9 Interdicted
10 To shelter, on a ship
11 Jeune fille
12 Fine spray
14 Type of wheat
20 Allusion
21 "Auld Lang __"
24 Redbreast
25 Draw forth
26 Battle of the __
27 Grimaces

22

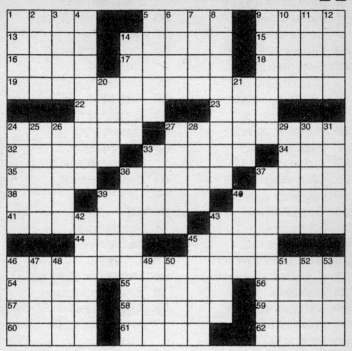

28 "__ She Sweet?":
1927 song
29 Booms
30 Canadian decree
31 __ Maupassant
33 Protracted
36 Arranges again
37 Large extinct bird
39 Honey bunch
40 Collection of Old
Norse poetry
42 Unsteady gait

43 ". . . __ and hungry
look": Shak.
45 Wig styles
46 Rumanian coins
47 Angers
48 Brooklet
49 Chimney duct
50 "__ boy!"
51 Long-eared
mammal
52 Ireland
53 The others

ACROSS

1 Venetian traveler
5 Golden Horde member
10 Novelist Wister
14 Composer Stravinsky
15 Dispense with nuptials
16 Member of the Hindu trinity
17 Actress from Washington
19 Misstep
20 Singer from Michigan
21 Troubles
22 Buddhist branch
23 Anagram for dote
25 Subsided gradually
29 TV performer's reward for reruns
33 Aids a felon
34 Triangular sail
35 Slow, to Mehta
36 Stinging sensation
37 Springsteen's birthplace
38 Spanish length unit
39 Actor Christopher
41 Hideaway
42 Yearned
43 Appraiser
45 Sews loosely
46 Bridge position

47 Small island
48 Peat, for one
50 Actor from Egypt
57 Brit.
58 Drummer from England
59 Suit to __
60 Singer John
61 Hautboy
62 Ripped
63 Revue components
64 Candy flavor

DOWN

1 __-à-terre
2 Make eyes at
3 Lounge
4 Preacher Roberts
5 Started to cry
6 Outlander
7 Whole step, in music
8 Gibbons
9 Adjusts the alarm clock
10 Actor-writer from Georgia
11 Historian from Massachusetts
12 Wicked
13 Siestas
18 Demolishes
24 Neat's-foot __
25 Insect's lips
26 "__ Irish Rose"

24

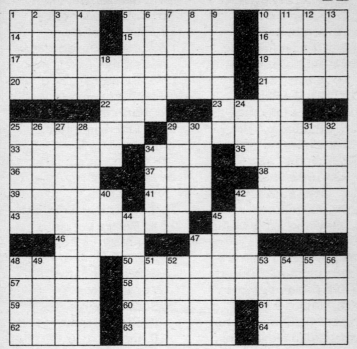

27 Singer from
New York
28 Entertainer
from New York
29 Staircase part
30 Author of
"My People"
31 Coincide
32 Oodles
34 A martial art
40 Curve
42 Tracks

44 Caches
45 Buffaloes
47 Patois
48 Daring deed
49 Word in the
Golden Rule
51 Exploit, in a way
52 Opponent
53 Energy source
54 Physics Nobelist
55 Do laundry work
56 Guitar part

ACROSS

1 At a distance
5 Ring
9 Hit show
14 Myrna Loy role
15 Soil: Comb. form
16 Cellist Casals
17 Tinsel, e.g.
18 Lynx becomes list maker
20 Collected
22 Weds
23 1963 Paul Newman film
24 Ice follower
26 Canonized woman of France
27 Speeder's snare
30 Invited
32 Toklas or Faye
33 Major follower
34 Relative of a shawm
38 Polio conqueror
39 Passé
40 __ voce
41 Upgrade
42 "Rock of __"
43 Fictional Pan
44 Gantry or Fudd
46 Passageways in the brain
47 Vol. measures
50 Like some rooms
51 Teachers' org.
52 Roofed-in gallery
54 Wounds

58 Otary becomes document closure
61 Simba, for one
62 Fruit for Eve
63 Japanese aborigine
64 Otherwise
65 Remains
66 Suffix meaning "inhabitants"
67 Like some hair

DOWN

1 Pilaster
2 Shape
3 Operatic highlight
4 Butter becomes shaky
5 Walked to and fro
6 Minced oath
7 Knack
8 Mauna __
9 Kind of cake
10 Crèche trio
11 Touches upon
12 Highway hazard
13 Kind of play or sense
19 Moved furtively
21 Certain
24 Cave dweller becomes source of light
25 Kefauver
27 Reckless
28 Jai __
29 __ pickle

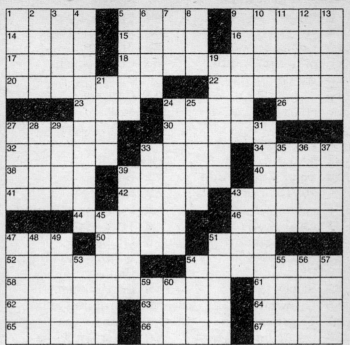

31 Bird becomes
neatly joined
33 Gung-ho
35 Munch
36 Finished
37 Parts of pitchers
39 Father __ (Joseph
de Veuster)
43 Mud formations
45 Speech beginning
47 These have
habitaciones

48 Moved like a
reptile
49 __ Flow
51 Tie
53 Co-fighter
54 Rustic road
55 Unctuous
56 Kind of dive
57 Prune: Scot.
59 Cheerful, in
Cherbourg
60 Quipper

ACROSS

1 A kind of waist
5 Dialect
10 Morose
14 Composer of the oratorio "Judith"
15 Ice-cream flavor
16 Assumed character
17 Blabbed
20 Rips into shreds
21 Mysteries
22 Seat of the Krupp steel works
23 Heck's cousin
24 Field of Merce Cunningham
27 Remember
32 Elec. unit
35 Places to go swimming
37 Tony's relative
38 Spoke imprudently
42 Nonrepresentational Swiss painter
43 Cristofori made the first one: 1709
44 Randy's skating partner
45 Crater lake near Rome
48 Attack
50 Shaft of a wheel
52 Vigorous vitality
56 Residential area of Queens

60 Saints' days in Sevilla
62 Flatter
64 High-strung
65 Accustom
66 Commune in Sicily
67 Concept
68 Mails
69 Rigel is one

DOWN

1 Scrap
2 Harps: Sp.
3 States of agitation
4 Threw stones
5 Mimic
6 Scarlet and cherry
7 Heater
8 Earthy pigment
9 Pertaining to the palm
10 Diver Louganis
11 Rich soil
12 Forearm bone
13 Chow
18 See 31 Down
19 Nosh
23 Comedian Dom
25 Dreamland
26 Leghorn's home
28 Camping gear
29 Touch upon
30 Turkish coin
31 With 18 Down, a Delaware tribe

14

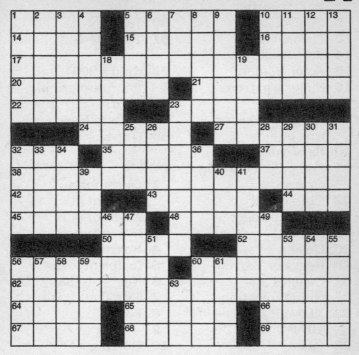

32 An Aleutian island
33 Shopping area
34 Commoner
36 ERA or RBI
39 Large parrot
40 Yoko __
41 __-me-not
46 Ex-capital of
   Japan
47 Binary
   compounds
49 Drives a dog team

51 "Mule Train"
   singer
53 Chore
54 Peruvian city
55 Actor Werner
56 Italian wine center
57 Plane or nail
58 Exam answer
59 Range in Greece
60 Glenn or Henry
61 Feminine suffixes
63 Cask

29

ACROSS

1 Bench garb
5 Split
10 Dome, e.g.
14 Soviet lake
15 Actor Romero
16 Sailor's patron saint
17 Reggie Jackson was one
20 Pass catcher
21 Followed a curving course
22 Chin cover
23 Bacon bringer
25 Put-on
26 Upsets
28 Boggs or Barrett
32 Coach's communication
33 NL MVP in 1971
35 Past
36 Musial was one
40 "You __ Love": Kern
41 Playing surface
42 Grumpy state
43 Post-loss reaction, sometimes
45 A Dahl
47 Connector
48 Profession
50 Cy Young, e.g.
53 Appointments
54 Actress Lupino
57 Comiskey Park team
60 Tease
61 Tommie and James
62 Cato's 2051
63 Roundup phrase: Abbr.
64 Bottom level
65 Dupes

DOWN

1 Quest for a pennant
2 Algerian port
3 U.S. symbols
4 Inventor Whitney
5 Incipient forest
6 Nez __, Indian tribe
7 TV's Lou Grant
8 Foray
9 __ la la
10 Goren goof
11 Gymnast Korbut
12 Ephah fraction
13 Sheep pen
18 Kind of team
19 Lowered
24 Florence's river
25 Actress Teri
26 Syrian statesman
27 Metric unit in England
28 Certain lingerie
29 Base-stealer's study re a pitcher

30

30 Twice
31 "The Prince of Tides" star
33 Autocrat
34 Lt.'s "birthplace"
37 Sudan neighbor
38 Crocus
39 England, to W.S.
44 Part's partner
45 Strikeout ___, such as Clemens
46 Repose

48 Quail
49 Whence the phoenix rises
50 Grange unit
51 Jot
52 Verdi opera
53 Kelly's swamp dweller
55 Charity
56 W.W. II foe
58 Trench: Scot.
59 Big bird

ACROSS

1 Witticisms
6 Brag
11 Brit. defenders
14 What "ye faithful" do
15 Printers' daggers
16 Wallach or Whitney
17 Seemingly contradictory
19 Bagel accompaniment
20 Comes forth
21 Make ineffective
23 Rouse
24 Saharan antelope
25 Saturn's wife
28 Ancient Jewish ascetic
30 Zhivago's love
33 Actor Neeson
35 Broadcast
36 Like __ of bricks
37 Skirt style
38 Crumbly earth deposits
40 The act of: Br. suffix
41 A Slaughter
42 Elec. unit
43 Bondage
44 Beat pounders
45 Wrestle
49 Goddess of night
50 Comics Viking

52 Vehicle for Judd Hirsch
54 Green stuff
56 Dressing ingredient
60 Have
61 Extremist socialist faction
63 Director Spike
64 Ryan or Dunne
65 For rent
66 Teeth spec.'s deg.
67 Curtain fabric
68 Attic promenades

DOWN

1 Make fun of
2 Cheese town
3 Carolina rail
4 Across: Prefix
5 Composed
6 Louis and Liston
7 Sashes in Sendai
8 N.R.C. predecessor
9 Defames
10 Like some roofs
11 Workaholic's need
12 "I'm quite illiterate, but I read __" Salinger
13 Idée __
18 Elevator man
22 Milky Way, e.g.
24 Indigo
25 Veracruz Indian
26 Serkin's instrument

32

16

27 Instruments for
Getz and Parker
29 Wyatt's family
31 Full of crows
32 Ell
34 Mass book
38 W.W. I spy
39 Asian river
46 Flower part
47 Words after
"ooh" and "tra"
48 Elevates

51 Street urchin
53 Dostoyevsky's
"The __"
54 Shape
55 Was indebted
56 __-Japanese War
57 Site of Akershus
Castle
58 Virginia willow
59 Utah Beach craft
62 Foreign: Comb.
form

ACROSS

1 Auricular
5 Take away
10 Réunion et al.
14 "Abide __ Me,"
   noted hymn
15 Vex
16 Get stuck, in a way
17 Suffix with depend
18 Made of a cereal
19 Nuisance
20 Symbol of high
   authority
23 But, to Virgil
24 Suffix with musket
25 Measures of length
28 Eleventh century
   date
31 "Watch your __!"
34 Timetable abbr.
35 Dyes
38 Cupid, to Athena
40 Symbol of treachery
43 South American
   monkey
44 Calm
45 Stage scenery
46 Times after sunsets,
   to poets
48 HI's former status
49 Lascivious looks
51 Pol. epithet since
   1880
53 Balsam, e.g.
54 "The __!"
   (Depression cry)

62 Half a game's name
63 Danger
64 Head table's locale
66 Tears
67 Opt
68 To be, to Cato
69 Elegant
70 Gives off fumes
71 Boil slowly

DOWN

1 Be under obligation
2 Light coloring
3 Yearn
4 Partner of crackers
5 Tolerated
6 Race
7 Word of disgust
8 Expression of
   understanding
9 "Honi soit qui
   mal y __"
10 International
   dealer
11 Stead
12 Formerly, formerly
13 One of Cain's
   brothers
21 German state
22 Engr. degrees
25 Gone by
26 Golfer Palmer
27 Container for eggs
28 He painted
   "Olympia"
29 British quart

34

30 "A nest of robins __ hair"

32 Wipe out

33 Tough question

36 Scale notes

37 Rep.'s counterpart

39 Fast planes

41 Cero or croaker

42 Very cold

47 Call for help

50 Decays gradually

52 Kind of tiger

53 Materials for fedoras

54 Loom threads

55 Hodgepodge

56 Track measures

57 TV part

58 Pear or apple

59 Rube

60 Kiln

61 Go skyward

65 "And __ a fine seam"

ACROSS

1 Bogged down
6 Sire, to a dam
10 Lights-out signal
14 Character in "The Seagull"
15 Actor Thicke
16 "I cannot tell __"
17 Shrewd; astute
18 Derby winner: 1966
20 Gunpowder or Twankay
21 Seattle __, Triple Crown winner
23 Hostess Perle
24 Deserves
26 Belmont winner: 1979
28 Highest point
30 Eschew
31 Jockey
32 Derby winner: 1974
36 Gerund's end
37 Garçon's handout
38 Gibbon
39 Preakness winner: 1972
42 Instrument for Nero
44 Subordinate to
45 Medicinal plants
46 Basketball's inflatable lining
49 Maker of toy trucks
50 Best
51 Blas and Hodges
52 See 64 Across
55 Derby winner: 1954
58 Likeness
60 Equal, in France
61 Middle of Q.E.D.
62 Classical farewells
63 Village of yore
64 With 52 Across and 45 Down, Derby winner: 1982
65 Put into use

DOWN

1 Fine spray
2 "Dies __"
3 Derby winner: 1972
4 P.O. purchase
5 Derby winner: 1878
6 Fashions
7 "There ought to be __"
8 Greek letter
9 Spanish queen
10 Assumes
11 Heeling, at sea
12 Caravel of 1492
13 Actor George
19 Insect stage
22 Superman foe __ Luthor
25 Soul, in Soissons
26 Tale
27 Caen's river
28 Nursery item
29 The odds
30 Way chaser

32 Pole for tossing
33 Derby winner: 1902
34 Actor Andrews
35 Aphrodite's son
37 Relinquish
40 He trained Spectacular Bid
41 The witch of __
42 Derby winner: 1944
43 Autograph

45 See 64 Across
46 Presaged
47 Hasta __
48 Rose essence
49 Append
51 No-see-um
53 City of Hungary
54 "__ we forget"
56 Ryan or Foster
57 Cash stash, for short
59 Boxer Baer

ACROSS

1 Captain of the Pequod
5 It must go on
9 Fundamentals
13 Salami shop
14 Man in a cage
16 Pinball problem
17 Spoken
18 Allan-__
19 Inter __ (among other things)
20 Snooker's relative
22 X years before Hastings
23 Garrison
24 Approved
26 Hercules's dozen
29 Brawny
31 Nimble
32 Outscores
33 Feed-bag morsel
36 Canasta play
37 Aluminum wraps
38 Unadorned
39 Adult elver
40 Genetic duplicate
41 Metric measure
42 Guarantee
44 Beach Boy Brian
45 Eli's rival
47 Medicine ball?
48 Ye follower
49 Quartering

54 Compete against the clock
55 Lake Geneva spa
56 Alley Oop's love
58 Cupid
59 Cut a rug
60 Exigency
61 Lorelei Lee's creator
62 __-do-well
63 Coaster

DOWN

1 Bother
2 Sage or mint
3 Jai __
4 Wallet
5 Elevator's alternative
6 Attacked
7 The Tentmaker
8 Fuse metal
9 Cossack chief
10 Certain butters
11 Barker or Barnes
12 Solemn
15 Vacation spots
21 Knowledge
25 Boxing stats
26 Kind of duck
27 Pulitizer Prize novelist: 1958

28 Whisper sweet nothings
29 Fishing net
30 Yarn
32 Ill-mannered lout
34 Mars: Comb. form
35 Sea bird
37 Bungled
38 Huge amounts
40 Letters for Lee
41 Swingy rhythm

43 Takes the wheel
44 Frankfurter
45 Shade of pink
46 Memorable shrine
47 Finish second
50 Terrible czar
51 End to end, on the gridiron
52 Coward
53 Jubilation
57 Do sum work

ACROSS

1 Scratch
5 "Take __ Train," 1941 song
9 German city
14 Performer Falana
15 Clumsy one's expression
16 Rectory
17 Tart
18 Enamel material
19 A Perón
20 Scowl, e.g.
22 Ward off
23 Promise solemnly
24 Tattered clothing
26 Twerp
29 Spoil
33 Irritate
37 Model T or Stanley Steamer
39 Nautical welcome
40 "__ Theme," in a Lean film
41 Where a spring gives zing
42 School in Savoie
43 Suffix with axiom
44 Oates novel
45 Actor Falk
46 Expunge
48 Show affection, with "on"
50 Sup
52 Lopped the crops
57 Slacken
60 Suffers embarrassment
63 Vote to accept
64 Grad
65 Knight's wreath
66 Bout
67 Fictional Wolfe
68 Actor Sharif
69 Pry
70 Active one
71 London art gallery

DOWN

1 Supporting device
2 Not regional
3 Similar
4 __ in (attacked strongly)
5 Londoner's candy
6 Israeli dance
7 Majestic
8 Late bloomer
9 Come forth
10 Avoids humiliation
11 Cut
12 Famous Italian family
13 Actress Patricia
21 "__ of God," play and movie
25 Foofaraw
27 Foolhardy
28 Hornswoggled
30 "Cat on __ Tin Roof"
31 Composer Porter

40

32	Observer	**53**	Walking
33	Dressed	**54**	Toscanini's
34	Detest		birthplace
35	Seed covering	**55**	Fanfare
36	Confronted boldly	**56**	Inventor of farm
38	"_ Shanter,"		machines
	Burns poem	**57**	Colleen
42	Swords of sorts	**58**	Delightful abode
44	Take _ (rest)	**59**	Dorothy Gale's
47	Very good		dog
49	Shudder	**61**	Butter substitute
51	African antelope	**62**	Positive

ACROSS

1 "Pomp and Circumstance" composer
6 Comedian Foxx
10 Bosom companion?
13 New York mayor before Koch
14 Fancy case
15 Anon
16 Gaucho weapons
17 Arrow poison
18 Something to knock on
19 Organized U.S. militia force
22 Syr. neighbor
23 Ex-frosh
24 __ Paulo, Brazil
27 Bugle call after tattoo
30 Loose robe
34 B.P.O.E. member
35 Captured
37 Wed stealthily
38 Group Woodrow Wilson fostered
42 Flower holder
43 Play about Sadie Thompson
44 Bishop's domain
45 Backbone
46 Kind of mother
48 Have lunch
49 Golden-rule preposition
52 Queue before Q
54 Group founded in '45
60 Persia updated
62 Chalk's need
61 Hebrew month
64 Smash review
65 __ good example
66 Painter's item
67 Foxy
68 Greek god of love
69 Makes cartoons

DOWN

1 Recede
2 Trotsky or Uris
3 Festive occasion
4 Violin-maker of Cremona
5 Withstand
6 Check
7 Volcano in Sicily
8 One-on-one contests
9 San __ Padres
10 Clodhopper
11 Crucifix
12 Also
15 Bantu language
20 Declaim
21 Surprising victory
24 Hawks
25 "With __ and a bound . . .": Coleridge
26 African mammal
28 Like a church mouse

42

21

29 Living-room items	**53** Kind of beer
31 Large ruminant	**54** Russia's __
32 Sleeper's breathing	Mountains
problem	**55** Defense arm
33 Adjust the alarm	**56** Pact since W.W. II
36 Contract the brows	**57** River in Turkish
39 Real	Armenia
40 Ending for fraud	**58** Space org.
41 Concerning	**59** Muddle or
47 Composed	mulligan
50 Rib	**60** Taxing initials
51 More peculiar	**63** Lofty trains

ACROSS

1 Repeat
5 Campus V.I.P.
9 __ Angelico
12 Horse or sheepskin
13 Existent
14 Press wax
15 Pepys's sign-off
17 Loathe
18 Force out
19 Revolves
21 Oak or elm
23 Waste
24 Cause of more fondness?
27 Fall flowers
30 Cheer heard at a bullfight
31 Worship
33 Wife of Abraham
34 Supplement
35 Viewpoint
37 Life story, for short
38 Hauled
41 Kefauver
43 Terminate
44 Spartacus and Nat Turner
46 Tasks for Junior
48 Send as payment
50 Writer Bombeck
51 Changeable fashion item
53 Roles for Ferrer and Plummer

56 Mind
57 Ease
61 Cockcrow
62 Lawlessness
63 Kennel noises
64 Printers' measures
65 Recolors
66 Comic Johnson

DOWN

1 Historic period
2 Ice cream holder
3 Pilgrimage to Mecca
4 Beginnings
5 Arafat's org.
6 Josh
7 Open
8 Hat for Mike Hammer
9 Type of mattress
10 Evaluate
11 Pub drinks
13 Is present at
14 California mount
16 Sheath of a leafstalk
20 Soviet news agency
22 French school
24 Perfume base
25 Pans with hot coals to keep sleepers cozy
26 Rub out
28 Showers

44

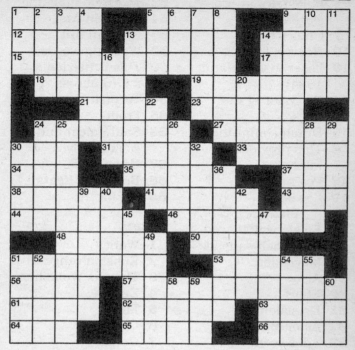

29 Aped
   blacksmiths
30 Ceral grain
32 __ nous
36 Scare
39 "Brideshead
   Revisited"
   author Waugh
40 Half: Prefix
42 Philippine isle
45 "Arabian Nights"
   voyager

47 Japanese city
   bombed in W.W. II
49 Wee
51 Where you live
52 Black, to Byron
54 Glacial ridges
55 Month between
   Aug. and Oct.
58 Female deer
59 Hindu
   incantations
60 Opposite of NNW

ACROSS

1 Philadelphia pro eleven
7 Child's toy
10 Hoover, for one
13 Loser to Cleveland: 1884
14 Neighbor of the Keys
15 Dutch commune
16 This provides interest
18 Pea holder
19 Locale
20 "__ Pinafore"
21 Steal away to wed
23 Sandwich sausage
26 Movie dog
27 Also
30 Effort
31 Do slaloms
32 Actor Marvin
33 Adolescent
34 Tried to lose
37 Chart
38 Alphabetical listings
40 Fury
41 Scents
43 Insincere statements
44 Quarter of four
45 D.A.R. counterpart
46 Billiard shot
47 Boy in "Little Men"
48 Londoner, for short
50 Says
52 Toolshop machine
54 It's often cast
55 Russian hut
59 Wedding words
60 This is needed for 16 Across
64 Tarnish
65 Profit
66 Sauté meat and cook slowly
67 Use a lever
68 Before, to Keats
69 Aslant

DOWN

1 Wanes
2 Russian range
3 Thomas Wolfe hero
4 Enjoys
5 Finish
6 Observe
7 Cough
8 Honshu sash
9 Foie gras, e.g.
10 Testimony under oath
11 Take in a foundling
12 Euripides play
14 Interchange of thoughts
17 Synchronized
22 Erie or Huron
24 Arrow poison
25 Mortgages
27 __ mater

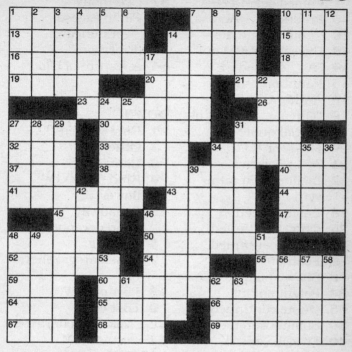

28 In the vicinity of
29 Place for storage
31 Nun
34 Thick
35 Sea bird
36 Legal document
39 Hindu groups
42 School subj.
46 Child's make-believe food
48 Item associated with Goodyear

49 "M*A*S*H" character
51 Rope material
53 Flange
56 Narrow cut
57 Cold Alpine wind
58 Mimicked
61 Unit of corn
62 Teamster org.
63 Prefix with cycle or angle

ACROSS

1 Famed seamstress
5 Product of 1 Across
9 __ out (made do)
13 Caesar's "And you!"
14 "A __ divided . . . "
15 Fountain order
16 Author of quote
19 "Oh __ . . . " start of partial quote
20 M.I.T. or R.P.I.
21 Actor Jeremy
22 Incline, as a mine vein
23 Basilica section
25 Quote continued
28 Quote continued
32 Footnote word
33 Showy plant
34 Potent ending
35 Quote continued
39 Somme summer
40 French capital
41 Bangkok native
42 Publications
44 Quote continued
46 Stew
47 Zadora and Lindstrom
48 Trattoria drink
51 What a legislature does
52 Era
55 Partial quote concluded
59 Tunes
60 "War and __"
61 Ceremony
62 Fill to excess
63 __ of Concord (Emerson)
64 A feature of Old Glory

DOWN

1 Ring V.I.P.'s
2 Other: Sp.
3 Remain
4 Kind of fish or flower
5 Broadway choreographer
6 Craving
7 Cinematographers' org.
8 Part of G.W.
9 Lost calf
10 "Mikado" character
11 Former P.M.
12 Week components
14 __ Kush, Asian range
17 So long, in Sorrento
18 Kettledrum
22 Anthem
23 Liberty and others
24 Slippery
25 Fall beverage
26 "__ which will live in infamy": F.D.R.
27 Stair post
28 Hindu garments

48

29 Compact
30 Sunken fences
31 La tia's spouse
33 Editor's mark
36 Used frugally
37 Life of Riley
38 Play __ it lays
43 Emanate
44 Willow twig
45 "Yond Cassius __ lean and hungry look"

47 Pie part
48 Audit makers
49 Scotto solo
50 Baltimore's McHenry
51 Plunder
52 Came down
53 "I __ kick . . . "
54 German dam or river
56 CD's ancestors
57 Affirmative vote
58 Apr. 15 collectors

ACROSS

1 Cygnet
5 Israelite leader
10 British streetcar
14 Small amount
15 Novel by Chateaubriand
16 Adventure story
17 Brisk pace
18 Temper tantrums
19 Eternally
20 Diamond arbiter
22 Ore processing plants
24 Hear ye!
26 Wading bird
27 Goals of the boys of summer
31 Mountain crests
35 Of birds
36 Satan's lure
38 Car pt.
39 Rod's companion
40 Of a region
41 __-kiri
42 Business abbr.
43 Catkin
44 More tender
45 "A Sentimental Journey" author
47 What Ruth was to Gehrig
49 Ireland, to Celts
51 Eject
52 Rickey Henderson specialty
56 Female monster
60 Infield covering, for short
61 Healed
63 Tree of Java
64 Otherwise
65 Sports stadium
66 Salamander
67 One's equal
68 Stair post
69 Red and Coral

DOWN

1 In __ (in its original place)
2 Early bird's breakfast
3 Upon
4 Mets' league
5 Lurch
6 One __ time
7 Falls behind
8 Fragrant resin
9 Aaron's game
10 African fly
11 Critic's laudation
12 Ripener
13 Planet or Roman god
21 Pitcher Nolan
23 Italian money
25 A long look
27 A fashion capital
28 Important occurrence
29 Brother's daughter

30 Used up
32 Jeweled headdress
33 Plumed wading bird
34 Pitfall
37 Tops of heads
40 Yankees' league
41 Specialty of Mantle and Maris
43 Plant used for blue dye
44 Self-satisfied
46 Farm machine

48 Without feet
50 Harden
52 Pace
53 O. Henry offering
54 Gaelic
55 Developed
57 Fencing sword
58 "I never __ Moor": Dickinson
59 Fast planes
62 Sevilla-to-Córdoba dir.

ACROSS

1 Canines
5 Like
9 Kitchen implement
14 Opera highlight
15 Nobelist in Literature: 1947
16 Sierra __
17 Home décor
19 "As You Like It" forest
20 Scheduled
21 Former Ugandan dictator
23 Historic time
24 Hot-weather home adjunct
27 Bit of butter
30 N.Y. canal
31 Where Springsteen was born
32 Lessen
34 Cell-nuclei substances
36 __ avis (oddity)
40 "Anna __," Yordan play
42 Ebbs
44 Cease
45 Invitation abbr.
47 Colt controls
48 Suffix with Japan
50 "Othello" villain
52 Heavy weight
53 Cold-weather home adjunct
58 Cries of delight
59 "Money __ everything"
60 Wild ass
64 Adhesive ornament
66 Type of gardener
68 "__ of Two Cities"
69 Taj Mahal site
70 Paul __, Swiss artist
71 Darnels
72 Affirmative votes
73 Search for

DOWN

1 Crows' cousins
2 Spoken
3 __ monster
4 Veteran sailors
5 Morocco quake site: 1960
6 Taste the soup
7 Think-tank occupants
8 Famed atomic physicist
9 Bell sounds
10 Above, to Key
11 Cowboys' contest
12 New Year's month, in Madrid
13 Of the kidney
18 Flycatchers
22 Occupied
25 Gold-making king
26 Gay __
27 Chums
28 Touch at the edge
29 Mexican snack

52

33 Diminish gradually
35 Hungarian hero
37 Mine entrance
38 A place to play keno
39 Y.M.C.A., e.g.
41 Tartan trousers
43 Royal headgear
46 Wine classification
49 Happy expressions
51 Heller's "__ Gold"
53 Mubarak's predecessor

54 Greek letter
55 Part of a Hepburn collection
56 Dental device
57 Attacks on quarterbacks
61 High wind
62 Blunted sword
63 Give off fumes
65 October brew
67 Gun fancier's org.

ACROSS

1 Veranda
6 Jahan built here
10 File
14 "Butterfield 8" author
15 "The Tonight Show" host: 1957–62
16 Athenian "Whoopee!"
17 Avifauna
18 When most people watch TV
20 Soviet symbol
22 Come through
23 Circumference
25 Energetic
28 Autocrat
29 Lebanese export
33 Querying word
34 Proper
35 Play with annoyingly
36 Make up for
38 Negative prefix
40 Old Roman port
41 Worked on a dirk
42 Mosel feeder
44 Baseball great Roush
45 Links star Sam
46 __ Mujeres, Mexico
47 Quarry
48 Sycamore
51 Service group?
54 Made soda

58 Everted
60 Winged
61 Campus figure
62 Senior citizen, in Köln
63 Drug from the leaves of a plant
64 Cap site
65 Beginning
66 Mystery writer's award

DOWN

1 Impoverished
2 Czech river
3 She wrote "The Fountainhead"
4 Like potato chips
5 Error causer
6 Informed
7 Needlefish
8 Corporate infiltrator
9 Medieval head-protector
10 Many Floridians
11 Tel __
12 Bother or trouble ending
13 Earl or duke
19 Presidential picker
21 Commedia dell'__
24 Fauvist painter
25 Former Iranian rulers
26 Don

27	Alpine flower	47	Rang
30	Postal machine	49	Neighborhoods
31	Player's sotto-voce remark	50	Efface
32	Set preceder	51	Flame holder
34	Intervened officiously	52	In a bit
37	Shore phenomenon	53	Fortune-teller's phrase
39	Took a leap	55	Bite
43	Swiss river	56	Heating device
46	Shoe part	57	Letter opener
		59	All-purpose veh.

ACROSS

1 Omaha Beach craft
5 Soaks flax
9 Long walks
14 Opera highlight
15 Upon
16 Nylon constituent
17 Copy
19 Standish
20 Flavorful seed
21 Musical half step
23 Moderately moist
25 Facts and figures
26 Feminine suffix
29 Implements
31 Sharp answer
35 Irritate
37 Layer
39 Composer Stravinsky
40 Volcanic output
41 Untidy
42 Filet border
43 Sir __ Guinness
44 Singles
45 Anoint, old style
46 Shorter
48 Agts.
50 Distress signal
51 Small French land masses
53 Part of a plane
55 Glazer
59 Coddle

63 Memento of a saint
64 Copy
66 Long-legged shore bird
67 On the ocean
68 Mild expletive
69 Kefauver
70 Adjacent
71 Congers

DOWN

1 Small apes
2 Canadian Indian
3 Tilts
4 Mixed dish of greens
5 Unbranched flower cluster
6 Greek letter
7 Small children
8 Swiftness
9 Descendant of a son of Noah
10 Copy
11 Unit of weight, for short
12 Adam's address
13 President Mobutu __ Seko of Zaire
18 Likeness
22 Take a spouse
24 Communion plate
26 Acclamation
27 Fragile layered rock

56

28 Thrifty one	**49** Abele
30 Stair part	**52** Family car
32 Monsters	**54** V.I.P. at a fete
33 Norse chieftain	**55** Gaelic
34 Kilmer classic	**56** Seines
36 Copy	**57** Landed
38 Big Bertha's birthplace	**58** Artifice
	60 Senate aide
41 Edible mushroom	**61** And others: Abbr.
45 Brazilian palm	**62** Bolsheviks
47 Votes into office	**65** Pod occupant

ACROSS

1 Edible kin of amaryllis
6 Most recent
10 Non-alcoholic
14 Mendelssohn masterwork
15 Biblical dry measure
16 Rights org.
17 Latin entertainer
18 Sandwich Islands goose
19 Film unit
20 Ice-cream treats
23 __ Haute
24 A Shoshonean
25 Site of Mongolia and Bhutan
29 British thank-you's
30 Hood and Rainier: Abbr.
31 Miner's need
33 __ de mer
34 Charge
37 Andiron
38 Summit site: 1986
40 Pub potation
41 Conk out
42 Locale
43 Abyss
44 Composer Rorem
45 Cart
46 Consent
49 Rebound
51 Vacillates
57 Proboscis
58 Riyadh native
59 Cabinet post
60 New York canal
61 Umpire's decision
62 Forte of O. Henry
63 Grains or drinks
64 Swiss painter: 1879–1940
65 Runs in neutral

DOWN

1 Lomond, for one
2 Sympathetic response
3 "L'__, c'est moi"
4 Saw cut
5 Stocky
6 Like some plans
7 Moslem bigwigs
8 Feel
9 Faithful, in Frankfurt
10 Capital of ancient Lydia
11 Sight at Fort Lauderdale
12 Swift
13 Oklahoma city
21 Motown
22 Pit or stone
25 __ Romeo
26 Ketch component
27 Concerning
28 Eroded

30 Home of a famous Philip
32 Fisher and Foy
33 Wretched
34 Just
35 Sicilian resort
36 Nervous
39 British business abbr.
43 Winged flycatchers
44 "Buon __ !"
46 Capp character
47 Splendor
48 The O'Grady girl
49 Yellowish pink
50 Mid-XVIth century year
52 Taxi
53 Amusing fellow
54 Ancient Greek coin
55 Solitary
56 Carrie Nation's supporters

ACROSS

1 First Arabic letter
5 Indianapolis NFL team
10 Hamsters, guppies et al.
14 Artist Bonheur
15 Not together
16 Upon
17 Type of bridge
18 Knot again
19 Island country near Key West
20 Ghost
22 More annoying
24 Mountain nymph
26 Singer Peggy
27 Pennant
30 Not merited
35 Obliterate
36 Tutelary god
37 Identical
38 The late Mr. Onassis
39 Grief
43 Name for the sun
44 Roam
46 Compete
47 Lessen
49 Adds sugar to
51 Stone monuments
52 Baseball tally
53 Suitor
55 Minnesota NFL team
59 Look-alikes
63 Actress Baxter
64 Fairylike; delicate
66 Wings for an angelus
67 Angers
68 Smiling
69 Citrus fruit
70 Small amphibian
71 Male deer
72 Back talk

DOWN

1 Companion of crafts
2 Circular area of a roadway
3 Small land mass
4 Atlanta NFL team
5 One's life work
6 "Norma" or "Carmen"
7 Caesar's lang.
8 Journey
9 Pittsburgh NFL team
10 Green Bay NFL team
11 Small case
12 "Oh, __ in England . . .": Browning
13 Bowsprit
21 Sylvan sights
23 Tar's milieu
25 Lack of luster
27 Chicago NFL team
28 Indian weapon
29 Unsophisticated
31 Scottish denial
32 Of a facial feature

60

33 Play to the
balcony
34 Strikes out
40 "The ___," TV spy
drama: 1966–69
41 Noise at Babel
42 Glossy fabric
45 Most weird
48 Cincinnati NFL team
50 Cask
51 New Orleans
NFL team
54 Squeeze out
water
55 Conceited
56 Concerning
57 Was aware of
58 Small opening
60 "Roast Pig"
dissertator
61 St. Louis
NFL team
62 Perceives
65 Air-traffic org.

ACROSS

1 Transport
5 Some musical compositions
10 Neighbor of Pelion
14 Actress Bancroft
15 Disease of cereals
16 Expensive
17 Australian bush song
20 Unmoving
21 Liquid for pickles
22 Common abbr.
23 Act
26 Numbers man: Abbr.
29 European deer
31 English cathedral town
32 Group of eight
34 Rope for Tarzan
37 Father of Menelaus
38 Yarn-making machine
41 Relative of mimosa
42 Heroine of "Crime and Punishment"
43 Proofreader's mark
44 Means of access
45 Does lawn work
49 Greek letter
50 Repeat
54 A feast __ famine
55 Frighten
57 Greeted
59 Moslem ascetic
63 Saturn, e.g.
64 Contention
65 Westernmost of the Aleutians
66 Profound
67 Condor's home
68 Eliot of "The Untouchables"

DOWN

1 Mooring rope
2 Yellowish-red dye
3 Loosen, as boots
4 Native of Riga
5 Apply antifreeze
6 Vase
7 Chick-to-be
8 Hoyden
9 Belle or Bart
10 Thor's dad
11 Person chosen
12 Mournful
13 Southern constellation
18 Energy
19 A grass grown for hay
24 Italian painter: 1575–1642
25 Crewman on a whaling ship
27 Vintner Masson
28 Newspaper items, for short
30 Cut
33 Elite

35 First
36 Literary collection
37 Wheat beard
38 "Go away, grimalkin!"
39 Hanger-on
40 "Maja" painter
41 Expert
44 With intensity
46 Limestone formation
47 Wrenches

48 Hindu holy men
51 Instant
52 Subject
53 Attention
56 Cut short
58 ___ IV, first czar
59 Ball of cotton
60 Vietnamese seaport
61 Needlefish
62 Twice CCLI

ACROSS

1 Fortune
5 Supply food for a fee
10 Bases of the decimal system
14 Harrow rival
15 Overhead
16 Oodles
17 Apt anagram for evil
18 Hay bundles
19 Big bean
20 French magazine for women
21 Wide-awake
22 Absolute ruler
23 Actress Remick
24 Ore pockets
25 Lemon drink
26 Mysterious power
29 Us, to Ovid
30 Shoot the breeze
32 Pedigree
35 Harass
39 Salad plant
40 Goaded
41 What hams chew up
43 Nips
44 Marry
45 Cash follower
47 Morse-code E
48 Wood for skis
50 Belief
52 Serve well
55 Mace
57 Church officer
58 Author Ernie or Howard
59 Part of TLC
60 "Brother, can you spare __?"
61 Like a wing
62 Ascend
63 Russian revolutionary
64 "__ fan tutte": Mozart
65 Social insects
66 Moved along a cliff
67 Scottish Gaelic

DOWN

1 Carpenter's device
2 Helpful, as a tool
3 Tony winner: 1961 and 1974
4 Joint below the femur
5 Plot
6 Edible mollusk
7 El Greco subject
8 Peak Norgay climbed
9 Relaxes
10 After-shave powder
11 Oscar winner: 1960 and 1966
12 Wanderer
13 Gape
27 French river

64

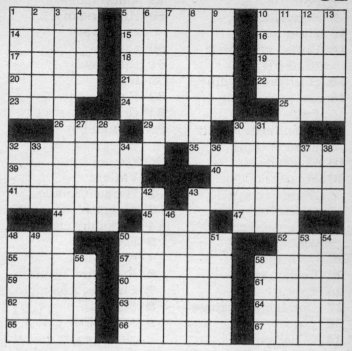

28	Did a road job	46	Conclusion
30	Lofty	48	Capital of
31	Friends, in Firenze		Ghana
32	Bandleader Brown	49	Done in
33	Co. tag	50	Nature writer
34	Eur. country		Edwin Way __
36	Sash in Sasebo	51	Drift
37	Originally called	53	Social rank
38	Six-pt. plays	54	Weird
42	Produced	56	Apiary denizens
43	Certain infant:	58	A New York
	Colloq.		university

ACROSS

1 Post
5 Irtysh feeder
10 Farm unit
14 British composer: 1710–78
15 Oneness, in Udine
16 Get an F on an exam
17 Algonquian Indian
18 Evita or Juan
19 Russian saint
20 Presley song in "King Creole": 1958
23 Surpasses other vendors
24 __ de mer
25 Certain moths
26 Capture
27 One-horse carriage
30 Yearns
34 Golfer's norm
35 Coffee: Slang
36 Elvis's TV debut song: 1956
40 Competent
41 Daily record
42 Overweight
43 However
44 Crow sound
45 Agt.'s concern
47 Help!
48 Affluent
53 "Elvis __," 1970 film

57 Juno, to Plato
58 Kilns
59 Husband of a countess
60 Cupid
61 Runs away
62 Goad
63 Habit
64 Charon's vessel
65 Roman boy

DOWN

1 Virile
2 Pianist Claudio
3 Sluggish
4 Yorkshire city
5 Elvis's hometown
6 Ryan and Tatum
7 Shuttlecocks
8 Siouan
9 Miss Liberty, to a sailor, e.g.
10 "__ and his money . . . "
11 Serene
12 Baltic port
13 Verve
21 Stickup
22 Joker
26 Ewe sound
27 Garden portal
28 Currier's partner
29 High wind
30 Melville captain

66

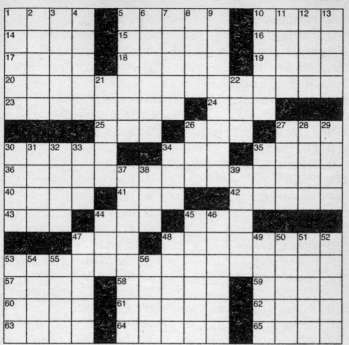

31 Philippine island

32 Sentry's word

33 Poet's before

34 Cribbage item

35 Chore

37 Rocket launching

38 Spat

39 In an angry way

44 Romaine

45 Tin-lead alloy

46 Elegant

47 Commence

48 North Sea feeder

49 Traffic jam

50 Hokkaido port

51 Solemn song

52 Famous Canadian physician

53 Melt

54 Blood: Comb. form

55 Part of Presley's signature

56 In good health

ACROSS

1 Spore
5 Wander
10 Gossip material
14 Eight: Comb. form
15 Seaport in SE England
16 Buffalo's lake
17 Russian sea
18 Fragrance
19 Daring
20 Deceived by trickery
23 "Hail!" to Caesar
24 Stannum
25 Seventh sign of the Zodiac
28 Collection of anecdotes
31 "Lost Horizon" director
35 Stop __ dime
36 Remove
39 Where Kashan is
40 Pitched a slow ball
43 Gaelic
44 An angel
45 Mary Lincoln, __ Todd
46 Unexpected obstacles
48 Alcoholic drink
49 Organic compound
51 River in Switzerland
53 Toward the stern
54 Moved out of town
62 Hindu woman's garment
63 "Water Lilies" painter
64 Dissolve
65 Part of Q.E.D.
66 Old-womanish
67 Mexican monetary unit
68 Depend (on)
69 Duchin or Nero
70 Exude

DOWN

1 Cleansing agent
2 Beige
3 And others: Abbr.
4 It once went far
5 Shovel
6 One-third of a 1970 film title
7 Place for a cupola
8 __ mater
9 Fermentation agent
10 Carefree
11 Press
12 Irritate
13 Actor Danson
21 Avoid
22 Muscular spasm
25 Easy, swinging gaits
26 Store ashes
27 Extremely light wood
28 Change
29 India's Prime Minister: 1947–64
30 TV series that featured Mr. T

32 Art copy
33 Indian queen
34 Wrath
37 McMahon and Ames
38 Sixth sense
41 Conformance with the law
42 Burglary
47 Bando of baseball
50 Philatelist's collection

52 Chart details again
53 Daisylike flower
54 Peel
55 Russian river
56 Completed
57 One
58 Soccer great
59 Retain
60 Otherwise
61 Store away
62 Sun. talk

ACROSS

1 Thespian
6 Gorged, perhaps
9 Incline
13 Cuomo or Lanza
14 Banner
15 Auto part
16 Lobbyist's activity
18 Rotate
19 Area on a liner
20 Inspiration for Kilmer
21 Actor Reginald
22 Observed
23 Land measure
27 Pitcher like Greg Maddux
28 Small masses of wool
29 Kind of land or boat
31 Lofty goal
33 Mrs., in Madrid
36 Push down
38 Less rational
40 Weight of India
41 Mennonite group
43 Ship's cranelike device
44 Brute preceders
46 Spinning toy
48 Unit of inheritance
49 Medical suffix
50 Reigned
52 Kind of rag
53 These are behind your nose

57 Step __ (accelerate)
58 Promoter's ploy
60 E.P.A. concern
61 Ovid's X's
62 Rousseau novel
63 Actress Russo
64 Tate display
65 Tealike shrub

DOWN

1 Elec. unit
2 Sights outside motels
3 Allowance for waste
4 River to the Seine
5 Flushed
6 Lined up
7 Jurist Roger Brooke __
8 Future chicken
9 Endured
10 Indicative
11 Noncitizen
12 Hawaii's state bird
14 First emperor of Austria
17 Compound used in making plastics
22 Side dish
23 Appends
24 Indian of Manitoba
25 Act of subduing
26 Corn unit

28 Armed conflict
30 Butcher's stock
32 Without auditory feedback
34 Check
35 Comic Johnson
37 A Dallas inst.
39 Zig follower
42 Romberg's prince, e.g.
45 Jot
47 Writes

49 Pound part
50 More unusual
51 Snow White's favorite
52 Go-getter
54 Van Druten's "__ Camera"
55 Leak
56 Norman city
58 Org. for Mom and Pop
59 Urge

ACROSS

1 River in central Europe
5 Surpass
10 Radar signal
14 Prediction from some voices
15 Medicine: Comb. form
16 Depend
17 Airborne canard?
20 Still
21 Is in distress
22 Make amends
23 Quarry
24 Bathhouses
26 Bracers
29 Savage
30 Hot spot
31 Measure of gold's fineness
32 Actress Gardner
35 News conference, in a way
39 Wapiti
40 Alex Haley masterwork
41 Being, to Brutus
42 Pennies
43 Semiprecious stones
45 Eternal
48 Ever and __
49 Of warships
50 Guardhouse
51 Axlike tool
54 On __ (fresh from the grapevine)
58 Monastery inmate
59 Pacific island group
60 Heavyweight Max
61 Baseball's Mel and family
62 Bridges
63 Woody Guthrie's son

DOWN

1 Nervous
2 Knowledge
3 __ camp
4 Australian bird
5 Makes neat
6 "Yes, we'll __ round the flag, boys"
7 Shoshoneans
8 A newlywed's title
9 Opposite of neg.
10 Harsh
11 Turkey
12 Actress Massey
13 Funeral piles
18 Special agent
19 Collar for a Pilgrim
23 In the __ (healthy)
24 Roman goddess
25 "To __ and a bone . . . ": Kipling
26 Soliloquy starter
27 Ellipsoid
28 Risk one's __
29 Data

72

31 Nautical miles, loosely
32 Prin.'s helper
33 Clamp
34 Mimes
36 Without restraint
37 Years on end
38 Actor Connery
42 Kent and Gable
43 Loos and Bryant
44 Discothèque's __ girl
45 Wind: Comb. form
46 French dance
47 Occasion
48 A felony
50 Basilica area
51 Seaweed substance
52 A sworded affair
53 Cipher
55 C.I.A.'s predecessor
56 Snooze
57 Lakers' org.

ACROSS

1 Off one's rocker
5 In fine spirits
9 Tiny particle
13 Shun
15 Easy, swinging gait
16 Heron's relative
17 Trey's neighbor
18 Youngman's forte
20 Flub
21 Do a sound job
23 Cheapen
24 Orchestral components
27 Horror movie attraction
28 Ferber's "Ice __"
30 Part of a cycle
32 Spew forth
33 Soapbox component
34 Day worker, for short
38 A sib
39 Needling literary works
42 Chit
43 "From Here to Eternity" setting
45 Greenback
46 Infidel
48 Danish coin
50 Like a Titan
51 Legume of India
52 Baby grand's cousin
54 Rock salt
56 Wayfarer's stop

57 Apparel for a young diner
60 Part of Arnie's arsenal
62 Duck
64 Schooner's spine
65 Adjective for a cad
66 Raises ire
67 Monty Python's Eric __
68 Administers the coup de grace
69 Surveyor's map

DOWN

1 Florida county
2 Attest
3 Bluff, as in poker
4 Minor facial malady
5 English theatre of note
6 Actor Chaney
7 Sincerely flattered
8 Convention attendee
9 Tower on a mosque
10 Adjective for Arbuckle
11 Become bored
12 Suffix with host
14 Discounts
19 Nigerian people
22 Wasatch Range native
25 Race term
26 Puts together
28 Money in Monterrey
29 Sills solo

74

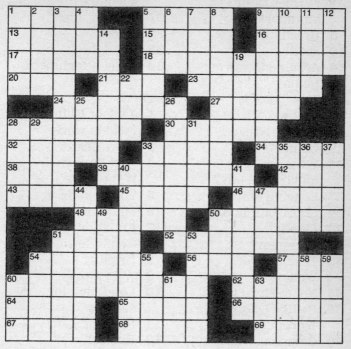

31 Listen!
33 Take aback
35 Bad thing to be behind
36 Castle defense
37 Like a runt
40 Fruitless
41 Angler's gadget
44 Godfrey played it
47 Grow wizened
49 "Don't __ on my parade!"

50 Sixty secs.
51 What the judge bangs
53 Conifers
54 Pay attention to
55 Ireland, to a poet
58 Notion
59 Defeat
60 Do some schussing
61 Antediluvian
63 Nabob

ACROSS

1 Former Berlin landmark
5 Brazilian dance
10 Exult
14 Assam silkworm
15 Red as __
16 The __ Eagle
17 Suitor
18 The Louvre, e.g.
19 Competent
20 What an oil millionaire has?
23 Fencing foil
24 Short-haired dog
25 Finally!
28 Iron men?
33 Take care of
34 Wellaway!
35 No, to Burns
36 Be like Daddy Warbucks
40 Compass heading
41 Actress Merkel et al.
42 Whittled
43 Made notches
46 Skinflints
47 Cobbler's tool
48 Logical
49 Sign of fiscal fitness?
56 Do some darning
57 Utopian
58 Medicinal plant
59 Mexican finger food

60 This gives Paris a white Christmas
61 Behind time
62 Check
63 Dead duck
64 Legal attachment

DOWN

1 Jack or Clifton
2 Field of work
3 Prevaricator
4 Poet Warren or Wilbur, e.g.
5 Young salmon
6 Maltreat
7 In the middle: Comb. form
8 Gripe
9 __ in a teapot
10 Loud metallic sounds
11 Morning garb
12 Exclusively
13 Itsy-bitsy
21 England's __ Downs
22 Suffix with prosper
25 Phoenix's remains
26 Junior, to Sis
27 Crowbar, e.g.
28 Entreat
29 Beams
30 Habituate
31 Less common

32 Dispatches
34 British princess
37 Remote
38 Suppose
39 Doubleday's game
44 "__ Harvest": Hilton
45 Reverential dread
46 Austrian composer-conductor: 1860–1911

48 Put on
49 Vegetarian's no-no
50 Formerly
51 Thought: Comb. form
52 German negative
53 Jai __
54 Distinction
55 Whetted
56 Atlas abbr.

ACROSS

1 Accumulate
6 Cold or ready follower
10 Like many a Texas ranch
14 Overalls material
15 On the China
16 Fashion magazine
17 Lapsus linguae
20 Sting a customer
21 Scary cinema sounds
22 "Raiders of the Lost __"
25 Cycle beginning
26 Hurry along
27 Speak thoughtfully
33 Westminster follower
34 Dizzy or Daffy
35 High mountain
37 Type of act
38 Jupiter or Zeus
40 Code predecessor
41 Asner and Ames
42 Play it close to the __
43 Sacrificial site
44 Rap
48 Cry of disgust
49 Hoover, for one
50 Color changer
51 Aftermath of a mistake
55 Press

57 Speak without result
62 Kitchen follower
63 Actor Robert De __
64 Uncanny
65 Peruse
66 Star of 67 Across
67 "I __ of Jeannie" (TV oldie)

DOWN

1 TV commercials
2 Brooks or Tillis
3 Black cuckoo
4 Drinks slowly
5 Slick talker
6 Ament
7 Bat wood
8 Comprehends
9 Deck opening
10 Wood overlay
11 Seaweed
12 Run-down part of a city
13 Golf-bag items
18 Gambling game
19 Artemis's victim
22 Cognizant
23 Some bridge calls
24 Put the __ on (squelch)
28 Obtain
29 Archie's "dingbat"
30 Tennis unit
31 Moved swiftly
32 Cheap; shoddy

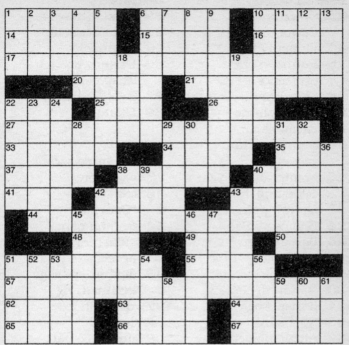

36 City associated with a farm exodus?

38 Remove from power

39 Dec., in N.Y.C.

40 Brewed beverage

42 Rival of 16 Across

43 Like some trucks

45 Dispossessed

46 Menlo Park name

47 Fishhook part

51 Pitcher

52 Give a 10, e.g.

53 Film dog

54 Site of Vance A.F.B.

56 __-do-well

58 Bard's preposition

59 "Chances __," Mathis hit

60 Avila aunt

61 Margin

ACROSS

1 Of the ear
5 Cicatrix
9 Communion table
14 Fibber
15 Rounded ear projection
16 Skin layer
17 Water plant
18 Paradise
19 Sharp-tasting vegetable
20 Fighter of the Year: 1956 and 1960
23 Cereal grain
24 Before, to Poe
25 Squandered, perhaps
28 Gumbo
30 __ Kett of comics
34 Indisposed
35 Roof edge
37 Altruistic person
39 Fighter of the Year: 1979
42 In the middle of
43 Deserve
44 Equal: Prefix
45 Give temporarily
46 Terminates
48 Organic compound
50 Mining find
51 Doctrine adherent
52 Fighter of the Year: 1937
60 Wanderer

61 On one's __ (alert)
62 Always
63 Existent
64 Twin of Jacob
65 Identical
66 Ustinov or Stuyvesant
67 Evaluate
68 Dilatory

DOWN

1 Norwegian king
2 Cultivate
3 Villain in "Othello"
4 French pencil
5 "Washington __ here"
6 Ending passage in music
7 Help a hood
8 Tenant
9 Revere
10 Magnifier
11 Music for three
12 Egyptian god
13 Operated
21 Post-office equipment
22 Chalk remover
25 Rope fiber
26 Feather
27 City WNW of Chicago
28 Eggs, to Cato
29 Attuned

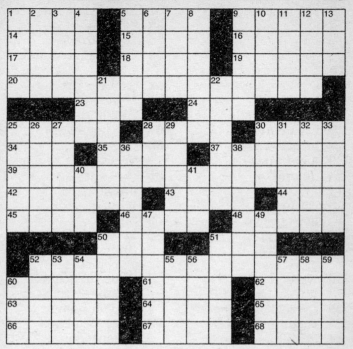

	30	Suffix with Jacob or Euclid		51	Offspring
31	Peculiarity		52	Aperture
32	Concise		53	Give forth
33	Passion		54	Part of a church
36	Aorta, e.g.		55	Parks of civil rights fame
38	Truthful		56	Gist
40	State further		57	Elliptical
41	Spanish article		58	Verne character
47	Less messy		59	Expanded
49	Strain		60	Siesta
50	Command			

ACROSS

1 Hammer part
5 Mil. addresses
9 Columbus sailed from here
14 Possess
15 Tibetan priest
16 O'Day or Bryant
17 Level
18 Where Qum is
19 Columbus's hometown
20 A patron of Columbus
22 Change
23 Doctor's prescription
25 Travesty
29 Mad. Ave. products
30 Waterston or Wanamaker
33 __ tenens (temporary substitute)
34 Penultimate Greek letter
35 Wine: Comb. form
36 E. M. Forster book
40 Astronaut Sally
41 Ship's record
42 "Beauty and the __"
43 Curve
44 Half a Kikuyu group's name
45 Author Laurence and painter Maurice
47 One who edits
49 Columbus, to 20 Across

52 Christopher, to 20 Across
57 Concerning
58 Witches
59 Tiny particle
60 One of Columbus's ships
61 Salinger girl
62 Actress Sommer
63 Toughness
64 Herring relative
65 Close

DOWN

1 Escoffier, e.g.
2 Wash
3 State
4 Make one's way
5 Brought into agreement
6 "Wooden Soldiers" action
7 Muscat native
8 Mold metal in a certain way
9 Heathens
10 Anoint, formerly
11 Fluff
12 Siouan
13 Mosel feeder
21 Mosque leaders
24 Personal: Comb. form
25 Irish county
26 Southwestern Indians
27 U.S.M.A. and U.S.N.A.
28 Trick

82

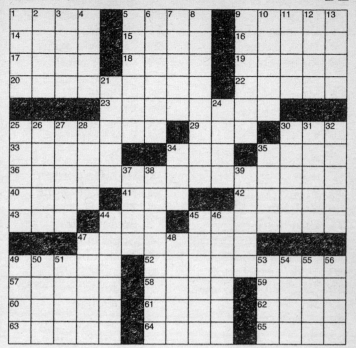

30 Family car
31 Parsley relative
32 Fortress ditches
34 Cribbage board insert
35 Unique person
37 "When I was ___ . . ."
38 Certain pigments or paintings
39 French composer
44 Like some arithmetic

45 Stain on one's reputation
46 Pitched
47 Way
48 Stock market disaster
49 Tops
50 Sad news item
51 Isolated
53 Portent
54 Tree trunk
55 Aleutian island
56 Evil look

ACROSS

1. Oscar in "The Odd Couple"
5. Counterfeit
9. Take aback
13. Radioactivity measure
15. Money in Milano
16. Ohio county
17. Florida city
18. Slightly open
19. Adjective for the Styx
20. Archer William and son
21. Bun holders
23. Longbow material
25. Hangs in there
26. Divine revelation
29. "High Noon" climax
31. Survey
32. Neck of land
34. Say
39. Garb for Pavlova
40. 1040's grist
42. A piece of cake
43. Thrusts
45. Birthday secret
46. Partake of food
47. Colonial patriot
49. Causes confusion
51. Korean shoemaking center
54. Out of kilter
55. Capone weapons
58. Top monk
62. "The Naked Maja" duchess
63. Cabell of baseball
64. Create cloth
65. Berliner's quaff
66. Kind of wire
67. Great quintet
68. Classify
69. RBI or ERA
70. Lease item

DOWN

1. Dundee denizen
2. Father of "Time"
3. Type of presentation
4. Cop's cudgel
5. Thick cuts
6. Son, in Córdoba
7. Bedouin tribesman
8. Cat's-eye or agate
9. Military vehicles
10. Glenn's lap
11. N.F.L. team
12. Billfold items
14. Canvas holder
22. Korean border river
24. Cardinal point
26. Makes a selection
27. One-sided melee
28. Can. province
29. Sun Belt segment
30. Shoshoneans
33. Ratchet's partner

35 Childhood keepsake
36 Comet part
37 Anglo-Saxon serf
38 Bar orders
41 "Pygmalion" creator
44 Holmes vehicle
48 Certain theater supporters
50 Speak slooooowly

51 Salk's conquest
52 Shade of brown
53 Chic or tony
54 Tangible wealth
55 Small projections
56 Group of troops
57 Celestial phenomenon
59 Make pastry
60 Kiln
61 Run-through

ACROSS

1 Capital of Norway
5 Domesticated
10 Vivacity
14 Satellite of a planet
15 Got up
16 Press
17 Bedouin
18 Playing card
20 Fragrant
22 Baxter and Meara
23 Melody
24 Completed
26 Terminates prematurely
29 Willy Loman et al.
33 Barter
34 Half gainer, e.g.
35 Hindu woman's garment
36 Scale notes
37 Graduates' get-together
40 Male descendant
41 Fruit drinks
43 Tater
44 Residence
46 Says again
48 Tea cakes
49 Bar orders
50 Parseghian of football
51 Chaplain, to a G.I.
54 Beget
59 Straightforward

62 Twofold
63 Prefix with vision or graph
64 Banks or Ford
65 Sea eagles
66 Snow vehicle
67 Keenly desiring
68 Uncontrolled anger

DOWN

1 __ Khayyám
2 Painful
3 Burden
4 Within a ship
5 Candles
6 Island off Ireland
7 Greatest amount
8 Superlative ending
9 Lowest passing grade
10 Jungle king's mother
11 Shah's former realm
12 Golfer's warning
13 Finishes
19 Poison
21 1.0567 liquid quart
24 Goliath's conqueror
25 Kitchen staple
26 Fragrance of roses
27 She said "I do"
28 Isolated fertile areas

86

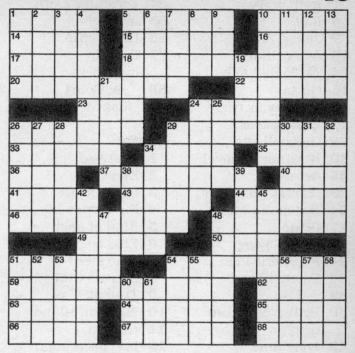

29	Skull cavity	51	Affectionate taps
30	__-Dixon line	52	Biblical shepherd
31	Wear away	53	Distribute
32	Cubs and Mets	54	Crew
34	Cheats	55	One of the
38	This, in Madrid		Great Lakes
39	Mother-of-pearl	56	Nimbus
42	Extremely hungry	57	Chinese dynasty
45	Lodger	58	Otherwise
47	Toward shelter	60	Classroom
48	Cabinet-maker's		competition
	tool	61	A feast __ famine

ACROSS

1 Irvin or Ty
5 Ray
9 Joker, e.g.
13 Actor Sharif
14 Taj Mahal site
15 Gluts
16 Monkey or tree
17 Come close
18 Catchall site
19 Hawthorne novel
22 Actor Ely
23 Pianist Templeton
24 Baseball's Mel
27 Grate
30 Wears away
34 Pâtisserie item
36 Finely honed
38 __ Lisa
39 British Museum display
42 Long time
43 Atlanta arena
44 Exploiters
45 Gymnast Mary Lou
47 Bridge term
49 Bean type
50 Kind of code
52 Cook's abbr.
54 "I Dreamt I Dwelt __"
60 Prospero's spirit
61 English river
62 Ange appendage
64 Velvetlike cloth
65 Invent
66 Bird's crop
67 Borscht ingredient
68 __ of Court
69 "Kiss Me, __"

DOWN

1 Tent bed
2 Elide
3 English spa
4 Pipe type
5 Kind of split
6 Elbe feeder
7 Fine steed
8 Actress Gibbs
9 Tunneled site
10 Aleutian island
11 Hold in
12 Mil. decoration
15 Less perilous
20 Mushroom
21 Actress Verdugo
24 Aquatic mammal
25 Western resort
26 English river
28 Ladle off
29 Famed Quaker family
31 Noted Washington couple
32 Juárez January

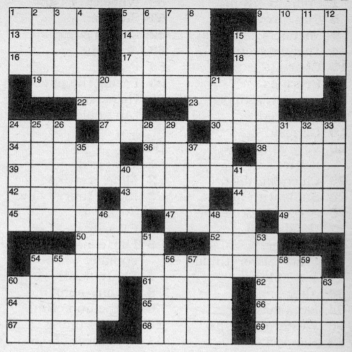

33 Pert
35 Old or New follower
37 Biographer Ludwig
40 Dead duck
41 Cuban dance
46 Vestment for John Paul II
48 Whence 39 Across came

51 Primitive calculators
53 Remiss
54 Dies __
55 Ennead
56 Jungle king
57 "__ go bragh!"
58 Turkish coin
59 Bed part
60 P.D. message
63 Female sheep

ACROSS

1 Spill the beans
5 Can. province
9 Michael Caine role
14 Theater section
15 Char
16 Bearings
17 Spanish seaport
18 Vocalized
19 Clumsy
20 Very generous nature
23 Calendar abbr.
24 Suffix with quack
25 Showy neckpieces
27 Mississippi explorer
31 "The __ Everything," 1959 film
33 Alter
34 Land map
35 Western campus
38 Henpecks
39 Plants' beginnings
40 Winter vehicle
41 Old tongue
42 Gridiron play
43 Filmdom's Keaton
44 Planets' paths
46 Long, narrow valley
47 Ceiling beam
49 Eggs' companion
50 __ at ease
51 Government leader

58 Winged
60 Wheeler or Lahr
61 Sulfuric __
62 Lexicons, e.g.
63 Armbone
64 Pealed
65 Facing the pitcher
66 High-schooler
67 "An apple __ . . ."

DOWN

1 Tasteless
2 Miner's strike
3 Indian tourist city
4 Yogi, e.g.
5 Classify
6 Like elms in summer
7 Sharp flavor
8 Jason's ship
9 In the hub of
10 Writer Yutang
11 Weakness of character
12 Computer data
13 Baritone Simon __
21 __ off (annoyed)
22 Endures
26 "My __ Rachel," 1952 film
27 Fonda or Wyman
28 The Tentmaker
29 Butcher-shop items
30 Envelope enclosure

31 Sanctify
32 Bridge at St. Louis
34 __ moss
36 Jay of comedy
37 Capital of South Yemen, once
39 Steeple top
43 Coulee and Boulder
45 Command
46 Loose garment

47 Cowboy's rope
48 Apportion
49 Lena or Marilyn
52 Be adjacent to
53 Remove
54 Home near Twelve Oaks
55 Specialized school: Abbr.
56 Singer Turner
57 Tense
59 Social

ACROSS

1 Leonine name
6 Dress
10 Dallas univ.
13 Regarding expanse
14 James __, U.S. author
15 Suffix with labor or victor
16 Vt. site of British defeat: 1777
18 Pretext
19 Finish
20 Travels
21 How we stand
23 Takes offense at
25 Big Broadway success
26 Actress Michele
27 Lee J. or Ty
28 Youth org.
31 Intense; violent
34 Roaring Twenties dances
36 Tucked in for the night
37 Flogged
39 Burden
40 French President: 1954–59
42 Versifier Nash
43 October brew
44 Firpo of boxing
45 Mrs., in Madrid
46 Dental __
48 Intermittent light
52 Narcotic
54 Usher's concern
55 Pitcher's stat
56 Choir member
57 Charitable
60 Golfers' pegs
61 Yale Bowl, e.g.
62 Sublease
63 Dejected
64 Shrill barks
65 Pantywaist

DOWN

1 One-edged sword
2 A Castle
3 Repairs
4 Prohibit
5 Straightened
6 Duelists' pledges
7 Business reps.
8 Antique auto
9 Stupefied
10 Fighting Irish campus site
11 Ponder dreamily
12 Employed
15 Eye part
17 Short letter
22 Arrests
24 Skip over
25 Audio measure
27 Buffalo Bill's family
29 Erupt
30 Org.

92

31 __ avis
32 Fourth person
33 Gained (from)
35 Robes for justices
37 Young servant
38 Medical suffix
41 Coagulate
42 Platform pundits
45 Serb or Croat
47 Cambodian neighbor

48 Senses
49 What celebrants kick up
50 Sea eagles
51 Shabby
52 Dobbin's dinner
53 __ bargain (legal stratagem)
54 Crisp cookie
58 Actress Le Gallienne
59 Hawaiian garland

ACROSS

1 Weaving machine
5 Famed fabulist
10 Hive dwellers
14 Prefix for potent
15 Serf
16 Home of the Jazz
17 So-so school grades
18 Seized
19 Hindu teacher
20 Musician
23 Permit
24 Fruit-flavored drink
25 Island east of Borneo
29 Self
30 High mountain
33 Choice
34 Foot: Comb. form
36 Wild plum
37 Musician in the reed section
40 Withered
41 Part of Q.E.D.
42 Indian princess
43 Compass point
44 Political officeholders
45 Climbers
47 Unit of work
48 Consumed
49 Musician in the brass section
58 Chinese dynasty

59 Of an hour
60 Novelist Ferber
61 __ homo (behold the man)
62 Raise one's spirits
63 Line of juncture
64 Decay through use
65 Cozy places
66 Wise

DOWN

1 Places
2 Portent
3 Units
4 Christmas decoration
5 Cunning
6 Its capital was Susa
7 Japanese beverage
8 Baking chamber
9 Five-sided building in Virginia
10 A signal horn
11 Small needle case
12 Fall on deaf __
13 Closed
21 Violin's precursor
22 Fuss
25 Halt
26 Actress Burstyn
27 Metric liquid measure
28 Boxes
29 Blue-pencils
30 Adjust

31 Defeated contestant
32 "For __ sake!"
35 Period in history
36 Vapidity
38 Extend, as a hemline
39 Muse of poetry
44 Anger
46 Wire ropes
47 Lawn trimmer
49 Fret

50 Nottingham product
51 Peruvian Indian
52 Romeo or Juliet
53 Old Danish money
54 Actor Dillon
55 Notion
56 Unexpected obstacle
57 Docile

ACROSS

1 Bible item
6 Sum total
9 Split
14 Strange
15 Comedienne Arthur
16 Russian coin
17 Frighten
18 Small ape
19 Hamburger topper
20 Nonplused
23 Ocean's little sister
24 Roman deity
25 Assist
28 Go by taxi
31 Waned
35 Israeli dance
37 Pinball machine no-no
39 Iris, lace or braid
41 Speechless
44 Swahili or Zulu
45 Take on hands
46 Departed
47 Short comic plays
49 N.J. five
51 Lost-weekend results
52 Flightless bird of yore
54 Author Fleming
56 Sack the quarterback
63 Haughty
64 A Gershwin
65 Lubricated
67 Walkway
68 What the old nylons did
69 Willow
70 Make haste
71 Whitney or Wallach
72 Donkey, in Devon

DOWN

1 Kind of soup
2 Ego
3 Soviet body of water
4 Turkish coins
5 One of a group
6 Qualified
7 Shakespearean king
8 Stately, to Solti
9 Weapon of old
10 Short one
11 He had an Irish Rose
12 Blockhead
13 Actor Olin
21 Taunts
22 Mimic
25 Jezebel's spouse
26 Specks
27 Consumed water
29 Menu item
30 Fey

32 High or low follower

33 Transgressed

34 "She __ Say Yes," 1931 song

36 High: Prefix

38 Ripped or ripped along

40 Fast planes

42 Passé

43 Neural systems

48 Swinish female

50 Pub's cousin

53 Burning

55 Din

56 Voyage

57 Gardener's need

58 Regulation

59 Spoken

60 Rajah's spouse

61 Skidded

62 Pit

63 Family members

66 Prohibitionist

ACROSS

1 Actress Moreno
5 Sourdough's deed
10 Saroyan hero
14 "Yes __": Sammy Davis Jr.
15 Capacious
16 Arrived
17 Jack
20 Individual
21 Stair part
22 Sluggish
23 Sound receiver
24 Snow, to Burns
25 Jack
33 Lawful
34 Start of a counting-out rhyme
35 Compass dir.
36 Fronton cheer
37 Evening meals
40 Margin
41 Nabokov novel
42 Use a harvester
43 Part of Hispaniola
45 Jack
49 Zilch
50 Tavern order
51 Crow
54 Take care of
57 Exist
60 Jack

63 Suffix with resist
64 Wood for bridges
65 Vice principal, e.g.
66 See 50 Across
67 Ways and __
68 Striplings

DOWN

1 Puerto __
2 Image
3 Domesticated
4 Witch bird
5 Actress Bloom
6 Varnish ingredients
7 Commedia dell'__
8 Operatic prince
9 Debussy's "La __"
10 "A man, a plan, __, Panama"
11 Gay blade
12 Afghan V.I.P.
13 Convene
18 Special skills
19 Sty sound
23 Inventor Whitney
24 Battle memento
25 Comic Radner
26 Watery expanse
27 Drive back
28 Neighbor of Tibet
29 Clumsy
30 High nest
31 Modules

1	2	3	4		5	6	7	8	9		10	11	12	13
14					15						16			
17				18					19					
20				21						22				
			23						24					
	25	26				27	28	29				30	31	32
33					34						35			
36				37	38				39		40			
41				42					43	44				
45			46	47				48						
		49						50						
51	52	53			54	55	56				57	58	59	
60				61					62					
63				64					65					
66				67					68					

32 Big rig, for short
33 Good soil
38 Russian river
39 Hebrew word meaning "peace"
44 Summer quaff
46 Ass or catapult
47 Suits
48 Appraisers
51 Snatch
52 Queue

53 Formerly
54 Shopper stopper
55 Wagnerian goddess
56 Paradise
57 Where Laos is
58 Comedian Foxx
59 Looks at
61 Floppy cap
62 Chum

ACROSS

1 Duration measure
5 Landed
9 Hardwood tree
12 First man
13 Spokes of a circle
15 Bar order
17 Oscar winner for "Sayonara"
19 Actress Samms
20 Daub
21 Found
23 Despot
25 Exist
26 Relating to mail
29 One-tenth: Comb. form
31 Part of a min.
34 Seed covering
35 Beseech
37 Wall Street term
39 Oscar winner for "Julia"
42 Piano exercise
43 Yield
44 Pulled
45 __ Moines
46 Barrel-bottom stuff
48 Takes sap from trees
50 Friend, in Paris
51 Ending for old or young
52 Star-shaped figure
57 Marner's creator
61 Bad
62 "I Am Woman" composer-singer
64 Brain tissue
65 Add up
66 Mud puddle
67 Thing, to Belli
68 Distribute
69 Withered

DOWN

1 __ and feathers
2 The same, to Severus
3 Constructed
4 Beset
5 Garfunkel
6 Subsequently
7 Words exchanged at a wedding
8 Color slightly
9 White poplar
10 Half: Prefix
11 Garment borders
14 Newton or Stern
16 Cheer word
18 __ Major
22 Take with one
24 Pennines, e.g.
26 Asphalted a road
27 Speak pompously
28 Cranial cavity
29 Defies
30 Gazed upon

100

31 Extra tire
32 Like chalets
33 Worker gangs
36 Running contest
38 Out of sequence
40 Alabama city
41 Liability
47 Figure in skating
49 Sly look
50 Book of maps
51 Sniff

52 Favorite
53 Always
54 World's longest river
55 Peruse
56 Different: Comb. form
58 Inactive
59 Aroma
60 Sort
63 U.S. humorist

ACROSS

1 Record
5 Recurring theme
10 Battle site: 1944
14 Taj Mahal site
15 "Gesundheit" getter
16 Pequod's captain
17 Worms or squids
18 Violinist Isaac __
19 TV staple
20 Samovar
21 Norse king
22 British bye-byes
24 Cato's 156
26 Galsworthy's "__ Devon"
28 Director Spielberg
30 Horse's motion
31 Cheerleader's encouragement
34 Singing group
35 "Common Sense" author
36 "__ Yankee Doodle Dandy"
37 Stereo
38 Costly fur
39 Read a bar code
40 Finish
41 Poi sources
42 Blame bearers
43 Scottish river
44 South Yemen's capital, once
45 Muse of astronomy
46 Dozed off
48 M-R connection
49 Divert
50 Scot's wear
52 Jersey letters for the Dream Team
55 North African port
56 Din
58 Golf gadgets
59 Geometric fig.
60 Sea eagles
61 Lease
62 Capture
63 Venetian V.I.P.s
64 __-European

DOWN

1 Forbidden
2 Seaweed product
3 Hamlet's title
4 Consume
5 Film critic Janet
6 Eight: Prefix
7 Friml operetta
8 Comparative suffix
9 Actress Joan
10 __ Domingo
11 Bogart-Hepburn title
12 Statutes
13 Dictionary abbr.
21 Finished
23 Sweeten the pot
25 Cato's 57
27 Posts

51

28 Itin.
29 Biblically yours
32 Violin for a
virtuoso
33 Medieval guild
35 Gay __
38 Cast down
39 It comes in
cakes
41 Youngsters
42 Poetic cave
45 Except

47 Sixteenth of a
pound
49 "Caro nome,"
for one
51 Words of
comprehension
53 Transmit
54 In re
55 Sept. chaser
57 Spanish gold
58 Prefix with corn
or color

ACROSS

1 Infield fly
6 Qualified
10 Atom grps.
14 Tickle pink
15 Conrad or Barbara
16 "__ Ben Adhem": Leigh Hunt
17 Mature
18 Assist an arsonist
19 Tender
20 __ turn (perfectly)
21 Mayor and council
24 "Phantom Lady" star Ella __
26 Spreads by rumor
27 Wisdom bits
29 Relative of a taw or steelie
31 Woodtrimming tool
32 Drag one's feet
33 Couple
36 Quite large
39 Cut a cuspid
41 Sètte preceder
42 Oodles
44 Ubangi feeder
45 __ Alighieri
46 Wooden shoes
48 In the neighborhood of
51 Helix
53 Renowned Boston event

55 June honoree
58 "__ a Kick Out of You"
59 Never, poetically
60 Metrical feet
62 Convinced
63 White-tailed eagles
64 Orderly pile
65 Hold court
66 Method of learning
67 Tied up in knots

DOWN

1 Saucy
2 Medley
3 They like shooting stars
4 Shoshonean
5 Blue-__ (edit)
6 Lessen
7 Tended a tot
8 Would as __ (gladly)
9 Complicate
10 Number 5 iron
11 Some woodwinds
12 Moto portrayer
13 Children's author Dr. __
22 Electees
23 Fabric for a summer frock
25 Vicinity
27 Card-player's decision
28 An Adams

30 Rods for hoods
32 Senator's spot
33 Papa or boss
34 Shoe feature
35 Keats favorites
37 Mel of many voices
38 Chelsea resident, e.g.
40 Big horn
43 Downward slope
45 Housecoat
46 Knight's title

47 Manet or Monet
48 Stupidly imitative
49 Mischiefmaker
50 "Louise" or "Norma"
52 Intrinsically
54 Claudius's successor
56 Basics
57 Embankment
61 Had dinner

ACROSS

1 Turkish title
5 Easter
10 Capuchin monkey
13 Robin of legend
14 "__ of Two Cities"
15 Some recs.
16 Cartoonist Peter
17 Light unit
18 Sector
20 Hit song of 1926
23 "__, though I walk . . ."
24 Knievel
25 Conducted
26 Commercials
28 Dull finish
31 Prefix for center
33 Boorish fellow
35 Second notes
36 Pelagic fish eaters
38 Conceal
40 Mankiewicz and Papp
43 Jaeger's cousin
44 Outlaw
45 Combine
46 Celtic Neptune
47 Challenged
49 Actor Fernando
50 Lex. or Mad.
52 "Till __," 1944 song
54 Emulate Stanislavsky
56 Hit song of 1926, with "The"
62 Cupid
63 Kind of guitar or drum
64 Alike, to Brigitte
65 "Born in the __"
66 __ firma
67 Kismet
68 Sun. speech
69 Fiery crime
70 Cole chaser

DOWN

1 One-legged whaler
2 Sanguinary
3 Hit song of 1929
4 Hacienda material
5 Washed out
6 "Three men in __"
7 Young salmon
8 Adhere or split
9 Therefore
10 Thick slice
11 Hit song of 1953
12 River to the Rhone
19 Append
21 Sweet potato's relative
22 Works of a Swiss painter
26 Hirt and Pacino
27 Deer
29 Tatum of jazz

30 Peg for Peete
32 Kind of school
34 Faithful
37 Sabot or clog
39 Inheritance of
the meek
40 Crock or shock
41 Quarter of four
42 Rocky portrayer
44 Teases
good-naturedly
47 More adroit

48 Pat
50 Vigoda or
Burrows
51 Body attacker
53 Ornamental herb
55 Musical symbols
57 Autocratic leader
58 Leander's love
59 Ardor
60 Do I dare to
__ peach?: Eliot
61 Large number

ACROSS

1 Make over
5 Superman portrayer
10 Woodwind instrument
14 Ireland
15 Presbyter
16 Stunning defeat
17 Curb
19 Fine dirt
20 Withdraw from a union
21 Jaunty headgear
22 Poker stake
23 Dory adjunct
25 Enraged
27 Having the same direction
32 Bridge holding
35 Ripeners
36 Catlike mammal
38 Jogged
39 Ascended
40 Kin of saxhorns
41 Robin or swallow
42 Food fragment
43 Edible mushroom
44 Strainer
45 Greater in size
47 Legally permitted
49 Winged
51 Drop bait lightly
52 Exchange premium
54 U.N. labor arm
56 __ Nevada
61 Scores in baseball
62 Curb
64 Companion of crafts
65 Riata
66 Word of woe
67 Occupied
68 One who inquires
69 Mother of 48 Down

DOWN

1 Beatty film
2 Lake or canal
3 Thin, circular plate
4 Formerly
5 Invalidate a law
6 Building addition
7 Prepare for publication
8 Open to bribery
9 Hermits
10 Confer holy orders upon
11 Curbs
12 Remove from office
13 Feminine suffix
18 False gods
24 Happen again
26 Former G.I.
27 Word of mouth, in law
28 Greek marketplace
29 Curbs
30 Exist
31 Printed slander

108

33 Whittle
34 Finished
37 Lawful
40 Steinbeck's "__ Flat"
41 Storage drawer
43 __ culpa
44 Brown pigment
46 Having a high shine
48 __ and Pollux
50 Hebrew prophet

52 Yemeni, e.g.
53 Hindu spiritual guide
55 Russian city east of Chelyabinsk
57 And others: Abbr.
58 Get one's goat
59 Highway
60 Handle, to Hadrian
63 Suffix with expert

ACROSS

1 Ducks for apples
5 "__ a dream . . .": Martin Luther King, Jr.
10 Spotted cavy
14 Hanging askew
15 Toe
16 Viva voce
17 Close by
18 Verbal contraction
19 Rend asunder
20 Words from King
23 G.I. oases
24 Usher's beat
25 Dull finish
28 Freedom March starting point
31 Creamy color
32 Puck stopper
34 New Guinea seaport
37 What King envisioned
40 Comical cry at a mouse
41 Depended (on)
42 Leontyne Price role
43 Actress Braga
44 Jewish festival
45 ". . . Montgomery to Oslo is __ . . .": King
48 Writer Hunter
50 King's credo
57 Singer Paul from Ottawa
58 Goof
59 Practical joke, e.g.
60 Have the lead
61 Declares with confidence
62 Pound or Stone
63 Wife of Zeus
64 "Giant" ranch
65 Consider

DOWN

1 Whimper's alternative, at world's end
2 Bread spread
3 "Michael, Row the __ Ashore"
4 Grow rapidly
5 Locale of 13 Down
6 Takes on
7 "Full many __ of purest ray . . .": Gray
8 Chianti, e.g.
9 Caesar's reproach to Brutus
10 Antonio's defender
11 Jessye Norman's stock-in-trade
12 Carp
13 Coeur d'__
21 Monogram of Old Possum's creator
22 Fingered, in a way
25 Dole out
26 Yearn
27 Arduous journey
28 Sheeplike antelope
29 Besides
30 Told a whopper
32 Enter

55

33 Atlanta arena
34 Hyena's home
35 "The King __"
36 Dutch cheese
38 Valerie Harper sitcom
39 Sent off a spacecraft
43 Vast desert in Africa
44 Normal condition
45 Inundated
46 French income

47 Werner of "Ship of Fools"
48 Chris of tennis
49 Vice follower
51 Angle iron
52 King's answer to human conflict
53 Draft classification
54 Exude
55 She ain't what she used to be
56 Quiz

111

ACROSS

1 Haley book
6 Ripens
10 Roscoe
13 Consent
14 Kipling's "__ Sea to Sea"
15 Host
16 Liberace's candelabra holder
18 Den
19 Sprite
20 "__ tu . . . ," Verdi aria
21 American, in Acapulco
23 Ancient ascetic
26 China preceder
27 Compelling
30 Pirates' craft
32 Corporeal channels
33 Have the flu
34 Mugger on the boards
37 Nucleic acid
38 Conceded
41 A Gershwin
42 Rather or McGrew
43 Stowe girl
44 Amati product
46 Electronic device
49 In a dry way
50 Movie dog
51 OPEC, for one
54 Star: Comb. form
56 Robert E. __
57 Baden-Baden, e.g.
60 Aped minnows
61 La Scala offering
65 Brother of Fritz, in comics
66 Handicapped, in a way
67 Warsaw inhabitants
68 Finish
69 Enough, to FitzGerald
70 Cut of halibut

DOWN

1 Duster or tatter
2 Monster
3 Spoken
4 Hoop's height in basketball
5 But, to Cato
6 Burning
7 Wheat or rye
8 Long, long time
9 One cause of heavy breathing
10 Prince Charles, to George VI
11 Mexican friend
12 Novice
15 Straighten
17 Annoyed
22 Josh
24 Obstruction
25 Egress
27 Ace, for one

28 Mrs. Chaplin
29 Stadium section
31 Raised
33 Memorabilia
35 Seed cover
36 "__ are called . . ."
39 With: Fr.
40 Calamitous
45 Ceramist's __ glaze
47 Newspaper entries
48 Scull adjunct

50 Egypt's great dam
52 Texas shrine
53 Extend a subscription
54 "Off the Court" author
55 Give the eye
58 Soccer great
59 Region
62 Scurried
63 Wife of Saturn
64 Inquire

ACROSS

1 Tradesman
7 Apparel
13 Earthy or earthly
14 Tryst
16 Reclusive
17 Exalt
18 Periods of prosperity
19 Had a leading role
21 Prohibition
22 Actor Max of "Barney Miller"
24 Solar year excess
25 Sora or rail
26 Homes for bees
28 Fr. holy woman
29 Kitchen appliance
30 Agreements between nations
32 Vocalist
33 Tear
34 Pleat
35 Graf's game
38 Fall apart
42 Man from Mars
43 __ Angeles
44 Crisp cookies
45 Tie together tightly
46 Lures
48 Landed
49 Cutting tool
50 Hush-hush matters
52 Fruit drink
53 Necklace of precious gems
55 Convalesce
57 Shaker for condiments
58 Pencil adjuncts
59 Plant sprouts
60 Checks

DOWN

1 Give up hope
2 Causing disintegration
3 Circle section
4 Hawaiian garlands
5 Related on mother's side
6 Slipped back to a former state
7 Fine
8 Doctrine
9 Care for
10 Judge in 1995 headlines
11 Veins of a leaf
12 Increase in size
13 Imparted knowledge
15 Male or female
20 Cry of disgust
23 Well educated
25 Neck scarf
27 Beer mug
29 Small brooks

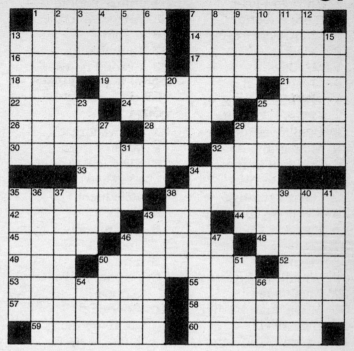

31 Electees
32 Name for the sun
34 Promoted
35 Knight's garment
36 Cure-alls
37 Ancient capital of Assyria
38 Coconut fiber
39 Prolonged discussion
40 Web weavers

41 Glycerides
43 Workers in a football plant
46 Chapeau for Corot
47 Cubic meter
50 State flower of Utah
51 Begone!
54 Wedding words
56 Carbohydrate suffix

ACROSS

1 Zhivago's love
5 Pfc.'s superior
8 Capital of Oregon
13 Yalies
14 Meadow
15 "Tosca" et al.
17 "Through the __ of Ruth . . .": Keats
19 Bind a certain way
20 Monogram of Prufrock's creator
21 "The Sun Also __"
23 Daisy's relative
24 Movie equipment
26 Ply with a potion
27 Exchange premium
30 Whodunit feature
32 Invalidates
35 Music man Michel
38 Big wheel
40 Persian Gulf wind
42 Small ropes on ships
44 __ of Capricorn
45 Amassed
46 Aerie
47 Prying
50 Braided; plaited
54 Spinach cousin
56 Stage direction
57 Martini ingredient
60 Beatrice of comedy
62 A Bogart role
64 Injury addition
65 Anagram for ire
66 Cupid
67 Valuable fur
68 Second notes
69 Actress Tuesday

DOWN

1 "__ we forget"
2 Woeful word
3 First U.S. woman in space
4 Residue
5 Stake
6 Intrinsically
7 Football pass
8 Sun god
9 Capital of Western Samoa
10 Capone contemporary
11 Muse of poetry
12 Spouses
16 Withered
18 Epoch
22 Soupy of radio and TV
24 Where the elite meet
25 Spectacle
27 Plane-launched weapon: Abr.
28 Growl
29 Swenson of "Benson"

116

31 Word with Rabbit or Fox
33 Tra chasers
34 Tour of duty
36 Scruff
37 Podium
39 Accustom
41 W.W. II craft
43 TV sleuth
47 __ me tangere
48 O'Neill character et al.

49 Popular chip dip
51 Rubberneck
52 Behemoths of the road
53 Forage plant
55 Mound
57 Plucky
58 Matinee __
59 Wimp's cousin
61 When Paris sizzles
63 Pussy foot

ACROSS

1 The Moslem faith
6 Detroit products
10 Nos. person
13 Ruth's mother-in-law
14 A woodwind
15 Skirmish
16 Hybridize
18 Tops
19 __ in Able
20 __ the line (conformed)
21 Tickles
23 First U.S. space traveler
25 Collars or jackets
26 Hawaiian liquor, for short
27 Cummerbunds' cousins
28 Charge
31 TV host
34 Kind of guard
36 Sharp-tasting
37 Kitchen wear
39 Math course
40 Transverse timber
42 Sorority members
43 Linen marking
44 "Sister" of Vesuvius
45 Actor Chaney
46 Flier from a fire
48 One of Lear's daughters
52 "Ivanhoe" heroine
54 Equitable
55 "Three men __ tub"
56 Actor Sharif
57 Major intersection
60 Gram or type preceder
61 "All __ Jazz," 1979 movie
62 Hit musical of 1977
63 Noah's vessel
64 Male heirs
65 Musical instrument of 50 Down

DOWN

1 Ancient Peruvians
2 Actress Bernhardt
3 Free
4 Morning hrs.
5 Error
6 Prepared apples for baking
7 Not up yet
8 Fish eggs
9 Act of calming via a drug
10 Brisk exchange of words or opinions
11 Window part
12 Affirmative votes
15 "Afternoon of a __": Debussy
17 Drill
22 Playwright Hart
24 Keats and Shelley
25 Spanish river

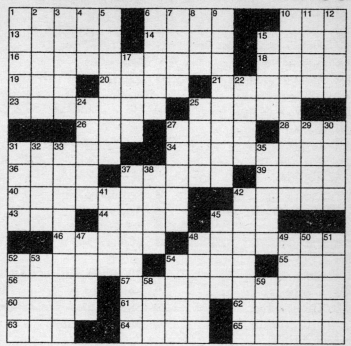

27 Sheath of a leafstalk

29 Geraint's wife

30 Leghorns' largess

31 Engrave with acid

32 French husband

33 Pedestrian's lane

35 "Platoon" director

37 Draws

38 Carnation

41 Actor Connery

42 Nicaraguan rebels

45 Profit's opposite

47 Mère's mate

48 Squalls

49 Laughing

50 Vast subcontinent

51 Intense light beam

52 Roster

53 Hebrew measure

54 Actress Crawford

58 Greek letter

59 Navy's C.I.A.

ACROSS

1 Raptorial flier
6 Cheer word
9 Extent
14 Canary's cousin
15 One of the ratites
16 Certain cockerel
17 Moment
18 Voracious flier
20 Met production
22 Type of grin
23 Standards
26 A Shoshonean
27 Turkey portions
30 "__ Andronicus"
32 Function
36 Farewell
38 Common or horse follower
40 Clothe, with "up"
41 Those who proverbially flock together
44 Building addition
45 Soul
46 "__ Foolish Things . . .": 1935 song
47 For fear that
49 Beer mug
51 Once, once
52 News agcy.
54 Clothe
56 Created anew
59 Homo sapiens, e.g.
62 European robin
65 Homes for 41 Across
67 Steps over a fence
68 Dove call
69 "Life __ Beautiful"
70 Heads, in France
71 Complexion
72 Relative on mother's side

DOWN

1 Superlative ending
2 It precedes dynamic
3 Props man
4 Authorized
5 Primero mes
6 Type of room, for short
7 First of a Latin trio
8 Aggrieve
9 Skedaddle
10 America's 39th President
11 Colorful marine fish
12 __ express
13 Suffix with exist
19 Puddinglike dessert
21 Actor Carney
24 One not suited for the job
25 Cooked, in a way
27 Tag
28 Roman official
29 Lasses
31 Inequitable

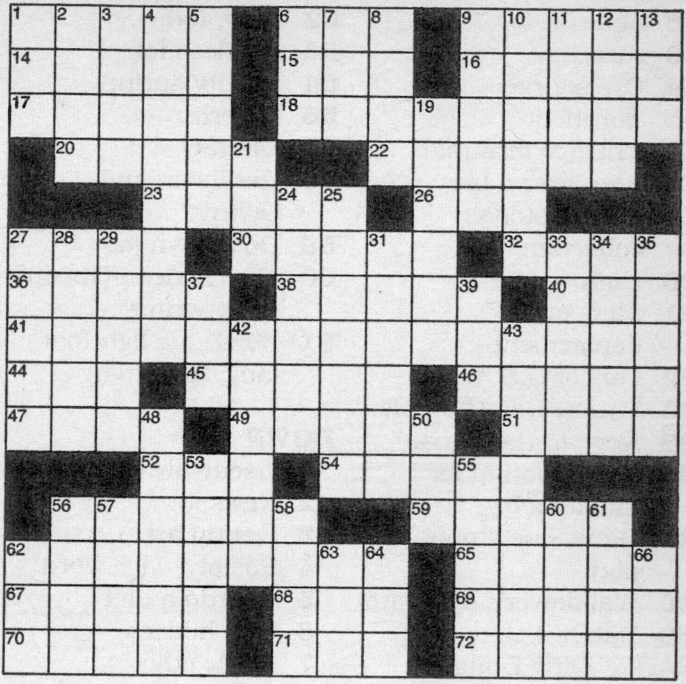

33 Different
34 Soil deposit
35 Everglades denizen
37 Springsteen's "Born in the __"
39 Gormandize
42 Kind of kick, in football
43 Actor
48 Fall
50 Beak

53 Shaves
55 Because
56 Anatomical network
57 Revise
58 Every's partner
60 Ferber or Best
61 Liability
62 Q-U connection
63 Old French coin
64 Tot's "piggy"
66 Bishopric

ACROSS

1 Related
5 Agile
9 Attacks
14 Ore source
15 Staunch
16 Chicago terminal
17 Soar over a bar
19 Early Astor's collection
20 High __ kite
21 Alencon's department
22 Part of U.S.A.
23 Plunge into the ether
25 Now, in the barrio
26 Underfooting for Yamaguchi
27 Game one stoops to play
30 Wallflower's opposite
33 Batter
34 "__ Ding Dong Daddy . . ."
35 Skating stunt
36 French assembly
37 Loutish one
38 Fat farm
39 Community folkways
40 Rawboned
41 First sergeants, to G.I.s
43 Mongrel
44 Lack of good sense
45 Bounded over a barrier

49 Conditional release
51 Adriatic seaport
52 Clay, today
53 Footless lot
54 Mighty spring
56 Severity
57 Old tar
58 Gershwin and Levin
59 Do a lawn job
60 "The African Queen" scriptwriter
61 "And __ a lightfoot lad": Housman

DOWN

1 Oscar-awarding org.
2 Newsstand
3 Dental art
4 Society-page word
5 Overdo a diet
6 Clip hedges
7 Hoyle edict
8 Still
9 Lively amphibian
10 Have __ (show mercy)
11 Dancing movement
12 TV's Johnson
13 Hardy lass
18 Express an opinion
22 Move boxcars about
24 Popular pickle
25 Cool colors
27 Units of sound
28 Running wild

122

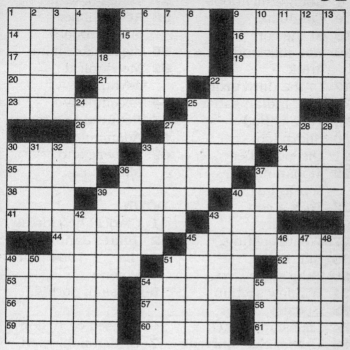

29 Cooper or Hart
30 Flax or hemp
31 Montreal player
32 Goes over another's head
33 Cheerful; brisk
36 Plinth
37 Minstrel
39 President Fillmore
40 Shockingly vivid
42 Striped antelope
43 Man of the cloth

45 Caucasian, in Hawaii
46 Tierney classic: 1944
47 Violinist Mischa
48 "__ Doodle," 1937 song
49 Young salmon
50 ". . . Baked in __"
51 Vaunt
54 Jamboree org.
55 Huck's raft-sharer

ACROSS

1 Communications
9 Conducts
15 At the core
16 Hot milk-and-wine drink
17 Of the third order
18 East Indian sailor
19 Time period
20 Sharp tool
21 Disencumber
22 Mohammed's son-in-law
23 Took a cab
25 Ruhr city
27 Went coasting
28 Side dish
30 Take steps
31 Window section
32 __ daisy
34 Like some cakes
35 Unit of elec. current
38 Goes to the meeting
40 Id follower
41 Skirt features
43 Judge twice
45 Nettled
46 D.C. bigwig
47 Mubarak's capital
50 Soviet news source
51 "Siddhartha" author
53 Spiders on stoves
55 Stein filler

56 Quip
57 Touch of winter
59 Actor Kilmer of "The Doors"
60 Flammable item
62 Mechanical advantage
64 Accompany
65 Reduced to a mean
66 Adamant
67 Scrooge and Marley, e.g.

DOWN

1 Clerical headdress
2 Juárez Januaries
3 "La __," 1954 film
4 Coterie
5 "Nessun dorma," e.g.
6 Caused corrosion
7 British noblemen
8 Vulpine
9 First-aid device
10 Natterjack
11 Hook shape
12 Increase
13 Straightens anew
14 Grating
21 Disavow
24 Overhead trains
26 Glossy fabrics
27 Bad Ems, e.g.
29 Triumphant cries

124

33 Lewis's "Main __"
34 Greek peak
35 Stirs up
36 Aesop, for one
37 Bearing
39 Cheat
42 Sullivan and Asner
44 Cant
46 1995 film "Get __"

48 Plunder
49 Ass or catapult
52 Indy champ: 1983
54 Luges
56 Blackbird
58 Impudent
61 Bambi's mother
62 Once around the track
63 Took charge of

ACROSS

1 Diner's faux pas
5 Pompous one
9 Helen's abductor
14 __ Minor
15 Verdi classic
16 Much too heavy
17 Dignitary's grand welcome
19 Soup scoop
20 Oppose boldly
21 Truck of a sort
23 Haw's companion
24 What a cheerleader has
26 Concealed matters
28 China of Germany
32 Buck or hart
33 Idyl or sonnet
34 Computer's diet
36 Agamemnon's war god
39 Actor Ray
40 Part of U.S.N.A.
41 Hangchow export
42 Bothersome individual
43 Kudos at the corrida
44 "__ You," Platters hit
45 Salamander
47 Orchestra section
50 Cut prices drastically
53 Matador's trophy
54 Faucet
55 Osiris's wife
57 Bone filler

62 Vail competitor
64 St. Basil's Cathedral site
66 Gaggle members
67 Shoe or family follower
68 Thrust
69 Miscue
70 Longbows-in-the-rough
71 Snakelike fish

DOWN

1 Nasty remark
2 Unscrupulous person
3 Astronaut Sally
4 S.A. rodent
5 Broke up
6 Actor Torn
7 Mid-month, to Virgil
8 Portcullises' kin
9 Shield carriers
10 Bedouin garment
11 Whodunit ingredient
12 Tiny land mass
13 Appears
18 African snakes
22 Hero's award
25 Part of a trike
27 Paine's "The Age of __"
28 Clinton rival
29 Gulf Coast menu item

30 Shows rage or sorrow
31 Church parts
33 Mush relative
35 A sense
37 Edifice extensions
38 Firmament
40 Observes
46 Puling person
48 Big name in old Egypt
49 Mesopotamian nation

50 Repertory showplace
51 Kind of disc or printer
52 Soiled
56 Withered
58 Clever trick
59 The going __
60 Exam type
61 Arachnids' traps
63 Inner: Prefix
65 Dawn's droplets

ACROSS

1 Creator of Li'l Abner
5 Home or bed follower
10 Bandicoots
14 Mountain range in the U.S.S.R.
15 Thanks, to Dumas
16 Author James __: 1909–55
17 Sacks
19 Distance measure
20 Bird dogs
21 Groups of fish
23 Express
25 Presidential nickname
26 Dreadful
28 Worked
33 Fall beverage
34 Harold of comics
35 U.N. arm
36 Linden and Holbrook
37 Factory
39 Cessation
40 Suffix with elephant
41 Part of Q.E.D.
42 Scenic view
43 Milton's "__ Lost"
45 Composer of "Comus"
46 Border
47 Triangle at a river mouth

50 Athenian's rival
54 Carl, Rob and Fritz
58 Nat or Natalie
59 Like some rainfalls
61 Vipers
62 Come onstage
63 Wreath on a knight's helmet
64 Take five
65 Pits
66 Require

DOWN

1 Bounders
2 "It's a Sin to Tell __"
3 A tense
4 Visualizes
5 Shrewd
6 Succinct
7 Unit of work
8 Experts
9 Prudent
10 Heroine of an old novel or song
11 Exchange premium
12 Swiss patriot
13 Understands
18 Other: Comb. form
22 Shofar
24 Followed in turn
26 Rigg or Ross
27 Loafer
29 Writing implement

128

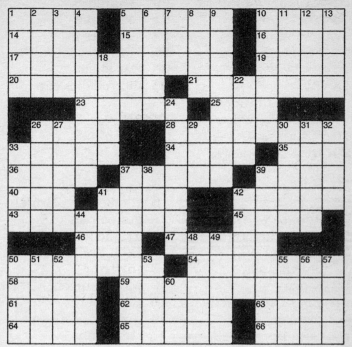

30 Gigantic person
31 Wed in secret
32 Nitwit
33 Casino item
37 Religious dignitaries
38 __ Vegas
39 Seat of Marywood College
41 Redact
42 Glossy fabric
44 Check

48 Made a mistake
49 Lascivious looks
50 Cicatrix
51 Do some modeling
52 The Dolomites, e.g.
53 Not any
55 Erin, to a Gael
56 Respiratory sound
57 Snow vehicle
60 Hwy.

ACROSS

1 Napkins for babies
5 Huckster, sometimes
10 Formless mass
14 Soviet sea
15 Twit
16 French fantasy
17 Off one's rocker
18 Discussed
20 Desk accessory, once
22 Holmes activity
23 Shoe size
24 Actress Merrill
25 Gets cracking
28 Provides gratuitously
32 Stops
33 Cry of surprised dismay
35 Satanic
36 Flood refuge
37 Spartan serf
38 Notable time
39 Chariot way
41 Spirit
42 Basque's topper
44 Mazurkalike dance
46 Snacks and feasts
48 Art movement
50 Aleutian island
51 Trooper's quarry
54 River in Hades
57 Retreated
59 Within: Prefix
60 "Thanks __"
61 Rich cake
62 Grouper
63 Porgy's woman
64 Ear shell
65 Pierre is its cap.

DOWN

1 Island off Java
2 Golf-bag item
3 Sassed
4 Least speedy
5 Clement __, British statesman
6 Traffic (in)
7 Bad: Prefix
8 Invited
9 Most indigent
10 Rich fabric
11 Jacob and Leah's third son
12 Chamber for Child
13 Titanic's undoing
19 Country duo Brooks and __
21 Tolkien creatures
25 Roaring Camp's creator
26 Musical Coward
27 Word with plexus or system
29 Upset
30 Cables

31 Bed support
32 Long-running musical
34 Dixie-style bread
37 Set a course for
40 Squirrels and chipmunks
42 British spa
43 Regards highly
45 Walk (through)
47 Green Bay gridder

49 Vined latticework shelter
51 Puncture
52 Whimper
53 God of love
54 Part of a Molière work
55 Other: Sp.
56 Recess
58 Humerus's locale

ACROSS

1 Savory jelly
6 Vegetables
10 Fish or singer
14 Kind of surgeon
15 N.Y.U. is one
16 Margarine
17 Famed twosome
20 Cattle locales
21 Utah city
22 Corn unit
23 Stallone's nickname
25 Streisand or Streep
28 Baden-Baden, e.g.
29 Bible book
33 Be frugal
34 British gun
35 Castle defense
36 Anonymous trio
39 Nobelist Wiesel
40 Penitential season
41 Addition
42 Marries
43 Assistance
44 Beams
45 Small hotel
46 Constrictor
48 Raced
51 Bunch of grapes
55 Apocalyptic quartet
59 Bridge seat
60 Decree

61 Slur
62 Picnic intruders
63 Chooses
64 Goat antelope

DOWN

1 Also
2 Char
3 Cougar
4 Work on laundry
5 Symphonic compositions
6 One who mopes
7 Football-pass catchers
8 Cleo's snake
9 Pig pen
10 Nobelist Niels __
11 "I cannot tell __"
12 Part of a baseball
13 Mayday's cousin
18 Cry of discovery
19 Plaything
23 Used up
24 Reach port
25 Fur scarf
26 Like Milquetoast
27 Mountains in Peru
28 Lose a lap
29 Radarange maker
30 Full of clichés
31 Weight allowances
32 Lower-world river

33 Mulligan or
    slumgullion
34 Coil of yarn
37 Closely knit
    group
38 Torments
45 Words at an altar
46 Smirches
47 Your and my
48 Thai tongue
49 Nuisance

50 Newts
51 Informal
    conversation
52 Far: Comb. form
53 Eastern V.I.P.
54 Fix over
55 Social
56 Sky sight, to
    some
57 Tear
58 Unused

ACROSS

1 Gooseneck, e.g.
5 Cries loudly
9 Court minutes
13 Woodwind
14 Name in spydom
15 __ rate (inferior)
17 Sluggards
19 Excessive enthusiasm
20 Doddering
21 Various
23 Unkempt abode
24 Short sketch
25 Bit of land amid water
26 Stadium cheers
28 Abandons
30 "The Greatest"
31 Word after door or place
32 "And __ shake the spheres": Dryden
36 Reflect
38 An explosive
39 Directed
41 Elec. unit
42 A Canadian export
43 Twelfth graders
45 Very, in Paris
46 Epochs
49 Spicy stew
50 Dull routine
51 Softened
53 Against
56 Night noise
57 Significant event
59 Canvas abodes
60 Vegetarian's anathema
61 Mandolin's cousin
62 Oater's locale
63 Slithering killers
64 Collar or jacket

DOWN

1 Forfeiture
2 Qualified
3 Illegal booze
4 Lapwings
5 Word with lace or tree
6 Acorn's source
7 What born losers don't get
8 Pantywaists
9 Vapor: Comb. form
10 Magnetic quality
11 Shades
12 "The Tempest" sprite
16 Miami's county
18 Layer
22 Rivers
24 Bridge reversal
26 Knocks
27 "Thanks __!"
28 "Letting 'I __' wait . . .": Shak.
29 What an R.N. takes

31 Nothing more than
33 Begins a journey
34 Decorated metalware
35 Bullfight cries
37 Sweets
40 Predicament
41 Ex-coach Parseghian
44 Songs of yore
45 Snapper

46 Formerly, formerly
47 Freshen
48 Solo
50 Legal matter
52 Bird's-__ soup
53 Animal docs
54 Golden-rule word
55 Homophone for scene
58 Toddler's favorite spot

ACROSS

1 Shadowbox
5 Dunces
10 Asian nanny
14 Kind of duck
15 Gallagher's vaudeville partner
16 Jay of late night
17 Ballplayer Amos
18 Inasmuch as
19 Famed suffragette
20 Call it quits
23 Captains' records
24 Was a candidate
25 Demonstrated
28 Petered out
33 Bathes
34 Auctioneer's warning
35 A feast __ famine
36 Elderly
37 Fetch
38 Serve the coffee
39 Buddhist sect
40 Set straight
41 Something worthless
42 Supposing
44 Bed linen
45 Mailing stations: Abbr.
46 Oil cartel
47 Speaks the unvarnished truth

55 Medicinal plant
56 Overact
57 Not new
58 Brewer's need
59 Moon or Spoon
60 Another kind of duck
61 Clumsy boats
62 Gawk
63 Hard to handle

DOWN

1 Kind of machine
2 Footway
3 Moslem V.I.P.
4 Made a decision
5 Designate
6 Climbs, in a way
7 Dispatched
8 Anagram for ache
9 Disdainful
10 Nutty flavoring
11 Kitten's cry
12 Create a pot
13 "The __ Baltimore," Wilson play
21 Troubles
22 Spicy taste
25 Shopping mall
26 Spreads unchecked
27 Hot spots
28 Busy with
29 Port or sherry

136

30 Shavetail
31 Explode
32 Takes a risk
34 Beam
37 Banes of tennis players
38 Head off
40 To me: Fr.
41 Quakers' pronoun
43 Disturbs

44 Globe or ball
46 Aquatic mammal
47 Tibetan priest
48 Winged
49 Main part of an egg
50 Leave out
51 Popular PBS show
52 "Got it!"
53 Actress Patricia
54 Mary Baker __

ACROSS

1 Pointed tools
5 Knights' wives
10 Arp's art
14 Cage for chicks
15 Archie Bunker's wife
16 Actor Jannings
17 Problem solvers
20 Becomes better
21 At a rapid tempo
22 "Let __ eat cake"
23 Health resorts
24 Diversifies
27 A basic human need
30 Actress/talk-show host Stewart
31 Task
32 Decay
34 Valuable vase
35 Serbs and Croats
36 A fine cotton
37 Wooden pin
38 Uncle Tom's creator
39 __ of the crop
40 Novelty
42 California raisin center
43 Product from sisal
44 Gets the point
45 Makes irate
48 Honeys
52 S.C. lawmaker
54 Iran's foe: Var.
55 Bête __ (bugbear)
56 Source of mohair
57 Does some planting
58 Break off
59 Partner of odds

DOWN

1 Start of a play
2 Robin's prey
3 Airplane maneuver
4 Old Faithful activity
5 Digs for data
6 Legally revoke, as a legacy
7 __ America
8 Numerical suffix
9 Malls are their meccas
10 Abhor
11 College town in Iowa
12 __ cheap
13 Moreover
18 Black tea
19 Papal cape
23 What push comes to
24 Seductive woman
25 Being from outer space
26 Grassland
27 Artie and Irwin
28 Hurons' kin

138

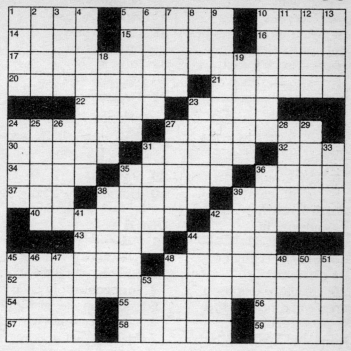

29 Kind of candle
31 Neck and neck
33 "__ Shanter," Burns poem
35 Relatives by marriage
36 Renown
38 A wee nip
39 Angler's basket
41 Inflicts
42 Tentacle

44 Took an oath
45 Sale sign
46 Notorious fiddler
47 Eat like a beaver
48 Hood's switchblade
49 A part of
50 Major Hoople's expletive
51 Giant jets
53 Caviar

ACROSS

1 "__ Lisa"
5 Decorous
10 The nouveaux riches put it on
14 Starbuck's captain
15 Jay Silverheels role
16 Spooky-sounding lake
17 Blushing
18 "__ of Murder," 1948 film
19 The Swedish Nightingale
20 With 51 Across, the pursuit of happiness?
23 British Teddy boys
24 Trim trees
25 African expedition
28 Overshoes for the pursuer
33 "The __ lama / He's a priest": Nash
34 Merganser
36 Fishing net
37 Balsam, e.g.
38 Kind of lantern
40 Faucet
41 Heart chambers
43 Castor's mother
44 Marquand sleuth
45 Pursuer's protector
47 Man of a Thousand Faces
49 Thun's river
50 __ Rabbit, Uncle Remus friend
51 See 20 Across
58 Beethoven's birthplace
59 Pile up
60 __-majesté
61 Piedmontese wine center
62 Belief
63 Oil cartel
64 Filmed
65 Vestibule
66 Home of the Jazz

DOWN

1 Antony or Connelly
2 Words of surprise
3 Spaced-out agcy.?
4 Immeasurably deep
5 Alden spoke for him
6 Hammer's partner
7 Medical-school subj.
8 Seven-year affliction
9 "You don't say!"
10 Backslide
11 Pupil's place
12 Touch with color
13 British omega
21 Super suffix
22 At large
25 Up to now
26 Bryant or Baker
27 Iron: Comb. form

28 Dramatist Jean
29 Filled with wonder
30 Find in a serendipitous way
31 Akin on Mom's side
32 Former Indian infantryman
35 "__ 18," 1961 Uris book
38 Chocolate source
39 Vestry
42 Teed off

44 Gymnast Retton
46 Rococo
48 Layer
50 More despicable
51 "Tommyrot!"
52 Golden-rule word
53 Sobeit
54 Carry on about
55 Govt. branch
56 On the briny
57 "Ugh!"
58 Kind of relief

ACROSS

1 Soft mineral
5 Beanstalk boy
9 Manifest
14 Cupid
15 Wight, e.g.
16 Abdul-Jabbar was one
17 The Censor
18 Nicholas II was the last
19 Mountain ridge
20 With 36 Across, used-car salesman's pitch
23 It's for the birds
24 Tot's muddy concoction
25 Equivalence in value
28 Chance happening
33 Correct
34 Jai __
35 Kanga's baby
36 See 20 Across
40 Not pro
41 Wimbledon winner: 1975
42 Sydney Carton's love
43 Mandarin's drink, perhaps
46 Actor Assante
47 Pothole
48 Gleason's "How sweet __!"
49 Customer's reply
57 ". . . by the __ early light": Key
58 King of comedy
59 Eye part
60 Funeral oration
61 Sandwich fish
62 Frog or year preceder
63 Invited
64 Skating maneuver
65 Cithara's cousin

DOWN

1 Diplomacy
2 Nanking nanny
3 Viaud's pen name
4 Intersection
5 Small bus
6 What 1 Down is to a consul
7 Thunder sound
8 Deborah, Jean or Walter
9 Patron saint of Norway
10 Diverse
11 Made do
12 Neural network
13 "__ bien!"
21 Surpass
22 In the work cited: Abbr.
25 Fruit for Melba's dessert
26 Perth __, N.J.
27 Horse's restraint
28 Greeting with the lei of the land
29 Solicitude
30 Writer Jong
31 Out

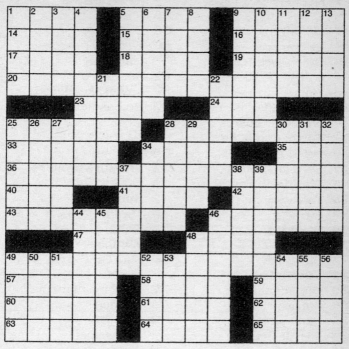

32 Trifled (with)
34 Basilica area
37 Page or LuPone
38 Patron saint of Augsburg
39 Chowderhead
44 Valencia or mandarin
45 Harbored, as a grudge
46 Dissonant
48 Silly

49 Brainstorm
50 "The Laughing Cavalier" painter
51 Furry "Return of the Jedi" creature
52 Informal farewell
53 Park of K.K.K.
54 Actress Judith or Dana
55 Close
56 Stare open-mouthed

ACROSS

1 Mediterranean isle
6 Whips
11 Mil. award
14 As crazy as __
15 Greek architectural order
16 Yoko __
17 Hit ahead of preceding golfers
19 Earth: Comb. form
20 Lyres' kin
21 Eyed amorously
23 Darling, in Yorkshire
26 Toolbox item
27 Attracts
28 Bounded
30 Moreno and Hayworth
31 Less ruddy
32 Lab animal
35 Singles
36 Class clown
37 Missile housing
38 For each
39 Solzhenitsyn subject
40 Tropical grass used for thatching
41 Listen
43 Eye protectors
44 His motto: "The puck stops here"
46 Guides
47 Demolished
48 Part of Hispaniola
50 Alias, for short
51 Par-plus-two score
57 Thrice, in prescriptions
58 Thread
59 Eat away
60 Tackle's teammate
61 Sommer's namesakes
62 He has nerves of steel

DOWN

1 Treasure hunter's aid
2 Sum total
3 Mauna __
4 Trifle
5 Hymns of praise
6 Like Oregonian forests
7 Airplane maneuver
8 Burden
9 Musician's engagement
10 Academic type
11 Slicer's favorite hole
12 Scoff
13 Feelings
18 November ring occupants
22 "The __ Game"
23 Excel
24 Duffer's downfall
25 Paleozoic and Mesozoic
26 Certain school, for short
27 Trim

144

28 Archfiend
29 Promote one's movie
31 Whimper
33 "A Lesson From __"
34 Lots
36 Gourd's "cuz"
37 Middling
39 Frying pan
40 Worth; distinction
42 Pub order
43 Low-fat, in product names

44 Abrade
45 Like a certain bucket
46 Accumulations
48 Part of an ear of corn
49 Qualified
52 Venezuelan export
53 Gold, in Granada
54 Tar
55 Nipponese capital, once
56 Eventually

ACROSS

1 Character in 53 Across
5 Served well
9 Pavarotti and Domingo
11 Drudges
13 First name of 21 Across
14 Happy
16 "Boléro" composer
17 At full speed: Poet.
19 Recompense
20 Ottoman imperial standard
21 Character in 53 Across
22 Subsist
23 One of a deadly septet
24 Jackie of jest
25 High hat
26 Fastened, in a way
28 Malcontents
30 Primitive plant
32 Gauguin's God
33 Sounds flustered
37 Safeguard
41 Fluffs
42 Picks for a role
44 Stephen of "The Crying Game"
45 Like the vulture
46 Character in 53 Across

47 Liverpool bars
48 Ecological org.
49 MTV offering
50 Peace Palace site, with "The"
51 Hide
53 Schulz strip
55 Jawaharlal and Motilal
56 Some pen drawings
57 Castile, e.g.
58 Character in 53 Across

DOWN

1 Yeast does this
2 Type of legal proceedings
3 Droop
4 "Exodus" hero
5 Beat
6 Calvados capital
7 Actress Gabor
8 Notwithstanding
9 Muse of comedy
10 Roebuck's partner
11 Engendered
12 Three-time Cy Young Award winner
13 Black Monday happening
15 Vatmen
18 Othello, e.g.
21 Shield

146

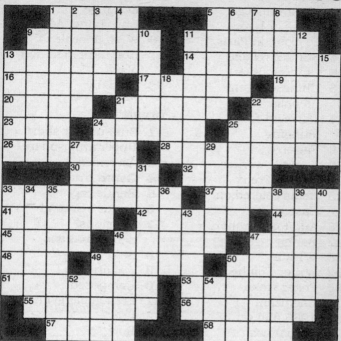

22 Character in
   53 Across
24 Emulates Frosty
25 Appearances
27 Character in
   53 Across
29 Devotion
31 Porticoes
33 Pivots
34 Character in
   53 Across
35 Loosens a corset

36 Garage event
38 Salto locale
39 Contradicts
40 Abates
43 Swill
46 Tummy
   tightener
47 Fright
49 Aloe __
50 Maori clan
52 Greek letter
54 Conger

ACROSS

1 Harvest
5 Macaroni, e.g.
10 Puma or lynx
13 To exist, in Paris
14 Surface related
15 Chinese desert
16 Chinese eating utensils
18 Garment for lounging
19 Fabulist
20 A textile worker
22 Before: Prefix
23 Items colored on Easter
26 Auditor, for short
27 Bare
28 Is irate
32 Writer Bombeck
35 Poker stake
37 Cognizant
38 1985 film set in Chinatown
41 Pass a law
42 The Eternal City
43 Roster
44 Girl in "The Wizard of Oz"
46 Nobleman
48 __ Dee, river in the Carolinas
49 Novelist Ferber
50 Guido's highest note
53 Losers in a race
57 Connection
59 Vaporize a liquid
60 Chinese fowl
63 Group in southwestern China
64 Expunge
65 Entertainer Adams
66 W.W. II locale
67 Golf term in match play
68 Close by

DOWN

1 Sum up, for short
2 Upper atmosphere
3 Ascended
4 Gourd fruit
5 Gentle tap
6 Jackie's second
7 Religious denominations
8 Seize
9 __-Lorraine
10 Composed
11 French clergyman's title
12 Row
15 Chinese tourist attraction
17 See 24 Down
21 Asparagus shoot
24 With 17 Down, German battleship
25 Singer Bobbie __
27 Venetian traveler in China
28 Appeared to be
29 Holy: Comb. form
30 Greek god of love
31 Dispatched
32 Spotted

148

33 City on the Truckee
34 Picasso's model, Dora __
36 Even if, briefly
39 Aquatic mammal
40 College official
45 Piled
47 Tolled
49 Mound of sand, gravel and rocks
50 Ooze

51 Donizetti's "__ di Lammermoor"
52 Inquirer
53 Qualified
54 Booty
55 Fodder holder
56 Emperor after Claudius I
58 Paradise
61 Doctrine
62 Napoleon's marshal

ACROSS

1 Roughage
5 Harry's helpmate
9 Settlements
14 Carson City neighbor
15 Montreal athlete
16 Athenians' meeting place
17 Former Ugandan strong man
18 Train in the ring
19 Courtroom event
20 Five-and-ten
22 Viet __
23 Road agent's quarry
24 Hide away
26 Tout's specialty
28 Sluggish
29 O.K. Corral lawman
30 Chanel
31 Subsidize
33 Brunch beverages
35 Different ones
39 Scuffle
40 Man of high rank
42 Exclusive group
43 Lots of moola
44 Marathon, e.g.
46 Golf club
50 Golden Gate City inst. of learning
51 __ firma
52 Ephron et al.
54 Skier's convenience

56 Insignificant
58 Hollandaise, e.g.
59 It's fit to be tied
60 Restrain
61 Affected by poison ivy
62 SW Indians
63 Aphrodite's lovable lad
64 Playmates for Poms
65 Exploit of yore
66 Unit of force

DOWN

1 Thin wire nails
2 Sends in payment
3 One of nature's kingdoms
4 One's external world, to a shrink
5 Outstrip
6 Took the cover off
7 Laconians' capital
8 Pitcher's nemesis
9 Mend
10 Soil: Comb. form
11 First official act at the Super Bowl
12 Calamitous
13 "They called her frivolous __"
21 Civil War Secretary of State
25 Ill will

27 Affectation
30 Romaine
32 Rhone feeder
34 Mr. Christian's crime
35 Former U.S.S.R. secret police
36 Pertaining to Ind.-Ill.-Mich., e.g.
37 Four bits
38 Compass pt.
41 Silencer of a sort

42 Spooky meetings
45 Fashion
47 Spoke loudly
48 Irascible
49 1920 League member
51 Three-spots
53 Meaning
55 Twinge
57 Vespiary
58 Tiny taste

ACROSS

1 Plod through clods
5 Fall beverage
10 Mideast gulf
14 Busy place
15 Author St. Johns
16 Do K.P.
17 Like __ of bricks
18 One-man fights
19 Famed Ferrara family name
20 Unwanted possession
23 Tragedy by Euripides
24 Spotted
25 Necktie fabric
28 Slept noisily
33 "Agnus __"
36 Cupid
39 Detroit's Joe Louis Sports __
40 Famed scout
43 Up to the time of
44 Have a meal
45 Jenny
46 Cuddle up
48 What some cars guzzle
50 Frontier lawman
53 Locale of Pular and Pili
58 Self-appointed tribunal
62 Seed coating
64 Tropical vine
65 Dust Bowl victim
66 "Rio __"
67 Organic compound
68 Cachet
69 Final word
70 Prophets
71 Puzzler's favorite serf

DOWN

1 Oboe's forerunner
2 Supple
3 Egg-shaped
4 People, in Pisa
5 Receptacle
6 Presley was one
7 Removes
8 Wed secretly
9 Dermal outbreaks
10 P.G.A. event
11 Topgallant
12 Tate treasures
13 Society-page word
21 Sound receiver
22 Year's record
26 Wriggler
27 Poke
29 "Jaws" vessel
30 Olds products
31 Finishes
32 Week component

33 Sight on Cape
Cod
34 Newts
35 Gide's "__ Die"
37 "Mikado" sash
38 Chant
40 Hot cross __
41 Tim or Woody
42 Meadow
47 Links delights
49 Pouch
51 Poker ploy

52 Chatter
54 Springe part
55 "Put up your __"
56 Of a Great Lake
57 Pillar of stone
58 Buzzard's
cousin
59 Arkin or Ladd
60 Corker
61 Trireme must
62 Altar on high
63 Brink

ACROSS

1 Strong scents
6 Actress Gardner
9 Complainer
13 Fall flower
14 Unless, in law
16 Tramp
17 Simple piano tune
19 Margarine
20 Kind of sphere
21 Yale name
22 Jacket parts
24 Harsh sounds
26 Kindergarten awards
28 Put away for safekeeping
30 Wash __, comic hero
34 Put two and two together
37 High nest
38 City in Pennsylvania
39 Authentic
41 Kind of rocket
43 Harvard rival
44 Theater org.
45 Stupefies
47 Composer Rorem
48 Post-office item
50 __ of one's own medicine
51 Deep voices
53 Merman or Waters
57 "A well boiled __" Spooner

60 Greek letters
62 Joie de vivre
64 41st president
65 Tennis swing
68 Ersatz butter
69 Race-track figure
70 What rookies must learn
71 Rung
72 Equal: Prefix
73 Immobile

DOWN

1 Sound-speed number
2 Theater employee
3 Leaf aperture
4 Military caps
5 Last year's jrs.
6 Blue dye
7 Changing
8 Inquire
9 Mott Street favorite
10 Part
11 Biblical brother
12 Hisses' kin
15 Mallorca, for one
18 Examiner
23 Buchwald or Linkletter
25 O.T. book
27 Heat: Comb. form
29 Sports centers
31 Breakfast dish
32 Choler
33 Spore

34 River to the Kura
35 Depression
36 Computer fodder
40 Butcher's item
42 Preoccupy
46 Collection
49 Buddy
52 Religious group
54 Wading bird
55 Wed on the run
56 Magic Johnson was one

57 Nigerian people
58 Satanists, for example
59 What "video" means
61 __ snuff (satisfactory)
63 Scene of a jay's robbery
66 __ polloi
67 Prefix meaning "three"

ACROSS

1 Rumanian dance
5 Platter
9 Basilica feature
13 Redact
15 To join, to Jeanne
16 Driblet
17 Pride of Kilgore, Texas
19 Puccini heroine
20 Set free
21 Marble of tennis fame
23 Suffix for south
24 Alternate
26 Indian weight
29 Shirt insert
31 Gorki loc.
34 Partner of true
37 A proportion: Abbr.
38 Brown bread
40 Deduce
41 "__ Didn't Say Yes"
42 Lassitude
43 Dijon daughter
44 Top ad spot: Abbr.
45 Adjective for purple
46 Charge
47 Trains
50 Building extension
51 Saskatchewan capital
53 German river
56 Orchid tubers
57 Peculiar
61 Skin
62 Unreachable
65 Prod
66 Somersault
67 Tors
68 Ginger or root follower
69 Kind of card
70 Irish Gaelic

DOWN

1 Part of H.M.S.
2 Persian name
3 Director Clair
4 This is sometimes right
5 Clubman's costs
6 Among schools
7 Pose
8 Design
9 Ticket word
10 Salesman's concern
11 Suffix for tooth
12 Upon: Prefix
14 Cervine creature
18 Resounded
22 Closer to the end
25 Bony
26 Brittle
27 Banks of baseball

156

28 Where shots
  are heard
30 Opposite of
  downdraft
32 Customary
33 Moonshiner's
  need
35 Conger, e.g.
36 Coat with flour
39 Follower of
  9 Down
48 Gyp

49 Vassal
52 Church V.I.P.
54 Actor Singer
55 Springe
56 Father
58 Imbibe
59 Growl
60 Fabergé items
61 Massage
63 Ending for
  "form"
64 Taiwan follower

ACROSS

1 Woodwind instrument
5 Kind of metabolism
10 Fort Worth inst.
13 Emulate an orant
14 Faye of films
15 Humbug
16 Becomes hortatory
19 Suffix with rest
20 ". . . lovely as __"
21 Bails
22 Tapers, e.g
24 Deface
25 Comparative ending
26 Certain wave crest
31 Concerning
34 Pan-fry
35 In the manner of
36 Old Glory features
40 Poetic dusk
41 River's little cousin
42 Bough home
43 Like some candies in boxes
45 Spot for a developer
47 Fam. member
48 Sounds of shots
52 Jeans fabric
55 Rhone feeder
57 Cry of discovery
58 Declaration commemoration
61 Bellow
62 ". . . home of the __"
63 Capp's Hyena
64 Wapiti
65 Certain exerciser
66 Gates and Burgoyne, e.g.

DOWN

1 Kind of nerve
2 Music to a diva's ears
3 Holmlike
4 CBS symbol
5 Pitcher's opponent
6 Then, in Toulon
7 Location
8 Twinge
9 Light-Horse Harry
10 Dull noise
11 Arrived
12 Refs' cousins
15 Rubberneck
17 Shopper's lure
18 Roofer, at times
23 Fashionable name
24 Glove for Mattingly
26 Forded
27 Coat for corn
28 Mantilla, at times
29 Bitters

30 Over
31 Bewildered
32 Fr. holy women
33 Thrashes
34 Snick-or-__
37 Cut corners
38 Partner of crafts
39 Double preposition
44 Willow
45 Loewe's lyricist
46 Oil cartel
48 "Superman" star

49 Copland
  composition
50 A title for Macbeth
51 Certain beans
52 Dreadful
53 Chemical
  compound
54 Minn. neighbor
55 Inits. at Calvary
56 See 54 Down
59 Wane
60 Brownie

ACROSS

1 Word of regret
5 Peacock in the sky
9 Distort
13 Big cat
14 Domesticated
15 Finished
16 Poet Pound
17 Coeur d'__, Idaho
18 "Splitsville"
19 Slogans
21 Twerp's cousin
22 Munro pen name
23 Japanese emigrant to the U.S.
25 Typical De Mille film
28 Precincts
31 Turf
34 Transfer design
36 Fall flower
38 Upon
40 Kind of colony
42 Volume
43 Havana product
45 Feasts
47 First word of "Home, Sweet Home"
48 Composer Franck
50 Ardor
51 The Queen of __
53 Previously
57 Flourished
60 Rallying cries
64 Nautical prefix
65 Cover-up name
66 Change the décor
67 Two of a kind
68 Leghorns' lodging
69 Post
70 Raced
71 Finished
72 A Peter Pan foe

DOWN

1 Actor Baldwin
2 Doolittle and Minnelli
3 Corporeal channel
4 Light meal
5 __ Alto
6 Melting-pot goal
7 Sells
8 Ukrainian city
9 Most talkative
10 Claim confidently
11 Italian painter: 1575–1642
12 Support
14 Marble
20 Hastened
24 Historic period
26 Vim
27 Chilled
29 Mighty mite
30 Half: Prefix
31 Black Hawk was one

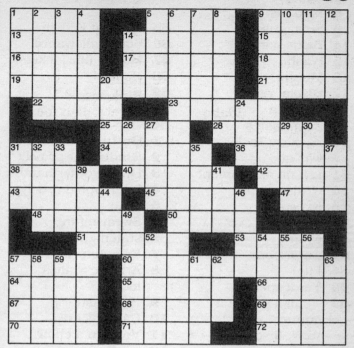

32 Auricular
33 Venetian ruler
35 Path
37 Embarrassed
39 Countersign
41 Meadow
44 Short cheer
46 Street sign
49 Bounty
52 Bear in Kipling tales
54 Standards

55 Peaches and __
56 Cantor or Murphy
57 Openings
58 Harvest
59 De Witt Clinton's canal
61 Something tried in a court
62 F.D.R.'s successor
63 Underfoot item

ACROSS

1 Collar
5 Mud hen
9 Sinai gulf
14 Baltic port
15 Wash
16 Muffles
17 Glacial ridges
18 Scintilla
19 Abominates
20 Zachary Taylor was one
21 Left on assignment
23 Cruise ships
25 Expensive
26 Call it a __
27 Craft
32 Enter port
35 Fit
38 Verdi opera
39 "__ of a gun of a gunner . . .": W.W. II song
40 Above a whisper
41 Don Juan's mother
42 The scoop
43 Steamer
44 Genetic duplicate
45 Boat or begin
47 Comic Piscopo
48 Clair or Lacoste
51 Coming up
55 Capsized
60 Lendl of tennis
61 Put the kibosh on
62 Three feet
63 Canceled, to NASA
64 __ trump (bridge bid)
65 Novelist Ferber
66 Waste allowance
67 Mae __ (life jackets)
68 Noticed
69 Rest on one's __

DOWN

1 Guttural warning
2 Hindu sage or poet
3 On the other hand
4 Interrupted rudely
5 Chic
6 Swearing-in statement
7 Egg-shaped
8 Arizone State's locale
9 Hold fast
10 Campus area
11 Voice in a choir
12 __ cheese
13 C.E.O's subordinate
22 __ the way (eased)
24 Emulated Flo-Jo
28 Attacked
29 Chinese: Prefix
30 Churchill's successor in 1955
31 Take it easy
32 Bucket
33 Annapolis inst.
34 Bean curd

35 __ in (tuckered out)
36 Scarf or snake
37 Abner's radio sidekick
40 Longed
44 Pro's antithesis
46 Doctrines
47 Amman's land
49 "The Highwayman" poet
50 Sidestep

52 City east of Lisbon
53 Hoopster
54 Speed measures set at sea
55 Be sure of
56 Part of a Mozart title
57 Former mates
58 Penitence period
59 Greenland aerie builder

ACROSS

1 Wash cycle
6 Save for later viewing
10 Additional
14 Perfect
15 Nonpareil
16 Admit
17 Kind of general
19 Mentally sound
20 Otherwise
21 Oven for annealing glass
22 Book of maps
23 This may be on tap
24 Lyric poem
25 Goo
29 Notice
33 Chemical compound
34 Iridescent gem
35 Wire measures
37 Of the limits of knowledge
40 Headcheese, e.g.
41 Wise one
42 Akin on Mom's side
43 British monarchy's symbol of authority
45 King of the English: 946–55
46 Anonymous Richard
47 London stoolie
50 Vermont ski spot
53 Chanteuse Horne
54 Aide: Abbr.
58 Trademark
59 Any Simon Legree
61 Hebrew measure
62 Actor Jannings
63 Odd job
64 Seven-day period
65 Nook at Notre Dame
66 Cheyenne's home

DOWN

1 Mature
2 Matinee __
3 Loch __ monster
4 Cloy
5 Shade tree
6 "We're off __ the wizard"
7 Study of man's development
8 Equal
9 Miss the mark
10 Pull the strings
11 Shape of a famed office
12 Columnist Barrett
13 Female sheep
18 Robin Hood's quaff
22 Summer quaff
23 Distorted
24 A European capital
25 Hold back
26 Certain gaits
27 Sacro attachment

28	Beethoven's Ninth, e.g.	50	Sign outside a school
30	Bundle of hay	51	Volume
31	Clergyman	52	Curved molding
32	Gladden	53	Gooseneck, e.g.
34	The Tentmaker	54	Late great tennis star
36	Snow vehicle	55	Desist
38	Town near Padua	56	Withered
39	Real dweeb	57	Family follower
44	Edgar Allan __	59	Earl Grey is one
48	Leg part	60	Statute
49	Smash into		

ACROSS

1 Broom made of twigs
6 His Rose was Irish
10 F.D.R. dog
14 "__ vincit amor"
15 Hoyden
16 Operatic prince
17 Army weapon
19 Gaelic
20 Certain painting
21 Squealer
22 Dregs
23 Charity
25 Church V.I.P.
27 Complete array
31 "__ Here to Eternity"
32 Hearing: Comb. form
33 Author Bombeck
35 Hens' pens
39 Without delay
42 Shortens sail
43 Oodles
44 Avoid
45 Words of comprehension
47 Assuage
49 Bikini description
51 Amazon dolphin
52 Telephone man
53 Corn unit
55 High regard
60 Wall Street ploy
61 Farm workers
63 Ferrara family name
64 Vase, in Vichy
65 Golfer Palmer
66 Source of venison
67 Caustics
68 Propound

DOWN

1 Box-office hit
2 Eastern V.I.P.
3 Dirk of yore
4 Lubricates
5 Impulsive
6 "__ Blue?"
7 Catafalques' cousins
8 Peruvian Indian of old
9 Cathedral city
10 Country rodent
11 Consent
12 Defeated one
13 War god
18 Hay-fever cause
24 Aromatic plant
26 Pixilated
27 Duo
28 Skin woe
29 Kind of job
30 DiMaggio was one
31 Card game

166

34 Cultural Revolution name

36 Fed. safety org.

37 In addition to

38 "Auld Lang __"

40 Org.

41 Caught sight of

46 Remarkable sight

48 Former Turkish titles

49 Taunt

50 Ten-point type

51 Goodnight girl of song

52 Raised

54 Breezy

56 Bakery item

57 Sicilian resort

58 Redact

59 An elec. engineer's degree

62 A Brown of renown

ACROSS

1 Farm structure
5 Oct. predecessor
9 Staggers
14 Jai __
15 __ blue (loyal)
16 Apportion
17 Bewildered
18 One, in Berlin
19 Down-Easter's state
20 Restrain
22 Speculate
23 "__ la Douce"
24 Wood smoothers
25 Coined money
28 Wood or Turner
29 Person's experience
31 __ the joint
35 Buenos __, Arg.
36 Garfunkel or Linkletter
37 Cleans the furniture
38 Affront
39 Dairies
41 Winter vehicle
42 Suave
43 Broke suddenly
47 Bullring cries
48 Headrest
49 Insolent retort
53 Aroma of flowers
54 Curse or pledge
55 Augury

56 British river
57 Word with cap or pad
58 State bird of Hawaii
59 Lesions
60 Put in the mail
61 Ample, to FitzGerald

DOWN

1 Thwart
2 Medicinal plant
3 Flatten a flat
4 One overly concerned with details
5 Large ship
6 Author Jong
7 Hoodlum
8 Golf gadget
9 A 1927 hit song
10 Large antelope
11 Leave out
12 Hermit
13 Suffixes for young and old
21 Lockups in the Navy
22 Magical baton
24 Toys man
25 Suffragette dollars: Abbr.
26 Beach toy
27 Beige
28 Tempted

168

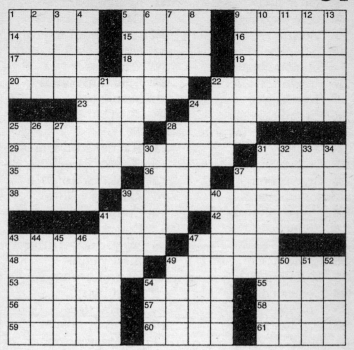

30 Propelled a bireme
31 Sidewalk section
32 Whence a flu flew in
33 British gun
34 To be, to Brutus
37 Bo of films
39 Ball of yarn
40 Protected the plants
41 Area once covered by Red Smith
43 Quarrels

44 Explosive, for short
45 Modify
46 Spitfire or Zero
47 Belonging to a cereal class
49 Nemesis
50 Verily
51 Comedian Jay
52 "If you __ Susie . . ."
54 Gives approval

ACROSS

1 Pay a visit
5 Asian serpent
10 "Aeneid" starter
14 "__ of the Mind," Shepard play
15 Browning's Ben Ezra, e.g.
16 Prejudice
17 Symphonic favorite
20 Guard
21 Dodger of yore
22 Guest room, sometimes
23 Mild expletives
25 Conquer
29 Tunes
30 Baste
33 Funnyman Johnson
34 Cook's cover
35 Employ
36 Popular piano piece
40 Prefix for bar or gram
41 Architectural ridge
42 Finished
43 Conger
44 Faded away
45 Accent
47 Otherwise
48 Dep.
49 Cinematic Superman
52 Rascal
57 Virtuoso's showpiece
60 Dock
61 Author Dahl
62 Clarinet, e.g.
63 Copy editor's term
64 Hitchcock film, with "The"
65 Bills that pay few bills

DOWN

1 Holmes's hansoms
2 Sailor's direction
3 Banker's word
4 Latvian
5 Coins of Copenhagen
6 "Nevermore" utterer
7 First victim
8 __-Saud
9 Common contraction
10 "__ Irish Rose"
11 Widespread
12 Wrestlers' pads
13 Tennis
18 Secrete
19 San Joachin valley city
23 Measures the circumference of
24 Greek Cupid
25 Ike's wife
26 "__ by any other name . . .": Shak.
27 Barfly's perch
28 "Perfect" number

29 Plant pest
30 Debonair
31 __ Park, Colorado
32 Has on
34 Concur
37 Soup server
38 Eye part
39 Neither's partner
45 Easels, e.g.
46 Soft mineral
47 Another tennis
great

48 Chide
49 Corded fabrics
50 Release
51 Fencer's weapon
52 Cicatrix
53 Dynamic prefix
54 St. Paul's
designer
55 To __ (precisely)
56 Asgard dwellers
58 Scepter's partner
59 King of France

ACROSS

1 Matures
5 State, in Soissons
9 Separated
14 Simone's husband
15 In the buff
16 More recent
17 Latin I word
18 Busy as __
19 Spiny shrub, also called furze
20 Pioneer suffragist
23 A solid alcohol
24 Williams's "Leave __ to Heaven"
25 Phoenix neighbor
28 Incendiary substance
33 Jai __
36 Perpetually
38 African plant
39 Temperance advocate
42 Take __ stride
43 Yorkshire river
44 Uncanny
45 Basque headgear
47 Tour
49 N.B.A. figure
51 Kind of light used in a theater
56 Dress-reform feminist
60 Campus fabric
62 Cambio coin
63 Key letter
64 Type of acid
65 Britain's Anthony
66 "__ Plenty o' Nuttin' . . ."
67 Dey or czar
68 Carnelian's kin
69 One-billionth: Comb. form

DOWN

1 Accumulate
2 Entire range
3 Undo
4 Shankar's instrument
5 Make possible
6 Saxhorn
7 Capital of South Yemen, once
8 Bicuspids, e.g.
9 Cat, goat or rabbit
10 Peasant
11 Askew
12 __ adjudicata
13 Due's follower
21 Customary; conventional
22 Matisse or Pétain
26 Blackfin snapper
27 Ward off
29 "Ride a __ Horse": MacInnes
30 Winged
31 South Seas parrot
32 What the dr. ordered

172

33 Johnson of "Laugh-In"
34 Den
35 Author Rice
37 Pitcher
39 Small lie
40 Studio prop
41 Thin; fine: Comb. form
46 Quake
48 Ellis or Long
50 Manicures

52 __ Hood
53 Last of a series
54 "Somebody __ de bay": S. Foster
55 Clio sidekick
56 Indigo source
57 Silver source
58 Met staple
59 Uncle Remus's __ Rabbit
60 Patriotic org.
61 Ostrich's kin

ACROSS

1 Demolished
6 Spring warming period
10 Mud puddle
14 "Abie's __ Rose"
15 Davenport milieu
16 Pocket bread
17 __ New Guinea
18 Historic times
19 Army outfit
20 Warm-weather attire
23 Kind of pal
24 Haw's partner
25 Cluck of disapproval
28 Exchange informally
31 Stormed
35 Math problem
37 Give forth
39 Hot spot
41 Dangerous section of the Atlantic
44 React to a June moon
45 Sixty minutes
46 Equipment
47 Theme
49 Peter Jennings's field
51 Color
52 Anonymous Richard
54 Under the weather
56 Yellow-skinned veggies
63 Presage
64 Join the chorus
65 Loses heat
67 Forearm bone
68 Ending for Jean or Nan
69 Poly attachment
70 Betelgeuse or Polaris
71 Essential being
72 Accomplishments

DOWN

1 Gymnastic feat
2 Yemeni or Omani
3 Tobacco holder
4 Seize illegally
5 London's river
6 United
7 Rumanian dance
8 Wave-tossed
9 Gasket's kin
10 Urge
11 Dryer clogger
12 Elevator name
13 Dab
21 Single
22 Gate City of the West
25 Keep __ on (observe)
26 Crinkly fabric
27 Edible submarines
29 Chinese nursemaid
30 Mountaineer's spike

174

32 Kind of plank or way
33 Rimmed
34 Stall
36 Biblical prophet
38 Faithful or factual
40 Dried up
42 Deprive of weapons
43 Hale of golf fame
48 "Oh, say can __ by the dawn's . . ."
50 Cut thin

53 Redacts
55 At liberty
56 Secure
57 Ferber or Millay
58 Kind of admiral
59 Picnic pests
60 Curved molding
61 Do, e.g.
62 Snow vehicle
63 Inge's "__ Stop"
66 Former jrs.

ACROSS

1 Appear
5 Valuable violin
10 Stitched joining
14 Nimbus
15 Planet second nearest to the sun
16 Seaweed
17 Toward the mouth
18 Cavities in bones
19 Layer
20 Complete
22 Female ballet dancers
24 "__ Depths," Gorky drama
26 Melody veil
27 Turkish inn
29 Nosher's delight
33 Comprehends
36 Neill or Houston
38 Be sorry about
39 Planet eighth nearest to the sun
41 Planet nearest to the sun
44 Collection of anecdotes
45 __ Mahal
47 Depends
48 Summer TV fare
51 Plate armor for a thigh
53 Joplin specialty
55 Takes the place of
59 Unmanned space probe launched Aug. 20, 1977

63 Claw
64 Esprit
65 False
67 Important food fish
68 Knee, to an M.D.
69 Arabian ruler
70 Road: Lat.
71 Inquiries
72 Concise
73 Ticked off

DOWN

1 Outcry
2 Planet third nearest to the sun
3 Make happy
4 Maker of toy planes
5 Actress Gardner
6 Tailor, at times
7 Giant red star in Scorpio
8 Revolve
9 "Your face, my thane, __ book . . ." Shak.
10 Planet sixth nearest to the sun
11 Connecticut Ivy Leaguers
12 Critic James
13 Planet fourth nearest to the sun
21 Broken, in Brest
23 Berliner's ice
25 Didn't exist
28 Cap for Scotty
30 African wild sheep
31 Heal

32 Florida islands
33 Snarl
34 Descartes or Magritte
35 On __ (equivalent)
37 Actress Oberon
40 Corrode
42 Find a new tenant
43 Plant called traveler's-joy
46 Planet fifth nearest to the sun
49 Planet seventh nearest to the sun

50 Slow horse
52 Yellow flags
54 Playwright Jean __
56 Planet farthest from the sun
57 Copier need
58 Trap
59 Star in Lyra
60 Bullring calls
61 G.I.
62 Apple variety
66 Galena is one

ACROSS

1 Stylish
5 Note from the boss
9 Crisp cookie
14 Tap dancer Coles
15 "Turandot" tune
16 Martini additive
17 Join the work force
18 Scary experiences
20 At no cost
21 Guarantee
22 J.F.K. sight
23 Shea denizen
25 Entity
27 Prize for a mystery
30 Tarts' cousins
33 L-Q link
36 __ culpa
37 Sparkles
39 Sandwich bread
40 Johnny Mercer song
43 Hawkeye portrayer
44 One way to go
45 Men and boys
46 Starfish arms
47 Rent
48 Access
50 Bird of 8 Down
52 Grazed
53 Onassis nickname
55 Pontificates
59 Curmudgeon
63 Policeman's weapon
65 Fast-food order finale
66 Western resort lake
67 Fairy-tale starter
68 Distinctive quality
69 Modify
70 House of Lords member
71 Bring up

DOWN

1 Restaurant V.I.P.
2 Rime
3 Apropos of
4 Pauline Kael's subject
5 "Olympia" painter
6 Emerald Isle
7 Russian jets
8 Surfer's paradise
9 D.H. Lawrence's "__ in Love"
10 Winglike structure
11 Broadway event
12 Second person's namesakes
13 Symbol on a staff
19 Bound
24 Work units
26 Zulu regiment
27 Imprison
28 __ Robbia, Florentine sculptor
29 Dorothy Sayers novel

30 Spotted pony
31 Prefix with active
32 Wharton's Frome
34 Different
35 Comedienne Kelly
38 Family of the
founder of
antiseptic surgery
41 Facility
42 U.N. vetoer's word
49 Olympian quaff
51 Observant one

52 Inquiring one
53 Theater org.
54 Iranian coin
56 At the summit of
57 Prong
58 "__ homo"
60 Rake
61 City on the
Jumna
62 Bristle source
64 Gardener's
tool

ACROSS

1 Like the American eagle
5 Athirst
10 "Dancing Queen" band
14 "I cannot tell __"
15 Turned rigid with fear
16 Topsoil
17 Menu
19 __ Domini
20 Raiment
21 Larch
23 Entry
25 Close a deal
26 Smokers' gadgets
30 Wheelchair-accessible
33 Incensed
34 Long-limbed
36 Cassowary's kin
37 Army meal
38 Kind of knife
39 Street sign
40 Bankbook abbr.
41 A suburb of Boston
42 Beat, old style
43 More pithy
45 Intervals of rest
47 Sharif and others
49 Prophet
50 Contrite
53 Clergyman or college bigwig
57 Organic compound
58 Not à la carte
60 Composer Harold
61 Give instruction to
62 Nobelist Wiesel
63 Secondhand
64 Hair-raising
65 Orlop, for one

DOWN

1 Ali chaser
2 Touched down
3 Spirited song
4 Joys
5 Worn-out
6 Sandy's comment
7 Nanny
8 Pound and Stone
9 Crop up again
10 Call to arms, to Shakespeare
11 Waiter's friendly words
12 Judge's bench
13 Frenzied
18 Declaim
22 Out of town
24 Flynn of flicks
26 Boundary
27 A Forsyte

28 Gourmet
29 Carpenter, at times
31 Mug
32 Hoodwinks
35 Southern French city
38 Hair clasp
39 Tarnished
41 Kind of belt
42 Velocity

44 Beamed
46 Tranquil
48 Noose
50 Andean nation
51 A son of Seth
52 Skier's transport
54 Lacquered metalware
55 Auricular
56 Strong odor
59 XXVI doubled

ACROSS

1 Untidy person
5 Lessen
10 Beer ingredient
14 "Just in __," 1956 song
15 Bundle binder
16 Malefic
17 Canal or lake
18 Weasel relative
19 Neck part
20 Floyd of boxing fame
22 Loafed
23 Was in session
24 Ancient times
26 __ Moines
29 Actress Miles of "Psycho"
32 Courage
35 Preposterous
38 Word to a king
40 Arose
41 Also
42 Soft drinks
43 Mint or sage, e.g.
44 Extravagance or abundance
46 "Superman" actor Christopher
48 Within: Comb. form
49 Vintage auto
50 Gamblers' paradise
52 Globe
54 Fritter away
57 Eric of football fame
63 Performs
64 Revere
65 Poker stake
66 Andrews Sisters, e.g.
67 Inhibit
68 Rods; heaters
69 Sea swallow
70 Pulls
71 Stain

DOWN

1 Pace
2 Italian monetary unit
3 Leave out
4 Red root vegetables
5 Cut short an aircraft flight
6 Nocturnal mammals
7 Low female voice
8 Wee
9 Do wrong
10 Rickey of baseball fame
11 Elliptical
12 Meerschaum, e.g.
13 Snow vehicle
21 Having roof overhangs
22 Wrath
25 Unit
26 Plate
27 Enrol
28 Make points
30 Moreno or Hayworth

31 Overhead

33 More repulsive

34 Expunge

36 Oscar of basketball fame

37 Cut of meat

39 Former name of Exxon

42 Task

44 Author Deighton

45 Furnace tenders

47 Victory sign

51 More unusual

53 Boasts

54 Unit of electricity

55 Land measure

56 Agitate

58 Ninth Greek letter

59 Rowing team

60 Break suddenly

61 __ the Great, German king

62 Cozy place

64 Combine in a sum

ACROSS

1 Denizen of the deep
5 Moral precept
10 Cob or pen
14 Give __ on the back
15 Hush breaker
16 Bok choy's kin
17 Owns up
19 On the Red
20 "__ Buttermilk Sky," 1946 tune
21 __ water (prove true)
22 Restraint
24 TV tear-jerkers
26 Actress Anouk __
27 Pindar product
28 Deeply absorbed
31 Kind of accounting
34 Copy a peacock
35 Earthly offering
36 Reserved
38 Tina's ex
39 Drench
41 N.B.A. whistler
42 Lotus-eater
44 Entry
45 Formed foam
47 Great fault
49 Caesar, for one
50 Absorbs
54 Rebukes
56 Dross
57 Lbs. upon lbs.
58 Endings for pay and plug
59 Loses one's shirt
62 Dry dishes
63 Cara or Papas
64 Te Kanawa specialty
65 Prying
66 Made crow sounds
67 Goulash

DOWN

1 Tortilla treats
2 Apia's island
3 Dubbed
4 Had lunch
5 Concert finale
6 Fares
7 Whipped along
8 Biblical bk.
9 Franc unit
10 Bonnie Blair, e.g.
11 Is eliminated
12 Downwind
13 Like some misses
18 Cast off
23 Edit
25 Explorer De __
26 Moslem mogul
28 Miffed
29 Gaelic

30 Judge
31 Comic Reiner
32 Olive genus
33 Butters up
34 Stacked
37 Pick up a grounder
40 Barnyard sound
43 Severe
46 Admiral Bull __
47 Plastered
48 "__ Camera"

50 Setting
51 Commence
52 Loosen knots
53 Fiddlesticks!
54 Seeded
55 Bruce Catton's Muse
56 Take a swerving course
60 Celestial Altar
61 Kind of relief

ACROSS

1 Nervous
5 Hidden treasure
10 Priestly vestment
13 Like a pittance
14 Earth tone
15 Barnyard noise
16 Genesis figure
17 July 4 noisemaker
20 Bellhop's expectation
21 Become awry
22 Body of troops
23 L. Frank Baum's __ City
25 Walks proudly
27 Like a villain
28 Not sharp
29 Juan's buddy
31 Move capriciously
32 Shakespearean exclamation
35 Certain Latin lands
39 Chopper
40 "Sixteen __"
41 Noted thesaurus compiler
42 Large antelope
44 Muni or Newman
45 Be playful
47 Tops in celerity
50 Groundwork
51 Sound-speed ratio number
52 Profound reverence
53 Baloney
56 __ the Terrible
57 Wrath
58 A deadly sin
59 Tear violently
60 Bolivian export
61 Sailboat's propellants
62 Inquires

DOWN

1 Act like a thespian
2 Dungaree cloth
3 Rumor source
4 Far Eastern money
5 Seashell
6 Yearned
7 Masticate
8 Common pronoun
9 Flub
10 Cancel
11 Tibetan monks
12 Treat tenderly
18 Tale
19 Very dry, as champagne
21 Where to get a bob
24 Latvian capital
25 Ship moorings
26 Ballerina's skirt
28 Mix thoroughly
29 Bedouin garment
30 Baer or Beerbohm
31 Facade

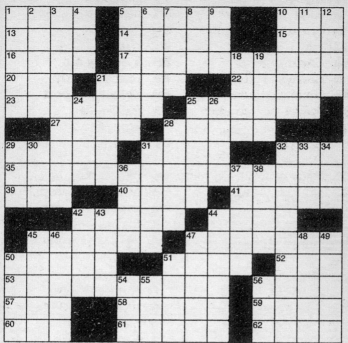

32 Genesis "clothing"

33 Summer treat

34 Clock setting in N.Y.C.

36 Salieri opera

37 Impudent

38 Clumsy boor

42 Pernicious

43 Be vanquished

44 Indianapolis cagers

45 Mediterranean isle

46 Tree variety

47 Gem surface

48 Posh

49 Takes care of

50 Angler's need

51 Cupboard items

54 Droop

55 Babylonian sky god

56 Author Levin

ACROSS

1 Campus buildings
6 __ Hari
10 Detect
14 Oil: Comb. form
15 Presage
16 Weighty book
17 Neighbor in "I Love Lucy"
18 Hindu woman's garment
19 Comedian King
20 Sarcastic term for a household head
23 Adriatic, e.g.
24 Pouch
25 Asner and Sullivan
28 Skin layer
31 Run away to be married
36 1996 candidate
38 "Norma __"
39 Coral islands
40 Impending evil or danger
43 Whole
44 "The Greatest"
45 Crack in flesh
46 Rabies
47 Luges
49 Twilight time, to Tennyson
50 Dieter's no-no
52 "My Gal __"
54 Visionary project
62 Taxi rider
63 Domesticated
64 Chemical combining form
65 Ajar
66 Cry of sorrow
67 Acting parts
68 Peruse
69 Doctrines
70 Vase handles

DOWN

1 End piece of a loaf
2 Lowest female voice
3 A memorable Bert
4 City on the Aire
5 Performed alone
6 Part of M.V.P.
7 Baby's nurse, in China
8 Singer Brewer
9 Life; soul
10 Getz or Kenton
11 Kind of shirt
12 General Bradley
13 Half a score
21 Denmark's __ Islands
22 Vinegar: Comb. form
25 Old car
26 Soft and fluffy
27 Narrow openings
29 U.K. airmen
30 Olympic award
32 Tress
33 Kukla, Fran and __

188

34 U.S.N.A. newcomer
35 German city
37 Greek goddess of strife
39 Surrounded by
41 Preliminary sketch
42 Cakes and __
47 Purloins
48 African desert
51 Central Asian range
53 Citrus fruit

54 Cloak
55 Region
56 Transmit
57 Moslem priest
58 "The Untouchables" man
59 Good for what __ you
60 Concept
61 Kennedy matriarch
62 Pro

ACROSS

1 Astrological fire sign
6 Map
10 Sugar source
14 A Columbus caravel
15 Hindu queen
16 Afresh
17 Luzon island
18 Eight: Comb. form
19 Agnomen
20 Grave; mirthless
22 Builder
24 Repetition
26 Grow older
27 Maple genus
31 Bassets and spaniels
33 Persona __ (one welcome)
37 Highly seasoned sausage
39 Sweet cherry
41 Gehrig or Groza of sports
42 Leo or Gemini
45 Historic period
46 Londoner's radial
47 Program
48 Pastry
50 Nobleman
52 Mrs. Truman
53 Priestly garment
55 Lowest passing grades
57 Made less dangerous
61 Erie and Panama
65 Above
66 Evaluate
68 Violinmaker
70 Bill of fare
71 Jacket or collar
72 "Chinatown" director Polanski
73 Finishes
74 Canvas shelter
75 Astrological air sign

DOWN

1 P.D. alert
2 Narrow inlets
3 Division word
4 And others: Abbr.
5 More rational
6 At once!
7 Resin
8 Poker stake
9 Pope's crown
10 Astrological water sign
11 Med. school subj.
12 Verne character
13 Water pitcher
21 Change
23 Yuletide drink
25 Longhair
27 Property, e.g.
28 North African capital
29 "King Olaf" composer
30 Operated
32 Observe

34 Adjust, as car wheels
35 Natterjacks
36 S.A. Indians
38 Roadside stopovers
40 Flowering shrub of the heath family
43 Three, in Venice
44 Young socialite
49 Astrological earth sign
51 New

54 Soft, visorless cap
56 Entangle
57 Rounded roof
58 Not odd
59 Ward (off)
60 Arabian staple
62 Mine, in Paris
63 Essayist Elia
64 Asterisk
67 Weighty weight
69 Tempest __ teapot

ACROSS

1 Biting remarks
6 Place for a sail
10 Appellation
14 Zodiacal Ram
15 Lotion ingredient
16 On the briny
17 Airy; gossamer
20 ". . . with the greatest of __"
21 Actor Andrews
22 Watches the waistline
23 Not up yet
25 Sticky stuff
26 "Old Marley was as __"
34 Cove
35 Unwrap
36 Musical syllable
37 Like Death Valley
38 Blockheads
40 Daytime TV feature
41 Tennis shot
42 "Clan of the Cave Bear" author
43 "Divine Comedy" author
44 Shifty; tricky
48 Diamond __
49 Microbe
50 __ Ababa, Ethiopia
53 Cowardly Lion portrayer
55 Nick and Nora's pooch
59 Clever; alert
62 "To __ His Own"
63 Words on a sale item
64 Courage
65 Editor's annotation
66 Exam for teens
67 One's strong point

DOWN

1 Large bundle
2 "Un bel di," e.g.
3 Semis
4 Guillotined
5 Fast flier
6 Historic hilltop fortress in Israel
7 Alda or Ladd
8 Parlor piece
9 Golfer's item
10 "The Birth of a __," film classic
11 Tennis great
12 Encounter
13 Little pitchers have big ones
18 Fruit drinks
19 Decorate
24 Belfry denizen
25 Departs
26 Timepiece faces
27 Register
28 Excuse
29 "Hello, __!"
30 Choose
31 Make amends
32 Furious
33 Place for a boutonniere
38 "__ in the Sun," Peck film

39 "__ the land of the free . . ."

40 City south of San Francisco

42 Like a chimp

43 Women's patriotic org.

45 __ one's troth

46 Horrified

47 Croat's neighbor

50 Lincoln and Vigoda

51 Goldurn!

52 Reno rollers

53 Highlands girl

54 __ Minor

56 "A __ Is Born"

57 Civil wrong in law

58 Poker-pot builder

60 Spigot

61 Letters on a TV set

ACROSS

1 Headstrong
5 Was indebted
9 Winners at the polls
12 Stare amorously
13 Barter
14 Cruising
15 Drinking place
17 Open-hand hit
18 Name of eight English kings
19 Derisive laughs
21 Young girl
23 A Stooge
24 Prepared
27 Taxing org.
30 Revere
34 Wings for Amor
35 Chooses
37 Receptacle for coal
38 Landscaped dwelling unit
41 W.W. II area
42 Entertain festively
43 "__ Quam Videri," N.C. motto
44 Spanish gentleman's title
46 Observe
47 Guide
48 Summit
50 Brogan or oxford
52 Teach
57 One-celled animal
61 Be overfond

62 "I Never Promised You a __"
64 Lecherous look
65 Williams's "The __ Menagerie"
66 Thought
67 Shade tree
68 Hearing organs
69 Toss

DOWN

1 Dressing gown
2 Matured
3 Smote
4 Announced publicized
5 Hockey great
6 Small soft masses
7 Tree-of-life site
8 Cloth for overalls
9 Man is one
10 Very close
11 Weakens
13 Young boys
14 Interrogated
16 Neutral shade
20 Seashore
22 Fodder
24 Short-lived fashions
25 Make happy
26 Hank of home-run fame
28 Compensate
29 Weighing devices
31 Corpulent

194

32 Laundry cycle
33 Enrol
35 Mecca-to-Karachi dir.
36 Three, in Milano
39 Miscue
40 Like a shooting star
45 Water mammal
47 Body of an organism
49 Cleanse of impurities

51 Witches
52 Inactive
53 Witty Coward
54 Flower part
55 Soft drink
56 Russian emperor
58 Norse saga
59 Spelling competitions
60 Med. school subject
63 Tee predecessor

ACROSS

1 Site of a Miami P.G.A. tournament
6 Finished
10 Intention
13 Sun-dried brick
14 Entice
15 __ time (never)
16 Corners of concern to carpenters
18 Shakespearean king
19 Kind of well
20 Capital of Cuba
22 Ernie __, U.S. Open champ: 1994
23 Chew candy
24 Wanderers
28 Recording ribbon
29 Acknowledge
30 Double-bogey on a par-five hole
31 Australian bird
34 British Open champ: 1988
38 Chemical suffix
39 October birthstones
40 Prong
41 Cuts off
42 Spinets, e.g.
44 House-to-house poll
48 __ Simpson, Southern Open champ: 1985
49 Woodwind player
50 Sketching material
55 Evaluate
56 Lawful
58 Hole-in-one golf scores
59 Level
60 Strike
61 Cover
62 Withered
63 Hourly

DOWN

1 Facts
2 Scent
3 Subterranean plant part
4 Competent
5 Rented
6 Korbut et al.
7 Wound: Heraldry
8 Before, in poesy
9 Forms anew
10 Mr. T series
11 Foolish
12 Ethical
15 Thomas __ Edison
17 Zeros
21 "Where there __ no Ten Commandments . . .": Kipling
23 Grottoes
24 Outer-space agcy.
25 Pizzeria fixture
26 Change location
27 Profound respect
28 Relates
30 Smacks
31 Leprechaun's land

196

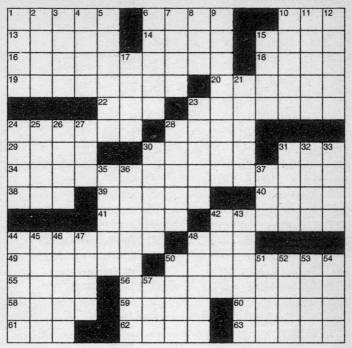

32 Opposite of
stereo
33 Employs
35 Gauchos' weapons
36 Christ's followers
37 Seventh Greek
letter
42 "Legends of the
Fall" star Brad
43 Mischievous
44 __ Gables
(Miami suburb)

45 Beaded
calculators
46 Famous
47 Contends
48 Threefold
50 Ripening agent
51 Bullets and shells,
for short
52 Couple
53 Kett of comics
54 Stagger
57 First woman

ACROSS

1 Trite writers
6 West Point inst.
10 Fury
14 Snowy bird
15 Kind of poker
16 Spoken
17 Kind of dress like 46 Across
19 Western Indians
20 __ acids
21 This is often cast
22 Cleo's river
23 Moslem ascetic
25 Knots or knobs
27 Utilities customer
31 Side-to-side distance
33 Farm building
34 Young woman
35 Speck
38 Egg white
40 Makes fast
43 Movie "Citizen"
44 Cajole
46 Hindu garment
47 Mark for misconduct
49 Heroic poetry
50 Arctic garb
52 Bullring cries
54 __ War, great race horse
55 Decimal point
57 Approaches
61 Damascene, e.g.

62 Circuitous
65 Big rig, for short
66 Prince William's aunt
67 Rent
68 Sharp
69 Marquis de __
70 Amati rel.

DOWN

1 Cut down
2 Taj Mahal site
3 Stuff
4 Cap de Gaulle wore
5 Getz and Kenton
6 Haven for a G.I.
7 Retreats for readers
8 He portrayed Pasteur
9 This helps to form a sum
10 Locomotive locale
11 Bandleader Shaw
12 Celts
13 Otherwise
18 Soviet coin: Var.
24 Writer Anatole __
26 Auricular
27 Washington is its cap.
28 Soft, lustrous fiber
29 Exile isle
30 Petition with names in circular form

198

32	Attack	51	"What's in __?"
36	Snare	53	Aquarium favorites
37	Prefix for nautical	54	Disguise
39	Docile; gentle	56	Mrs. Chaplin
41	Lengthen	58	Assist a hood
42	Sibling's nickname	59	Loud noise
45	Bombastic	60	Capital of ancient Elam
48	Striped or plaid fabric	63	Word in a wedding announcement
50	"Gay" city	64	A Kennedy

ACROSS

1 Indulge, with "to"
6 Commoner
10 Trick
14 Endure
15 Wander
16 Unlock
17 Flowery luxury
19 Employed
20 Ginger __
21 Wail
22 Novice
23 Decrease
25 Lukewarm
27 Outshine
30 Contribute
33 Beer ingredient
36 Harem room
38 Bizarre
39 Upon: Prefix
40 Chauffeurs
42 Droop
43 Kind of energy
45 Actress Garr
46 Hoopla
47 Sanctuary
49 Martha Graham's field
51 Bet
53 Classified
57 "Oz" lion Bert
59 Crown
62 "__ Yankee Doodle dandy"
63 Take __ view of (disapprove)
64 Flowery dreamer
66 Spouse
67 Fruit drinks
68 Scottish noble
69 Produced offspring
70 Emit fumes
71 Employees, as on a ranch

DOWN

1 Secret group
2 White poplar
3 High and low waters
4 Tokyo's former name
5 Involuntary response
6 Graduation ball
7 Misplace
8 Occurrence
9 Defeated
10 Habitual ritual
11 Flowery baby talk
12 Prophet
13 Inner: Comb. form
18 Bitterness
24 Tennis segment
26 Mil. captives
28 Prepare for publication
29 Washed
31 Snare
32 Border

200

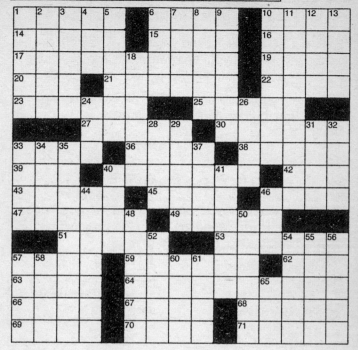

33 Isolated plateau

34 Mil. addresses

35 Flowery segregationist

37 Queen of heaven, to Homer

40 Slip a Mickey to

41 Hair tints

44 Unnerved

46 Part of H.M.S.

48 Applelike fruit

50 "The Iceman __"

52 __ Janeiro

54 Large, powerful person

55 Correct

56 Defies

57 Gentle, meek one

58 Jewish month

60 To __ (precisely)

61 Twilight

65 Exclamation of surprise

Help us puzzle you better and get . . .

¹F R E E ²P U Z Z L E S !

That's right! We'll send you a set of **free** puzzles—just for checking off your answers to the two questions below and dropping it in your nearest mailbox.

Your responses will enable us to offer you more of the puzzles that you're interested in.

Thanks for your help!

PUZZLER PROFILE

I have checked off my responses to the two questions below. Please send me my FREE puzzles!

1. I like these kind of Crosswords (please check all that apply):
   - __ Daily-size
   - __ Sunday-size
   - __ Very difficult
   - __ Large-print
   - __ Acrostics (quotations)
   - __ Cryptics (British-style)
   - __ Variety word games

   (Like those in GAMES and other puzzle magazines.)

2. Approximate number of puzzle books from all publishers (not including magazines) that I buy each year:
   - __ 1 to 2
   - __ 3 to 5
   - __ 6 to 10
   - __ 11 or more

NAME_____

ADDRESS_____

CITY_____STATE_____ZIP_____

SEND TO: **PUZZLER PROFILE**
P.O. BOX 124
MEDFORD, NY 11763

SOLUTIONS

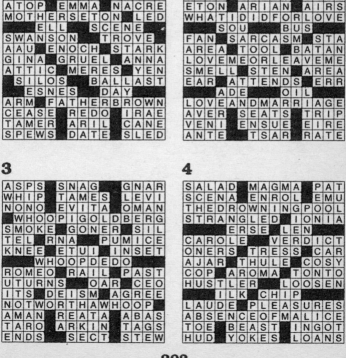

1

M	A	S	H		O	A	T	S		B	O	U	T	S
A	L	L	Y		V	I	O	L		A	R	N	I	E
A	T	O	P		E	M	M	A		N	A	C	R	E
M	O	T	H	E	R	S	E	T	O	N		L	E	D
		E	L	L				S	C	E	N	E		
S	W	A	N	S	O	N			T	R	O	V	E	
A	A	U		E	N	O	C	H		S	T	A	R	K
G	I	N	A		G	R	U	E	L		A	N	N	A
A	T	T	I	C		M	E	R	E	S		Y	E	N
	S	I	L	O	S			B	A	L	L	A	S	T
		E	S	N	E	S			D	A	Y			
A	R	M		F	A	T	H	E	R	B	R	O	W	N
C	E	A	S	E		R	E	D	O		I	R	A	E
T	A	M	E	R		A	R	I	L		C	A	N	E
S	P	E	W	S		D	A	T	E		S	L	E	D

2

S	P	A	R		G	A	E	L			D	I	M	E
T	A	R	A		R	U	N	E	S		I	D	E	S
E	T	O	N		A	R	I	A	N		A	I	R	S
W	H	A	T	I	D	I	D	F	O	R	L	O	V	E
			S	O	U				B	U	S			
F	A	N		S	A	R	C	A	S	M		S	T	A
A	R	E	A		T	O	O	L		B	A	T	A	N
L	O	V	E	M	E	O	R	L	E	A	V	E	M	E
S	M	E	L	L		S	T	E	N		A	R	E	A
E	A	R		A	T	T	E	N	D	S		E	R	R
			A	D	E				O	I	L			
L	O	V	E	A	N	D	M	A	R	R	I	A	G	E
A	V	E	R		S	E	A	T	S		T	R	I	P
V	E	N	I		E	N	S	U	E		E	I	R	E
A	N	T	E			T	S	A	R			R	A	T	E

3

A	S	P	S		S	N	A	G			G	N	A	R
W	H	I	P		T	A	M	E	S		L	E	V	I
N	O	N	O		E	V	I	T	A		O	M	A	N
	W	H	O	O	P	I	G	O	L	D	B	E	R	G
S	M	O	K	E		G	O	N	E	R		S	I	L
T	E	L		R	N	A		P	U	M	I	C	E	
K	N	E	E		E	T	U	I		I	N	S	E	T
			W	H	O	O	P	D	E	D	O			
R	O	M	E	O		R	A	I	L		P	A	S	T
U	T	U	R	N	S		O	A	R		C	E	O	
I	T	S		D	E	I	S	M		A	G	R	E	E
N	O	T	W	O	R	T	H	A	W	H	O	O	P	
A	M	A	N		R	E	A	T	A		A	B	A	S
T	A	R	O		A	R	K	I	N		T	A	G	S
E	N	D	S			S	E	C	T			S	T	E	W

4

S	A	L	A	D		M	A	G	M	A		P	A	T
S	C	E	N	A		E	N	R	O	L		E	M	U
T	H	E	D	R	O	W	N	I	N	G	P	O	O	L
S	T	R	A	N	G	L	E	D		I	O	N	I	A
				E	R	S	E			L	E	N		
C	A	R	O	L	E		V	E	R	D	I	C	T	
O	N	E	R	S		T	R	E	S	S		C	A	R
A	J	A	R		T	H	U	L	E		C	O	S	Y
C	O	P		A	R	O	M	A		T	O	N	T	O
H	U	S	T	L	E	R		L	O	O	S	E	N	
			I	L	K		C	H	I	P				
L	A	U	D	E		P	L	E	A	S	U	R	E	S
A	B	S	E	N	C	E	O	F	M	A	L	I	C	E
T	O	E		B	E	A	S	T		I	N	G	O	T
H	U	D		Y	O	K	E	S		L	O	A	N	S

5

```
MEAL ANIL  MAZES
ARMA DODO  AMINO
GROUNDHOG  SANDY
MORROS LETS  COS
AREARUG  OIL
     SPRINGFEVER
PROVE ONEA  NEVE
LEVI APACE  TAIL
ONES KEPT  FOLLY
WINTERSTALE
     ADO  RETINAL
JAB INIT  ACNODE
AVAST  THESHADOW
MOLTO SAVE  LUPE
SWEAR AWED  LSTS
```

6

```
RHOS ABLER  TSAR
EARP DRAPE  ETNA
GREATDANES  EBON
STONELIKE  SPENT
     INES  EWER
ABBES  ELOQUENT
BILLET ARUM  AWE
BOOS RUMBA  WREN
ATO FUSE  LOADED
ADVISERS  SYSTS
     HAFT  ASIF
WHOLE  MALLEABLE
HAUL  FOXTERRIER
ARNE IDLED  EDNA
TIDY REEDS  REAL
```

7

```
EBBS MARSH  WOLF
LEAP IDAHO  APAR
ELSA DENIM  TUBA
CLINGINGVINES
TACKY    EAR
   SPASM  ROLLER
ISA SHOO  MOOLA
SHRINKINGVIOLET
LAUDE PELE  LES
EGGERS  TEXAS
    AVE  SPREE
  BLEEDINGHEART
DALI SADIE  ADAH
EROS ATOLL  RITA
WATT WALES  SOON
```

8

```
CASA AREA  RACKS
ODES RAVI  ABOUT
ROCHESTER  WORRY
ART DEAN  ADAPT
LESSEN  SABER
  OMAR  LEADING
BUFFALOBILL  GAR
ELIA LYE  IOTA
ENG HELENOFTROY
PASTIME  SURE
   ETUDE  TEMPTS
LUNTS VALE  ROE
NURSE  JAMESTOWN
ALGER ADIT  ONES
BLESS REDS  PERE
```

9

```
OWNS AFAR  TSPS
NOONS ZONE  ETON
COMICSTRIP  TRIO
ELEVATE SRA  ILO
   ELECT  OUTPUT
MOSLEM REVEAL
AMT  EMERGING
LARS RASPS  SNEE
TRINKETS  GAT
  PALATE  COASTS
BAGGED SMART
ALE EYE  AMATEUR
STAB STRIPTEASE
TARE ECOL  ESSEN
ERST THIS  TYRE
```

10

```
MOTH STEAM  ALAN
ALEE TARDO  WARE
SEAR ORGAN  ASEA
HOLDONTOYOURHAT
    DES  LVE
AMAZES ALIA  HAS
LONE SCOTT  ONE
GONEWITHTHEWIND
ESE IDEES  ASIA
REX DENS  MARTEN
   LEO  AAR
FLYINGDOWNTORIO
LEAN ROMAN  DOOR
INRE ALIKE  ETNA
PADS METED  REAL
```

11

```
GAFF   SLAB  BALM
URAL  SHALL  ALAI
LOLA  PILAU  NESS
FEATHERONESNEST
    TILT  BYE
RESENT  MAINDRAG
OVERT  LOIRE  ORU
BOXY  ROUND  GARY
IKE  BENET  ERRED
NESTEGGS  ADESTE
    OER  ALDA
BIRDSOFAFEATHER
ARID  ULTRA  AARE
NELL  PUTON  URIS
ISLE  SEAS   KENT
```

12

```
POLO  TATAR  OWEN
IGOR  ELOPE  SIVA
ELLARAINES  SLIP
DELLAREESE  ILLS
      ZEN  TOED
LAPSED  RESIDUAL
ABETS  JIB  LARGO
BITE   USA   VARA
REEVE  DEN  PINED
ASSESSOR  BASTES
    EAST  AIT
FUEL  OMARSHARIF
ENGL  RINGOSTARR
ATEE  ELTON  OBOE
TORN  SKITS  MINT
```

13

```
AFAR  PEAL  SMASH
NORA  AGRO  PABLO
TRIM  CATALOGUER
AMASSED   UNITES
   HUD  BERG  STE
RADAR    ASKED
ALICE  ETTE  OBOE
SALK  DATED  VIVA
HILL  AGES  PETER
    ELMER  ITERS
CCS  AIRY  NEA
ARCADE   LESIONS
SEALINGWAX  LION
APPLE  AINU  ELSE
STAYS  ITES  DYED
```

14

```
WASP  ARGOT  GLUM
ARNE  PEACH  ROLE
SPILLEDTHEBEANS
TATTERS  ENIGMAS
ESSEN    DRAT
    DANCE  RECALL
AMP  POOLS  OBIE
TALKEDOUTOFTURN
KLEE  PIANO  TAI
ALBANO   STORM
    AXLE   GUSTO
ASTORIA  FIESTAS
SPREADITONTHICK
TAUT  ENURE  ENNA
IDEA  SENDS  STAR
```

15

```
ROBE  APART  ROOF
ARAL  CESAR  ELMO
CALIFORNIAANGEL
END  ARCED  BEARD
   EARNER  GAG
ALARMS   BASEMAN
SIGN  TORRE  AGO
STLOUISCARDINAL
ARE  GRASS  SNIT
DESPAIR   ARLENE
   AND  CAREER
AWARD  POSTS  IDA
CHICAGOWHITESOX
RIDE  AGEES  MMLI
ETAL  WORST  USES
```

16

```
JESTS  BOAST  RAF
ADORE  OBELI  ELI
PARADOXICAL  LOX
EMANATES  NEGATE
    STIR  ADDAX
OPS  ESSENE  LARA
LIAM   AIR   ATON
MAXI  MARLS  XION
ENOS   AMP   YOKE
COPS  TUSSLE  NYX
   HAGAR  TAXI
MOOLAH  SALADOIL
OWN  MAXIMALISTS
LEE  IRENE  TOLET
DDS  NINON  STOAS
```

17

```
O T I C   S T R I P   I L E S
W I T H   T E A S E   M I R E
E N C E   O A T E N   P E S T
  T H E H O R S E S M O U T H
  S E D         E E R
P A C E S   M L I   S T E P
A R R   S T A I N S   E R O S
S N A K E I N T H E G R A S S
T I T I   S E R E N E   S E T
E E N S   T E R   L E E R S
    G O P         F I R
W O L F S A T T H E D O O R
A L A I   P E R I L   D A I S
R I P S   E L E C T   E S S E
P O S H   R E E K S   S T E W
```

18

```
M I R E D   M A T E   T A P S
I R I N A   A L A N   A L I E
S A V V Y   K A U A I K I N G
T E A   S L E W   M E S T A
    R A T E S   C O A S T A L
C L I M A X   F O R G O
R I D E R   C A N N O N A D E
I N G   C A R T E   L A R
B E E B E E B E E   P I A N O
    U N D E R   S E N N A S
B L A D D E R   T O N K A
O U T D O   G I L S   D E L
D E T E R M I N E   I M A G E
E G A L   E R A T   V A L E S
D O R P   G A T O   E X E R T
```

19

```
A H A B   S H O W   A B C S
D E L I   T A M E R   T I L T
O R A L   A D A L E   A L I A
  B I L L I A R D S   M L V I
    F O R T   O K A Y E D
L A B O R S   S T R O N G
A G I L E   B E A T S   O A T
M E L D   F O I L S   B A R E
E E L   C L O N E   L I T E R
  A S S U R E   W I L S O N
C A N T A B   P I L L
O L D E   B I L L E T I N G
R A C E   E V I A N   O O L A
A M O R   D A N C E   N E E D
L O O S   N E E R   S L E D
```

20

```
C L A W   T H E A   E S S E N
L O L A   O O P S   M A N S E
A C I D   F R I T   E V I T A
M A K E A F A C E   R E P E L
P L E D G E   R A G S
    N E R D   D E F A C E
C H A F E   A U T O   A H O Y
L A R A S   S P A   E C O L E
A T I C   T H E M   P E T E R
D E L E T E   D O T E
    D I N E   R E A P E D
L E T U P   L O S E S F A C E
A D O P T   A L U M   O R L E
S E T T O   N E R O   O M A R
S N O O P   D O E R   T A T E
```

21

```
E L G A R   R E D D   B R A
B E A M E   E T U I   S O O N
B O L A S   I N E E   W O O D
  N A T I O N A L G U A R D
    I S R   S O P H
S A O   T A P S   S I M A R
E L K   T O O K   E L O P E
L E A G U E O F N A T I O N S
L A P E L   R A I N   S E E
S P I N E   S T E P   E A T
    U N T O   N O P
  U N I T E D N A T I O N S
I R A N   A D A R   S L A T E
R A V E   S E T A   E A S E L
S L Y   E R O S   D R A W S
```

22

```
E C H O   P R O F   F R A
R O A N   A L I V E   S E A L
A N D S O T O B E D   H A T E
  E J E C T   R O T A T E S
    T R E E   T R A S H
A B S E N C E   A S T E R S
O L E   A D O R E   S A R A H
A D D   S L A N T   B I O
T O W E D   E S T E S   E N D
S L A V E S   E R R A N D S
    R E M I T   E R M A
H E M L I N E   I A G O S
O B E Y   B E D O F R O S E S
M O R N   A N O M Y   Y A P S
E N S   D Y E S   A R T E
```

23

```
EAGLES   TOP  DAM
BLAINE  CUBA  EDE
BANKDEPOSIT   POD
SITE   HMS  ELOPE
    SALAMI   ASTA
AND  NISUS   SKI
LEE  TEEN DIETED
MAP  INDICES  IRE
AROMAS  CANT  ONE
   SAR  MASSE NED
BRIT   UTTERS
LATHE  DIE   ISBA
IDO  DEPOSITSLIP
MAR  GAIN  BRAISE
PRY  ERE   TILTED
```

24

```
ROSS   FLAG  EKED
ETTU  HOUSE  SODA
FRANCISSCOTTKEY
SAY  INST   IRONS
    HADE  BEMA
CANYOU  SEEBYTHE
IDEM   CALLA  IAL
DAWNSEARLYLIGHT
ETE  PARIS   THAI
RELEASES  WHATSO
    FRET  PIAS
CAFFE   SITS   AGE
PROUDLYWEHAILED
AIRS  PEACE  RITE
SATE  SAGE   STAR
```

25

```
SWAN  CALEB  TRAM
IOTA  ATALA  SAGA
TROT  RAGES  EVER
UMPIRE  SMELTERS
   OYES   IBIS
PENNANTS  ARETES
AVIAN  APPLE  IGN
REEL  AREAL  HARA
INC  AMENT  SORER
STERNE  TEAMMATE
    EIRE  SPUE
STEALING  OGRESS
TARP  CURED  UPAS
ELSE  ARENA  NEWT
PEER  NEWEL  SEAS
```

26

```
DOGS  ASIF  CORER
ARIA  GIDE  LEONE
WALLPAPER   ARDEN
SLATED  AMIN  ERA
   SWIMMINGPOOL
PAT  ERIE   USA
ABATE  DNAS  RARA
LUCASTA  RECEDES
STOP  RSVP  REINS
   ESE  IAGO  TON
STORMWINDOWS
AHS  ISNT  ONAGER
DECAL  LANDSCAPE
ATALE  AGRA  KLEE
TARES  YEAS  SEEK
```

27

```
PORCH  AGRA  RASP
OHARA  PAAR  EVOE
ORNIS  PRIMETIME
REDSTAR  DELIVER
    PERIMETER
SPRY  TSAR  CEDAR
HUH  MEET  TEASE
ATONE  DIS  OSTIA
HONED   SAAR  EDD
SNEAD  ISLA  PREY
    PLANETREE
WAITERS  AERATED
INSIDEOUT  ALATE
COED  ALTE  SENNA
KNEE  SEED  EDGAR
```

28

```
LCTS  RETS  HIKES
ARIA  ATOP  AMIDE
REPLICATE   MILES
SESAME  SEMITONE
    DAMP  DATA
ESS  GEAR  RETORT
CHAFE  TIER  IGOR
LAVA  MESSY  ORLE
ALEC  ONES  ANELE
TERSER  REPS  SOS
    ILES  NOSE
ENAMELER  PAMPER
RELIC  DUPLICATE
STILT  ASEA  EGAD
ESTES  NEAR  EELS
```

29

```
LEEKS LAST SOFT
OCTET OMER ACLU
CHARO NENE REEL
HOTFUDGESUNDAES
    TERRE  UINTA
ASIA TAS MTS
LANTERN MAL FEE
FIREDOG ICELAND
ALE DIE SETTING
   PIT NED DRAY
AGREE CAROM
BLOWSHOTANDCOLD
NOSE ARAB LABOR
ERIE CALL IRONY
RYES KLEE IDLES
```

30

```
ALIF COLTS PETS
ROSA APART ATOP
TOLL RETIE CUBA
SPECTER PESKIER
   OREAD LEE
BANNER UNEARNED
ERASE LAR SAME
ARI SADNESS SOL
ROVE VIE ABATE
SWEETENS STELES
   RUN SWAIN
VIKINGS RINGERS
ANNE ELFIN ALAE
IRES RIANT LIME
NEWT STAGS SASS
```

31

```
HAUL DUETS OSSA
ANNE ERGOT DEAR
WALTZINGMATILDA
STATIC BRINE
ETC PERFORM CPA
ROES ELY OCTAD
  LIANE ATREUS
SPINNINGWHEEL
ACACIA SONYA
CARET KEY MOWS
ETA ITERATE ORA
  SCARE HAILED
WHIRLINGDERVISH
AUTO CLAIM ATTU
DEEP EYRIE NESS
```

32

```
LUCK CATER TENS
ETON ABOVE ALOT
VILE BALES LIMA
ELLE ALERT CZAR
LEE LODES ADE
  ESP NOS GAB
LINEAGE TORMENT
ENDIVE BAITED
SCENERY PINCHES
  WED IER DIT
ASH TENET ACE
CLUB ELDER PYLE
CARE ADIME ALAR
RISE LENIN COSI
ANTS EDGED ERSE
```

33

```
MAIL TOBOL ACRE
ARNE UNITA FAIL
CREE PERON OLGA
HARDHEADEDWOMAN
OUTSELLS MAL
  IOS BAG GIG
ACHES PAR JAVA
HEARTBREAKHOTEL
ABLE LOG OBESE
BUT CAW PCT
  SOS WELLTODO
THATSTHEWAYITIS
HERA OASTS EARL
AMOR FLEES URGE
WONT FERRY PUER
```

34

```
SEED STRAY DIRT
OCTO POOLE ERIE
ARAL AROMA BOLD
PULLEDAFASTONE
AVE TIN
LIBRA ANA CAPRA
ONA DELETE IRAN
PULLEDTHESTRING
ERSE SERAPH NEE
SNAGS RUM ESTER
AAR AFT
PULLEDUPSTAKES
SARI MONET MELT
ERAT ANILE PESO
RELY PETER SPEW
```

35

```
ACTOR   ATE  LEAN
MARIO  FLAG  AXLE
PRESSURING   SPIN
  STEERAGE   TREE
     DENNY   SEEN
ACRE  ACE   WADS
DREAM  IDEAL  SRA
DEPRESS   CRAZIER
SER  AMISH  DAVIT
  ETTU  TOP  GENE
OSIS   RULED
DUST   ADENOIDS
ONIT   PRESSPARTY
ECOL  TENS  EMILE
RENE   ART  YAPON
```

36

```
ELBE  TRUMP  BLIP
DOOM  IATRO  RELY
GROUNDLESSRUMOR
YET  AILS   ATONE
    PREY  CABANAS
TONICS  FERAL
OVEN   KARAT   AVA
BACKFENCEGOSSIP
ELK  ROOTS   ESSE
   CENTS  AGATES
AGELESS   ANON
NAVAL  BRIG  ADZ
EVERYONESTONGUE
MONK  SAMOA  BAER
OTTS  SPANS  ARLO
```

37

```
DAFT  GLAD  MOTE
AVOID  LOPE  IBIS
DEUCE  ONELINERS
ERR  DUB  DEBASE
  FLUTES   GORE
PALACE   PHASE
ERUPT  SLAT  TEMP
SIS  SATIRES  IOU
OAHU  BUCK  PAGAN
  KRONE  MIGHTY
  GUAR  SPINET
HALITE  INN  BIB
SEVENIRON  EVADE
KEEL  VILE  RILES
IDLE  ENDS  PLAT
```

38

```
WALL   SAMBA  CROW
ERIA  ABEET  LONE
BEAU  MUSEE  ABLE
BARRELSOFMONEY
    EPEE   PUG
ATLAST  PRESSERS
SEETO  ALAS   NAE
HAVEMONEYTOBURN
ESE  UNAS   PARED
SERRATED  MISERS
   AWL   SANE
MONEYINTHEBANK
MEND  IDEAL  ALOE
TACO  NEIGE  LATE
STEM  GONER  LIEN
```

39

```
AMASS   CASH  VAST
DENIM  ASEA  ELLE
SLIPOFTHETONGUE
  SOAK   SCREAMS
ARK  TRI   HIE
WEIGHONESWORDS
ABBEY   DEAN  ALP
RIOT  DEITY  AREA
EDS  VEST   ALTAR
SHOOTTHEBREEZE
UGH   DAM   DYE
ERASURE   IRON
WASTEONESBREATH
ETTE  NIRO  EERIE
READ  EDEN  DREAM
```

40

```
OTIC   SCAR  ALTAR
LIAR  LOBE  DERMA
ALGA  EDEN  ONION
FLOYDPATTERSON
    OAT   ERE
SPENT  OKRA  ETTA
ILL  EAVE  SHARER
SUGARRAYLEONARD
AMIDST  EARN  ISO
LEND  ENDS  ESTER
    ORE   IST
HENRYARMSTRONG
NOMAD  TOES  EVER
ALIVE  ESAU  SAME
PETER  RATE  SLOW
```

41

```
C L A W   A P O S   P A L O S
H A V E   L A M A   A N I T A
E V E N   I R A N   G E N O A
F E R D I N A N D   A L T E R
      M E D I C I N E
C H A R A D E   A D S   S A M
L O C U M   P S I   O E N O
A P A S S A G E T O I N D I A
R I D E   L O G   B E A S T
E S S   M A U   S T E R N E S
      R E D A C T O R
C O L O N   C R I S T O B A L
A B O U T   H A G S   M O T E
P I N T A   E S M E   E L K E
S T E E L   S H A D   N E A R
```

42

```
S L O B   S H A M   J O L T
C U R I E   L I R A   E R I E
O C A L A   A J A R   E B O N
T E L L S   B O B B Y P I N S
      Y E W S   L A S T S
O R A C L E   D U E L
P O L L   S P I T   U T T E R
T U T U   T A X E S   E A S Y
S T A B S   W I S H   D I N E
      H A L E   A D D L E S
  P U S A N   A W R Y
T O M M Y G U N S   A B B O T
A L B A   E N O S   W E A V E
B I E R   L I V E   L A K E S
S O R T   S T A T   R E N T
```

43

```
O S L O   T A M E D   L I F E
M O O N   A R O S E   I R O N
A R A B   P A S T E B O A R D
R E D O L E N T   A N N E S
      A I R   D O N E
A B O R T S   S A L E S M E N
T R A D E   D I V E   S A R I
T I S   R E U N I O N   S O N
A D E S   S P U D   A B O D E
R E S T A T E S   S C O N E S
      A L E S   A R A
P A D R E   G E N E R A T E
A B O V E B O A R D   D U A L
T E L E   E R N I E   E R N S
S L E D   E A G E R   R A G E
```

44

```
C O B B   B E A M   C A R D
O M A R   A G R A   S A T E S
T I T I   N E A R   A T T I C
  T H E M A R B L E F A U N
      R O N   A L E C
O T T   R A S P   E R O D E S
T A R T E   K E E N   M O N A
T H E E L G I N M A R B L E S
E O N S   O M N I   U S E R S
R E T T O N   S L A M   S O Y
      A R E A   T B S
  I N M A R B L E H A L L S
A R I E L   A I R E   A I L E
P A N N E   C O I N   C R A W
B E E T   I N N S   K A T E
```

45

```
B L A B   A L T A   A L F I E
L O G E   S E A R   M I E N S
A D R A   S A N G   I N E P T
H E A R T O F G O L D   T U E
      E R Y   A S C O T S
J O L I E T   B E S T O F
A M E N D   P L A T   U C L A
N A G S   S E E D S   S L E D
E R S E   P A S S   D I A N E
    O R B I T S   C A N Y O N
R A F T E R   H A M
I L L   H E A D O F S T A T E
A L A T E   B E R T   A C I D
T O M E S   U L N A   R A N G
A T B A T   T E E N   A D A Y
```

46

```
S I M B A   G A R B   S M U
A R E A L   A G E E   I O U S
B E N N I N G T O N   R U S E
E N D   G O E S   U N I T E D
R E S E N T S   S M A S H
      L E E   C O B B   B S A
R A B I D   O N E S T E P S
A B E D   H I D E D   O N U S
R E N E C O T Y   O G D E N
A L E   L U I S   S R A
  F L O S S   F L A S H E R
O P I A T E   S E A T   E R A
A L T O   B E N E V O L E N T
T E E S   O V A L   R E L E T
S A D   Y A P S   S I S S Y
```

47

```
LOOM AESOP BEES
OMNI SLAVE UTAH
CEES TAKEN GURU
INSTRUMENTALIST
   LET    ADE
CELEBES EGO ALP
ELITE PEDO SLOE
ALTOCLARINETIST
SERE ERAT RANEE
ENE INS SCALERS
   ERG    ATE
SLIDETROMBONIST
TANG HORAL EDNA
ECCE ELATE SEAM
WEAR NESTS SAGE
```

48

```
PSALM ALL CRACK
EERIE BEA RUBLE
ALARM LAR ONION
 FLABBERGASTED
   SEA   OPS
AID RIDE EBBED
HORA TILT ORRIS
ATALOSSFORWORDS
BANTU HIRE WENT
SKITS NETS DTS
   MOA   IAN
 THROWFORALOSS
PROUD IRA OILED
AISLE RAN OSIER
SPEED ELI NEDDY
```

49

```
RITA CLAIM ARAM
ICAN LARGE CAME
COMICACTOROAKIE
ONE RISER INERT
  EAR    SNA
 GOLFERNICKLAUS
LICIT EENA ENE
OLE SUPPERS RIM
ADA REAP HAITI
MANOFALLTRADES
  NIL    ALE
GLOAT SEETO ARE
RINGSTARDEMPSEY
ANCE ALDER AIDE
BEER MEANS LADS
```

50

```
TIME ALIT ASH
ADAM RADII BEER
REDBUTTONS EMMA
SMEAR ESTABLISH
   TSAR   ARE
POSTAL DECI SEC
ARIL PRAY NOPAR
VANESSAREDGRAVE
ETUDE CEDE DREW
DES LEES BLEEDS
  AMI    STER
PENTAGRAM ELIOT
EVIL HELENREDDY
TELA TALLY SLOP
 RES DOLE SERE
```

51

```
TAPE MOTIF STLO
AGRA ACHOO AHAB
BAIT STERN NEWS
URN OLAV TATAS
  CLVI AMANOF
STEVEN GAIT RAH
CHOIR PAINE IMA
HIFI SABLE SCAN
END TAROS GOATS
DEE ADEN URANIA
 NODDED NOPQ
AMUSE KILT USA
ORAN NOISE TEES
CIRC ERNES RENT
TAKE DOGES INDO
```

52

```
POPUP ABLE MOLS
ELATE BAIN ABOU
RIPEN ABET SORE
TOA CITYFATHERS
  RAINES NOISES
PEARLS AGGIE
ADZE STALL TWO
SIZABLE TEETHED
SEI LOADS UELE
 DANTE SABOTS
AROUND SPIRAL
POPSCONCERT DAD
IGET NEER IAMBI
SURE ERNS STACK
HEAR ROTE TENSE
```

53

```
AGHA  PASCH  SAI
HOOD  ATALE  LPS
ARNO  LUMEN  AREA
BYEBYEBLACKBIRD
   YEA  EVEL  LED
ADS  MATTE  EPI
LOUT  RES  ERNS
SECRETE  JOSEPHS
SKUA  BAN  POOL
 LER  OARED  REY
AVE  THEN  ACT
BIRTHOFTHEBLUES
EROS  STEEL  EGAL
USA  TERRA  FATE
SER  ARSON  SLAW
```

54

```
REDO  REEVE  OBOE
ERIN  ELDER  ROUT
DISCIPLINE  DUST
SECEDE  TAM  ANTE
     OAR  LIVID
PARALLEL  TENACE
AGERS  CIVET  RAN
ROSE  TUBAS  BIRD
ORT  MOREL  SIEVE
LARGER  LICENSED
   ALATE  DAP
AGIO  ILO  SIERRA
RUNS  LIMITATION
ARTS  LASSO  ALAS
BUSY  ASKER  LEDA
```

55

```
BOBS  IHAVE  PACA
ALOP  DIGIT  ORAL
NEAR  ARENT  RIVE
GOTOTHEMOUNTAIN
   USOS  AISLE
MATTE  SELMA
ECRU  GOALIE  LAE
THEPROMISEDLAND
EEK  HINGED  AIDA
  SONIA  PURIM
AROAD  EVAN
WESHALLOVERCOME
ANKA  BONER  HOAX
STAR  AVERS  EZRA
HERA  REATA  DEEM
```

56

```
ROOTS  AGES  GAT
AGREE  FROM  ARMY
GRANDPIANO  LAIR
 ELF  ERI  GRINGO
  ESSENE  INDO
COGENT  XEBEC
AORTAE  AIL  HAM
RNA  GRANTED  IRA
DAN  EVA  VIOLIN
  DIODE  ARIDLY
ASTA  CARTEL
ASTERO  LEE  SPA
SWAM  GRANDOPERA
HANS  LAME  POLES
END  ENOW  STEAK
```

57

```
 DEALER  ATTIRE
TERRENE  MEETING
ASOCIAL  ENNOBLE
UPS  STARRED  BAN
GAIL  EPACT  BIRD
HIVES  STE  RANGE
TREATIES  SINGER
   REND  FOLD
TENNIS  COLLAPSE
ALIEN  LOS  SNAPS
BIND  BAITS  ALIT
AXE  SECRETS  ADE
RIVIERE  RECOVER
DREDGER  ERASERS
 SHOOTS  DETERS
```

58

```
LARA  CPL  SALEM
ELIS  LEA  OPERAS
SADHEART  LIGATE
TSE  RISES  ASTER
   CAMERAS  DOSE
AGIO  ALIBI
ANNULS  LEGRAND
MAGNATE  SHEMAAL
 RATLINS  TROPIC
  RANUP  NEST
NOSY  TRESSED
ORACH  ENTER  GIN
LILLIE  SAMSPADE
INSULT  ERI  AMOR
SABLE  RES  WELD
```

59

I	S	L	A	M		C	A	R	S			C	P	A
N	A	O	M	I		O	B	O	E			F	R	A	Y
C	R	O	S	S	B	R	E	E	D			A	O	N	E
A	A	S		T	O	E	D		A	M	U	S	E	S
S	H	E	P	A	R	D		E	T	O	N	S		
		O	K	E		O	B	I	S		F	E	E
E	M	C	E	E		C	R	O	S	S	I	N	G
T	A	R	T		A	P	R	O	N		T	R	I	G
C	R	O	S	S	T	I	E		C	O	E	D	S
H	I	S		E	T	N	A		L	O	N		
	S	P	A	R	K		G	O	N	E	R	I	L
R	O	W	E	N	A		J	U	S	T		I	N	A
O	M	A	R		C	R	O	S	S	R	O	A	D	S
T	E	L	E		T	H	A	T		A	N	N	I	E
A	R	K		S	O	N	S		S	I	T	A	R

60

	E	A	G	L	E		R	A	H		S	C	O	P	E
S	E	R	I	N		E	M	U		C	A	P	O	N
T	R	I	C	E		C	O	R	M	O	R	A	N	T
	O	P	E	R	A			T	O	O	T	H	Y
		N	O	R	M	S		U	T	E		
L	E	G	S		T	I	T	U	S		R	O	L	E
A	D	I	E	U		S	E	N	S	E		T	O	G
B	I	R	D	S	O	F	A	F	E	A	T	H	E	R
E	L	L		A	N	I	M	A		T	H	E	S	E
L	E	S	T		S	T	E	I	N		E	R	S	T
		U	P	I		D	R	E	S	S		
R	E	M	A	D	E			B	I	P	E	D
R	E	D	B	R	E	A	S	T		N	I	D	E	S
S	T	I	L	E		C	O	O		C	A	N	B	E
T	E	T	E	S		H	U	E		E	N	A	T	E

61

A	K	I	N		S	P	R	Y		H	A	S	A	T
M	I	N	E		T	R	U	E		O	H	A	R	E
P	O	L	E	V	A	U	L	T		P	E	L	T	S
A	S	A		O	R	N	E		S	T	A	T	E	S
S	K	Y	D	I	V	E		A	H	O	R	A
		I	C	E		S	Q	U	A	T	T	A	G
B	E	L	L	E		P	O	U	N	D		I	M	A
A	X	E	L		S	E	N	A	T		B	O	O	R
S	P	A		M	O	R	E	S		L	A	N	K	Y
T	O	P	K	I	C	K	S		C	U	R		
	F	O	L	L	Y		H	U	R	D	L	E	D
P	A	R	O	L	E		B	A	R	I		A	L	I
A	P	O	D	A		B	R	O	A	D	J	U	M	P
R	I	G	O	R		S	A	L	T		I	R	A	S
R	E	S	O	D		A	G	E	E		M	A	N	Y

62

M	E	S	S	A	G	E	S		S	T	E	E	R	S
I	N	T	E	R	N	A	L		P	O	S	S	E	T
T	E	R	T	I	A	R	Y		L	A	S	C	A	R
E	R	A		A	W	L		R	I	D		A	L	I
R	O	D	E		E	S	S	E	N		S	L	I	D
	S	A	L	A	D		A	C	T		P	A	N	E
		S	H	A	S	T	A		O	A	T	E	N
A	M	P		A	T	T	E	N	D	S		E	S	T
G	O	R	E	S		R	E	T	E	S	T		
I	R	E	D		S	E	N		C	A	I	R	O
T	A	S	S		H	E	S	S	E		P	A	N	S
A	L	E		M	O	T		N	I	P		V	A	L
T	I	N	D	E	R		L	E	V	E	R	A	G	E
E	S	C	O	R	T		A	V	E	R	A	G	E	D
S	T	E	E	L	Y		P	A	R	T	N	E	R	S

63

B	U	R	P		P	R	I	G		P	A	R	I	S
A	S	I	A		A	I	D	A		O	B	E	S	E
R	E	D	C	A	R	P	E	T		L	A	D	L	E
B	R	E	A	S	T		S	E	M	I		H	E	M
		P	E	P		S	E	C	R	E	T	S
	D	R	E	S	D	E	N		D	E	E	R	
P	O	E	M		D	A	T	A		A	R	E	S
A	L	D	O		N	A	V	A	L		S	I	L	K
P	E	S	T		O	L	E	S		O	N	L	Y
	N	E	W	T		S	T	R	I	N	G	S	
S	L	A	S	H	E	D		E	A	R		
T	A	P		I	S	I	S		M	A	R	R	O	W
A	S	P	E	N		R	E	D	S	Q	U	A	R	E
G	E	E	S	E		T	R	E	E		S	T	A	B
E	R	R	O	R		Y	E	W	S		E	E	L	S

64

C	A	P	P		S	T	E	A	D		R	A	T	S
A	L	A	I		M	E	R	C	I		A	G	E	E
D	I	S	C	H	A	R	G	E	S		M	I	L	E
S	E	T	T	E	R	S		S	C	H	O	O	L	S
		U	T	T	E	R		R	O	N		
	D	I	R	E		O	P	E	R	A	T	E	D
C	I	D	E	R		T	E	E	N		I	L	O
H	A	L	S		P	L	A	N	T		S	T	O	P
I	N	E		E	R	A	T		S	C	A	P	E
P	A	R	A	D	I	S	E		A	R	N	E	
		R	I	M		D	E	L	T	A		
S	P	A	R	T	A	N		R	E	I	N	E	R	S
C	O	L	E		T	O	R	R	E	N	T	I	A	L
A	S	P	S		E	N	T	E	R		O	R	L	E
R	E	S	T		S	E	E	D	S		N	E	E	D

65

```
BIBS ADMAN BLOB
ARAL TEASE REVE
LOCO TALKEDOVER
INKWELL EDUCING
    TENE DINA
HASTENS ENDOWS
HALTS OOPS EVIL
ARK HELOT ERA
ITER ELAN BERET
REDOWA REPASTS
   DADA ATTU
SPEEDER ACHERON
TURNEDBACK ENTO
ALOT TORTE MERO
BESS ORMER SDAK
```

66

```
ASPIC PEAS BASS
NEURO INST OLEO
DAMONANDPYTHIAS
RANCHES OREM
    EAR SLY
STAR SPA ACTS
STINT STEN MOAT
TOMDICKANDHARRY
ELIE LENT ANNEX
WEDS AID RAYS
    INN BOA
SPED CLUSTER
THEFOURHORSEMEN
EAST FIAT ELIDE
ANTS OPTS SEROW
```

67

```
LAMP SOBS ACTA
OBOE HARI THIRD
SLOWPOKES MANIA
SENILE ASSORTED
STY SKIT ISLE
RAHS DESERTS
ALI MAT SEEMSTO
PONDER AMATOL
STEERED AMP ALE
SENIORS TRES
ERAS OLLA RUT
RELENTED VERSUS
SNORE MILESTONE
TENTS MEAT LUTE
WEST ASPS ETON
```

68

```
SPAR ASSES AMAH
LAME SHEAN LENO
OTIS SINCE MOTT
THROWINTHETOWEL
    LOGS RAN
PROVEN DWINDLED
LAVES GOING ORA
AGED BRING POUR
ZEN ALINE TRIPE
ASSUMING SHEETS
    POS OPEC
LAYSITONTHELINE
ALOE EMOTE USED
MALT RIVER DEAD
ARKS STARE EELY
```

69

```
AWLS DAMES DADA
COOP EDITH EMIL
TROUBLESHOOTERS
IMPROVES PRESTO
    THEM SPAS
VARIES SHELTER
ALANA CHORE ROT
MING SLAVS PIMA
PEG STOWE CREAM
NEWNESS FRESNO
    ROPE SEES
ANGERS SWEETIES
SENATORHOLLINGS
IRAK NOIRE GOAT
SOWS SEVER ENDS
```

70

```
MONA STAID RITZ
AHAB TONTO ERIE
ROSY ANACT LIND
CHASINGTHELAST
    MODS LOP
SAFARI GALOSHES
ONEL SMEW SEINE
FIR CHINESE TAP
ATRIA LEDA MOTO
RAINCOAT CHANEY
    AAR BRER
BUSONARAINYDAY
BONN AMASS LESE
ASTI TENET OPEC
SHOT ENTRY UTAH
```

71

```
T A L C . J A C K . O V E R T
A M O R . I S L E . L A K E R
C A T O . T S A R . A R E T E
T H I S O N E P R O V I D E S
. . . S U E T . . . P I E . .
P A R I T Y . A C C I D E N T
E M E N D . A L A I . . R O O
A B I G O P P O R T U N I T Y
C O N . . A S H E . L U C I E
H Y S O N T E A . A R M A N D
. . R U T . . I T I S . . . .
I H E A R I T K N O C K I N G
D A W N S . A L A N . U V E A
E L O G E . T U N A . L E A P
A S K E D . A X E L . L Y R E
```

72

```
M A L T A . F L O G S . D S M
A L O O N . I O N I C . O N O
P L A Y T H R O U G H . G E O
. . . H A R P S . O G L E D .
S W E E T Y . . P L I E R S .
C H A R M S . S P R A N G . .
R I T A S . P A L E R . R A T
O N E S . C U T U P . S I L O
P E R . G U L A G . C O G O N
. . H A R K E N . L A S H E S
. G O A L I E . P I L O T S .
R A Z E D . H A I T I . . . .
A K A . D O U B L E B O G E Y
T E R . L I S L E . E R O D E
E N D . E L K E S . R O B O T
```

73

```
. L I L A . . . A C E D . . .
. T E N O R S . S L A V E S .
C H A R L I E . P L E A S E D
R A V E L . A M A I N . P A Y
A L E M . B R O W N . L I V E
S I N . M A S O N . M I T E R
H A S P E D . R E P I N E R S
. . A L G A . D I E U . . . .
S P U T T E R S . E N S U R E
L I N T S . C A S T S . R E A
U G L Y . S A L L Y . P U B S
E P A . V I D E O . H A G U E
S E C R E T E . P E A N U T S
. N E H R U S . S E P I A S .
. . S O A P . . . L U C Y . .
```

74

```
R E A P . P A S T A . C A T
E T R E . A R E A L . G O B I
C H O P S T I C K S . R O B E
A E S O P . T E A S E L E R .
P R E . E G G S . C P A . . .
. . M E R E . . S E E T H E S
E R M A . A N T E . A W A R E
Y E A R O F T H E D R A G O N
E N A C T . R O M E . L I S T
D O R O T H Y . E A R L . . .
. . P E E . E D N A . E L A .
A L S O R A N S . N E X U S
B O I L . P E K I N G D U C K
L O L O . E R A S E . E D I E
E T O . D O R M Y . N E A R
```

75

```
B R A N . B E S S . P A C T S
R E N O . E X P O . A G O R A
A M I N . S P A R . T R I A L
D I M E S T O R E . C O N G .
S T A G E . S T A S H . T I P
. S L O W . E A R P . C O C O
. . . A I D . M I M O S A S .
O T H E R S . . . T U S S L E
. G R A N D E E . S E T . . .
P I L E . R A C E . I R O N .
U S F . T E R R A . N O R A S
. T B A R . P E N N Y A N T E
S A U C E . L A C E . R E I N
I T C H Y . U T E S . E R O S
P E K E S . G E S T . D Y N E
```

76

```
S L O G . C I D E R . O M A N
H I V E . A D E L A . P A R E
A T O N . S O L O S . E S T E
W H I T E E L E P H A N T . .
M E D E A . . S E E N . . . .
. . . R E P . . . S N O R E D
D E I . E R O S . A R E N A .
B U F F A L O B I L L C O D Y
. U N T I L . D I N E . A S S
N E S T L E . G A S . . . . .
. . . . E A R P . . A N D E S
. K A N G A R O O C O U R T .
A R I L . L I A N A . O K I E
R I T A . E S T E R . S E A L
A M E N . S E E R S . E S N E
```

77

```
M U S K S   A V A   C R A B
A S T E R   N I S I   H O B O
C H O P S T I C K S   O L E O
H E M I   E L I   L A P E L S
  R A S P S   S T A R S
      S T A S H   T U B B S
A D D   A E R I E   E R I E
R E A L   R E T R O   Y A L E
A N T A   N U M B S   N E D
S T A M P   A D O S E
    B A S S I   E T H E L
I C I C L E   N U S   E L A N
B U S H   C H O P S T R O K E
O L E O   T O U T   R O P E S
S T E P   I S O   I N E R T
```

78

```
H O R A   D I S C   A P S E
E M E N D   U N I R   D R O P
R A N G E R E T T E   M I M I
  R E L E A S E   A L I C E
      E R N   R O T A T E
S E R   G U S S E T   R U S
T R I E D   P C T   T O A S T
I N F E R   S H E   E N N U I
F I L L E   P O A   R E G A L
F E E   D R I L L S   E L L
  R E G I N A   E M S
S A L E P   S T R A N G E
R I N D   O U T O F R A N G E
U R G E   F L I P   C R A G S
B E E R   F A C E   E R S E
```

79

```
O B O E   B A S A L   T C U
P R A Y   A L I C E   S H A M
T A K E S T O T H E S T U M P
I V E   A T R E E   L A D E S
C A N D L E S   M A R
    I E R   W H I T E C A P
A S T O   S A U T E   A L A
S T A R S A N D S T R I P E S
E E N   C R E E K   N E S T
A S S O R T E D   L O T
    S I S   R E P O R T S
D E N I M   I S E R E   O H O
I N D E P E N D E N C E D A Y
R O A R   B R A V E   L E N A
E L K   B I K E R   F O E S
```

80

```
A L A S   P A V O   W A R P
L I O N   T A M E D   O V E R
E Z R A   A L E N E   R E N O
C A T C H W O R D S   D R I P
  S A K I   I S S E I
      E P I C   A R E A S
S O D   D E C A L   A S T E R
A T O P   P E N A L   T O M E
C I G A R   D I N E S   M I D
C E S A R   Z E A L
  S H E B A   O N C E
G R E W   W A T C H W O R D S
A E R O   A L I A S   R E D O
P A I R   R O O S T   M A I L
S P E D   D O N E   S M E E
```

81

```
G R A B   C O O T   A Q A B A
R I G A   L A V E   D U L L S
O S A R   A T O M   H A T E S
W H I G   S H I P P E D O U T
L I N E R S   D E A R
    D A Y   V E S S E L
P U T I N   A B L E   A I D A
A S O N   A L O U D   I N E Z
I N F O   C L A M   C L O N E
L A U N C H   J O E
    R E N E   O N D E C K
K E E L E D O V E R   I V A N
N I X E D   Y A R D   N O G O
O N E N O   E D N A   T R E T
W E S T S   S E E N   O A R S
```

82

```
R I N S E   T A P E   M O R E
I D E A L   O N E R   A V O W
P O S T M A S T E R   S A N E
E L S E   L E H R   A T L A S
    B E E R   O D E
S L I M E   O B S E R V E
T O L A N   O P A L   M I L S
E P I S T E M O L O G I C A L
M E A T   S A G E   E N A T E
S C E P T R E   E D R E D
    R O E   N A R K
S T O W E   L E N A   A S S T
L O G O   T A S K M A S T E R
O M E R   E M I L   C H O R E
W E E K   A P S E   T E P E E
```

83

B	E	S	O	M		A	B	I	E		F	A	L	A
O	M	N	I	A		M	I	N	X		I	G	O	R
F	I	E	L	D	P	I	E	C	E		E	R	S	E
F	R	E	S	C	O		R	A	T		L	E	E	S
			A	L	M	S		E	L	D	E	R		
P	A	N	O	P	L	Y		F	R	O	M			
A	C	O	U		E	R	M	A		C	O	O	P	S
I	N	S	T	A	N	T	A	N	E	O	U	S	L	Y
R	E	E	F	S		L	O	T	S		S	H	U	N
		I	S	E	E		A	P	P	E	A	S	E	
T	E	E	N	Y		I	N	I	A					
B	E	L	L		E	A	R		E	S	T	E	E	M
R	A	I	D		F	I	E	L	D	H	A	N	D	S
E	S	T	E		U	R	N	E		A	R	N	I	E
D	E	E	R		L	Y	E	S		S	T	A	T	E

84

B	A	R	N		S	E	P	T		R	E	E	L	S
A	L	A	I		T	R	U	E		A	L	L	O	T
L	O	S	T		E	I	N	E		M	A	I	N	E
K	E	E	P	B	A	C	K		W	O	N	D	E	R
			I	R	M	A		S	A	N	D	E	R	S
S	P	E	C	I	E		L	A	N	A				
B	A	C	K	G	R	O	U	N	D		C	A	S	E
A	I	R	E	S		A	R	T		D	U	S	T	S
S	L	U	R		C	R	E	A	M	E	R	I	E	S
				S	L	E	D		U	R	B	A	N	E
S	N	A	P	P	E	D		O	L	E	S			
P	I	L	L	O	W		B	A	C	K	T	A	L	K
A	T	T	A	R		O	A	T	H		O	M	E	N
T	R	E	N	T		K	N	E	E		N	E	N	E
S	O	R	E	S		S	E	N	D		E	N	O	W

85

C	A	L	L		K	R	A	I	T		A	R	M	A
A	L	I	E		R	A	B	B	I		B	I	A	S
B	E	E	T	H	O	V	E	N	S	F	I	F	T	H
S	E	N	T	I	N	E	L			R	E	E	S	E
				D	E	N		G	E	E	S			
M	A	S	T	E	R		A	I	R	S		S	E	W
A	R	T	E			A	P	R	O	N		U	S	E
M	O	O	N	L	I	G	H	T	S	O	N	A	T	A
I	S	O		A	R	R	I	S			O	V	E	R
E	E	L		D	I	E	D		S	T	R	E	S	S
			E	L	S	E		S	T	A				
R	E	E	V	E			S	C	A	L	A	W	A	G
E	M	P	E	R	O	R	C	O	N	C	E	R	T	O
P	I	E	R		R	O	A	L	D		R	E	E	D
S	T	E	T		B	I	R	D	S		O	N	E	S

86

A	G	E	S		E	T	A	T		A	P	A	R	T
M	A	R	I		N	U	D	E		N	E	W	E	R
A	M	A	T		A	B	E	E		G	O	R	S	E
S	U	S	A	N	B	A	N	T	H	O	N	Y		
S	T	E	R	O	L			H	E	R				
			M	E	S	A		N	A	P	A	L	M	
	A	L	A	I		E	V	E	R		A	L	O	E
F	R	A	N	C	E	S	E	W	I	L	L	A	R	D
I	T	I	N		A	I	R	E		E	E	R	Y	
B	E	R	E	T	S		T	R	I	P				
	R	E	F			S	T	R	O	B	E			
A	M	E	L	I	A	B	L	O	O	M	E	R		
D	E	N	I	M		L	I	R	A		B	E	T	A
A	M	I	N	O		E	D	E	N		I	G	O	T
R	U	L	E	R		S	A	R	D		N	A	N	O

87

K	A	P	U	T		T	H	A	W		S	L	O	P
I	R	I	S	H		I	O	W	A		P	I	T	A
P	A	P	U	A		E	R	A	S		U	N	I	T
	B	E	R	M	U	D	A	S	H	O	R	T	S	
				P	E	N			H	E	M			
T	C	H		S	W	A	P		R	A	G	E	D	
A	R	E	A		E	M	I	T		H	A	D	E	S
B	E	R	M	U	D	A	T	R	I	A	N	G	L	E
S	P	O	O	N			H	O	U	R		G	E	A	R
	E	S	S	A	Y		N	E	W	S		D	Y	E
			R	O	E			I	L	L				
	B	E	R	M	U	D	A	O	N	I	O	N	S	
B	O	D	E		S	I	N	G		C	O	O	L	S
U	L	N	A		E	T	T	E		E	S	T	E	R
S	T	A	R		E	S	S	E		D	E	E	D	S

88

S	E	E	M		A	M	A	T	I		S	E	A	M
H	A	L	O		V	E	N	U	S		A	L	G	A
O	R	A	D		A	N	T	R	A		T	I	E	R
U	T	T	E	R		D	A	N	S	E	U	S	E	S
T	H	E	L	O	W	E	R			A	I	R		
				I	M	A	R	E	T		S	N	A	C	K
G	R	A	S	P	S		S	A	M		R	U	E
N	E	P	T	U	N	E		M	E	R	C	U	R	Y
A	N	A		T	A	J		R	E	L	I	E	S	
R	E	R	U	N		T	U	I	L	L	E			
			R	A	G		P	R	E	E	M	P	T	S
V	O	Y	A	G	E	R	I	I		T	A	L	O	N
E	L	A	N		N	O	T	S	O		T	U	N	A
G	E	N	U		E	M	E	E	R		I	T	E	R
A	S	K	S		T	E	R	S	E		S	O	R	E

89

```
C H I C   M E M O   W A F E R
H O N I   A R I A   O L I V E
E A R N   N I G H T M A R E S
F R E E   E N S U R E   S S T
      M E T       U N I T
E D G A R   P I E S   M N O P
M E A   G L I N T S   P I T A
B L U E S I N T H E N I G H T
A L D A   S T E A D Y   H E S
R A Y S   T O R N   E N T R Y
    N E N E       A T E
A R I   O R A T E S   C R A B
N I G H T S T I C K   T O G O
T A H O E   O N C E   A U R A
A L T E R   P E E R   R E A R
```

90

```
B A L D   E A G E R   A B B A
A L I E   F R O Z E   L O A M
B I L L O F F A R E   A N N O
A T T I R E   T A M A R A C K
      G A T E   S E W U P
L I G H T E R S   R A M P E D
I R A T E   R A N G Y   E M U
M E S S   B O W I E   S T O P
I N T   S A L E M   S M I T E
T E R S E R   R E S P I T E S
    O M A R S   S E E R
P E N I T E N T   R E C T O R
E N O L   T A B L E D H O T E
R O M E   T R A I N   E L I E
U S E D   E E R I E   D E C K
```

91

```
S L O B   A B A T E   H O P S
T I M E   B A L E R   E V I L
E R I E   O T T E R   N A P E
P A T T E R S O N   I D L E D
      S A T   Y O R E
D E S   V E R A   N E R V E
I N C R E D I B L E   S I R E
S T O O D   T O O   C O L A S
H E R B   L A V I S H N E S S
R E E V E   E N T O   R E O
      R E N O   O R B
W A S T E   D I C K E R S O N
A C T S   A D O R E   A N T E
T R I O   D E T E R   G A T S
T E R N   D R A W S   S P O T
```

92

```
T U N A   E T H I C   S W A N
A P A T   N O I S E   K A L E
C O M E S C L E A N   A S E A
O L E   H O L D   T E T H E R
S U D S E R S   A I M E E
    O D E   I M M E R S E D
C O S T   P R E E N   O R E
A L O O F   I K E   D O U S E
R E F   I D L E R   I T E M
L A T H E R E D   S I N
    S A L A D   S O A K S U P
S C O L D S   S C U M   T N S
O L A S   T A K E S A B A T H
W I P E   I R E N E   A R I A
N O S Y   C A W E D   S T E W
```

93

```
E D G Y   C A C H E   A L B
M E R E   O C H E R   B A A
O N A N   C H E R R Y B O M B
T I P   S K E W   A R R A Y
E M E R A L D   S T R U T S
    V I L E   B L U N T
A M I G O   F L I T   F I E
B A N A N A R E P U B L I C S
A X E   T O N S   R O G E T
    E L A N D   P A U L
C A V O R T   F A S T E S T
B A S I S   M A C H   A W E
A P P L E S A U C E   I V A N
I R E   A N G E R   R E N D
T I N   G U S T S   A S K S
```

94

```
H A L L S   M A T A   S P O T
E L A E O   O M E N   T O M E
E T H E L   S A R I   A L A N
L O R D O F T H E M A N O R
      S E A   S A C
E D S   D E R M A   E L O P E
D O L E   R A E   A T O L L S
S W O R D O F D A M O C L E S
E N T I R E   A L I   K I B E
L Y S S A   S L E D S   E E N
      F A T   S A L
C A S T L E I N T H E A I R
F A R E   T A M E   A M I D O
O P E N   A L A S   R O L E S
R E A D   I S M S   A N S A E
```

95

```
ARIES PLAT  CANE
PINTA RANI  ANEW
BATAN OCTA  NAME
 SOLEMN ERECTOR
    ROTE AGE
ACER DOGS  GRATA
SALAMI GEAN  LOU
SIGNOFTHEZODIAC
ERA  TYRE AGENDA
TORTE EARL  BESS
    ALB DEES
DEFUSED CANALS
OVER RATE  AMATI
MENU ETON  ROMAN
ENDS TENT  LIBRA
```

96

```
BARBS MAST  NAME
ARIES ALOE  ASEA
LIGHTASAFEATHER
EASE DANA  DIETS
    ABED GOO
DEADASADOORNAIL
INLET OPEN  TRA
ARID DOLTS  SOAP
LOB  AUEL DANTE
SLIPPERYASANEEL
    LIL GERM
ADDIS LAHR  ASTA
BRIGHTASABUTTON
EACH ASIS  HEART
STET PSAT  FORTE
```

97

```
RASH  OWED  INS
OGLE TRADE  ASEA
BEERGARDEN SLAP
EDWARD SNICKERS
    LASS MOE
READY IRS  ADORE
ALAE ELECTS  BIN
GARDENAPARTMENT
ETO REGALE  ESSE
SENOR EYE  STEER
    TOP SHOE
INSTRUCT AMOEBA
DOTE ROSEGARDEN
LEER GLASS  IDEA
ELM  EARS  CAST
```

98

```
DORAL OVER  AIM
ADOBE LURE  ATNO
TOOLANGLES LEAR
ARTESIAN HAVANA
   ELS CARAMEL
NOMADS TAPE
AVOW SEVEN  EMU
SEVEBALLESTEROS
ANE OPALS  TINE
    LOPS PIANOS
CANVASS TIM
OBOIST ARTPAPER
RATE LEGITIMATE
ACES EVEN  SMITE
LID  SERE HORAL
```

99

```
HACKS USMA  RAGE
EGRET STUD  ORAL
WRAPAROUND UTES
 AMINO DIE NILE
    SUFI NODES
USER  BREADTH
SILO LASS  IOTA
ALBUMEN SECURES
KANE COAX  SARI
DEMERIT EPOS
 PARKA OLES
MANO DOT  NEARS
ARAB ROUNDABOUT
SEMI ANNE  LEASE
KEEN SADE  STRAD
```

100

```
CATER PLEB  RUSE
ABIDE ROVE  OPEN
BEDOFROSES USED
ALE LAMENT  TYRO
LESSEN  TEPID
    EXCEL DONATE
MALT ODAH  WEIRD
EPI DRIVERS  SAG
SOLAR TERI  HYPE
ASYLUM DANCE
 WAGER  SORTED
LAHR DIADEM  IMA
ADIM LOTUSEATER
MATE ADES  THANE
BRED REEK  HANDS
```

The PDQ
(Pretty Darn Quick!)
Vegetarian
Cookbook

240 Healthy and Easy
No-Prep Recipes for Busy Cooks

Donna Klein

HPBooks

HPBooks

Published by The Berkley Publishing Group

A division of Penguin Group (USA) Inc.

375 Hudson Street

New York, New York 10014

Copyright © 2004 by Donna Klein

Cover design by Liz Sheehan

Text design by Tiffany Estreicher

First HPBooks paperback edition: December 2004

Visit our website at

www.penguin.com

Library of Congress Cataloging-in-Publication Data

Klein, Donna.

The PDQ (Pretty Darn Quick) vegetarian cookbook / Donna Klein.

p. cm.

Includes index.

ISBN 1-55788-438-2

1. Vegetarian cookery. 2. Quick and easy cookery. I. Title.

TX837.K547 2004

641.5'636—dc22

2004049723

Printed in the United States of America

10 9 8 7 6 5 4 3 2 1

To my husband, Jeff,
for everything and to my daughters,
Emma and Sarah, for inspiring this book

Contents

Acknowledgments

Sincere thanks to my literary agent, Linda Konner, for her steadfast support and abiding faith in my writing endeavors.

Many thanks to John Duff, and to Jeanette Egan for her expert guidance and careful editing of the manuscript.

Special thanks to my vegetarian friends and acquaintances for their invaluable advice and continuing encouragement.

Finally, deep appreciation to the animal rights community for broadening my horizons and helping me to see vegetarianism as much more than a health issue.

Introduction

How did you let another day of healthy eating get away from you?

You meant to pack that easy vegetable wrap for lunch last night. You'd even roasted a red bell pepper alongside the baked potatoes you'd had for supper, and then placed it in a paper bag to cool like the recipe said. But after loading the dishwasher and paying bills, you lost your enthusiasm for coring, seeding, and ribbing the slippery capsicum, let alone peeling off its blistered skin. Besides, your favorite TV show was almost on. So this afternoon, when a coworker going to McDonald's asked if you wanted anything, weak from lack of a good breakfast and tired of peanut butter crackers from the vending machine, you said yes.

You meant to prepare that quick vegetarian stir-fry for your family this evening—you'd even made a careful shopping list during lunch hour. But traffic was heavy, and when you arrived at the supermarket along with the rest of the rush-hour crowd, both express lanes stretched far down the food aisles. As you eyed all the vegetables in the busy produce section, you pictured all the chopping and the mincing and the shredding and the grating and the stemming and the trimming in your cluttered kitchen. Even with the help of your food processor, dinner would be late. So you tossed a couple of three-cheese frozen pizzas into your cart instead and promised yourself that tomorrow you'd do better—besides, you'd already blown it with that large order of French fries.

If any of this rings true, this book's for you!

The PDQ Vegetarian Cookbook is for people who want to make nutritious vegetarian meals for themselves (and their families), but who often don't have the time (or energy) for prepping the fruits and vegetables before they ever make it into the skillet or salad bowl. With no chopping, peeling, slicing, coring, seeding, whipping, or blending required, these recipes are simple and fast; most are ready in 30 minutes or less. With no cutlery, graters, juicers, electric mixers, blenders, or food processors required, the recipes are safe and reliable. Consequently, this cookbook is also ideal for teenagers cooking without supervision, college students and young adults lacking expensive culinary equipment, and senior citizens losing the comfortable use of their hands due to arthritic or other conditions. But, mostly, The PDQ Vegetarian Cookbook is for anyone who's ever tried to follow an "easy" vegetarian recipe only to discover that the devil's in the preparation.

How Does a Vegetarian Cookbook Eliminate the Preparation?

For many people, "no-prep" and "vegetarian" are contradictory terms. Indeed, not too long ago, the task of putting together a repertoire of quick vegetarian meals without picking up a knife would have been daunting, if not downright impossible. Fortunately, times have changed. From appetizing hors d'oeuvres to impressive desserts, for casual weeknight suppers or elegant dinner parties, many of the recipes in The PDQ Vegetarian Cookbook are designed to take full advantage of the best new convenience foods that have flooded the supermarkets in recent years, such as ready-washed salad greens, precut fruits and vegetables, already-shredded cheese blends, and refrigerated pesto. Several showcase the natural adaptability of fresh whole foods like tiny new potatoes, sugar snap peas, cherry tomatoes, and numerous types of berries. Others incorporate a wide variety of frozen vegetables, from artichoke hearts to winter squash. Still others rely on old pantry standbys: canned tomatoes, cooked beans, chopped pimientos, and pitted olives. Bakery items such as pre-baked pizza shells and sponge tarts, as well as refrigerated piecrusts and frozen puff pastry, are occasionally required. A standard assortment of dried herbs, spices, and seasonings is essential, with a few gourmet items—coarse sea salt, Cajun seasoning, Szechuan pepper, for example—rounding out the list. Extra-virgin olive oil, canola oil, sesame oil, and peanut oil are pantry basics. Add to that an exciting array of flavored oils, vinegars, and world-class bottled cooking sauces, dressings, and pastes—including Asian black bean sauce, Mexican chipotle sauce, Moroccan harissa sauce, Thai curry paste, and Japanese wasabi mayonnaise—and you have all the ingredients to create great-tasting vegetarian dishes without the time-consuming and often labor-intensive preparation.

While practical activities such as washing and scrubbing fruits and vegetables, rinsing and draining a can of beans, defrosting frozen vegetables, and softening butter are required for many of the recipes, the bottom line is: No cutlery (save for a table knife) or kitchen appliances are necessary to prepare any of the ingredients for use in the recipes. You do not even need a cheap blender to puree a finished soup. While a serrated bread knife is a beautiful thing for tasks such as slicing garlic bread or splitting hamburger buns, a standard table knife does the trick almost as well; it even works as a pizza cutter when you are desperate! Regarding cooking equipment, only the basics are necessary to execute the overwhelming majority of the recipes—a large non-stick skillet with a lid (ideally one with an ovenproof handle), a stockpot, assorted saucepans, and a baking sheet top the list. While a wok is a wonderful thing for preparing stir-fries, all of the stir-fries in this book were tested in an inexpensive Teflon-coated 12-inch skillet. Although a microwave oven is not necessary, it can be useful if a recipe ingredient needs to be precooked, heated, softened, or defrosted before use in the recipe (in most of the recipes calling for cooked frozen vegetables, I must confess to taking advantage of mine).

Are Convenience Foods Really Healthy?

Purists often pooh-pooh commercially prepared foods as being overloaded with fat and sodium. Yet the majority of recipes in *The PDQ Vegetarian Cookbook* contain 10 grams or less of fat per serving and 600 milligrams or less of sodium per serving, well within the mainstream medical community's guidelines for healthy eating. Almost two-thirds of the recipes are cholesterol-free, and the majority of the recipes contain only 2 grams or less of saturated fat, which is little more than 10 percent of the FDA's recommended Daily Value (DV) based on a 2,000-calorie-per-day diet.

Happily, many recipes are centered around fresh fruits and vegetables anyway; already-shredded cabbage, presliced mushrooms, ready-washed spinach, bagged baby carrots, new potatoes, cherry tomatoes, and fresh berries are just a few. Yet fresh isn't always the best; according to recent studies, plain frozen vegetables may be more nutritious than fresh, depending on how fresh the latter really are and how they have been handled. This is because frozen vegetables are processed at the highest point of their nutritional content (within hours of picking) and retain their nutrients almost indefinitely, while fresh vegetables tend to lose nutrients 24 hours after picking and continue to lose them in the shipping process. Although sodium is added in the freezing process, the amount is negligible for those who are not on a severely sodium-restricted diet.

Because canned vegetables do tend to have a greater sodium content than their fresh or frozen counterparts, they are seldom used in *The PDQ Vegetarian Cookbook*. Major exceptions are canned tomato products and canned beans. Regarding canned tomato products, recent studies have confirmed that processed tomato products contain up to eight times as much lycopene, a carotenoid and antioxidant that may help prevent certain cancers, as fresh tomatoes. Furthermore, the lycopene in cooked and processed tomatoes is more easily absorbed than that in raw tomatoes. Concerning canned cooked beans, with the exception of canned cooked lentils, rinsing them is requested in all recipes to greatly reduce their sodium content.

The PDQ Vegetarian Cookbook achieves nutritional soundness in other important ways. Reduced-fat and low-sodium ingredients (light sour cream, reduced-fat shredded cheese, low-sodium vegetable broth, reduced-sodium soy sauce, no-salt-added tomato sauce, for example) are suggested for most recipes whenever practical. Olive oil and canola oil, both low in saturated fat, are the principal sources of fat used throughout the book. Butter (high in saturated fat) and vegetable shortening (high in trans fat) are used in only a small number of recipes. High-trans-fat margarines are not used at all; a trans-fat-free margarine is suggested to convert a dairy recipe to vegan. Certain convenience foods, such as canned soups, bottled salad dressings, packaged sauce or dip mixes, Velveeta cheese, and instant potatoes, are avoided altogether because of their high amounts of sodium and additives.

The Physical Health Benefits of Eating More Vegetables

Among the many reasons for eating a diet rich in vegetables are its demonstrated health benefits. Studies have shown that vegetarians generally have lower rates of heart disease, diabetes, and cancer. Researchers strongly suspect that this is because diets that are predominately plant-based tend to be lower in fat and higher in fiber and other key disease-fighting antioxidants (including vitamins C and E and beta-carotene) than typical meat-eaters' diets.

Conversely, studies have shown that a diet rich in animal products increases the threat of heart disease, diabetes, and cancer. This is probably because animal products contribute all the cholesterol and most of the saturated fat to the human diet. Furthermore, animal products contain zero fiber, and fiber is essential for proper evacuation and a healthy colon. Plant-based foods, on the other hand, contain no cholesterol, small amounts of saturated fat, and contribute all the fiber to the human diet.

Because eggs and dairy foods are both animal products, they are not a mainstay in these recipes. Almost two-thirds of the recipes in this book are vegan, or completely plant-based. Getting enough protein and calcium shouldn't be a problem for a vegan who eats a wide variety of foods. Beans, legumes, nuts, and seeds are excellent sources of protein. Because scientists now know that the body can store essential amino acids (the building blocks of protein) throughout the day, the protein from the barley you had for lunch will complement the protein in the lentils you had for dinner, forming a "complete" protein, the best meat substitute of all. Regarding calcium, many green vegetables—such as broccoli, collard greens, kale, okra, and Swiss chard—are good sources of this important mineral. As an added boon for vegans, recent studies have indicated that the calcium from vegetable sources may actually be better absorbed than that from dairy products.

Regardless of your eating persuasion—aspiring vegetarian, strict vegan, or occasional meat-eater—the inclusion of fruits, vegetables, whole grains, and legumes are obvious contributors to a healthier lifestyle.

The Mental Health Benefits of No-Prep Cooking

The transition to a healthier lifestyle is as much about incorporating balance and ease into daily life as it is about eating more vegetables. While the physical benefits of vegetarianism are well documented, so are the mental health benefits of sitting down to a relaxed meal, and still finding time afterwards to take a walk, play a game of cards, read the kids a bedtime story, write in your journal, or phone an old friend.

Let's face it: Countless shopping lists, long food lines, and the real rush hour that happens every night in the kitchen are huge energy zappers, which often prevent us from savoring the healthy fruits, vegetables, grains, and legumes we are attempting to eat more of. Yet many of us cling to the belief that food that is made from scratch, and only from the freshest of ingredients, is fundamentally better for us, so we trudge on, determined to prove our point. With so much time and effort put into meals and their planning, on top of everything else we have to do, we're usually toast by the time the dishwasher is loaded. It's no wonder that so many of us spend our evenings collapsed in front of the TV.

That's why I am excited about sharing the following recipes with you. At the very least, they will present you with easy answers to the daily question, "What's for dinner?" Ultimately, they will help you let go of your packaged-food guilt so that the possibilities in the kitchen—and in life—become endless.

About the Nutritional Numbers

All of the nutritional analyses in this book were compiled using MasterCook Deluxe 4.06 software, from SierraHome. However, as certain ingredients (light coconut milk, caponata, potato gnocchi) were unknown to the software at the time of compilation, substitutes of equivalent caloric and nutritional value were used in their place. All of the recipes using rinsed and drained canned beans have been analyzed using freshly cooked dried beans. Unless salt is listed as a measured ingredient (versus to taste, with no preceding suggested measurement) in the recipe, no salt has been included in the analysis; this applies to other seasonings (black pepper, cayenne, nutmeg) and any ingredient that is not preceded by a specified amount (chips or raw vegetables for dipping). None of the recipes' optional ingredients (salsa, sour cream, guacamole) have been included in the nutritional analyses. If there is a choice of two or more ingredients in a recipe (for example, nonfat or light mayonnaise), the first ingredient has been used in the analysis. Likewise, if there is a choice in the amounts of a particular ingredient in a recipe (for example, 2 to 3 tablespoons pine nuts), the first amount has been used in the analysis. If there is a range in the number of servings a recipe yields (for example, 4 to 6 main-course servings), the analysis has been based on the first amount.

About Meat, Egg, and Dairy Substitutes

No tofu or other food substitutes are required to make any of the recipes in this book. However, I have made many of the nonvegan recipes user-friendly for those who do not consume eggs, dairy, or honey by suggesting a vegan substitute in the recipe's headnote or providing a vegan alternative in the recipe's list of ingredients, or both. The nonvegan recipes that do not present these alternatives either cannot be converted or, in my opinion, are not well suited for conversion. These recipes generally include all those where eggs are the primary ingredient (for example, all of the recipes containing eggs in the chapter "Brunch and Egg Dishes") or where cheese is a cooked or melted ingredient (for example, Chili-Bean and Cheese Casserole, page 114, or Broccoli with Cheese Sauce, page 135).

Regarding eggs, to my knowledge there are no substitutes for eggs that are to be left whole in recipes (for example, poached or shirred eggs). Furthermore, the liquid egg substitutes on the market appropriate for scrambling contain egg products.

In the case of cheese, I find that the soy cheese substitutes on the market that actually cook or melt like real cheese contain casein, which is a milk product. The truly vegan cheeses, on the other hand, have a somewhat grainy texture that doesn't hold up well when heated; moreover, they are somewhat harsher in flavor. In some recipes where cheese is not a primary ingredient (for example, Refried Bean Tostadas, page 78), it's just as easy to convert a recipe by leaving the cheese out. Of course, all of the nonvegan recipes can be altered at your discretion. To assist you in making any conversions, the following are suggested substitutions for the dairy products used in this book:

- Soymilk, rice milk (preferred in heated dishes such as soups), or coconut milk (in some recipes) instead of regular milk or skim milk

- Soy creamer (Silk brand recommended) or nondairy coffee creamer (note that many of the leading brands contain a casein derivative, which is a milk product) instead of half-and-half or light cream

- Soy cheese (note that many brands contain casein, a milk product, to help them "melt")

- Crumbled firm tofu for ricotta cheese in lasagna and similar dishes

- Nondairy cream cheese (Tofutti brand highly recommended)

- Nondairy sour cream (Tofutti or Rice Dream brand recommended)

- Soy margarine (preferably Earth Balance brand, which contains no trans-fatty acids)

- Soy yogurt (Silk brand recommended)

- Nondairy frozen desserts (Tofutti, Soy Delicious, or Rice Dream brand recommended) for ice cream or frozen yogurt

The following substitutions can be made for eggs or products that normally contain eggs:

- Two ounces (¼ cup) of mashed soft tofu for an egg used for binding (as in a filling or stuffing)

- Soy creamer or nondairy coffee creamer in lieu of an egg wash when baking (as for brushing on puff pastry to make it shiny)

- Soy mayonnaise (Nasoya brand recommended)

The following substitutions can be made for honey:

- Maple syrup (preferably pure) or brown sugar

Please keep in mind that the above substitutions are suggestions for the recipes in this book and do not represent an all-inclusive list. If you do decide to use substitutes, please note that all of the recipes in this book were tested primarily without them. While I am reasonably certain, based on experience, that the substitutes will work in the recipes where indicated, I am afraid that their use in the recipes where a substitute has not been recommended will result in a disappointing dish.

What Do the Terms Mean?

Dairy-free: Contains eggs but no dairy products.

Dairy-free option: Can be made with dairy substitutes or the dairy product can be omitted.

Egg-free: Contains dairy products but no eggs.

Egg-free option: Can be made without eggs or products containing eggs.

Lacto-ovo: Contains dairy products and eggs.

Vegan: No animal products, including honey, are used in the recipe, although optional ingredients may contain dairy products or eggs.

Vegan options: The recipe contains eggs, dairy products and/or honey, but suggestions are given for making it vegan.

Tempting Starters, Snacks, and Tidbits

Awaken your guests' appetites, and say "welcome" at the same time, with any one of this chapter's tasty appetizers. Many, such as chilled Artichoke Bottoms with Hummus or hot Gnocchi with Caponata, can be enjoyed sitting around a coffee table or standing about an open-house buffet. Others, such as Cheesy Roasted Corn Dip with Red, White, and Blue Tortilla Chips, are ideal for Fourth of July celebrations or feeding a Super Bowl crowd. Some, such as Broiled Portobello Mushroom Caps with Gorgonzola Butter or Toasted Pot Stickers with Wasabi Cream, are better suited for the formality of a first course served at the dinner table. Whatever the occasion, the following stress-free recipes are sure to start it off on a relaxed and happy note!

ARTICHOKE BOTTOMS WITH HUMMUS

Vegan

MAKES 10 TO 12 APPETIZERS

This virtually effortless appetizer is always popular. Hummus, a Middle Eastern dip or spread made from chickpeas, sesame tahini, lemon, and garlic, can be found in the refrigerated section of most well-stocked supermarkets. Other tasty store-bought fillings include deli-quality tabbouleh and potato and egg salads. If you have a little more time, the artichoke bottoms are scrumptious filled with Tahini-Yogurt Sauce (page 142) or served heated with Creamed Spinach (page 155). Grain salads, such as Greek-Style Bulgur Salad with Chickpeas, Feta, and Olives (page 51) and Mediterranean Couscous Salad (page 53), are other delicious options; use your imagination—the possibilities are endless!

    2 (14-ounce) cans artichoke bottoms
        (10 to 12 pieces), rinsed and well drained
    10 to 12 tablespoons prepared hummus
    Sweet paprika (optional)
    10 to 12 grape tomatoes or small cherry
        tomatoes and/or pitted black olives, for
        garnish (optional)

Fill each artichoke bottom with 1 tablespoon of the hummus. Sprinkle lightly with paprika, if using. Cover and refrigerate a minimum of 30 minutes or up to 2 days and serve chilled, garnished with a grape tomato and/or olives, if desired.

PER APPETIZER
Calories 38 ▪ Protein 1g ▪ Total Fat 1g ▪ Sat. Fat 0g ▪ Cholesterol 0mg ▪ Carbohydrate 5g ▪ Dietary Fiber 2g ▪ Sodium 204mg

Cook's Tip Use 2 (14-ounce) cans whole artichokes (do not use marinated variety) in lieu of the artichoke bottoms. Drain well by turning them upside down. You will need to push open the leaves gently with your fingers and, depending upon size, fill each with about half the amount of hummus.

SPICY BLACK BEAN DIP WITH PLANTAIN CHIPS

Vegan

MAKES 6 SERVINGS

Ready in just about 10 minutes, this lively appetizer offers your guests a nice change of pace from chips and salsa. Plantain chips are highly popular in Caribbean cuisine; they can be found in the international food aisle of most major supermarkets. Corn tortilla chips can be substituted, if desired. The bean dip also makes a terrific wrap filling.

    ½ tablespoon extra-virgin olive oil
    ½ cup frozen chopped onion
    ½ tablespoon refrigerated bottled minced garlic
    1 (4-ounce) can diced mild green chilies,
        drained
    ½ teaspoon ground cumin
    ⅛ teaspoon cayenne pepper, or to taste
    Salt and freshly ground black pepper, to taste
    1 (16-ounce) can vegetarian refried black beans
    Sour cream or nondairy sour cream (optional)
    6 ounces plantain chips

In a small saucepan, heat the oil over medium heat. Add the onion and cook, stirring, until softened and thawed, about 3 minutes. Add the garlic and cook, stirring, 1 minute. Add the chilies, cumin, cayenne, salt, and black pepper; cook, stirring, 1 minute. Add the refried beans and cook, stirring, until heated through, about 5 minutes. Serve hot, garnished with sour cream, if desired, and accompanied by the chips for dipping.

PER SERVING (INCLUDES PLANTAIN CHIPS)
Calories 244 ▪ Protein 6g ▪ Total Fat 12g ▪
Sat. Fat 9g ▪ Cholesterol 0mg ▪ Carbohydrate 33g ▪
Dietary Fiber 7g ▪ Sodium 325mg

BAKED BRIE WITH CAPONATA

Egg-free

MAKES 6 SERVINGS

A 2-cup ceramic Corning Ware baking dish works beautifully in this easy yet elegant recipe. Caponata, a sweet-and-sour Italian eggplant relish, can be found near the olives and pimientos in most supermarkets.

1 (8-ounce) round Brie, top rind removed
1 (4.75-ounce) can caponata
Packaged crostini or bruschetta toasts, bread
sticks, or water crackers

Preheat oven to 350F (175C).

Place the Brie in a round shallow baking dish just large enough to accommodate its size. Spread the caponata evenly over the top. Bake 20 to 25 minutes, or until the Brie is softened and slightly runny. Let stand 10 minutes before serving. Serve warm with the toasts.

PER SERVING (WITHOUT BREAD)
Calories 147 ▪ Protein 8g ▪ Total Fat 12g ▪
Sat. Fat 7g ▪ Cholesterol 38mg ▪ Carbohydrate 2g ▪
Dietary Fiber 1g ▪ Sodium 594mg

Variations

Baked Brie with Chutney: Substitute ½ cup mango chutney for the caponata; bake and serve as directed.

Baked Brie with Raspberries: Substitute ½ cup raspberry preserves for the caponata; bake and serve as directed.

Plain Baked Brie: Do not remove the top rind. Omit the caponata; bake and serve as directed.

EASY APPETIZER BURRITOS

Vegan

MAKES 24 APPETIZERS

If you're searching for a quick and easy alternative to nachos that's also crowd-pleasing, look no further. Cherry or grape tomatoes can replace the olive garnish, if desired. You can also omit the garnishes altogether and serve the burritos whole for a quick and easy dinner for four. Should you opt to use cheese, I don't recommend using vegan soy cheese substitutes for this recipe as they typically don't melt well.

2 cups water
1 cup long-grain white rice
1 (15-ounce) can vegetarian chili
1 cup (4 ounces) already-shredded reduced-fat
    cheddar, Monterey Jack, or Mexican blend
    cheese (optional)
1 cup canned vegetarian refried beans, heated
4 (10-inch) flour tortillas, preferably spinach- or
    sun-dried tomato–flavored, warmed
24 pickled jalapeño chili slices, for garnish
    (optional)
24 whole pitted black olives, for garnish
Toppings: salsa, guacamole, and/or sour
    cream or nondairy sour cream

In a medium saucepan, bring the water to a boil over high heat. Add the rice, reduce the heat to low, cover, and simmer until all of the water has been absorbed, 17 to 20 minutes. Stir in the chili. Cover and cook 5 more minutes. Remove the pan from the heat, stir in the cheese (if using), and let stand, covered, 5 minutes. Uncover and stir again.

Spread ¼ cup of the refried beans over each tortilla, leaving about a 1-inch border all around. Top with one-fourth of the rice mixture. Roll up each tortilla from the edge nearest you, tucking in the sides as you roll. Cut each burrito crosswise on a diagonal into 6 equal pieces for a total of 24 pieces. Top each piece with a slice of jalapeño chili (if using), then top the jalapeño with an olive; secure the garnishes with a wooden pick. (If not serving immediately, place the appetizers on a baking sheet, cover loosely with foil, and hold in a warm oven up to 1 hour.)

To serve, place the salsa, guacamole, and/or sour cream in the center of a large round serving platter. Arrange the appetizer burritos around the toppings and serve at once.

PER APPETIZER (WITHOUT TOPPINGS)

Calories 84 ▪ Protein 5g ▪ Total Fat 1g ▪
Sat. Fat 0g ▪ Cholesterol 0mg ▪ Carbohydrate 14g ▪
Dietary Fiber 1g ▪ Sodium 195mg

CHÈVRE-PESTO CROSTINI

Egg-free

MAKES 6 SERVINGS

The union of tangy goat cheese and garlicky pesto is heavenly. This versatile spread also makes a fine topping for baked potatoes or sauce for hot cooked pasta.

1 (5.3-ounce) container spreadable goat
    cheese (about ⅔ cup), at room temperature
3 tablespoons refrigerated prepared pesto (see
    Cook's Tip, page 14)

Packaged crostini or bruschetta toasts, thin melba toast rounds, crackers, or toasted flat breads

Place the goat cheese in a small bowl and mash well with a fork. Add the pesto and mix until thoroughly blended. Serve at room temperature. Or cover and refrigerate a minimum of 30 minutes or up to 2 days and serve chilled (or return to room temperature). Serve with the toasts for spreading.

PER SERVING (WITHOUT BREAD)
Calories 151 ■ Protein 9g ■ Total Fat 12g ■ Sat. Fat 7g ■ Cholesterol 28mg ■ Carbohydrate 1g ■ Dietary Fiber 0mg ■ Sodium 138mg

Cook's Tip To serve the crostini as ready-assembled appetizers, count on using about 2 dozen packaged crostini or bruschetta toasts and spreading each with about 1½ teaspoons of the chèvre-pesto mixture. If the spread has been well chilled, the appetizers will stay fresh for up to 1 hour at room temperature. To turn them into canapés, top each with a sliced black olive or piece of pimiento.

CHICKPEAS WITH CURRIED MAYONNAISE IN LETTUCE CUPS

Dairy-free with vegan options
MAKES 4 SERVINGS

This no-fuss first course, appetizer, or snack is also good prepared with plain yogurt. Omit the lettuce cups and serve the chickpea mixture wrapped in Indian-style flatbread (naan or roti) or stuffed in pita bread for a light lunch. To create a vegan dish, replace the regular mayonnaise with soy mayonnaise, such as Nasoya, or plain soy yogurt, such as Silk.

1 (19-ounce) can chickpeas, rinsed and drained
¼ cup reduced-fat regular mayonnaise, soy mayonnaise, or plain soy yogurt
½ teaspoon mild curry powder, or more to taste
Salt and freshly ground black pepper, to taste
Small butter lettuce, radicchio, and/or Belgian endive leaves

In a medium bowl, toss the chickpeas, mayonnaise, curry powder, salt, and pepper until well combined. (At this point, the mixture can be stored, covered, in the refrigerator up to 2 days before using chilled or returning to room temperature.) Spoon into lettuce cups and serve.

PER SERVING
Calories 175 ■ Protein 7g ■ Total Fat 6g ■ Sat. Fat 1g ■ Cholesterol 5mg ■ Carbohydrate 24g ■ Dietary Fiber 3g ■ Sodium 76mg

CHEESY ROASTED CORN DIP WITH RED, WHITE, AND BLUE TORTILLA CHIPS

Lacto-ovo with egg-free option

MAKES 12 SERVINGS

Ideal for serving a Fourth of July or Super Bowl crowd, this cheesy dip consists entirely of packaged ingredients readily available at most major supermarkets. As an added boon, it can be assembled and refrigerated a day or two ahead of baking. While you can serve it with any tortilla chip, the contrast of the red, white, and blue ones against the yellow dip is especially appealing. A vegan cream cheese substitute, such as Tofutti's Better than Cream Cheese, can be used instead of the regular variety, but add ¼ teaspoon onion powder when you mix the corn with the mayonnaise and other ingredients. Vegan substitutes for the shredded cheese are not recommended here, as they don't melt well.

3 cups frozen yellow corn, thawed and drained

2 tablespoons canola or other mild vegetable oil

Salt and freshly ground black pepper, to taste

8 ounces (2 cups) already-shredded reduced-fat Monterey Jack and cheddar cheese, with jalapeño chilies, if desired

¾ cup reduced-fat regular mayonnaise or soy mayonnaise

½ cup (4 ounces) reduced-fat cream cheese with chives or nondairy cream cheese

2 to 3 tablespoons diced pimiento, drained

Dash Tobasco sauce, or more to taste

Red, white, and blue corn tortilla chips

Preheat oven to broil. Lightly oil an 11 × 7 inch shallow casserole or baking dish and set aside.

Place the corn on a large ungreased baking sheet and toss with the oil. Season with salt and pepper and spread out in a single layer. Broil 4 to 6 inches from heating element, stirring and turning a few times, until lightly browned, 5 to 8 minutes. Set aside to cool slightly. Turn oven temperature to 400F (205C).

Transfer the corn to a large bowl and add 1 cup of the shredded cheese, the mayonnaise, cream cheese, pimiento, and Tabasco sauce. Mix well to thoroughly combine. Transfer to the prepared dish, spreading evenly with the back of a large spoon. Sprinkle evenly with the remaining cheese. Bake 10 to 15 minutes, or until very hot and bubbly. Serve warm with tortilla chips.

PER SERVING (DIP ONLY)
Calories 159 ■ Protein 7g ■ Total Fat 10g ■ Sat. Fat 3g ■ Cholesterol 16mg ■ Carbohydrate 11g ■ Dietary Fiber 1g ■ Sodium 234mg

Variation

Egg-free version: For an egg-free dish, use soy mayonnaise, such as Nasoya, in lieu of the regular mayonnaise.

Cook's Tip If you're really pressed for time, instead of thawing and broiling the corn, cook the frozen corn according to package directions, omitting the oil from the recipe.

GNOCCHI WITH CAPONATA

Vegan

MAKES 5 TO 6 SERVINGS

Gnocchi, chewy Italian potato dumplings, and caponata, a sweet-and-sour Italian eggplant relish, are a tasty duo in this ultra-simple appetizer. It's an ideal choice to serve in a chafing dish on a buffet table, but add a bit more caponata to ensure that it doesn't dry out. It also makes a quick and delicious weeknight supper for up to three.

8 ounces frozen or vacuum-packed potato gnocchi
1 (4.75-ounce) can caponata
Pine nuts, toasted (see Cook's Tip below; optional)

Select an 8½- or 9-inch pie dish and set aside.

Cook the gnocchi in a stockpot filled with boiling salted water according to package directions until al dente, 3 to 5 minutes. Drain in a colander and set briefly aside.

Add the caponata to the cooking pot and cook over medium-low heat, stirring, until heated through. Return the drained gnocchi and toss gently yet thoroughly to combine. Transfer to the pie dish and sprinkle with the pine nuts, if desired. Serve warm, accompanied by wooden picks or small cocktail forks.

PER SERVING

Calories 189 ■ Protein 5g ■ Total Fat 2g ■
Sat. Fat 0g ■ Cholesterol 0mg ■ Carbohydrate 37g ■
Dietary Fiber 3g ■ Sodium 453mg

Variation

Gnocchi with Pesto: Omit the caponata and toss the hot cooked gnocchi with 3 tablespoons refrigerated prepared pesto; sprinkle with the optional pine nuts and shredded Parmesan cheese, if desired. Serve warm.

Cook's Tip *Toasting nuts:* To toast chopped walnuts, slivered almonds, pine nuts, or other small nut shapes or pieces in the oven: Preheat the oven to 350F (175C). Spread the nuts in a single layer on an ungreased light-colored baking sheet. Bake until lightly golden, about 5 minutes, stirring halfway through the cooking time. Immediately remove from the baking sheet and set aside briefly to cool.

To toast on the stovetop: Heat a small dry skillet over medium heat. Add the nuts and cook, stirring constantly, until lightly golden, 3 to 5 minutes. Immediately remove from the skillet and set aside briefly to cool. For larger whole nuts and nuts pieces, increase the cooking time by a few minutes.

GREEK-STYLE CHICKPEA AND OLIVE BRUSCHETTA

Vegan

MAKES 6 TO 8 SERVINGS

This unusual bruschetta topping is ideal for cold-weather entertaining when the fresh tomatoes and basil of the classic version are in short supply. Six ½-inch-thick slices of Italian or peasant-style bread, lightly toasted, can be used in lieu of the pita, if desired.

1 cup canned chickpeas, rinsed and
  drained
3 tablespoons canned chopped black olives
1½ tablespoons garlic-flavored olive oil (see
  Cook's Tip below)
1½ tablespoons balsamic or red wine
  vinegar
¼ teaspoon dried oregano leaves
¼ teaspoon salt, preferably the coarse variety,
  or to taste
Freshly ground black pepper, to taste
6 to 8 (4-inch-round) mini pita breads
  (about 1 ounce each), preferably whole
  wheat, lightly toasted

In a small bowl, toss all the ingredients except the bread until well combined. Mash with a fork into a coarse consistency. Set aside at room temperature about 10 minutes to allow the flavors to blend; mash briefly again. (At this point, mixture can be stored, covered, in the refrigerator up to 3 days before returning to room temperature and using.) Spread about 2 tablespoons evenly over each piece of bread. Serve at room temperature.

PER SERVING
Calories 157 ▪ Protein 5g ▪ Total Fat 5g ▪
Sat. Fat 1g ▪ Cholesterol 0mg ▪ Carbohydrate 24g ▪
Dietary Fiber 3g ▪ Sodium 275mg

Cook's Tip If you don't have garlic-flavored olive oil, replace the ¼ teaspoon coarse salt with garlic salt.

MINI GREEK PITA PIZZAS

Egg-free

MAKES 8 MINI PIZZAS

These delicious appetizer pizzas can serve as a quick and easy dinner for four served with soup and a salad. If you can't locate the 4-inch pitas, use 6 of the 6-inch size and divide the toppings accordingly.

½ cup prepared pizza sauce (see second
  Cook's Tip, page 70)
8 (4-inch) pita breads (about 1 ounce each),
  preferably whole wheat
¾ cup (3 ounces) crumbled feta cheese
2 tablespoons plus 2 teaspoons canned
  chopped black olives
2 teaspoons extra-virgin olive oil
Dried oregano

Preheat oven to 375F (190C).

Spread 1 tablespoon of the pizza sauce evenly over each pita bread. Top each with 1½ tablespoons of the feta, followed with 1 teaspoon of the olives. Drizzle each with ¼ teaspoon of the oil, then sprinkle lightly with oregano. Transfer to an ungreased baking sheet. Bake in the center of the oven until the cheese is softened and the pitas are lightly browned, about 10 minutes. Serve at once.

Variations

Mini Neapolitan-Style Pita Pizzas: Substitute already-shredded mozzarella cheese for the feta cheese. Omit the olives, if desired.

Mini Pesto Pita Pizzas: Substitute ⅓ cup refrigerated prepared pesto sauce for the pizza sauce (you will only need about 2 teaspoons pesto per pita), already-shredded mozzarella cheese for the feta cheese, and chopped pimiento for the olives. Omit the oregano.

LAYERED SOUTH-OF-THE-BORDER PARTY DIP

Egg-free with vegan options

MAKES 8 SERVINGS

A chilled, make-ahead answer to hot, last-minute nachos, this colorful layered party dip is always a crowd-pleaser, particularly among young people. Nondairy sour cream, such as Tofutti Better than Sour Cream, can easily be substituted for the dairy sour cream, if desired. Vegan soy cheese substitutes will work here because the dish is not heated. Another option is to omit the cheese altogether; I do this often, and it's rarely ever missed!

1 (16-ounce) can vegetarian refried beans
½ cup medium salsa
1 (12-ounce) container guacamole (about 1½ cups)
1 cup light sour cream or nondairy sour cream
⅓ cup (about 1½ ounces) already-shredded reduced-fat cheddar cheese or vegan equivalent
2½ to 3 tablespoons canned chopped black olives or ¼ cup canned sliced black olives
12 to 16 grape or cherry tomatoes, for garnish
Corn tortilla chips

In a small bowl, mix the refried beans and salsa until thoroughly combined. Spread evenly over the bottom of an ungreased 10-inch pie plate or quiche dish. Carefully spread the guacamole over the top, leaving about a ½-inch border of the bean mixture exposed. Carefully spread the sour cream over the guacamole, leaving about a ½-inch border of the guacamole exposed. Sprinkle the cheese evenly over the sour cream, then sprinkle evenly with the olives. Cover and refrigerate a minimum of 1 hour, or overnight. Just before serving, garnish with the tomatoes. Serve chilled, with chips.

CURRIED LENTILS WITH INDIAN FLATBREAD

Vegan
MAKES 4 TO 6 SERVINGS

This warm and fragrant appetizer capitalizes on the convenience of canned cooked lentils, available in health food stores and some well-stocked supermarkets. The tiny black beluga heirloom variety is highly recommended here as the legumes cook down into a creamy consistency faster than regular red or brown lentils. You can also wrap the lentils in 4 (10-inch) flour tortillas or stuff into 4 (6-inch) pita breads for a satisfying light meal.

1 (15-ounce) can cooked lentils, briefly drained (do not rinse)

¼ cup water or low-sodium vegetable broth

1½ tablespoons tomato paste

1 tablespoon extra-virgin olive oil

2 to 3 teaspoons mild curry powder, or to taste

½ teaspoon onion powder

½ teaspoon garlic powder

Salt and freshly ground black pepper, to taste

Indian flatbread, lavosh, pita, or flour tortillas for dipping

In a small saucepan, bring the lentils, water, tomato paste, oil, curry powder, onion powder, garlic powder, salt, and pepper to a simmer over medium heat, stirring occasionally. Reduce the heat and simmer gently, uncovered, stirring occasionally, until thickened and creamy, about 10 minutes. Transfer to a warm serving bowl and serve as a dip for the flatbread.

PER SERVING (WITHOUT BREAD)
Calories 164 ■ Protein 10g ■ Total Fat 4g ■ Sat. Fat 1g ■ Cholesterol 0mg ■ Carbohydrate 24g ■ Dietary Fiber 6g ■ Sodium 51mg

Cook's Tip Because of their rather fragile consistency, canned cooked lentils—particularly the black beluga heirloom variety—are the only canned beans or legumes in this book that are not recommended for rinsing before use in the recipe. However, as most canned lentils are manufactured by organic and/or natural food companies, they generally have a much lower sodium content than most of the other leading brands of canned beans and legumes.

FRESH MOZZARELLA, CHERRY TOMATO, AND BASIL SPEARS

Egg-free
MAKES 24 APPETIZERS

A skewered variation of insalata caprese, this colorful combination in the red, white, and green of the Italian flag is an hors d'oeuvre that everyone seems to love.

24 bite-size fresh mozzarella cheese balls (about 8 ounces)

24 small fresh basil leaves or 12 medium to large fresh basil leaves, torn in half

24 small cherry or grape tomatoes (1½ to 2 cups)

3 tablespoons extra-virgin olive oil

1 tablespoon balsamic vinegar

1 tablespoon red wine vinegar

Salt and freshly ground black pepper, to taste

Alternate a cheese ball, basil leaf, and cherry tomato on each of 24 wooden picks. Arrange in a shallow container, preferably in a single layer. In a small bowl, whisk together the oil, vinegars, salt, and pepper. Pour over the skewered mixture, turning to thoroughly coat.

Cover and refrigerate a minimum of 30 minutes or overnight, turning once. Serve chilled or return to room temperature before serving.

PER APPETIZER

Calories 50 ■ Protein 2g ■ Total Fat 4g ■
Sat. Fat 2g ■ Cholesterol 8mg ■ Carbohydrate 1g ■
Dietary Fiber 0g ■ Sodium 41mg

Preheat oven to 350F (175C). Combine all the ingredients in a small baking dish just large enough to hold the olives in a single layer. Bake, uncovered, about 20 minutes, or until the olives are heated through, stirring a few times. Cool slightly. Serve warm or at room temperature. (Completely cooled olives can be stored, covered, in the refrigerator 3 or 4 days before returning to room temperature and serving).

PER SERVING

Calories 130 ■ Protein 0g ■ Total Fat 12g ■
Sat. Fat 0g ■ Cholesterol 0mg ■ Carbohydrate 3g ■
Dietary Fiber 0g ■ Sodium 641mg

Cook's Tip For easier eating, you can use pitted olives, but the pits help the olives hold their shape during baking.

BAKED OLIVES WITH RED WINE AND HERBS

Vegan

MAKES 6 SERVINGS

The aroma of baking olives, red wine, and herbs is nothing short of heady in this good-for-you appetizer. Although black olives are relatively high in fat, it's the healthy monounsaturated variety that contains a small amount of saturated fat and no cholesterol. While wine, of course, contains alcohol, studies continue to demonstrate that the flavonols in the red variety are not only beneficial to heart health by reducing blood cholesterol, but also may protect against certain cancers.

1 cup unpitted kalamata olives or other good-
    quality brine-cured black olives
½ cup dry red wine
½ tablespoon extra-virgin olive oil
½ teaspoon refrigerated bottled minced garlic
¼ teaspoon fennel seeds or aniseeds
¼ teaspoon dried thyme leaves

MARINATED OLIVES WITH ORANGE

Vegan
MAKES 6 SERVINGS

This easy, no-cook appetizer from Provence is a delight for olive lovers. While you can use any type of olive, try to make sure that they are deli-quality and not straight from a can.

> ½ cup pitted Niçoise, kalamata, or other good-quality black olives
>
> ½ cup pitted Provençal, picholine, Italian, or other good-quality green olives
>
> 2 tablespoons tiny white cocktail onions, drained (optional)
>
> ¼ cup orange juice made from frozen concentrate
>
> 3 tablespoons extra-virgin olive oil
>
> 2 teaspoons dried chopped orange peel
>
> ½ teaspoon garlic powder
>
> Freshly ground black pepper, to taste
>
> Cayenne pepper, to taste (optional)

In a small bowl, combine all the ingredients. Refrigerate, covered, a minimum of 12 hours, or up to 2 days, stirring a few times. Serve at room temperature for the best flavor.

PER SERVING
Calories 130 ▪ Protein 0g ▪ Total Fat 13g ▪
Sat. Fat 1g ▪ Cholesterol 0mg ▪ Carbohydrate 4g ▪
Dietary Fiber 0g ▪ Sodium 413mg

BROILED PORTOBELLO MUSHROOM CAPS WITH GORGONZOLA BUTTER

Egg-free
MAKES 4 SERVINGS

Serve these succulent, tangy mushroom caps on their own as an elegant appetizer or first course, or in split buns as gourmet blue-cheese burgers.

> ½ cup (2 ounces) crumbled Gorgonzola or other mild blue cheese, at room temperature
>
> 2 tablespoons Neufchâtel (a reduced-fat cream cheese), at room temperature
>
> 1 tablespoon unsalted butter, softened
>
> 4 large (about 2 ounces each) packaged portobello mushroom caps
>
> 1 teaspoon extra-virgin olive oil
>
> Salt and freshly ground black pepper, to taste

Preheat oven to broil. Lightly oil a baking sheet and set aside.

In a small bowl, mash together the Gorgonzola, Neufchâtel, and butter until well combined. Set aside.

Rub the smooth sides of the mushroom caps evenly with the oil and arrange on the prepared baking sheet, smooth sides up. Broil 6 to 8 inches from heating element until lightly browned, about 5 minutes. Remove from the oven and season lightly with salt and pepper, then turn mushroom caps over. Fill each cap with equal amounts (about 2½ tablespoons) of the Gorgonzola mixture. Return to oven and broil until lightly browned and bubbly, 1 to 2 minutes. Serve at once.

PER SERVING

Calories 117 ▪ Protein 5g ▪ Total Fat 10g ▪
Sat. Fat 6g ▪ Cholesterol 23mg ▪ Carbohydrate 3g ▪
Dietary Fiber 1g ▪ Sodium 240mg

EASY NACHOS

Egg-free

MAKES 6 SERVINGS

Heating the refried beans before baking ensures nice and hot nachos. Vegan soy substitutes for the cheddar cheese are not recommended, as they don't melt well.

1 (16-ounce) can vegetarian refried beans, heated

1 cup medium salsa

6 ounces corn tortilla chips

1½ cups (6 ounces) already-shredded reduced-fat cheddar cheese

Sliced pickled jalapeño chilies (optional)

Light sour cream or nondairy sour cream, and/or guacamole, for garnish (optional)

Preheat oven to 400F (205c). Lightly oil a pizza pan.

Mound the warm beans in the center of the prepared pan. Spoon half of the salsa over the beans. Arrange the chips over the beans and exposed surface of pan. Spoon the remaining salsa evenly over the chips. Sprinkle evenly with the cheese. Top with jalapeño chilies (if using). Bake in the center of the oven 4 to 5 minutes, or until the cheese is melted. Serve at once, garnished with mounds of sour cream and/or guacamole, if desired.

PER SERVING

Calories 265 ▪ Protein 13g ▪ Total Fat 10g ▪
Sat. Fat 3g ▪ Cholesterol 6mg ▪ Carbohydrate 31g ▪
Dietary Fiber 7g ▪ Sodium 749mg

PESTO DIP WITH RAW VEGETABLES

Egg-free

MAKES 6 SERVINGS; 1½ CUPS DIP

While I prefer a pronounced basil flavor to come through in this delicious appetizer, you can use as little as half the amount of pesto to create a tangier and less rich dip. Precut, ready-washed fresh vegetables, such as broccoli, cauliflower, carrots, and celery, are available in the produce section of most supermarkets. Although I've never come across a commercially prepared pesto that didn't contain cheese, you can greatly reduce the amount of dairy in the recipe by opting for nondairy sour cream or plain soy yogurt; the dip will still be quite tasty!

1 cup light sour cream, nondairy sour cream, or plain low-fat dairy or soy yogurt

½ cup refrigerated prepared pesto, or less to taste

Salt and freshly ground black pepper, to taste

Assorted fresh raw vegetables, to serve

In a small bowl, mix together the sour cream and pesto until well blended. Season with salt and pepper, if necessary. Cover and refrigerate a minimum of 30 minutes or up to 2 days. Serve chilled, accompanied with the vegetables for dipping.

PER SERVING (¼ CUP DIP WITHOUT VEGETABLES)

Calories 115 ▪ Protein 4g ▪ Total Fat 10g ▪
Sat. Fat 2g ▪ Cholesterol 9mg ▪ Carbohydrate 2g ▪
Dietary Fiber 0g ▪ Sodium 147mg

Variations

Chipotle Chile Dip: Substitute ½ cup prepared chipotle sauce for the pesto and serve with tortilla chips as well as raw vegetables. Chipotle sauce is a spicy, smoky, sweet condiment made from smoked dried jalapeño chiles (chipotle chilies). It can be found in specialty stores and many well-stocked supermarkets.

Red Pepper Dip: Substitute ½ cup prepared sweet red pepper spread for the pesto and serve with raw vegetables. This is also an excellent topping for baked potatoes.

Chutney Dip: Substitute ½ cup mango chutney for the pesto and add 1 teaspoon mild curry powder, if desired. Serve with raw vegetables.

Cook's Tip Leftover dip makes an excellent topping for baked potatoes.

PESTO TOASTS

Egg-free
MAKES 6 SERVINGS

Serve these versatile toasts as appetizers, snacks, or a light lunch accompanied by a soup or salad. Vegan soy cheese substitutes are not recommended for the mozzarella cheese as they don't melt well.

- 6 tablespoons refrigerated prepared pesto
- 6 large slices Italian bread (about 1¼ ounce each), lightly toasted
- 2 tablespoons diced pimiento, drained (optional)
- 9 tablespoons (about 2 ounces) already-shredded part-skim mozzarella cheese

Preheat oven to broil.

Spread 1 tablespoon pesto evenly over each bread slice, then sprinkle with 1 teaspoon of the pimiento (if using). Sprinkle each with 1½ tablespoons of the cheese. Place on an ungreased baking sheet and broil 4 to 6 inches from heat source until cheese is melted, 1 to 2 minutes. Serve at once.

PER SERVING
Calories 202 ■ Protein 9g ■ Total Fat 10g ■
Sat. Fat 3g ■ Cholesterol 10mg ■ Carbohydrate 19g ■
Dietary Fiber 1g ■ Sodium 366mg

Cook's Tip Pesto is an Italian sauce made from basil, pine nuts, Parmesan cheese, garlic, and olive oil. The refrigerated prepared variety tastes closest to homemade and is highly recommended for use in all of this book's recipes where pesto is required. Plastic containers of prepared pesto can be found in the refrigerated section of most well-stocked supermarkets, next to the fresh pastas. Refrigerated reduced-fat pesto can be used in lieu of the regular pesto, if desired.

TOASTED POT STICKERS WITH WASABI CREAM

Lacto-ovo with vegan options
MAKES 6 SERVINGS

Cabbage is typically the main ingredient in vegetarian pot stickers—the Asian equivalent of Italian ravioli, located in Asian and specialty markets, such as Trader Joe's. Though typically sautéed (see the variation below), baking them cuts down on the amount of oil needed. While you can offer these as finger foods, I like to provide small plates and forks or serve them as a first course at the dinner table.

For a vegan variation, serve with the Pineapple-Orange Mirin Dipping Sauce (page 18) in lieu of the Wasabi Cream.

16 ounces frozen vegetarian pot stickers (16 to 18 pieces)
2 to 3 teaspoons toasted (dark) sesame oil
Wasabi Cream (below) or Pineapple-Orange Mirin Dipping Sauce (page 18)

Bring a large pot of salted water to a boil over medium-high heat. Preheat oven to broil. Lightly oil a baking sheet and set aside.

Add the pot stickers to the boiling water; stir and return to a boil. Reduce the heat to medium and cook until just softened, about 2 minutes, stirring occasionally. Drain well and transfer, flat side down, to the prepared baking sheet. Brush the tops evenly with the sesame oil.

Broil 6 to 8 inches from the heating element until the tops are lightly brown, 3 to 5 minutes, turning the baking sheet a few times to promote even browning.

To serve, place the Wasabi Cream in the center of a large round serving platter (providing a spoon for serving), arrange the warm pot stickers around the sauce, and serve at once. Or divide the pot stickers among 6 small plates, and pass the Wasabi Cream separately.

PER SERVING (INCLUDES ABOUT
1 TABLESPOON WASABI CREAM)
Calories 213 ▪ Protein 5g ▪ Total Fat 10g ▪
Sat. Fat 1g ▪ Cholesterol 8mg ▪ Carbohydrate 27g ▪
Dietary Fiber 1g ▪ Sodium 299mg

Variation

Sautéed Pot Stickers: Boil and drain the pot stickers as directed. Heat 1 tablespoon peanut oil and ½ tablespoon toasted (dark) sesame oil in a large nonstick skillet over medium heat. Working in batches, if necessary, add pot stickers, flat sides down, and cook until lightly browned on just the flat side, 2 to 3 minutes. Serve at once, with Wasabi Cream, below.

WASABI CREAM

Lacto-ovo
MAKES ABOUT ½ CUP

A little of this spicy dip or condiment goes a long way; allow for about 1 teaspoon per pot sticker. It is also excellent served with raw vegetables. Wasabi mayonnaise is made with Japanese horseradish, distinctive for its vivid green color and head-rushing heat. It can be purchased at Trader Joe's and other specialty markets.

¼ cup nonfat sour cream
¼ cup wasabi mayonnaise
2 teaspoons honey
½ teaspoon reduced-sodium soy sauce

In a small bowl, mix together all the ingredients until well combined. Cover and refrigerate a minimum of 30 minutes, or up to 3 days.

PER SERVING (ABOUT 1 TABLESPOON)
Calories 51 ▪ Protein 0g ▪ Total Fat 5g ▪
Sat. Fat 1g ▪ Cholesterol 3mg ▪ Carbohydrate 2g ▪
Dietary Fiber 0g ▪ Sodium 48mg

SAUTÉED APPETIZER RAVIOLI

Lacto-ovo
MAKES 8 SERVINGS

This popular appetizer is terrific for carefree entertaining as it can be assembled in stages and held in a warm oven up to 1 hour before serving. It can also serve four for a special dinner. In that instance, use 2 cups pasta sauce, ladle equal amounts over warmed dinner plates, then top with equal amounts of ravioli—*delizioso!*

12 ounces fresh cheese-filled ravioli
¾ cup cornmeal
3 tablespoons already-shredded Parmesan cheese
⅛ teaspoon ground nutmeg
Salt and freshly ground black pepper, to taste
2 tablespoons extra-virgin olive oil
1 to 1½ cups favorite prepared pasta sauce, heated

In a large stockpot filled with boiling salted water, cook the ravioli according to package directions until just al dente; drain.

Meanwhile, in a small bowl, toss the cornmeal, Parmesan cheese, nutmeg, salt, and pepper until thoroughly combined. Transfer to a dinner plate or shallow soup bowl. While still quite warm yet able to be handled, lightly dredge the ravioli in the cornmeal mixture. (At this point, the ravioli can be held up to 1 hour at room temperature before continuing with the recipe.)

Preheat oven to 170F (75C). In a large nonstick skillet, heat half of the oil over medium heat. Add half of the ravioli and cook until lightly browned, about 2 minutes per side. Transfer to a serving platter and place in the warm oven. Add the remaining oil to the skillet and sauté the remaining ravioli. Add to serving platter. (At this point, ravioli can be held in warm oven up to 1 hour before serving.) Serve warm, with the heated pasta sauce passed separately for dipping.

PER SERVING (INCLUDES PASTA SAUCE)
Calories 195 ■ Protein 6g ■ Total Fat 9g ■ Sat. Fat 3g ■ Cholesterol 45mg ■ Carbohydrate 24g ■ Dietary Fiber 2g ■ Sodium 439mg

WARM WHITE BEAN BRUSCHETTA

Vegan
MAKES 4 TO 6 SERVINGS

Available at gourmet markets and rather expensive, the optional truffle oil provides a musky, sophisticated touch to this otherwise rustic appetizer.

1 (15-ounce) can great northern, navy, or other white beans, rinsed and drained
½ cup low-sodium vegetable broth
1 teaspoon refrigerated bottled minced garlic
½ teaspoon dried rubbed sage
1 bay leaf, broken in half
1 tablespoon extra-virgin olive oil
1 teaspoon white truffle oil (optional)
½ teaspoon salt, preferably the coarse variety, or to taste
¼ teaspoon freshly ground black pepper, or to taste
Packaged bruschetta toasts or sliced Italian bread, lightly toasted, cut in half

In a medium saucepan, combine the beans, broth, garlic, sage, and bay leaf; bring to a boil over medium-high heat, stirring occasionally. Reduce the heat to medium-low and simmer, stirring occasionally, until the mixture is slightly reduced, about 10 minutes.

Reduce the heat to low and remove the bay leaf halves. Cook, stirring and mashing the mixture against the sides and bottom of the pan with a large wooden spoon until smooth and of a spreadable consistency, about 5 minutes.

Remove from heat and add the olive oil, truffle oil (if using), salt, and pepper. Stir until well combined. Transfer to a warm serving bowl and surround with the bruschetta toasts. Serve at once.

PER SERVING (WITHOUT BREAD)
Calories 131 ▪ Protein 8g ▪ Total Fat 4g ▪
Sat. Fat 1g ▪ Cholesterol 0mg ▪ Carbohydrate 18g ▪
Dietary Fiber 4g ▪ Sodium 304mg

BAKED VEGETABLE WONTONS WITH PINEAPPLE-ORANGE MIRIN DIPPING SAUCE

Vegan

MAKES 30 APPETIZERS; 6 TO 8 SERVINGS

These light and crunchy appetizers are almost as fun to make as they are to eat. Canned straw mushrooms are located in Asian markets and the specialty food aisles of most major supermarkets. Select the tiniest ones you can find from among those in a 12-ounce can, and save the remainder to add to rice dishes or stir-fries. If pressed for time, skip the dipping sauce and serve with duck sauce, slightly heated or at room temperature. These are also delicious with Wasabi Cream (page 15).

3 tablespoons toasted (dark) sesame oil
½ cup frozen chopped onion
1½ cups already-shredded green cabbage
½ cup already-shredded carrots
30 tiny canned straw mushrooms, drained
    (about ⅔ cup from 12-ounce can)
1 tablespoon reduced-sodium soy sauce
1 tablespoon mirin (sweet rice wine)
½ tablespoon bottled chopped ginger
½ tablespoon curry powder
30 small square wonton wrappers
Pineapple-Orange Mirin Dipping Sauce (below)

Preheat oven to 375F (190C). Lightly grease a large baking sheet and set aside.

In a large nonstick skillet, heat 2 tablespoons of the oil over medium heat. Add the onion and cook, stirring often, until thawed and softened, 2 to 3 minutes. Increase the heat to medium-high and add the cabbage and carrots and cook, stirring often, until softened and wilted, about 5 minutes. Quickly add the mushrooms, soy sauce, mirin, ginger, and curry powder, stirring well to thoroughly combine. Cook, stirring constantly, 1 minute. Immediately remove from the heat. Set aside to cool. (At this point, the filling may be set aside at room temperature up to 1 hour before using, or covered and refrigerated up to 24 hours before returning to room temperature and using.)

Lay out about one-third of the wonton wrappers on a cutting board or other flat surface. Including 1 mushroom per tablespoon, arrange 1 tablespoon of the filling slightly off to the center of each wonton. Fold one corner of the sheet over to the opposite corner, handkerchief-style. Press the two sides of each wonton with your thumbs to seal. Fold in the three pointed edges, pressing with your thumbs to seal. Repeat the filling process with remaining wonton sheets.

Arrange the filled wontons on the prepared baking sheet. Brush the tops with half of the remaining oil. Bake 6 minutes on the middle rack. Turn the wontons over and brush with the remaining oil. Bake about 5 minutes, or until the tops are lightly browned.

To serve, place the dipping sauce in the center of a large round serving platter. Arrange the wontons around the dipping sauce and serve at once.

PER 1 WONTON (WITHOUT DIPPING SAUCE)
Calories 41 ▪ Protein 1g ▪ Total Fat 2g ▪
Sat. Fat 0g ▪ Cholesterol 0mg ▪ Carbohydrate 6g ▪
Dietary Fiber 0g ▪ Sodium 82mg

In a small saucepan, combine all the ingredients. Bring to a simmer over medium heat, stirring often. Immediately remove from heat and set aside to cool to room temperature. Whisk again before serving.

PER SERVING (ABOUT 1 TABLESPOON)
Calories 16 ▪ Protein 0.1g ▪ Total Fat 0g ▪
Sat. Fat 0g ▪ Cholesterol 0mg ▪ Carbohydrate 3g ▪
Dietary Fiber 0g ▪ Sodium 45mg

PINEAPPLE-ORANGE MIRIN DIPPING SAUCE

Vegan

MAKES ABOUT 1 CUP

This versatile sauce is also excellent with egg rolls and vegetable tempura. Apricot or plum preserves can be used in lieu of the marmalade, if desired. Mirin is a sweet rice wine available at Asian markets, specialty stores, and several well-stocked supermarkets. In a pinch, substitute with a medium-dry or sweet sherry.

½ **cup pineapple juice or pineapple fruit juice blend**

2 **tablespoons orange marmalade, preferably the bitter Seville style**

2 **tablespoons mirin**

1 **tablespoon reduced-sodium soy sauce**

1 **tablespoon rice vinegar**

¼ **teaspoon Chinese chili paste, or cayenne pepper, to taste**

¼ **teaspoon ground ginger**

Savory Soups, Stews, and Chilis

This chapter deliciously abolishes the myth that soups have to be long-simmering affairs, prepared by people who have nothing but time on their hands to make broth from scratch and chop copious amounts of vegetables. What the recipes prove is that good soup can be made from canned broth, canned tomatoes, canned beans, frozen vegetables, and, in the case of Chunky Tomato-Rice Soup, even leftover Chinese takeout rice! The first section offers lighter soups appropriate for lunch and first courses; consider Creamy Artichoke Soup with Thyme for your next dinner party. The second section features heartier soups, stews, and chilis that are typically more than 250 calories; these are ideal for quick weeknight suppers, or, in the case of Bulgur–Chili Bean Stew over Tortilla Chips and Moroccan Vegetable Stew over Couscous, for feeding a crowd. As an added boon, many of the following recipes provide a highly palatable cover to sneak some of the more suspect greens and vegetables—arugula, broccoli, kale, okra, spinach—into a healthy diet. If you've always shunned kale, try out the Italian-Style Kale and Kidney Bean Soup and chances are you'll bookmark the page for future reference. If you're not from the South and have never even heard of okra, cook up a pot of Black-Eyed Pea Jambalaya and you may find yourself wondering what other good things you've been missing out on in life!

First-Course and Lighter Soups

CREAMY ARTICHOKE SOUP WITH THYME

Egg-free with vegan option

MAKES 4 SERVINGS

This simple yet elegant soup makes an impressive first course to serve on special occasions. If you are converting it to a vegan recipe, rice milk is the preferred alternative to the skim milk, but you can certainly use soymilk; just be aware that the latter tends to separate when heated. Soy creamer is the suggested alternative to the half-and-half, because other nondairy coffee creamers typically contain a casein derivative, which is a milk product.

2 tablespoons extra-light olive oil, canola oil, or other mild vegetable oil

2 tablespoons all-purpose flour

1 (14-ounce) can (1¾ cups) low-sodium vegetable broth

2 (8-ounce) packages frozen quartered artichoke hearts, thoroughly thawed

1 teaspoon onion powder

½ teaspoon garlic powder

½ teaspoon dried thyme leaves

½ teaspoon sugar

½ teaspoon salt, or to taste

¼ teaspoon freshly ground black pepper, or to taste

2 large bay leaves

1⅔ cups skim milk or rice milk

⅓ cup half-and-half or soy creamer

In a medium stockpot, heat the oil over medium heat. Add the flour and cook, stirring constantly, 2 minutes. Slowly whisk in the broth and bring to a gentle boil. Boil, stirring, 1 minute. Stir in the artichokes, onion powder, garlic powder, thyme, sugar, salt, pepper, and bay leaves; return to a gentle boil. Reduce the heat to low, cover, and simmer, stirring occasionally, 15 minutes.

Stir in the milk and half-and-half. Return to a gentle simmer over medium heat, stirring to break up the artichokes with a wooden spoon and taking care not to allow the mixture to boil. Remove the bay leaves and serve hot.

PER SERVING

Calories 207 ▪ Protein 12g ▪ Total Fat 10g ▪ Sat. Fat 3g ▪ Cholesterol 9mg ▪ Carbohydrate 20g ▪ Dietary Fiber 6g ▪ Sodium 320mg

Cook's Tip Extra-light olive oil is a mild-tasting, highly filtered oil that contains the same amount of calories and fat as regular olive oil. It is ideal for use in recipes where a subtle flavor of olive oil is desirable, such as in creamy dishes or baked goods. It also has a higher smoking point than regular olive oil and is therefore an excellent choice for high-heat cooking.

ITALIAN-STYLE KALE AND KIDNEY BEAN SOUP

Vegan

MAKES 6 TO 8 SERVINGS

Beans and greens—in this case, kale, an excellent source of vitamins A and C, calcium, and iron—are frequently paired in Italian cooking. Serve this soup with crusty peasant bread and a simple tossed salad for a satisfying lunch or light supper. Frozen chopped spinach or collard greens can stand in for the kale, if desired.

2 tablespoons extra-virgin olive oil

1 cup frozen chopped onion

2 teaspoons refrigerated bottled minced garlic

2 (14-ounce) cans (3½ cups) low-sodium vegetable broth

2 cups water

1 (14.5-ounce) can no-salt-added diced tomatoes, juice included

1 (10-ounce) package frozen chopped kale, thawed under cold running water and drained

½ teaspoon dried oregano

¼ teaspoon sugar, or to taste (optional)

Salt and freshly ground black pepper, to taste

2 bay leaves

1 (15-ounce) can kidney beans, rinsed and drained

1 (15-ounce) can sliced potatoes, rinsed and drained

Pinch sweet paprika (optional)

In a medium stockpot, heat the oil over medium heat. Add the onion and cook, stirring, until thawed and softened, about 3 minutes. Add the garlic and cook, stirring constantly, 2 minutes. Add the broth, water, tomatoes with their juice, kale, oregano, sugar (if using), salt, pepper, and bay leaves. Bring to a boil over high heat.

Stir in the beans, potatoes, and paprika (if using). Bring to a boil; reduce the heat to medium-low. Simmer, uncovered, until slightly reduced, about 15 minutes, adjusting heat to maintain a simmer and stirring occasionally with a large wooden spoon to break up the potatoes. Serve hot.

PER SERVING

Calories 192 ▪ Protein 14g ▪ Total Fat 5g ▪ Sat. Fat 1g ▪ Cholesterol 0mg ▪ Carbohydrate 25g ▪ Dietary Fiber 8g ▪ Sodium 536mg

MEXICAN BEAN AND TORTILLA SOUP

Vegan

MAKES 4 SERVINGS

This soup can begin a Mexican-style meal on a lively note or become a satisfying light lunch served with a tossed green salad. Refried black beans can be substituted for the regular pinto bean variety, if desired.

> 2 cups water
> 1 (14-ounce) can (1¾ cups) low-sodium vegetable broth
> 1 (16-ounce) can refried vegetarian beans
> 1¼ cups mild or medium picante sauce·
> About 2 ounces corn tortilla chips, broken into bite-size pieces

In a medium stockpot, combine the water, broth, beans, and picante sauce. Bring to a boil over medium-high heat, stirring often to incorporate the beans. Reduce the heat and simmer, covered, 10 minutes, stirring a few times.

To serve, divide the soup evenly among 4 bowls and top with equal amounts of tortilla chips. Serve immediately.

PER SERVING

Calories 213 ▪ Protein 13g ▪ Total Fat 5g ▪
Sat. Fat 1g ▪ Cholesterol 0mg ▪ Carbohydrate 30g ▪
Dietary Fiber 8g ▪ Sodium 1,365mg

Variation

Mexican Rice and Bean Soup: Omit the tortilla chips and stir in 1 cup cooked white or brown rice and 1 cup frozen yellow corn after the mixture comes to a boil.

Cook's Tip Refried canned beans often contain lard, which is fat rendered from hogs. If the can is not labeled "vegetarian," be sure to check the ingredients.

MISO SOUP WITH POT STICKERS

Vegan

MAKES 4 SERVINGS

Miso is a fermented soy paste that is used frequently in Japanese cooking to flavor and thicken soups and sauces. While just 1 tablespoon of miso contains 2 grams of protein and 1 gram of dietary fiber, it also contains about 800 milligrams of sodium. If you are watching your salt intake, use the lesser amount in the recipe. Vegetarian pot stickers, a ravioli-like Asian pasta, are typically filled with a combination of cabbage, carrots, and radishes. Both miso and pot stickers can be found in Asian markets as well as specialty and health food stores; I get mine at Trader Joe's.

> 2½ cups water
> 1 (14-ounce) can (1¾ cups) low-sodium vegetable broth
> 1 teaspoon freeze-dried chopped chives
> 8 ounces frozen vegetarian pot stickers
> ½ cup canned straw mushrooms, drained (optional)
> 1½ to 2 tablespoons miso, preferably the brown variety, mixed with 2 tablespoons water
> 1 teaspoon toasted (dark) sesame oil

In a medium stockpot, bring the water, broth, and chives to a boil over medium-high heat. Add the pot stickers and mushrooms (if using); stir and return to a boil. Reduce the heat to medium and cook until pot stickers are softened but still firm to the bite, about 3 minutes, stirring occasionally. Remove from heat and add the miso mixture and sesame oil, stirring well to combine. (If not serving immediately, keep warm over low heat, but do not allow mixture to boil.) Serve hot.

PER SERVING

Calories 135 ▪ Protein 9g ▪ Total Fat 2g ▪
Sat. Fat 0g ▪ Cholesterol 0mg ▪ Carbohydrate 21g ▪
Dietary Fiber 2g ▪ Sodium 629mg

Variations

Miso-Noodle Soup: Substitute 2 to 3 ounces of somen noodles, broken in half, for the pot stickers.

Miso Soup: Omit the pot stickers and optional mushrooms. After the broth mixture comes to a boil, remove from heat and stir in the miso mixture and sesame oil. Serve hot.

MUSHROOM-BARLEY SOUP

Vegan

MAKES 4 TO 6 SERVINGS

This comforting soup is nice to serve when there's a nip in the air. For a slightly earthier flavor, substitute sliced cremini mushrooms for all or half of the white variety. While the recipe calls for regular pearl barley, you can use the quick-cooking variety and reduce the simmering time by about 15 minutes; however, the soup's flavors will be slightly less developed.

1½ tablespoons extra-virgin olive oil
½ cup frozen chopped onion
½ cup frozen chopped green bell pepper
1 (8-ounce) package presliced fresh white
    mushrooms
1 teaspoon refrigerated bottled minced garlic
2 (14-ounce) cans (3½ cups) low-sodium
    vegetable broth
2½ cups water
½ cup pearl barley
1 teaspoon dried crumbled thyme leaves
Salt and freshly ground black pepper, to taste

In a medium stockpot, heat the oil over medium heat. Add the onion and bell pepper and cook, stirring, until softened and thawed, about 3 minutes. Add the mushrooms and garlic and cook, stirring often, until mushrooms begin to release their liquids, about 3 minutes. Add the broth, water, barley, thyme, salt, and pepper; bring to a boil over high heat. Reduce the heat, cover, and simmer 45 minutes, stirring occasionally, or until the barley is tender. Serve hot.

PER SERVING

Calories 196 ▪ Protein 14g ▪ Total Fat 6g ▪
Sat. Fat 1g ▪ Cholesterol 0mg ▪ Carbohydrate 24g ▪
Dietary Fiber 8g ▪ Sodium 461mg

CURRIED PUMPKIN AND PEANUT SOUP

Vegan
MAKES 4 TO 6 SERVINGS

Loaded with vitamin A and fiber, canned pumpkin has a much greater role to play in a healthy diet than as the main ingredient in holiday pie. In this yummy soup, peanut butter adds protein and creaminess; if you are using an unsweetened variety of peanut butter, you may need to add a bit more sugar. Though optional, coconut milk lends an unmistakable taste of Thailand.

½ tablespoon canola oil

1 cup frozen chopped onion

¼ cup cider vinegar

½ tablespoon mild curry powder, or to taste

1 (14-ounce) can (1¾ cups) low-sodium vegetable broth

½ cup water

1 (15-ounce) can pumpkin puree

⅓ cup creamy peanut butter

1 teaspoon sugar

Salt and freshly ground black pepper, to taste

½ cup canned light coconut milk, half-and-half, or light cream (optional)

Chopped peanuts (optional)

In a medium stockpot, heat the oil over medium heat. Add the onion and cook, stirring, until softened and thawed, about 3 minutes. Increase the heat to medium-high and add the vinegar; cook, stirring often, until all the liquids have evaporated. Add the curry powder and cook, stirring constantly, until fragrant, about 15 seconds. Carefully add the broth, then the water. Stir in the pumpkin, peanut butter, sugar, salt, and pepper; let come to a gentle simmer, stirring occasionally, taking care as the mixture tends to spatter. Reduce the heat, cover, and simmer 10 minutes, stirring occasionally. Stir in the coconut milk (if using) the last few minutes of cooking. Serve hot, garnished with the chopped peanuts, if desired.

PER SERVING
Calories 221 ■ Protein 12g ■ Total Fat 13g ■ Sat. Fat 2g ■ Cholesterol 0mg ■ Carbohydrate 19g ■ Dietary Fiber 7g ■ Sodium 340mg

EASY RED PEPPER BISQUE

Egg-free with vegan option
MAKES 4 SERVINGS

Though it is short on ingredients, you and your guests will linger over each spoonful of this super-easy first-course soup. Sweet red pepper spread can be found among the olives and pimientos in most well-stocked supermarkets. The use of coconut milk in lieu of the traditional half-and-half or light cream will result in an equally delicious vegan bisque that is decidedly more exotic, an ideal opener to a Thai, Indonesian, or tropical-style meal. If you opt for a nondairy coffee creamer other than a soy creamer (Silk is a reliable brand), beware that most of these products contain a casein derivative, which is a milk product.

1 tablespoon cornstarch

1 tablespoon water

2¼ cups low-sodium vegetable broth

1 cup half-and-half, light cream, canned light coconut milk, soy creamer, or other nondairy coffee creamer

1 (6-ounce) jar sweet red pepper spread
Salt and freshly ground black pepper, to taste

In a small container, stir together the cornstarch and water until smooth. Set briefly aside.

In a medium saucepan, bring the broth, half-and-half, and red pepper spread to a gentle simmer over medium heat, stirring occasionally. Add the cornstarch mixture and cook, stirring constantly, until slightly thickened, 1 to 2 minutes. Season with salt and pepper and serve hot.

PER SERVING
Calories 126 ■ Protein 8g ■ Total Fat 7g ■
Sat. Fat 4g ■ Cholesterol 22mg ■ Carbohydrate 8g ■
Dietary Fiber 3g ■ Sodium 317mg

CURRIED SQUASH SOUP WITH FRESH GREENS

Vegan
MAKES 4 SERVINGS

It's hard to believe that not a single drop of dairy products (or dairy substitutes) are used in this rich and creamy plant-based soup. Even so, when prepared with fresh arugula leaves, a single serving provides about 35 percent of the recommended daily amount of calcium, not to mention 200 percent of the vitamin A, 60 percent of the vitamin C, and 25 percent of the iron! To turn this into a main course for four, stir in 2 cups hot cooked rice.

2 tablespoons canola oil
2 tablespoons all-purpose flour
1 to 1½ teaspoons mild curry powder, or to taste
1 (14-ounce) can (1¾ cups) low-sodium vegetable broth

3 cups water
1 (12-ounce) package frozen butternut squash, partially thawed
1 teaspoon sugar
½ teaspoon salt, preferably the coarse variety
1 to 2 pinches ground nutmeg
Freshly ground black pepper, to taste
3 cups fresh arugula, spinach, chard, and/or dandelion leaves, torn into bite-size pieces

In a medium stockpot, heat the oil over medium-low heat. Add the flour and curry powder and cook, stirring constantly, until smooth and beginning to bubble, about 5 minutes. Gradually stir in the broth and water. Increase the heat to medium-high and bring to a boil, stirring frequently. Boil, stirring, 1 minute. Add the squash, sugar, salt, nutmeg, and pepper. Reduce the heat to medium and simmer, stirring occasionally to break up the squash, about 5 minutes. Add the greens and reduce the heat to low. Cook, stirring occasionally, until the greens are wilted but still bright green, about 5 minutes. Serve hot.

PER SERVING
Calories 193 ■ Protein 11g ■ Total Fat 8g ■
Sat. Fat 1g ■ Cholesterol 0mg ■ Carbohydrate 24g ■
Dietary Fiber 3g ■ Sodium 522mg

CHUNKY TOMATO-RICE SOUP

Vegan
MAKES 6 SERVINGS

I get the yen to make this chunky tomato soup whenever I spot a leftover pint container of rice from Chinese takeout in the refrigerator. To make basic tomato soup with a smooth consistency reminiscent of Campbell's, see the first variation, below.

1 (14-ounce) can (1¾ cups) low-sodium
    vegetable broth
2 cups water
2 (14-ounce) cans sliced stewed tomatoes,
    juice included
1 (15-ounce) can no-salt-added tomato sauce
1 tablespoon extra-virgin olive oil
1½ teaspoons sugar, or to taste
½ teaspoon onion powder
½ teaspoon dried oregano leaves
½ teaspoon dried thyme leaves
¼ teaspoon garlic powder
Salt and freshly ground black pepper, to taste
2 cups cooked white or brown rice (see Cook's
    Tip, page 126)

In a medium stockpot, bring the broth, water, tomatoes with their juice, tomato sauce, oil, sugar, onion powder, oregano, thyme, garlic powder, salt, and pepper to a boil over high heat, stirring occasionally and breaking apart the tomatoes with a large wooden spoon. Add the rice, separating any clumps with your fingers. Reduce the heat; simmer, partially covered, stirring occasionally, until slightly thickened, about 15 minutes. Serve hot.

PER SERVING
Calories 182 ■ Protein 7g ■ Total Fat 3g ■
Sat. Fat 0g ■ Cholesterol 0mg ■ Carbohydrate 34g ■
Dietary Fiber 4g ■ Sodium 495mg

Variations

Basic Tomato Soup: For soup with a smooth consistency, omit 1 cup of the water, the stewed tomatoes, the oil, and the rice (unless smooth tomato-rice soup is desired). Use an additional 14-ounce can of vegetable broth and an additional 15-ounce can of tomato sauce. Adjust the amount of sugar to taste. After bringing to a boil, simmer only 5 minutes or so. The following variations can easily be adapted to this one, as well.

Chunky Tomato-Basil Soup: Omit the rice, if desired, and stir in 1 cup packed fresh basil leaves, torn in half or in quarters, depending on size, the last few minutes of simmering.

Chunky Tomato-Cheese Soup: Omit the rice and add 1 cup (4 ounces) already-shredded reduced-fat cheddar cheese immediately before serving, stirring until just melted. Garnish each serving with 1 tablespoon cheese, if desired.

Cook's Tip All canned tomatoes have varying degrees of acidity. Sugar is a commonly used neutralizer. A few tablespoons of dry white or red wine can be used in lieu of the sugar.

Heartier Soups, Stews, and Chilis

HEARTY BLACK BEAN SOUP

Vegan

MAKES 4 SERVINGS

Serve this speedy version of Mexican black bean soup with corn bread and a tossed green salad for a delicious and nutritious meal. Smaller portions are ideal as a casual first-course.

- 2 (15-ounce) cans black beans, rinsed and drained
- 1 (14-ounce) can (1¾ cups) low-sodium vegetable broth
- 1 (14-ounce) can sliced stewed tomatoes, juice included
- 1 cup water
- 2 tablespoons canned minced mild green chilies
- 1 tablespoon canola oil
- 1 teaspoon ground cumin
- 1 teaspoon dried thyme leaves
- ½ teaspoon onion powder
- ½ teaspoon garlic powder
- Salt and freshly ground black pepper, to taste
- 2 bay leaves

Place half the beans in a medium stockpot. Add a little of the broth and, using a potato masher, mash the beans until they are of a pastelike consistency. Add the remaining beans, broth, tomatoes with their juice, water, chilies, oil, cumin, thyme, onion powder, garlic powder, salt, pepper, and bay leaves; bring to a boil over medium-high heat, stirring occasionally. Reduce the heat to medium-low and simmer, uncovered, stirring occasionally, until nicely thickened, about 25 minutes. Serve hot.

PER SERVING

Calories 284 ▪ Protein 19g ▪ Total Fat 5g ▪ Sat. Fat 1g ▪ Cholesterol 0mg ▪ Carbohydrate 45g ▪ Dietary Fiber 9g ▪ Sodium 461mg

BLACK-EYED PEA JAMBALAYA

Vegan

MAKES 6 SERVINGS

This hearty vegetarian version of the spicy Cajun specialty is my favorite stew in the book. The secret is to allow the floured bell pepper and onion mixture to brown, so try not to rush this step; dinner will still be ready in less than 30 minutes!

3 tablespoons canola oil

1 cup frozen chopped green bell pepper

½ cup frozen chopped onion

3 tablespoons all-purpose flour

1 teaspoon refrigerated bottled minced garlic

1 (14-ounce) can (1¾ cups) low-sodium vegetable broth

½ cup water

1 (16-ounce) package frozen cut okra

1 (15-ounce) can black-eyed peas, rinsed and drained

1 (14-ounce) can diced tomatoes with jalapeño chilies, juice included

1 cup uncooked long-grain white rice

1 tablespoon dried celery flakes

½ teaspoon dried thyme leaves

¼ teaspoon cayenne pepper, or to taste

Salt and freshly ground black pepper, to taste

Tabasco sauce (optional)

In a medium stockpot, heat the oil over medium heat. Add the bell pepper and onion and cook, stirring, until softened and thawed, about 3 minutes. Stir in the flour and reduce the heat to medium-low. Cook, stirring often, until the flour turns a light brown, 5 to 8 minutes, adding the garlic the last few minutes or so. Gradually stir in the broth, then the water. Add the okra, black-eyed peas, tomatoes with their juice, rice, celery flakes, thyme, cayenne, salt, and black pepper; bring to a boil over medium-high heat, stirring from the bottom occasionally to prevent scorching. Reduce the heat, cover, and simmer until the rice is tender, 15 minutes, stirring occasionally. Serve hot, with the Tabasco sauce passed separately, if desired.

PER SERVING

Calories 298 ▪ Protein 11g ▪ Total Fat 8g ▪ Sat. Fat 1g ▪ Cholesterol 0mg ▪ Carbohydrate 48g ▪ Dietary Fiber 7g ▪ Sodium 300mg

Cook's Tip Rich in fiber and calcium, okra is a podlike green vegetable highly popular in American Southern cooking. When cooked, it exudes a gel-like substance that serves as a natural thickening agent in jambalaya and the gumbos of Louisiana. Whole and cut okra can be found in the frozen food section of most well-stocked supermarkets.

BULGUR-CHILI BEAN STEW OVER TORTILLA CHIPS

Vegan

MAKES 8 SERVINGS

This is a great dish to serve nacho-style at casual gatherings, as even young children can help themselves and forks really aren't necessary. Bulgur, a precooked cracked-wheat product dating back to ancient times, can be found in health food stores and most major supermarkets. Toss leftovers with penne or other small tubular-shaped pasta for another quick and easy meal. If you opt to use cheese as a topping, vegan substitutes are not recommended as they don't melt well.

3 tablespoons extra-virgin olive oil

2 cups frozen chopped onion

1 cup frozen chopped green bell pepper

1 tablespoon refrigerated bottled minced garlic

3 to 4 tablespoons chili powder

2 teaspoons ground cumin

1 teaspoon dried oregano

⅛ teaspoon cayenne pepper, or to taste

1 (28-ounce) can plum tomatoes, juice included

2 (15.5-ounce) cans red kidney beans, rinsed and drained

1 (8-ounce) can tomato sauce

1 cup water, plus additional as necessary

1 cup fine-grain (fancy) bulgur

1 (4-ounce) can diced mild green chilies, drained

½ teaspoon salt, or to taste

¼ teaspoon black pepper, or to taste

Stone-ground corn tortilla chips, preferably the round variety

Assorted optional toppings: already-shredded cheddar cheese, sliced pickled jalapeño peppers, and/or sour cream or nondairy sour cream

In a medium stockpot, heat the oil over medium heat. Add the onion and bell pepper and cook, stirring often, until thawed and softened, about 3 minutes. Add the garlic, chili powder, cumin, oregano, and cayenne; cook, stirring constantly, until most of the liquid given off from the frozen vegetables has evaporated, 3 to 4 more minutes.

Add the tomatoes with their juice, squeezing the tomatoes through your fingers as you add them to the pot or breaking them up with a large wooden spoon. Stir in the beans, tomato sauce, water, bulgur, chilies, salt, and black pepper. Bring to a simmer over medium-high heat. Reduce the heat, partially cover, and simmer, stirring occasionally, until the bulgur is tender and the mixture is thickened, 25 to 30 minutes. If the mixture becomes too thickened, add water as desired.

To serve, arrange a layer of tortilla chips in individual deep-sided plates and ladle with desired amounts of hot stew. Serve at once, with the optional toppings passed separately, if desired.

PER SERVING (WITHOUT CHIPS)
Calories 251 ▪ Protein 10g ▪ Total Fat 7g ▪
Sat. Fat 1g ▪ Cholesterol 0mg ▪ Carbohydrate 42g ▪
Dietary Fiber 11g ▪ Sodium 556mg

BUTTER BEAN SOUP

Vegan

MAKES 4 TO 5 SERVINGS

Savor this melt-in-your-mouth, straight-from-the-pantry soup any time the urge for a hot meal-in-a-bowl strikes. For a thinner consistency, add more broth or water as desired. Canned green lima beans can replace the butter beans, if desired. Smaller portions make an inviting first course for casual gatherings.

> 2 tablespoons extra-virgin olive oil or canola oil
> 2 tablespoons all-purpose flour
> 2 (14-ounce) cans (3½ cups) low-sodium vegetable broth
> 2 (16-ounce) cans large butter beans, rinsed and drained
> 1 (14.5-ounce) can no-salt-added diced tomatoes, juice included
> ½ teaspoon onion powder
> ½ teaspoon garlic powder
> ½ teaspoon dried oregano leaves
> ¼ teaspoon dried thyme leaves
> Salt and freshly ground black pepper, to taste

In a medium stockpot, heat the oil over medium heat. Add the flour and cook, stirring constantly, 2 minutes. Slowly whisk in the broth and bring to a gentle boil over medium-high heat. Boil and stir 1 minute. Add the beans, tomatoes with their juice, onion powder, garlic powder, oregano, thyme, salt, and pepper; return to a gentle boil. Reduce the heat and simmer, uncovered, stirring occasionally, until slightly thickened, 15 to 20 minutes. Serve hot.

PER SERVING
Calories 303 ■ Protein 22g ■ Total Fat 8g ■ Sat. Fat 1g ■ Cholesterol 0mg ■ Carbohydrate 39g ■ Dietary Fiber 15g ■ Sodium 469mg

QUICK CHILI BEAN POSOLE

Vegan

MAKES 4 SERVINGS

In this low-fat vegetarian version of the classic southwestern stew known as posole (pronounced poh-SOL-ay), canned chili beans replace the traditional pork. Canned hominy (dried corn that has been treated with lye to remove the hulls) has a rather bland taste that surprisingly grows on you. It can be found near the canned corn in most major supermarkets. I like to garnish this with traditional chili toppings and serve with lots of tortilla chips for a complete meal. If you opt to use cheese, vegan soy substitutes are not recommended as they don't melt well.

> 1 (16-ounce) can chili beans in mild sauce
> 1 (15.5-ounce) can white or yellow hominy, rinsed and drained
> 6 tablespoons mild or medium salsa
> 4 tablespoons canned diced mild green chilies
> ½ teaspoon ground cumin
> Salt and freshly ground black pepper, to taste
> Shredded cheddar cheese and/or sour cream or nondairy sour cream (optional)
> Corn tortilla chips (optional)

In a medium saucepan, combine all the ingredients except the optional toppings and chips; bring to a simmer over medium-high heat, stirring occasionally. Reduce the heat to low and simmer, uncovered, stirring occasionally, until slightly thickened, 5 to 10 minutes. Serve hot, with the optional toppings and chips passed separately, if desired.

PER SERVING (STEW ONLY)

Calories 194 ▪ Protein 7g ▪ Total Fat 2g ▪
Sat. Fat 0g ▪ Cholesterol 0mg ▪ Carbohydrate 41g ▪
Dietary Fiber 10g ▪ Sodium 738mg

TEXAS-STYLE TWO-BEAN CHILI

Vegan

MAKES 4 TO 6 SERVINGS

There's nothing quite like a piping hot bowl of chili on a chilly day. You can easily make it a "one-bean" chili by using all kidney or all pinto beans. If you opt to use cheese, vegan soy substitutes are not recommended as they don't melt well.

2 tablespoons extra-virgin olive oil

1 cup frozen chopped onion

½ cup frozen chopped green bell pepper

2 teaspoons refrigerated bottled minced garlic

1 (28-ounce) can crushed tomatoes

1 (15-ounce) can red kidney beans, rinsed and drained

1 (15-ounce) can pinto beans, rinsed and drained

1 (14-ounce) can no-salt-added stewed tomatoes, juice included

2 tablespoons chili powder, or more to taste

1 tablespoon ground cumin

1 tablespoon dried oregano

1 teaspoon sweet paprika

2 large bay leaves

Salt and freshly ground black pepper, to taste

Tabasco sauce, to taste

Shredded cheddar cheese and/or sour cream or nondairy sour cream (optional)

In a medium stockpot, heat the oil over medium heat. Add the onion and bell pepper and cook, stirring, until the onion is translucent but not browned, about 5 minutes. Add the garlic and cook, stirring, 1 minute. Stir in the crushed tomatoes, kidney beans, pinto beans, stewed tomatoes with their juice, chili powder, cumin, oregano, paprika, bay leaves, salt, pepper, and Tabasco sauce. Bring to a simmer over medium-high heat. Reduce the heat and simmer, uncovered, stirring occasionally, until the mixture is thickened, about 25 minutes. Serve hot, with the optional toppings passed separately, if desired.

PER SERVING

Calories 344 ▪ Protein 16g ▪ Total Fat 10g ▪
Sat. Fat 1g ▪ Cholesterol 0mg ▪ Carbohydrate 55g ▪
Dietary Fiber 15g ▪ Sodium 494mg

Variations

Red and White Bean Chili: Substitute 1 (15-ounce) can cannellini, great northern, or navy beans for the pinto beans.

Black Bean Chili: Substitute 2 (15-ounce) cans black beans for the kidney and pinto beans. Stir in 1 to 2 cups frozen yellow corn the last 15 minutes or so of simmering, if desired.

Chili with Lentils: Substitute 1 (15-ounce) can cooked lentils, preferably the black beluga variety, available in health food stores, for the kidney or the pinto beans. Briefly drain, but do not rinse the lentils (see Cook's Tip, page 10).

CURRIED TOMATO-LENTIL SOUP WITH BASMATI RICE

Vegan

MAKES 4 TO 5 SERVINGS

Ready in just about 20 minutes, this delicious curried soup takes advantage of canned cooked lentils, available in health food stores and some well-stocked supermarkets. Serve with Indian flatbread (naan or roti) or pita bread and a tossed green salad for a complete meal. Smaller portions make a pleasant opener to just about any gathering.

2 (14-ounce) cans sliced stewed tomatoes, juice included
1 (14-ounce) can (1¾ cups) low-sodium vegetable broth
1 cup water
1 teaspoon onion powder
½ teaspoon garlic powder
Salt and freshly ground black pepper, to taste
½ cup basmati or long-grain white rice
1 (15-ounce) can cooked lentils, drained (see Cook's Tip, page 10)
1½ tablespoons tomato paste
1 tablespoon extra-virgin olive oil
2 to 3 teaspoons mild curry powder, or to taste
½ teaspoon sugar, or to taste

In a medium stockpot, bring the tomatoes with their juice, broth, water, onion powder, garlic powder, salt, and pepper to a boil over high heat, stirring occasionally and breaking up the tomatoes with a large wooden spoon. Add the rice, reduce the heat to medium-high, and boil, stirring occasionally, until the rice is barely tender, 8 minutes.

Reduce the heat to medium-low and stir in the lentils, tomato paste, oil, curry powder, and sugar. Simmer, partially covered, stirring occasionally, until the rice is tender yet firm to the bite, about 10 minutes. Serve hot.

PER SERVING
Calories 317 ▪ Protein 18g ▪ Total Fat 5g ▪
Sat. Fat 1g ▪ Cholesterol 0mg ▪ Carbohydrate 53g ▪
Dietary Fiber 10g ▪ Sodium 323mg

INDONESIAN-STYLE PEANUT SOUP WITH COCONUT

Vegan

MAKES 4 TO 5 SERVINGS

Serve this rich, creamy, dairy-free soup with a tossed green salad for a complete meal, or on its own as an exotic first course for up to eight people.

2 (14-ounce) cans (3½ cups) low-sodium vegetable broth
1½ cups water
1 teaspoon onion powder
½ teaspoon garlic powder
Salt and freshly ground black pepper, to taste
½ cup unsalted chunky peanut butter
¾ cup canned light coconut milk
1 teaspoon curry powder, or to taste
1 teaspoon sugar
½ cup chopped roasted peanuts (optional)

In a medium stockpot, combine the broth, water, onion powder, garlic powder, salt, and pepper; bring to boil over high heat. Reduce the heat to low and add the peanut butter, stirring until thoroughly combined. Stir in the coconut milk, curry powder, and sugar. Increase the heat to medium and cook, stirring, until the mixture comes just to a simmer. Serve hot, garnished with the peanuts, if desired.

PER SERVING

Calories 317 ▪ Protein 19g ▪ Total Fat 23g ▪
Sat. Fat 10g ▪ Cholesterol 0mg ▪ Carbohydrate 13g ▪
Dietary Fiber 5g ▪ Sodium 471mg

HEARTY MINESTRONE SOUP

Vegan
MAKES 4 TO 5 SERVINGS

Minestrone is essentially Italian vegetable soup that typically takes a few hours to make from scratch. Taking advantage of canned beans, stewed tomatoes, and frozen vegetables, this delicious and nutritious meal-in-a-bowl minestrone is as quick as it gets. Smaller portions can begin any casual gathering on a welcome note, as well.

1½ tablespoons extra-virgin olive oil
½ cup frozen chopped onion
1 teaspoon refrigerated bottled minced garlic
2 (14-ounce) cans (3½ cups) low-sodium
  vegetable broth
1 (14-ounce) can no-salt-added stewed
  tomatoes, juice included
1 cup water
½ teaspoon dried oregano
¼ teaspoon dried thyme leaves
Salt and freshly ground black pepper, to taste
1 (15-ounce) can red kidney beans, rinsed and
  drained

1 (10-ounce) package frozen peas and carrots
½ cup ditalini or other small pasta

In a medium stockpot, heat the oil over medium heat. Add the onion and cook, stirring, until softened and thawed, about 3 minutes. Add the garlic and cook, stirring, 1 minute. Add the broth, tomatoes with their juice, water, oregano, thyme, salt, and pepper; bring to a boil over high heat, stirring occasionally and breaking up the tomatoes with the back of a large wooden spoon. Add the beans, peas and carrots, and pasta; return to a boil, stirring occasionally to break up the vegetables. Reduce the heat to medium and simmer, uncovered, stirring occasionally, until the pasta is tender yet firm to the bite, 10 to 15 minutes. Serve hot.

PER SERVING

Calories 302 ▪ Protein 21g ▪ Total Fat 6g ▪
Sat. Fat 1g ▪ Cholesterol 0mg ▪ Carbohydrate 44g ▪
Dietary Fiber 10g ▪ Sodium 517mg

Variation

Middle Eastern–Style Minestrone: Replace the kidney beans with chickpeas and the ditalini with couscous. If desired, add 1 to 2 teaspoons harissa or Chinese chili paste (or crushed red pepper flakes, to taste) the last few minutes of cooking.

BAKED POTATO SOUP

Egg-free with vegan options
MAKES 4 SERVINGS

This has all the flavors of a loaded baked potato, but with about half the fat. Serve with crusty whole grain bread and a green salad for a complete meal. For a vegan variation, I recommend rice milk over soymilk as the latter tends to separate when heated. If you use a vegan cream cheese substitute, double the amount of onion powder used. Vegan soy substitutes are not recommended for the optional cheddar cheese as they don't melt well.

24 ounces small red-skin potatoes

1 (14-ounce) can (1¾ cups) low-sodium
    vegetable broth

¼ teaspoon salt, or to taste

¼ teaspoon onion powder

¼ teaspoon garlic powder

½ cup (4 ounces) light cream cheese with
    chives or nondairy cream cheese, in 4 pieces

1½ cups skim milk or rice milk

¼ teaspoon black pepper, or to taste

Light sour cream or nondairy sour cream
    and/or reduced-fat shredded cheddar
    cheese, for garnish (optional)

Preheat oven to 425F (220C). Place the potatoes on an ungreased baking sheet and prick with a fork. Bake 45 to 60 minutes, or until fork-tender through the center, depending on size.

Transfer the potatoes to a medium stockpot and mash coarsely with a potato masher. Add the broth, salt, onion powder, and garlic powder; mash until slightly lumpy and skins are in bite-size pieces. Bring to a gentle simmer over medium-high heat, stirring occasionally. Reduce the heat to low and add the cream cheese; cook, stirring, until smooth and incorporated. Add the milk and pepper; bring to a gentle simmer over medium-high heat, stirring occasionally, taking care not to allow the mixture to boil. Reduce the heat to low and cook, uncovered, stirring occasionally, until slightly thickened, 5 to 10 minutes. Serve hot, garnishing each serving with a dollop of sour cream and/or a sprinkling of cheddar cheese, if desired.

PER SERVING
Calories 255 ▪ Protein 15g ▪ Total Fat 5g ▪
Sat. Fat 3g ▪ Cholesterol 18mg ▪ Carbohydrate 38g ▪
Dietary Fiber 4g ▪ Sodium 577mg

POTATO, BROCCOLI, AND CORN CHOWDER

Egg-free with vegan options
MAKES 4 SERVINGS

Serve this hearty chowder with lots of crusty bread and a tossed green salad for a satisfying, warming winter supper. Its rich and creamy flavor comes from Neufchâtel, a time-saving thickening agent used in lieu of the traditional flour-based roux. For a vegan variation, a nondairy cream cheese alternative (Tofutti makes an excellent brand that tastes and heats up like the real thing) and unflavored rice milk can replace the Neufchâtel and skim milk with equally tasty results. Smaller portions also make an inviting first-course soup for casual gatherings.

1 (14-ounce) can (1¾ cups) low-sodium
    vegetable broth

2 cups frozen broccoli cuts

¼ teaspoon garlic powder

¼ teaspoon onion powder

Salt, to taste

½ cup Neufchâtel (a reduced-fat cream cheese) or nondairy cream cheese, in 4 pieces

1½ cups skim milk or rice milk

2 (15-ounce) cans sliced potatoes, rinsed and drained

1 cup frozen yellow corn

Freshly ground black pepper, to taste

2 tablespoons diced pimiento, drained (optional)

In a medium stockpot, combine the broth, broccoli, garlic powder, onion powder, and salt. Bring to a boil over high heat. Reduce the heat to medium, cover, and cook 5 minutes. Reduce the heat to low and add the cream cheese; cook, stirring, until smooth and incorporated. Add the milk, potatoes, corn, and pepper; bring to a gentle simmer over medium-high heat, stirring occasionally. Reduce the heat to low and add the pimiento (if using); cook, uncovered, stirring occasionally, until thickened, 7 to 10 minutes. Serve hot.

PER SERVING

Calories 238 ▪ Protein 16g ▪ Total Fat 4g ▪ Sat. Fat 2g ▪ Cholesterol 12mg ▪ Carbohydrate 38g ▪ Dietary Fiber 9g ▪ Sodium 966mg

ROASTED HERBED TOMATO AND WHITE BEAN SOUP

Vegan

MAKES 4 SERVINGS

Roasting concentrates and intensifies the flavor of tomatoes in this nourishing, soul-satisfying soup. For even heartier soup, add ½ cup ditalini or other small pasta once the soup comes to a boil; simmer the soup an extra 5 minutes, or until the pasta is al dente. Smaller portions can also be served as an inviting first-course soup for casual gatherings.

1 (28-ounce) can no-salt-added plum tomatoes, drained, juice reserved

2 tablespoons extra-virgin olive oil

2 teaspoons refrigerated bottled minced garlic

1 teaspoon dried rubbed sage

½ teaspoon dried thyme leaves

½ teaspoon dried oregano

½ teaspoon salt, preferably the coarse variety

¼ teaspoon black pepper

1 (19-ounce) can cannellini or other white beans, rinsed and drained

1 (14-ounce) can (1¾ cups) low-sodium vegetable broth

2 tablespoons dry white wine (optional)

1 teaspoon sugar, or to taste

Preheat oven to 450F (230C). Lightly oil an 8½- or 9-inch pie dish and set aside.

Place the tomatoes in a medium bowl; crush each tomato lightly with a large wooden spoon to break apart. Drain, adding any accumulated juice to the reserved juice. Add the oil, garlic, sage, thyme, oregano, salt, and pepper to the tomatoes; toss until thoroughly combined. Transfer to the prepared pie dish and roast in the center rack of the oven 10 to 15 minutes, or until the tomatoes are just beginning to brown. Stir and turn the tomatoes over. Roast 10 more minutes, or until the tomatoes are browned but not charred and the juice is slightly caramelized. Remove from the oven and break up into small chunks with a large wooden spoon.

Meanwhile, place the beans in a medium stockpot and coarsely mash with a potato masher. Add the roasted tomatoes and all the accumulated cooking juice, the reserved tomato juice, broth, wine (if using), and sugar. Bring to a gentle boil over medium-high heat, stirring occasionally. Reduce the heat and simmer gently, uncovered, stirring occasionally, until slightly thickened, about 10 minutes. Serve hot.

PER SERVING

Calories 253 ■ Protein 16g ■ Total Fat 8g ■
Sat. Fat 1g ■ Cholesterol 0mg ■ Carbohydrate 34g ■
Dietary Fiber 10g ■ Sodium 493mg

TORTELLINI AND SPINACH SOUP

Lacto-ovo

MAKES 4 SERVINGS

This hearty main-course soup is a great way to get kids, as well as adults, to eat their spinach. If you don't have stewed tomatoes with Italian seasonings, stir in ½ teaspoon dried oregano leaves and ½ teaspoon dried basil leaves when you add the tomatoes.

  1 tablespoon extra-virgin olive oil
  ½ cup frozen chopped onion
  ½ teaspoon refrigerated bottled minced garlic
  3¼ cups water
  1 (14-ounce) can (1¾ cups) low-sodium
      vegetable broth
  1 (14-ounce) can no-salt-added stewed
      tomatoes, preferably with Italian
      seasonings, juice included
  Salt and freshly ground black pepper, to taste
  1 (9-ounce) package fresh tortellini
  1 (10-ounce) package frozen chopped spinach,
      thawed under cold running water and
      drained

Freshly grated Parmesan cheese, for garnish (optional)

In a medium stockpot, heat the oil over medium heat. Add the onion and cook, stirring often, until thawed and softened, 2 to 3 minutes. Add the garlic and cook, stirring, 1 minute. Add the water, broth, tomatoes with their juice, salt, and pepper; bring to a boil over high heat. Add the tortellini and spinach. Bring to a boil, reduce the heat slightly, and cook, stirring occasionally, until the tortellini are tender yet firm to the bite, 2 to 3 minutes. Serve hot, garnished with the Parmesan cheese, if desired.

PER SERVING

Calories 277 ■ Protein 18g ■ Total Fat 8g ■
Sat. Fat 2g ■ Cholesterol 43mg ■ Carbohydrate 37g ■
Dietary Fiber 7g ■ Sodium 554mg

MOROCCAN VEGETABLE STEW OVER COUSCOUS

Vegan

MAKES 6 TO 8 SERVINGS

Feed a hungry crowd with this spicy vegetable stew, or tagine, from Morocco. It gets its punch from harissa, a hot chili pepper sauce redolent of garlic, cumin, coriander, and caraway. Harissa can be found in Middle Eastern markets and many specialty stores. Chinese chili paste, available in many well-stocked supermarkets, is a good substitute.

  2 tablespoons extra-virgin olive oil
  ½ cup frozen chopped onion
  ½ cup frozen chopped green bell pepper
  1 teaspoon refrigerated bottled minced garlic

2 (14-ounce) cans (3½ cups) low-sodium
vegetable broth

1 (14-ounce) can stewed tomatoes, juice
included

1 (16-ounce) bag frozen mixed stew vegetables
(carrots, celery, potatoes, pearl onions)

½ teaspoon dried thyme leaves

Salt and freshly ground black pepper, to taste

1 (19-ounce) can chickpeas, rinsed and
drained

Crushed red pepper flakes, to taste (if not
using harissa or chili paste, below)

3 cups water

2 cups instant couscous, preferably whole
wheat

1½ to 2 tablespoons red wine vinegar

2 teaspoons harissa or Chinese chili paste, or
to taste

In a medium stockpot, heat 1½ tablespoons of the
olive oil over medium heat. Add the onion and bell
pepper and cook, stirring, until softened and
thawed, about 3 minutes. Add the garlic and cook,
stirring, 1 minute. Add the broth, tomatoes with
their juice, frozen vegetables, thyme, salt, and pepper. Bring to a boil over high heat, stirring occasionally and breaking up the tomatoes with a large
wooden spoon. Reduce the heat to medium-high
and boil 2 minutes, stirring occasionally.

Add the chickpeas and crushed red pepper
flakes (if using); reduce the heat to medium. Simmer briskly, uncovered, stirring occasionally, until
the vegetables are tender and the mixture is
slightly thickened, about 10 minutes. Cover and
keep warm over low heat if not using immediately.

Meanwhile, in a large saucepan, bring the water to a boil. Stir in the couscous and the remaining ½ tablespoon of oil. Cover and remove from
the heat. Let stand until all the water has been absorbed, 7 minutes. Uncover and fluff with a fork.

Just before serving, add the vinegar and harissa
to the stew, stirring well to thoroughly blend. Divide the couscous evenly among deep-welled serving plates or large soup bowls. Ladle equal
portions of the stew over the top and serve at
once.

PER SERVING
Calories 451 ▪ Protein 22g ▪ Total Fat 7g ▪
Sat. Fat 1g ▪ Cholesterol 0mg ▪ Carbohydrate 78g ▪
Dietary Fiber 9g ▪ Sodium 518mg

Cook's Tip You can easily make two meals to
serve four by using only half of the stew and
preparing just half the amount of couscous. Refrigerate the remaining portion of the stew up to 3
days and serve over rice, pasta, or polenta instead
of couscous, if desired.

Simply Salads

Not too long ago, salads were a luxury for many home cooks, even for vegetarians who, like most busy people, couldn't always muster the energy to wash, tear, and spin lettuce leaves at the end of an exhausting workday. These days, with a wide assortment of ready-washed bagged salad mixes readily available at most supermarkets, the tossed salad is back on the table. At the same time, the increased availability of precut fresh vegetables has fueled the popularity of nonlettuce salads such as broccoli slaw, carrot slaw, and coleslaw, which not only can be made in advance, but whose flavor typically improves with age.

Whether you're looking for a tossed green salad (see Mixed Green Salad with Honey Mustard–Raspberry Vinaigrette), a crunchy marinated side (see Broccoli Slaw with Raisins and Crystallized Ginger), a spicy bean medley (see Black Bean Salad with Lime-Cumin Vinaigrette), a substantial main course (see Greek-Style Bulgur Salad with Chickpeas, Feta, and Olives), or a pasta dish to bring to the next picnic or potluck (see Picnic Macaroni and

Cheese Salad), there's something for everyone in the following selection of fast and fabulous salad recipes.

Side Salads

BLACK BEAN SALAD WITH LIME-CUMIN VINAIGRETTE

Vegan

MAKES 4 SERVINGS

This spicy yet refreshing side dish provides a nice alternative to refried beans or baked beans. Kidney, pinto, or black-eyed peas can replace the black beans, if desired.

1 (15-ounce) can black beans, rinsed and drained

¼ cup canned diced mild green chilies, drained

¼ cup canned diced tomatoes with jalapeño chilies, drained

1 tablespoon bottled lime juice

1 tablespoon cider vinegar

1 tablespoon extra-virgin olive oil

½ tablespoon light brown sugar or honey, or to taste

½ teaspoon ground cumin

Salt and freshly ground black pepper, to taste

In a medium bowl, toss all the ingredients together until well combined. Let stand 15 minutes at room

temperature to allow the flavors to blend. Toss again and serve at room temperature. Alternatively, cover and refrigerate 1 hour or up to 3 days and serve chilled or return to room temperature.

PER SERVING

Calories 132 ▪ Protein 6g ▪ Total Fat 4g ▪ Sat. Fat 1g ▪ Cholesterol 0mg ▪ Carbohydrate 20g ▪ Dietary Fiber 3g ▪ Sodium 34mg

SOUTHWESTERN BLACK-EYED PEA, CORN, AND TOMATO SALAD

Vegan

MAKES 4 SERVINGS

This versatile side salad also makes a great salsa served with tortilla chips. If diced canned tomatoes seasoned with jalapeño chilies are unavailable, use regular canned diced tomatoes and add canned sliced jalapeño chilies to taste.

1 (15.5-ounce) can black-eyed peas, rinsed and drained

1 (14.5-ounce) can diced tomatoes with jalapeño chilies, liquid included

1 cup frozen yellow corn, cooked according to package directions, rinsed under cold running water to cool, drained

1 tablespoon extra-virgin olive oil

1 tablespoon red wine vinegar

1 tablespoon sugar

½ teaspoon ground cumin

Salt and freshly ground black pepper, to taste

In a medium bowl, toss all the ingredients together until well combined. Let stand at room temperature 10 to 15 minutes to allow the flavors to blend. Toss again and serve at room temperature. Alternatively, cover and refrigerate a minimum of 1 hour or up to 3 days and serve chilled.

PER SERVING

Calories 174 ▪ Protein 7g ▪ Total Fat 4g ▪ Sat. Fat 1g ▪ Cholesterol 0mg ▪ Carbohydrate 30g ▪ Dietary Fiber 6g ▪ Sodium 222mg

BUTTER BEAN SALAD

Vegan
MAKES 6 TO 8 SERVINGS

Perfect for picnics or barbecues, this southern-style bean salad can be made up to 3 days ahead of serving. Green lima beans can replace the butter beans, if desired.

> 2 (15-ounce) cans butter beans, rinsed and drained
> 1 (14.5-ounce) can diced tomatoes with mild green chilies, drained
> 2 tablespoons canola oil
> 1 tablespoon bottled lime juice
> 1 tablespoon lemon juice, preferably prepared from frozen concentrate
> 1 tablespoon light brown sugar
> 1 teaspoon ground cumin
> ½ teaspoon garlic powder
> Salt and freshly ground black pepper, to taste

In a medium bowl, toss all the ingredients together until well combined. Let stand at room temperature 10 to 15 minutes to allow the flavors to blend. Toss again and serve at room tempera-

ture. Alternatively, cover and refrigerate a minimum of 1 hour or up to 3 days and serve chilled.

PER SERVING

Calories 174 ▪ Protein 8g ▪ Total Fat 5g ▪ Sat. Fat 0g ▪ Cholesterol 0mg ▪ Carbohydrate 26g ▪ Dietary Fiber 7g ▪ Sodium 148mg

MARINATED THREE-BEAN, WHOLE WHEAT COUSCOUS SALAD

Vegan
MAKES 6 SERVINGS

The delightful flavor of this sweet-and-sour marinated salad improves with age, and the colder it is when served, the better. Whole wheat couscous, made from 100 percent whole durum wheat semolina, is available in health food stores and the specialty aisle of many well-stocked supermarkets. Regular couscous may be substituted.

> ¾ cup water
> 1 tablespoon extra-virgin olive oil
> 1 cup instant whole wheat couscous
> 1 (16-ounce) jar marinated three-bean salad, marinade included
> Salad greens (optional)

In a medium saucepan, bring the water and oil to a boil over high heat. Stir in the couscous, then the bean salad with its liquid. When the mixture comes to a brisk simmer, cover and remove from the heat. Let stand until all the liquid has been absorbed (the mixture should still be moist), 7 minutes. Uncover and toss lightly with a fork. Transfer to a serving bowl and let cool to room temperature. Cover and refrigerate a minimum of 3 hours, or up to 2 or 3 days, and serve well chilled, over salad greens, if desired.

WHITE BEAN AND BLUE CHEESE SALAD

Egg-free
MAKES 4 SERVINGS

The combination of white beans and blue cheese is truly a wonderful taste sensation. Serve with crusty peasant bread for a satisfying lunch, or add a soup and serve for supper. Crumbled feta or goat cheese can be used in lieu of the blue variety, if desired.

- 2 tablespoons cider vinegar
- 1 tablespoon extra-virgin olive oil
- ½ teaspoon dried oregano
- ¼ teaspoon garlic powder
- Salt and freshly ground black pepper, to taste
- 1 (16-ounce) can cannellini beans or other white beans, rinsed and drained
- ½ cup canned diced tomatoes, preferably petite-cut, drained
- ¼ cup (1 ounce) crumbled blue cheese

In a medium bowl, whisk together the vinegar, oil, oregano, garlic powder, salt, and pepper. Add the beans, tomatoes, and blue cheese; toss gently yet thoroughly to combine. Let stand at room temperature 10 to 15 minutes to allow the flavors to blend. Toss again and serve at room temperature.

Alternatively, cover and refrigerate a minimum of 1 hour or up to 2 days and serve chilled.

WARM BROCCOLI AND MUSHROOM SALAD WITH BALSAMIC VINAIGRETTE

Vegan
MAKES 4 TO 5 SERVINGS

The trick to this yummy salad is to add the mushrooms at the very end of cooking, tossing until just warm so they do not release their liquid. Ready-washed packages of fresh broccoli florets are available at most supermarkets in the produce section; near the refrigerated dips; or, loose, at the salad bar.

- ½ cup low-sodium vegetable broth
- ½ teaspoon onion powder
- 1 (10-ounce) package (about 4 cups) ready-washed fresh broccoli florets
- 2 tablespoons balsamic or raspberry vinegar
- 2 tablespoons extra-virgin olive oil
- 1 (8-ounce) package presliced fresh white mushrooms
- Salt and freshly ground black pepper, to taste

In a large nonstick skillet with a lid, bring the broth and onion powder to a boil over medium-high heat. Add the broccoli and let return to a boil. Reduce the heat to medium-low, cover, and simmer until the broccoli is crisp-tender, about 3 minutes, shaking the pan occasionally to redistribute the broccoli. Stir in the vinegar and oil and increase the heat to medium-high; cook, uncovered, stirring often, until the liquid is reduced by half, about 3 minutes. Add the mushrooms, tossing quickly until the mushrooms are just warm. Immediately remove from heat and season with salt and pepper. Serve warm.

PER SERVING

Calories 102 ▪ Protein 5g ▪ Total Fat 7g ▪
Sat. Fat 1g ▪ Cholesterol 0mg ▪ Carbohydrate 7g ▪
Dietary Fiber 3g ▪ Sodium 79mg

BROCCOLI SLAW WITH RAISINS AND CRYSTALLIZED GINGER

Dairy-free with vegan option

MAKES 4 TO 6 SERVINGS

This exotic salad is always popular at parties or potlucks. If broccoli slaw is unavailable, 4 cups of ready-cut fresh broccoli florets can be substituted. Crystallized ginger can be found in the spice aisle of most well-stocked supermarkets. For a vegan dish, soy mayonnaise can easily replace the regular variety.

- ⅓ cup reduced-fat regular mayonnaise or soy mayonnaise
- 2 tablespoons rice vinegar
- ⅛ teaspoon ground ginger
- ¼ teaspoon salt, or to taste
- ⅛ teaspoon freshly ground black pepper, or to taste
- ⅓ cup dark raisins
- 3 tablespoons tiny crystallized ginger pieces
- 1 (8-ounce) package broccoli/slaw mix

½ cup sliced almonds and/or unsalted sunflower seeds, for garnish (optional)

In a large bowl, whisk together the mayonnaise, vinegar, ground ginger, salt, and pepper. Stir in the raisins and crystallized ginger. Let stand 10 minutes at room temperature to allow the raisins and crystallized ginger to soften.

Add the broccoli coleslaw to the bowl and toss well to combine with the dressing. Cover and refrigerate a minimum of 1 hour, or overnight. Serve chilled, garnished with the nuts and/or seeds, if desired.

PER SERVING

Calories 128 ▪ Protein 2g ▪ Total Fat 6g ▪
Sat. Fat 1g ▪ Cholesterol 14mg ▪ Carbohydrate 13g ▪
Dietary Fiber 1g ▪ Sodium 243mg

Variation

Carrot Salad with Raisins and Crystallized Ginger: Substitute 1 (8-ounce) bag shredded carrots for the broccoli coleslaw mix. Use ½ cup raisins and 1½ tablespoons crystallized ginger; replace the optional almonds with walnut pieces, if desired. Proceed as otherwise directed in recipe.

MARINATED OLD-FASHIONED CABBAGE SALAD

Vegan

MAKES 6 SERVINGS

A tangy alternative to mayonnaise-based coleslaw, this old-time picnic classic's flavor improves if made a day ahead of serving. The use of instant minced onion adds to the unique flavor of the recipe; I've prepared it using fresh minced onion before, and was surprised by the taste difference.

1/3 cup distilled white vinegar

2 tablespoons canola or other mild vegetable oil

2 tablespoons sugar

2 tablespoons diced pimiento, drained

1½ teaspoons instant minced onion

½ teaspoon celery seeds

½ teaspoon dry mustard

½ teaspoon salt, or to taste

¼ teaspoon black pepper, or to taste

Pinch cayenne pepper, or to taste (optional)

1 (16-ounce) bag (about 8 cups) coleslaw mix

In a large bowl, whisk together all the ingredients except the coleslaw. Let the dressing stand 10 minutes to allow the sugar to dissolve and the onion to rehydrate. Whisk again. Add the coleslaw mix and toss well to combine. Cover and refrigerate a minimum of 8 hours, or up to 2 days, tossing a few times. Toss again before serving. Serve chilled.

PER SERVING

Calories 81 ▪ Protein 1g ▪ Total Fat 5g ▪
Sat. Fat 0g ▪ Cholesterol 0mg ▪ Carbohydrate 10g ▪
Dietary Fiber 2g ▪ Sodium 192mg

MEXICAN-STYLE CARROT SLAW WITH CURRANTS

Vegan

MAKES 4 TO 6 SERVINGS

This crunchy side dish is a great accompaniment to burritos, quesadillas, or enchiladas. Like most vinegar and oil-based slaws, its flavor improves with age. While I love the contrast of the chewy currants with the crunchiness of the carrots, you can omit them, if desired.

3 tablespoons orange juice

2 tablespoons red wine vinegar

2 tablespoons extra-virgin olive oil

1 tablespoon sugar

½ teaspoon ground cumin

½ teaspoon salt

¼ teaspoon freshly ground black pepper

Pinch cayenne pepper, or more to taste

1 (8-ounce) bag shredded carrots

¼ cup zante currants or raisins

In a large bowl, whisk together the orange juice, vinegar, oil, sugar, cumin, salt, black pepper, and cayenne. Add the carrots and currants; toss until well combined. Cover and refrigerate a minimum of 3 hours, or up to 2 days. Serve chilled.

PER SERVING

Calories 128 ▪ Protein 1g ▪ Total Fat 7g ▪
Sat. Fat 1g ▪ Cholesterol 0mg ▪ Carbohydrate 17g ▪
Dietary Fiber 2g ▪ Sodium 286mg

ASIAN-STYLE COLESLAW

Vegan
MAKES 6 SERVINGS

This unusual coleslaw is always a hit at picnics and potlucks. It's a terrific companion to most of the book's chilled Asian-style noodle dishes.

- 3 tablespoons rice vinegar, preferably the brown rice variety
- 1 tablespoon plain sesame oil or peanut oil
- 1 tablespoon toasted (dark) sesame oil
- 2 tablespoons light brown sugar
- ½ teaspoon onion powder
- ½ teaspoon salt
- ¼ teaspoon garlic powder
- Freshly ground black pepper, to taste
- Pinch cayenne pepper, or to taste (optional)
- 1 tablespoon bottled chopped ginger
- 1 (16-ounce) bag (about 8 cups) coleslaw mix
- 2 tablespoons toasted sesame seeds (optional; see Cook's Tip, at right)

In a large bowl, whisk together the vinegar, plain and toasted sesame oil, sugar, onion powder, salt, garlic powder, black pepper, and cayenne (if using). Stir in the ginger and set aside about 5 minutes until the sugar is dissolved. Stir again. Add the coleslaw mix; toss several times until the cabbage begins to wilt. Cover and refrigerate a minimum of 3 hours, or overnight. Serve chilled, tossing with the sesame seeds, if desired, just before serving.

PER SERVING
Calories 80 ▪ Protein 1g ▪ Total Fat 5g ▪
Sat. Fat 1g ▪ Cholesterol 0mg ▪ Carbohydrate 10g ▪
Dietary Fiber 2g ▪ Sodium 193mg

Cook's Tip To toast sesame seeds, heat a small heavy-bottomed skillet over medium heat. Add sesame seeds and cook, stirring often, until lightly browned, 2 to 3 minutes. Immediately remove from skillet and cool.

TROPICAL COLESLAW

Lacto-ovo with vegan options
MAKES 6 TO 8 SERVINGS

Kids typically love this fruited slaw, loaded with vitamin C. It's a great accompaniment to many of the book's Mexican- or Caribbean-style dishes. Nondairy sour cream (Tofutti's Better than Sour Cream is my favorite brand) or soy yogurt can replace the regular sour cream or yogurt for a dairy-free dish. To also make it egg-free, use soy mayonnaise (Nasoya makes a reliable brand) instead of the regular variety. For a completely vegan recipe, replace the honey, a bee product, with brown sugar.

- ½ cup light sour cream, low-fat plain yogurt, or a vegan equivalent of either
- ¼ cup reduced-fat regular mayonnaise or soy mayonnaise
- 2½ tablespoons honey or light brown sugar
- 1 tablespoon bottled lime juice
- ½ teaspoon salt, or to taste
- ¼ teaspoon black pepper, or to taste
- 1 (16-ounce) bag (about 8 cups) coleslaw mix
- 1 (11-ounce) can mandarin orange segments, drained
- 1 (8¼-ounce) can pineapple chunks, drained

In a large bowl, whisk together the sour cream, mayonnaise, honey, lime juice, salt, and pepper. Add the coleslaw mix, orange segments, and pineapple; toss well to combine. Cover and refrigerate a minimum of 1 hour, or up to 1 day, tossing a few times. Toss again before serving. Serve chilled.

PER SERVING

Calories 111 ▪ Protein 2g ▪ Total Fat 3g ▪
Sat. Fat 0g ▪ Cholesterol 5mg ▪ Carbohydrate 22g ▪
Dietary Fiber 2g ▪ Sodium 251mg

FRISÉE SALAD WITH WARM MAPLE-WALNUT DRESSING

Vegan

MAKES 4 SERVINGS

The sweetness of maple and the richness of walnuts are perfect counterpoints for frisée, a member of the somewhat bitter chicory family. Any combination of bitter greens—escarole, radicchio, Belgian endive, curly endive—typically found in the European-blend packaged salads, as well as spinach or arugula, can be substituted for the frisée.

6 to 7 cups loosely packed washed and torn
    frisée (chicory) or other bitter greens
2 tablespoons canola oil
⅓ cup walnut pieces
¼ cup pure maple syrup
2 tablespoons cider vinegar
Salt and freshly ground black pepper, to taste

Place the frisée in a large salad bowl and set briefly aside.

In a small heavy-bottomed saucepan, heat the oil over medium heat. Add the walnuts and cook, stirring constantly, until fragrant and lightly toasted, 1 to 2 minutes. Add the maple syrup, vinegar, salt, and pepper; cook, stirring constantly, 30

seconds. Pour over the frisée and toss well to thoroughly combine. Serve at once.

PER SERVING

Calories 191 ▪ Protein 4g ▪ Total Fat 13g ▪
Sat. Fat 1g ▪ Cholesterol 0mg ▪ Carbohydrate 18g ▪
Dietary Fiber 2g ▪ Sodium 10mg

MIXED GREEN SALAD WITH HONEY MUSTARD-RASPBERRY VINAIGRETTE

Egg-free and dairy-free, with vegan option

MAKES 4 SERVINGS

Though optional, a garnish of fresh raspberries is a lovely touch if this dish is served as a first-course salad. Use the vinaigrette to dress up already-shredded carrots or sliced canned beets, as well. To create a vegan recipe, use brown sugar or pure maple syrup in lieu of the honey, which is produced by bees.

2 tablespoons extra-light olive oil, canola oil,
    or other mild vegetable oil
2 tablespoons raspberry vinegar
2 tablespoons honey, light brown sugar, or
    pure maple syrup
1 tablespoon water
1 tablespoon Dijon mustard
½ tablespoon freeze-dried chopped chives
Salt and freshly ground black pepper, to taste
1 (10-ounce) bag (about 7 cups loosely
    packed) ready-washed mixed salad greens
Fresh raspberries, for garnish (optional)

In a small bowl, whisk together the oil, vinegar, honey, water, and mustard. Stir in the chives. Season with salt and pepper. Let stand a few minutes to allow the flavors to blend. Whisk again.

Place the salad greens in a large salad bowl. Add the dressing, tossing well to combine. Serve at once, garnished with the raspberries, if desired.

PER SERVING
Calories 111 ▪ Protein 2g ▪ Total Fat 7g ▪
Sat. Fat 1g ▪ Cholesterol 0mg ▪ Carbohydrate 12g ▪
Dietary Fiber 2g ▪ Sodium 69mg

Cook's Tip Bags of ready-washed lettuce and salad greens typically come in a 10-ounce size, which holds about 7 cups loosely packed greens, enough for 4 side salads.

MESCLUN SALAD WITH HERB VINAIGRETTE

Vegan
MAKES 4 SERVINGS

Mesclun is a French term for a mix of young field greens, which often includes arugula, radicchio, oak leaf lettuce, curly endive, and dandelion greens. Some well-stocked supermarkets offer loose ready-mixed mesclun, often calling them spring mixes or spring blends. Bagged salads labeled "mixed spring greens," or any mixed salad greens, will work in this recipe. Though optional, the addition of fresh herbs provides a nice touch of fragrance as well as flavor.

1½ tablespoons extra-virgin olive oil
1½ tablespoons canola oil
2 tablespoons red wine vinegar
1 tablespoon water
½ to 1 tablespoon fresh herbs such as whole fresh thyme leaves and/or torn fresh tarragon leaves (optional)
1 teaspoon freeze-dried chopped chives
½ teaspoon Dijon mustard
1 teaspoon sugar
¼ teaspoon garlic powder
¼ teaspoon dried tarragon
¼ teaspoon dried thyme
¼ teaspoon dried parsley
¼ teaspoon dried basil
¼ teaspoon salt, or to taste
Freshly ground black pepper, to taste
7 cups loosely packed mesclun or "spring mix," washed and blotted dry, or 1 (10-ounce) bag ready-washed mixed spring greens or other mixed greens

In a large bowl, whisk together all the ingredients except the salad greens until well blended. Let stand about 5 minutes to allow the flavors to blend. Whisk again. Add the greens and toss well to thoroughly coat with the dressing. Serve at once.

PER SERVING
Calories 119 ▪ Protein 2g ▪ Total Fat 10g ▪
Sat. Fat 1g ▪ Cholesterol 0mg ▪ Carbohydrate 6g ▪
Dietary Fiber 2g ▪ Sodium 163mg

PICNIC MACARONI AND CHEESE SALAD

Lacto-ovo with vegan options
MAKES 6 TO 8 SERVINGS

Don't be put off by the long list of ingredients; this warm-weather version of the classic casserole can be tossed together in minutes, then chilled in the cooler en route to the picnic. While you can easily make the recipe egg-free by using soy mayonnaise in lieu of the regular variety, the availability of shredded vegan cheese substitutes is limited, so you will probably need to alter the varieties and amounts according to taste.

8 ounces elbow macaroni

¾ cup reduced-fat regular mayonnaise or soy mayonnaise

2 tablespoons diced pimiento, drained

½ tablespoon sweet pickle relish

1 to 1½ teaspoons celery seeds

½ teaspoon onion powder

½ teaspoon garlic salt

½ teaspoon prepared horseradish (optional)

¼ teaspoon freshly ground black pepper, or to taste

¼ teaspoon dry mustard

⅛ teaspoon cayenne pepper, or to taste (optional)

½ cup (2 ounces) already-shredded reduced-fat cheddar cheese or vegan equivalent of choice

¼ cup (1 ounce) already-shredded part-skim mozzarella or reduced-fat Swiss cheese or vegan equivalent of choice

¼ cup (1 ounce) already-shredded Parmesan cheese or vegan equivalent of choice

¼ cup canned sliced black olives, drained

Sweet paprika, for garnish (optional)

Cook the macaroni in a large stockpot of boiling salted water according to package directions until al dente, 6 to 8 minutes. Drain in a colander and rinse under running cold water until cool. Drain well and let stand several minutes to further dry.

Meanwhile, in a small bowl, mix together the mayonnaise, pimiento, relish, celery seeds, onion powder, garlic salt, horseradish (if using), black pepper, mustard, and cayenne (if using) until thoroughly blended. Transfer the drained macaroni to a large bowl and add the cheeses and olives; toss to combine. Add the mayonnaise mixture to the macaroni and cheese mixture; toss well to combine. Cover and refrigerate a minimum of 1 hour, or up to 1 day. Serve chilled, garnished with a dusting of paprika, if desired.

PER SERVING
Calories 282 ▪ Protein 11g ▪ Total Fat 10g ▪ Sat. Fat 3g ▪ Cholesterol 19mg ▪ Carbohydrate 35g ▪ Dietary Fiber 1g ▪ Sodium 553mg

MARINATED MEDITERRANEAN SALAD WITH CHERRY TOMATOES

Vegan

MAKES 4 TO 5 SERVINGS

This tangy marinated salad is an easy, make-ahead alternative to a last-minute tossed green salad. Not surprisingly, it complements many of this book's pasta and other Mediterranean-style dishes.

1 pint (2 cups) cherry or grape tomatoes

1 (6-ounce) jar marinated quartered artichoke hearts, marinade included

½ cup jarred small whole onions, drained

12 pitted kalamata olives

2 tablespoons balsamic vinegar

1 tablespoon extra-virgin olive oil

1 tablespoon capers, drained

½ cup whole fresh basil leaves, torn (optional)

Salt and freshly ground black pepper, to taste

Place all ingredients in a medium salad bowl. Toss gently yet thoroughly to combine. Let stand 20 minutes at room temperature to marinate. Toss again and serve.

Alternatively, cover and refrigerate up to 24 hours; add the basil (if using) shortly before serving instead of with the other ingredients. Serve chilled or return to room temperature.

Variation

Marinated Mediterranean Pantry Salad: Omit the cherry tomatoes and basil. Add 1 (15-ounce) can chickpeas, rinsed and drained, 2 tablespoons sun-dried tomato bits that have been reconstituted in warm water to cover 10 minutes and drained, and 1 tablespoon diced pimiento, drained. Proceed as otherwise directed in the recipe.

MARINATED BABY BELLA MUSHROOM AND GRAPE TOMATO SALAD

Vegan
MAKES 4 TO 5 SERVINGS

I love this salad. Even my younger daughter, who typically shuns mushrooms, loves this salad. While she and I both agree that baby bella mushrooms have the better flavor here, you can use the cultivated white variety (or a combination of the two) instead, and the recipe will still be delicious.

1 pint (2 cups) grape or cherry tomatoes
1 (8-ounce) package presliced baby bella mushrooms (see Cook's Tip at right)

3 tablespoons balsamic vinegar
2 tablespoons extra-virgin olive oil
1 teaspoon dried oregano
Salt and freshly ground black pepper, to taste

Place all the ingredients in a medium salad bowl. Toss gently yet thoroughly to combine. Let stand 20 minutes at room temperature to marinate, tossing a few times. Toss again and serve. Alternatively, cover and refrigerate up to 24 hours. Serve chilled or return to room temperature.

Cook's Tip A baby bella mushroom is actually a small portobello or cremini mushroom. Cremini mushrooms are cultivated brown mushrooms that have a stronger, earthier flavor than their white counterparts. As such, they replicate the flavor of wild mushrooms nicely in most recipes.

NEW POTATO SALAD

Dairy-free with vegan option
MAKES 6 SERVINGS

Keeping the skins on potatoes not only adds important fiber to the diet, but slows the body's glycemic reaction to this starchy, yet mineral-rich tuber. The following recipe can easily be made vegan by using soy mayonnaise in lieu of the regular variety.

¾ cup reduced-fat regular mayonnaise or soy mayonnaise
1 tablespoon freeze-dried chopped chives

1 tablespoon Dijon mustard

½ tablespoon celery seeds

½ teaspoon lemon pepper seasoning

½ teaspoon onion powder

½ teaspoon salt

1½ pounds tiny new red-skin potatoes

In a large serving bowl, mix together the mayonnaise, chives, mustard, celery seeds, lemon pepper seasoning, onion powder, and salt until well combined. Set aside about 15 minutes to allow the flavors to blend. (Or cover and refrigerate up to 2 days before continuing with the recipe.)

Meanwhile, place the potatoes in a large pot and add enough salted water to cover; bring to a boil over high heat. Reduce the heat to medium-high and cook until tender but not mushy, 10 to 15 minutes, depending on size. Drain and let cool slightly.

Add the warm potatoes to the mayonnaise mixture and toss gently yet thoroughly to combine. Serve slightly warm or at room temperature. Alternatively, cover and refrigerate a minimum of 3 hours, or up to 2 days, and serve chilled.

PER SERVING

Calories 142 ■ Protein 2g ■ Total Fat 6g ■
Sat. Fat 1g ■ Cholesterol 11mg ■ Carbohydrate 21g ■
Dietary Fiber 1g ■ Sodium 392mg

HEARTS OF ROMAINE WITH LEMON-BALSAMIC VINAIGRETTE

Vegan

MAKES 4 SERVINGS

This tangy salad is a fine accompaniment to many of this book's Italian-style pasta entrées. For easy entertaining, you can prepare the dressing a few days ahead of using. If you're really pressed for time, substitute 1 (10-ounce) bag torn romaine lettuce leaves for the hearts.

3 tablespoons extra-virgin olive oil

2 tablespoons balsamic vinegar

2 tablespoons lemon juice, preferably prepared from frozen concentrate

½ teaspoon sugar

½ teaspoon salt

¼ teaspoon onion powder

¼ teaspoon garlic powder

¼ teaspoon dried oregano

¼ teaspoon lemon pepper seasoning

Freshly ground black pepper, to taste

2 (4-ounce) hearts of romaine, torn into salad-size pieces (about 8 cups loosely packed)

In a large bowl, whisk together all the ingredients except the romaine until well blended. Let stand about 5 minutes to allow the flavors to blend. Whisk again. Add the romaine and toss well to thoroughly coat with the dressing. Serve at once.

PER SERVING

Calories 114 ■ Protein 2g ■ Total Fat 10g ■
Sat. Fat 1g ■ Cholesterol 0mg ■ Carbohydrate 5g ■
Dietary Fiber 3g ■ Sodium 297mg

SPINACH-MUSHROOM SALAD WITH TARRAGON-DIJON DRESSING

Vegan

MAKES 4 SERVINGS

Redolent of tarragon, the quintessential French herb, this vegetarian variation of the Dijon classic is a favorite of mine. Dehydrated minced shallots can be found in gourmet shops and in the spice aisle of some well-stocked supermarkets. Dehydrated minced onion can be substituted.

1½ tablespoons tarragon vinegar

1½ tablespoons water

½ tablespoon Dijon mustard

1 tablespoon dehydrated minced shallots or onions

½ tablespoon sugar

1 teaspoon dried tarragon leaves

½ teaspoon salt

¼ teaspoon freshly ground black pepper

2 tablespoons plus 2 teaspoons extra-virgin olive oil

1 (9-ounce) bag (about 6 cups loosely packed) ready-washed baby spinach

4 ounces pre-sliced fresh white mushrooms

In a small bowl, whisk together the vinegar, water, mustard, shallots, sugar, tarragon, salt, and pepper; slowly whisk in the oil. Let stand about 5 minutes to allow the shallots to rehydrate. Whisk again.

Place half the spinach and half the mushrooms in a large bowl and toss to combine. Add half the dressing and toss well to thoroughly coat. Add remaining spinach and mushrooms and toss to combine. Add remaining dressing and toss well to thoroughly coat. Serve at once.

PER SERVING

Calories 111 ■ Protein 3g ■ Total Fat 10g ■ Sat. Fat 1g ■ Cholesterol 0mg ■ Carbohydrate 6g ■ Dietary Fiber 2g ■ Sodium 342mg

Cook's Tip One tablespoon of dehydrated minced shallots or minced onion equals ¼ cup minced raw.

WARM BROILED MUSHROOM AND BABY SPINACH SALAD

Vegan

MAKES 4 SERVINGS

I look forward to making this simple salad as much for the tantalizing aroma of broiled mushrooms as for its excellent taste. Mature spinach is a bit too substantial for the mushrooms; they shrink considerably after broiling, so use baby spinach if at all possible. If you're making it for company and need a little extra time, immediately after broiling, the mushrooms can be transferred to the lowest oven rack and held up to 20 minutes or so with the broiler turned off and the oven door shut. Proceed as otherwise directed in the recipe.

1 (8-ounce) package presliced fresh white mushrooms

2 tablespoons extra-virgin olive oil

Garlic salt, to taste

2 tablespoons low-sodium vegetable broth

1 tablespoon balsamic vinegar

Freshly ground black pepper, to taste

1 (9-ounce) bag (about 6 cups loosely packed) ready-washed baby spinach

Preheat oven to broil.

Place the mushrooms on an ungreased baking sheet with sides. Toss with the oil and garlic salt, then spread out in a single layer. Broil 6 to 8 inches from heating element until lightly browned and beginning to sizzle, about 3 minutes. Turn with a spatula and broil until golden and sizzling, about 2 minutes. Remove from the oven and transfer the mushrooms and all accumulated juice to a large bowl. Add the broth, vinegar, and pepper, tossing well to combine. Add half the spinach and toss to combine. Add the remaining spinach, toss to combine, and serve at once.

PER SERVING
Calories 90 ▪ Protein 3g ▪ Total Fat 7g ▪
Sat. Fat 1g ▪ Cholesterol 0mg ▪ Carbohydrate 5g ▪
Dietary Fiber 3g ▪ Sodium 69mg

Cook's Tip Instead of spinach, toss the broiled mushrooms with 10 to 16 ounces cooked vegetables (broccoli, asparagus, green beans, sugar snap peas, and new potatoes are good choices) to create delicious vegetable side dishes. The mushrooms also make great toppings for veggie burgers or baked potatoes. Or, if you are a mushroom lover like me, enjoy them on their own!

Main-Course Salads

GREEK-STYLE BULGUR SALAD WITH CHICKPEAS, FETA, AND OLIVES

Egg-free with vegan option

MAKES 4 MAIN-DISH OR
8 SIDE-DISH OR APPETIZER SERVINGS

A Greek rendition of Lebanese tabbouleh, this salad gets its kick from tangy feta and salty kalamata olives. For a vegan dish, replace the feta with about ½ cup marinated artichoke hearts, drained and quartered, or additional olives.

¾ cup plus 2 tablespoons low-sodium vegetable broth or water

2 tablespoons lemon juice, preferably prepared from frozen concentrate

½ teaspoon onion powder

¼ teaspoon garlic powder

1 cup fine-grain (fancy) bulgur

2 tablespoons extra-virgin olive oil

1 tablespoon red wine vinegar

½ teaspoon dried oregano

Salt and freshly ground black pepper, to taste

1 (15-ounce) can chickpeas, rinsed and drained

12 pitted kalamata or other good-quality black olives

2 to 3 ounces (½ to ¾ cup) crumbled feta cheese

Ready-washed romaine lettuce leaves, to serve (optional)

Cherry tomatoes, for garnish (optional)

In a medium saucepan over medium heat, bring the broth, lemon juice, onion powder, and garlic powder barely to a simmer. Remove from the heat and let cool 5 minutes. Add the bulgur, stirring well to combine. Let stand until the bulgur has absorbed all of the liquid and feels dry, about 30 minutes, stirring occasionally.

In a large bowl, whisk together the oil, vinegar, oregano, salt, and pepper. Add the chickpeas, olives, and cheese; stir well to combine. Add the bulgur, tossing well to combine. Season with additional salt and pepper, if necessary. Cover and refrigerate a minimum of 2 hours, or up to 2 days, and serve chilled or at room temperature. If desired, serve over romaine lettuce leaves, garnished with cherry tomatoes.

PER SERVING

Calories 362 ▪ Protein 14g ▪ Total Fat 15g ▪
Sat. Fat 3g ▪ Cholesterol 13mg ▪ Carbohydrate 46g ▪
Dietary Fiber 11g ▪ Sodium 461mg

COUSCOUS SALAD WITH MARINATED GREEK VEGETABLES

Vegan

MAKES 5 TO 6 MAIN-DISH OR 8 SIDE-DISH SERVINGS

Giardiniera, found in the specialty aisle of most major supermarkets, is a salty Greek mélange of crunchy vegetables, typically including cauliflower, carrots, cucumbers, red bell peppers, and celery, marinated in vinegar brine. Add some plump chickpeas and sliced black olives and you have a virtually instant salad blend to toss with couscous, bulgur, or small pasta. Leftovers stuffed into pita pockets make great sandwiches.

2¼ cups water

1½ cups instant whole wheat couscous

¼ teaspoon dried grated lemon peel

¼ teaspoon salt

2½ tablespoons extra-virgin olive oil

1 (16-ounce) jar giardiniera, rinsed and drained

1 (15-ounce) can chickpeas, rinsed and drained

¼ cup canned sliced black olives, drained

Dried oregano, to taste

Freshly ground black pepper, to taste

In a medium saucepan, bring the water to a boil over high heat. Stir in the couscous, lemon peel, salt, and ½ tablespoon of the oil. Let return to a boil, cover, and remove from the heat. Let stand until all the liquid is absorbed, 7 minutes. Uncover and fluff with a fork.

Transfer the couscous mixture to a large bowl. While still warm, add the giardiniera, chickpeas, olives, oregano, pepper, and remaining oil; toss well to combine. Serve warm or at room temperature. Alternatively, refrigerate a minimum of 3 hours, or up to 3 days, and serve chilled.

PER SERVING

Calories 367 ▪ Protein 12g ▪ Total Fat 9g ▪
Sat. Fat 1g ▪ Cholesterol 0mg ▪ Carbohydrate 59g ▪
Dietary Fiber 4g ▪ Sodium 263mg

MEDITERRANEAN COUSCOUS SALAD

Vegan

MAKES 5 TO 6 MAIN-DISH OR
8 SIDE-DISH SERVINGS

Variations of this popular salad abound throughout the Middle East. While the inclusion of peas, raisins, and pine nuts is fairly common, feel free to substitute with other ingredients that suit your fancy.

1 (14-ounce) can (1¾ cups) low-sodium
   vegetable broth
¼ cup water
½ teaspoon onion powder
¼ teaspoon garlic powder
1 cup frozen baby green peas
1½ cups instant couscous, preferably whole
   wheat
½ cup dark raisins
2 tablespoons pine nuts (optional)
2 tablespoons chopped pimiento, drained
3 tablespoons extra-virgin olive oil
2 tablespoons white wine vinegar
Salt and freshly ground black pepper,
   to taste

In a medium saucepan, bring the broth, water, onion powder, and garlic powder to a boil over high heat. Add the peas. When the mixture returns to a boil, stir in the couscous and raisins and remove from the heat. Cover and let stand until all the liquid has been absorbed, 7 minutes. Uncover and fluff with a fork.

Transfer to a serving bowl and add the pine nuts (if using), pimiento, oil, vinegar, salt, and pepper; toss well to combine. Let cool to room temperature and serve. Alternatively, cover and refrigerate a minimum of 3 hours, or overnight; serve chilled or return to room temperature.

PER SERVING
Calories 354 ▪ Protein 13g ▪ Total Fat 9g ▪
Sat. Fat 1g ▪ Cholesterol 0mg ▪ Carbohydrate 57g ▪
Dietary Fiber 6g ▪ Sodium 221mg

MISO NOODLE AND MIZUNA SALAD

Vegan

**MAKES 2 MAIN-DISH OR
4 FIRST-COURSE OR SIDE-DISH SERVINGS**

Miso, a protein-packed soy paste available in brown, white, or yellow varieties, is used as a thickening and flavoring agent in Asian cooking. The white or yellow ones are milder in taste than the brown, which is better suited for cooked soups and sauces. Mizuna is a frilly-leafed Japanese green available in the spring and summer. Both can be found in Asian and gourmet markets, as well as natural food stores.

- 4 ounces somen or soba noodles, broken in half (see Cook's Tip, page 101)
- 2 tablespoons rice vinegar
- 1 tablespoon white or yellow miso or 2 teaspoons brown miso
- 1 tablespoon water
- ½ tablespoon peanut oil
- ½ tablespoon toasted (dark) sesame oil
- ½ teaspoon onion powder
- ½ teaspoon sugar
- ¼ teaspoon garlic powder
- Freshly ground black pepper, to taste
- 4 cups mizuna, arugula, or spinach leaves, coarsely torn
- 1 cup grape or cherry tomatoes, for garnish

In a large stockpot, cook the noodles in salted water according to package directions until al dente. (Or see Chilled Somen Noodles with Spicy Peanut Sauce, page 100, for method.) Drain and rinse under running cold water until completely cooled. Drain well.

In a small nonreactive bowl, whisk together the vinegar, miso, water, peanut oil, sesame oil, onion powder, sugar, garlic powder, and pepper until well combined. Set aside.

In a medium bowl, combine the noodles and mizuna. Add the vinaigrette and toss until well combined. Divide evenly into servings, garnish with the tomatoes, and serve at once.

PER SERVING
Calories 330 ■ Protein 10g ■ Total Fat 9g ■
Sat. Fat 1g ■ Cholesterol 0mg ■ Carbohydrate 54g ■
Dietary Fiber 3g ■ Sodium 338mg

ORZO SALAD WITH BALSAMIC-TOMATO VINAIGRETTE

Vegan

**MAKES 6 MAIN-DISH OR
8 TO 10 SIDE-DISH SERVINGS**

This pretty pasta salad is perfect for a party or picnic as it holds up well at room temperature. Orzo is a rice-shaped pasta that varies in size, from plump to long grained. Though it is available in most well-stocked supermarkets, 12 ounces of small shell pasta or elbow macaroni can be substituted.

- 12 ounces (about 1¾ cups) orzo pasta
- 1½ cups frozen peas and pearl onions
- 1½ tablespoons balsamic vinegar
- 1 teaspoon tomato paste
- 3 tablespoons extra-virgin olive oil
- ½ teaspoon sugar, or more to taste
- ¼ teaspoon salt, or to taste
- ¼ teaspoon freshly ground black pepper, or to taste
- 1 cup canned diced tomatoes, drained

Bring a large stockpot of salted water to a boil. Add the orzo and cook according to package directions until al dente, 8 to 10 minutes. When the orzo is almost finished cooking, place the peas and pearl onions in a colander and set in sink. Slowly pour the cooked orzo into the colander. Rinse under cold running water to cool. Drain well and transfer to a large bowl.

In a small bowl, combine the vinegar and tomato paste; slowly whisk in the oil. Add the sugar, salt, and pepper; whisk well to combine.

Add the tomatoes to the orzo; toss well to combine. Add the vinaigrette, tossing well to combine. Season with additional salt and pepper as necessary. Serve at room temperature, or cover and refrigerate a minimum of 1 hour and serve chilled.

PER SERVING

Calories 304 ▪ Protein 9g ▪ Total Fat 8g ▪
Sat. Fat 1g ▪ Cholesterol 0mg ▪ Carbohydrate 49g ▪
Dietary Fiber 3g ▪ Sodium 213mg

CURRIED ORZO SALAD WITH CHUTNEY AND ASIAN VEGETABLES

Vegan

MAKES 6 MAIN-DISH
OR 8 TO 10 SIDE-DISH SERVINGS

Perfect for buffets or picnics, this outstanding pasta salad can be served slightly warm, chilled, or at room temperature. Orzo, a rice-shaped pasta, is available in most well-stocked supermarkets. Look for mango chutney, a spicy-sweet, jellylike condiment, in the specialty food aisle. Any frozen vegetable can be substituted for the Asian mix, if desired.

12 ounces (about 1¾ cups) orzo pasta (see Cook's Tip below)
1 (16-ounce) package frozen mixed Asian vegetables
1 cup mango chutney
1 tablespoon mild curry powder
1 tablespoon toasted (dark) sesame oil
Salt and freshly ground black pepper, to taste

In a large stockpot, cook the orzo in salted water according to package directions until al dente, 8 to 10 minutes, adding the vegetables the last 2 to 3 minutes of cooking (do not overcook the vegetables). Drain in a colander and transfer to a large bowl. Set aside.

Meanwhile, in a small bowl, stir together the chutney, curry powder, sesame oil, salt, and pepper until well combined. Add to the orzo mixture, tossing gently yet thoroughly to combine. Serve warm or at room temperature. Alternatively, cover and refrigerate a minimum of 2 hours, or up to 1 day, and serve chilled.

PER SERVING

Calories 387 ▪ Protein 10g ▪ Total Fat 4g ▪
Sat. Fat 1g ▪ Cholesterol 0mg ▪ Carbohydrate 79g ▪
Dietary Fiber 5g ▪ Sodium 50mg

Cook's Tip About 12 ounces (dry weight) small shells or elbow macaroni, cooked according to package directions, can be substituted for the orzo, if desired.

MEXICAN-STYLE PASTA SALAD WITH BLACK BEANS AND CORN

Vegan

MAKES 5 TO 6 MAIN-DISH OR
8 TO 10 SIDE-DISH SERVINGS

When you need something quick, easy, and delicious to bring to a picnic or potluck, this spicy pasta salad always rises to the occasion. Its heat can be controlled according to the strength of the salsa selected; mango and peach salsas are especially refreshing.

12 ounces medium shells, elbows, bow ties, or other similar pasta shape
1 cup frozen yellow corn
2 cups salsa, preferably medium
1 (15-ounce) can black beans, rinsed and drained
1 tablespoon extra-virgin olive oil
Salt and freshly ground black pepper, to taste

In a large stockpot of boiling salted water, cook the pasta according to package directions until al dente. Before it is done, place the corn in a colander in the sink. When the pasta is done cooking, slowly drain the pasta over the corn. Drain well.

Meanwhile, in a large bowl, combine the salsa, beans, and oil. While still quite hot, add the pasta and corn mixture, tossing well to thoroughly combine. Season with salt and pepper. Serve warm or at room temperature. Alternatively, cover and refrigerate a minimum of 3 hours, or up to 3 days, and serve chilled or return to room temperature.

PER SERVING
Calories 396 ■ Protein 15g ■ Total Fat 5g ■
Sat. Fat 1g ■ Cholesterol 0mg ■ Carbohydrate 75g ■
Dietary Fiber 7g ■ Sodium 275mg

PASTA SALAD WITH BROCCOLI AND HONEY-DIJON DRESSING

Egg-free and dairy-free, with vegan option

MAKES 6 MAIN-DISH OR
8 TO 10 SIDE-DISH SERVINGS

Great for picnics and potlucks, this pasta salad can be made up to 24 hours before serving; I actually prefer it the next day. For a vegan dish, substitute brown sugar for the honey.

12 ounces rotelle or other twist pasta
4 tablespoons extra-virgin olive oil
2 tablespoons red wine vinegar
2 tablespoons honey or light brown sugar
1 tablespoon Dijon mustard
½ teaspoon onion powder
Salt and freshly ground black pepper, to taste
2 cups ready-washed broccoli florets
¼ cup already-shredded carrots

In a large stockpot of boiling salted water, cook the pasta according to package directions until al dente, about 9 minutes. Drain and rinse under running cold water until completely cooled. Drain again.

Meanwhile, in a large bowl, whisk together the oil, vinegar, honey, mustard, onion powder, salt, and pepper. Add the pasta, broccoli, and carrots; toss well to combine. Cover and refrigerate a minimum of 1 hour, or up to 1 day, stirring a few times. Season with additional salt and pepper, as necessary. Serve chilled or return to room temperature.

PER SERVING

Calories 323 ■ Protein 8g ■ Total Fat 10g ■
Sat. Fat 1g ■ Cholesterol 0mg ■ Carbohydrate 51g ■
Dietary Fiber 2g ■ Sodium 41mg

PANTRY PASTA SALAD WITH OLIVES, ARTICHOKES, AND DRIED HERBS

Vegan

MAKES 6 MAIN-DISH OR
8 TO 10 SIDE-DISH SERVINGS

An olive lover, I make this pasta salad often, using any variety of good-quality black and green olives. It also helps to use up many of my dried herbs before their recommended shelf life of one year is up.

12 ounces rainbow rotini or other twist pasta

4 tablespoons extra-virgin olive oil

2 tablespoons white wine vinegar

1 teaspoon dried oregano leaves

1 teaspoon dried thyme leaves

1 teaspoon dried fennel seeds

½ teaspoon dried basil

½ teaspoon dried parsley

½ teaspoon garlic powder

½ teaspoon onion powder

½ teaspoon salt, preferably the coarse variety,
    or to taste

Freshly ground black pepper, to taste

Cayenne pepper, to taste (optional)

12 pitted kalamata olives or other good-quality
    black olives

12 pitted green Italian-style green olives or
    other good-quality green olives

1 (6-ounce) jar marinated quartered artichoke
    hearts, drained

1 (4-ounce) jar diced pimiento, drained

In a large stockpot filled with boiling salted water, cook the pasta according to package directions until al dente, about 9 minutes. Drain and rinse under running cold water until completely cooled. Drain again.

Meanwhile, in a large bowl, whisk together the oil, vinegar, oregano, thyme, fennel seeds, basil, parsley, garlic powder, onion powder, salt, black pepper, and cayenne (if using). Let stand about 10 minutes to allow the flavors to blend; whisk again.

Add the pasta, black and green olives, artichokes, and pimiento; toss well to combine. Season with additional salt and pepper, as necessary. Cover and refrigerate a minimum of 1 hour, or up to 3 days, turning a few times. Serve chilled or return to room temperature.

PER SERVING

Calories 344 ■ Protein 9g ■ Total Fat 13g ■
Sat. Fat 2g ■ Cholesterol 0mg ■ Carbohydrate 49g ■
Dietary Fiber 3g ■ Sodium 387mg

COLD SOMEN NOODLE SALAD WITH ENOKI MUSHROOMS AND TAHINI DRESSING

Vegan

**MAKES 4 MAIN-DISH OR
6 TO 8 SIDE-DISH SERVINGS**

Slender enoki mushrooms blend nicely with somen noodles in this exotic pasta salad. Tahini is an oily, peanut butter–like paste made from ground sesame seeds. It can be found in Middle Eastern markets as well as most major supermarkets.

8 ounces somen or soba noodles or other thin pasta, broken in half (see Cook's Tip, page 101)

2 tablespoons sesame tahini

1½ tablespoons rice vinegar

1 tablespoon reduced-sodium soy sauce

1 tablespoon water

½ tablespoon toasted (dark) sesame oil

½ teaspoon onion powder

½ teaspoon sugar

Salt and freshly ground black pepper, to taste

4 ounces enoki mushrooms, rough stems twisted off, separated into individual strands

½ cup already-shredded carrots

In a large stockpot, cook the noodles in boiling salted water according to package directions until al dente. (Or see Chilled Somen Noodles with Spicy Peanut Sauce, page 100, for method.) Drain and rinse under running cold water until completely cooled. Drain well.

In a large bowl, whisk together the tahini, vinegar, soy sauce, water, sesame oil, onion powder, sugar, salt, and pepper. Let stand 5 minutes to allow the flavors to blend, then whisk again. Add the noodles, mushrooms, and carrots; toss to thoroughly combine. Serve at room temperature, or cover and refrigerate up to 12 hours and serve chilled.

PER SERVING

Calories 290 ▪ Protein 10g ▪ Total Fat 7g ▪
Sat. Fat 1g ▪ Cholesterol 0mg ▪ Carbohydrate 49g ▪
Dietary Fiber 2g ▪ Sodium 161mg

Sandwiches, Wraps, Pizza, Breads, and Other Lighter Fare

This chapter is for all you fast-food junkies out there—no need to hide in the closet, because these recipes are good for you! If you're dying to sink your teeth into a juicy sandwich, heat up the grill and treat yourself to a Grilled Portobello Mushroom Sandwich with Paprika Aïoli. For something a bit spicier, serve Cajun-Style Veggie-Rice Cakes with Creole-Honey Mustard Mayonnaise inside hamburger buns. For something a bit more dignified, there's always the scrumptious open-faced Asparagus on Rye Toasts with Welsh Rarebit Sauce. If you're into more trendy wraps, there's no less than four such styles—Asian, Caribbean, Thai, and Mediterranean—from which to choose. Pizza lovers can indulge every night of the week on seven different varieties, from Classic Cheese-less Pizza alla Marinara to contemporary Pesto Pizza with Fresh Mozzarella and Cherry Tomatoes. Want a little more than regular pizza? Check out the Spinach and Cheese Stromboli or the Three-Cheese Calzones. If Mexican food is your ultimate weakness, the

Black Bean Tacos are great and the Bean Enchiladas with Green Sauce even better—though the Rice and Bean Empanadas may be the best!

ARTICHOKE AND FETA CHEESE PHYLLO PIZZA

Egg-free

MAKES 6 SERVINGS

This rustic yet sophisticated take on pizza is highly popular among those with adult taste buds. To make a more kid-friendly version, substitute shredded mozzarella for the feta. Lightly pricking the tomatoes ensures that they won't burst when baking at a high temperature.

8 sheets frozen phyllo dough, thawed according to package directions
7½ teaspoons extra-virgin olive oil
6 ounces (1½ cups) crumbled feta cheese
1 (6-ounce) jar marinated quartered artichoke hearts (about 12 pieces), drained
24 cherry or grape tomatoes
12 pitted whole kalamata olives
Dried oregano, to taste
Freshly ground black pepper, to taste

Preheat oven to 400F (205C). Lightly grease an extra-large baking sheet or 17½ × 11 inch jelly roll pan.

Place a phyllo sheet on the baking sheet, pressing down to fit the pan. Fold in any excess edges to form a crust. Brush the top with 1 teaspoon of the oil. Repeat with remaining phyllo sheets, leaving the top sheet oil-free. Arrange the cheese evenly over the top, followed by the artichoke quarters, then the tomatoes. Using a fork, lightly prick the top of each tomato. Using a pastry or basting brush, dab the tomatoes with the remaining ½ teaspoon oil. Intersperse the olives evenly among the artichokes and tomatoes. Lightly sprinkle the top of the pizza with oregano and pepper.

Place the pizza on the center rack of the oven and bake 10 minutes. Place on the lower rack and bake 5 to 10 minutes, or until the edges are crisp and golden. To serve, cut lengthwise in half, then cut crosswise into thirds for a total of 6 pieces. Serve warm.

PER SERVING (1 SLICE)

Calories 249 ▪ Protein 7g ▪ Total Fat 15g ▪
Sat. Fat 5g ▪ Cholesterol 25mg ▪ Carbohydrate 21g ▪
Dietary Fiber 2g ▪ Sodium 591mg

ASIAN NOODLE AND BROCCOLI SLAW WRAP WITH BLACK BEAN MAYONNAISE AND SPROUTS

Dairy-free with vegan option

MAKES 4 SERVINGS

These noodle wraps are as fun to eat as they are delicious. Black bean sauce (a salty blend of fermented black soybeans and garlic) can be found in Asian markets as well as the international aisle of many well-stocked supermarkets. While you can use any sprout in this recipe, the onion variety adds a nice flavor. For a vegan dish, use soy mayonnaise; Nasoya is a reliable brand.

- 1 (3.75-ounce) package uncooked cellophane noodles (bean threads) (see Cook's Tip at right)
- ¼ cup reduced-fat regular mayonnaise or soy mayonnaise
- ¼ cup Asian black bean sauce
- ½ tablespoon toasted (dark) sesame oil
- 8 ounces (about 3½ cups) broccoli slaw with carrots
- 2 ounces (about 1½ cups) onion sprouts
- Freshly ground black pepper, to taste
- 4 (10-inch) flour tortillas
- 4 large leaves of curly-leaf or hearts of romaine lettuce
- 4 tablespoons sunflower seeds (optional)

In a large stockpot of boiling water, cook the cellophane noodles 1 minute. Drain and rinse under running cold water to thoroughly cool. Set aside to thoroughly drain.

In a large bowl, stir together the mayonnaise, black bean sauce, and oil until well combined. Remove 2 tablespoons of the mayonnaise mixture and reserve. Add the broccoli slaw and sprouts to the large bowl; toss until the vegetables begin to soften. Season generously with pepper.

To assemble the wraps, spread ½ tablespoon of the reserved mayonnaise mixture along the center of each tortilla. Place a lettuce leaf on top. Arrange the cellophane noodles (pull apart with your fingers) evenly over the lettuce. Spread vegetable mixture evenly over the noodles. Sprinkle the vegetables evenly with sunflower seeds (if using). Fold over either side of each tortilla (do not tuck in sides), securing with a toothpick, if desired. Serve immediately. Alternatively, cover with plastic wrap and refrigerate up to 3 hours, but no longer, as the wraps may become soggy.

PER SERVING
Calories 295 ■ Protein 5g ■ Total Fat 10g ■ Sat. Fat 1g ■ Cholesterol 5mg ■ Carbohydrate 48g ■ Dietary Fiber 3g ■ Sodium 438mg

Cook's Tip Cellophane noodles, or bean threads, are transparent wheat-free noodles made from mung bean and potato starch. Typically, they are soaked in warm water for 10 minutes before simmering in soups or adding to stir-fries the last few minutes or so of cooking. Blanching in boiling water for 30 seconds accomplishes the same thing, while boiling for 1 minute thoroughly cooks them for use in cold dishes. They can be found in Asian markets as well as the international aisle of many well-stocked supermarkets.

ASPARAGUS ON RYE TOASTS WITH WELSH RAREBIT SAUCE

Egg-free

MAKES 4 SERVINGS

These open-faced sandwiches are perfect for special lunches or light suppers served with a tossed salad. For an added brunch treat, serve with a shirred, or baked, egg (see Baked Eggs, page 160) on the side.

1 (8-ounce) package frozen asparagus spears, cooked according to package directions and drained
4 slices lightly toasted rye bread
½ recipe Welsh Rarebit Sauce (page 165)

Arrange equal amounts of asparagus over each slice of toast. Top with equal amounts (about 5 tablespoons each) of rarebit sauce. Serve at once.

PER SERVING

Calories 237 ▪ Protein 13g ▪ Total Fat 10g ▪ Sat. Fat 4g ▪ Cholesterol 16mg ▪ Carbohydrate 23g ▪ Dietary Fiber 3g ▪ Sodium 569mg

BAKED FOCACCIA SANDWICH WITH MARINATED VEGETABLES AND OLIVES

Vegan

MAKES 6 TO 8 SERVINGS

This gourmet sandwich couldn't be any easier to create for a special lunch or easy supper. It is superb with a cup of Chunky Tomato-Rice Soup (page 26). Giardiniera, found in the specialty aisle of most major supermarkets, is a Greek mélange of crunchy marinated vegetables, typically including cauliflower, carrots, cucumbers, red bell peppers, and celery. Because it's already quite salty, standard canned black olives work better than the tangier, more expensive Greek kalamata variety. If opting for cheese, I don't recommend using vegan soy substitutes for this recipe as they typically don't melt well.

1 (about 16-ounce) herbed or plain focaccia bread loaf, cut horizontally in half
1 (12-ounce) jar giardiniera, rinsed and drained
1 (4-ounce) can sliced black olives, drained
1 tablespoon extra-virgin olive oil
Dried oregano
4 ounces sliced provolone or mozzarella cheese (optional)

Preheat oven to 400F (205C).

Place the bottom half of the bread on a sheet of aluminum foil large enough to enclose the entire loaf. Top with the giardiniera and olives. Drizzle evenly with the oil, then sprinkle lightly with oregano. Arrange the cheese (if using) evenly over the top. Cover with the top half of the bread. Enclose the loaf in the foil and bake 20 minutes, or until heated through. Cut into wedges and serve warm.

PER SERVING (⅙ OF THE LOAF)
Calories 351 ▪ Protein 9g ▪ Total Fat 8g ▪
Sat. Fat 1g ▪ Cholesterol 0mg ▪ Carbohydrate 61g ▪
Dietary Fiber 4g ▪ Sodium 257mg

Note: If you use full-fat provolone cheese in the recipe, each serving will contain 418 calories, 13 grams of fat (4 saturated), and 13 milligrams of cholesterol.

Variation

Baked Focaccia Sandwich with Roasted Red Bell Peppers: Replace the giardiniera with 1 (12-ounce) jar roasted red bell peppers, well drained, torn into long strips, and patted dry with paper towels. Replace the canned sliced black olives with 12 to 16 pitted whole black kalamata olives. Yum!

BEAN ENCHILADAS WITH GREEN SAUCE

Lacto-ovo with egg-free option
MAKES 4 SERVINGS

This yummy sauce gets its unique taste from green taco sauce, which is made from tomatillos, or Mexican green tomatoes. It can be found in the international aisle of most well-stocked supermarkets. While you can make this recipe egg-free by using soy mayonnaise and reduce the amount of dairy by using nondairy sour cream, I don't recommend using vegan cheese substitutes here; not only are the shredded varieties limited, but I find they do not melt particularly well. I often omit the cheese altogether and the enchiladas are still quite delicious.

- 2½ cups vegetarian refried beans
- ½ cup salsa, preferably medium
- 4 (10-inch) flour tortillas
- 1¼ cups (5 ounces) already-shredded reduced-fat Mexican-blend or Monterey Jack cheese
- ⅔ cup light sour cream or nondairy sour cream
- ½ cup green taco sauce
- 2 tablespoons reduced-fat mayonnaise or soy mayonnaise
- 2 tablespoons canned diced mild green chilies, drained

Preheat oven to 425F (220C). Lightly oil a 13 × 9-inch baking dish and set aside.

In a medium bowl, stir together the beans and salsa until well combined. Place one-fourth of the refried bean mixture down the center of each tortilla. Sprinkle each with 2 tablespoons of the cheese. Roll up each tortilla, tucking in both ends; place, seam sides down, in the prepared baking dish.

In a small bowl, stir together the sour cream, taco sauce, mayonnaise, and chilies until well combined. Pour the sour cream mixture evenly over the tortillas, spreading to cover. Sprinkle with the remaining cheese. Cover tightly with foil and bake 20 to 25 minutes, or until the sauce begins to bubble. Uncover and bake 3 to 5 more minutes, or until the cheese is completely melted and the sauce is bubbly. Serve hot.

PER SERVING
Calories 395 ▪ Protein 23g ▪ Total Fat 10g ▪
Sat. Fat 3g ▪ Cholesterol 13mg ▪ Carbohydrate 56g ▪
Dietary Fiber 10g ▪ Sodium 1,314mg

BLACK BEAN BURRITOS

Vegan

MAKES 4 SERVINGS

These spicy burritos get their punch from green salsa, or salsa verde, made from tomatillos and jalapeño chilies. It can be found in the international aisle of most supermarkets. If desired, regular tomato salsa can be used instead. Should you opt to use cheese, I don't recommend using vegan soy cheese substitutes here as they typically don't melt well.

1 tablespoon canola oil

½ cup frozen chopped green bell pepper

¼ cup frozen chopped onion

1 bay leaf, crumbled into tiny pieces

1 (16-ounce) can vegetarian refried black beans

½ cup medium to hot green salsa or salsa verde

4 (10-inch) flour tortillas, warmed

½ cup already-shredded reduced-fat Monterey Jack or Mexican-blend cheese (optional)

Sour cream (or nondairy sour cream) and/or guacamole (optional)

In a medium saucepan, heat the oil over medium heat. Add the bell pepper, onion, and bay leaf; cook, stirring, until vegetables are softened but not browned and most of the liquid from the frozen vegetables has evaporated, about 4 to 5 minutes. Add the refried beans and salsa; let come to a simmer, stirring occasionally.

Spoon one-fourth of the bean mixture (about ½ cup) along the center of each tortilla. Sprinkle each with 2 tablespoons of the cheese (if using). Roll up and serve at once, with the optional toppings passed separately, if desired.

PER SERVING

Calories 280 ■ Protein 11g ■ Total Fat 7g ■ Sat. Fat 1g ■ Cholesterol 0mg ■ Carbohydrate 44g ■ Dietary Fiber 8g ■ Sodium 734mg

BLACK BEAN PATTIES

Vegan

MAKES 4 SERVINGS

Serve these versatile patties on their own topped with salsa, guacamole, or sour cream, or inside hamburger buns with a smear of Chipotle Mayonnaise (below). Chili-Lime Corn (page 140) and Mexican-Style Carrot Slaw with Currants (page 43) make colorful companions.

1 cup canned black beans, rinsed and drained, slightly mashed

1 cup canned vegetarian refried black beans

¼ cup medium salsa, well drained

1 teaspoon ground cumin

Salt and freshly ground black pepper, to taste

About 1 cup all-purpose flour

1½ tablespoons extra-virgin olive oil

Guacamole, salsa, and/or sour cream or nondairy sour cream, for topping

Chipotle Mayonnaise (below; if not using above toppings)

In a medium bowl, mix together the black beans, refried beans, salsa, cumin, salt, and pepper until well combined. Gradually mix in ¼ cup to ½ cup, or more, of the flour until the mixture forms a loose ball. With floured fingers, divide the mixture into 4 equal patties. Dredge in the remaining flour, shaking off any excess.

In a large nonstick skillet, heat the oil over

medium heat. Add the bean patties and cook until golden brown on each side, 4 to 5 minutes per side. Serve at once, with the toppings or the Chipotle Mayonnaise, if desired.

PER SERVING (WITHOUT TOPPINGS)
Calories 288 ▪ Protein 11g ▪ Total Fat 6g ▪
Sat. Fat 1g ▪ Cholesterol 0mg ▪ Carbohydrate 47g ▪
Dietary Fiber 6g ▪ Sodium 312mg

Variations

Lentil and Black Bean Patties: Substitute 1 cup canned cooked lentils (preferably the black beluga variety, available at health food stores), drained but not rinsed, unmashed, for the black beans. Proceed as otherwise directed in the recipe.

Falafel Patties: Substitute 1 cup canned chickpeas, rinsed and drained, slightly mashed, for the black beans; 1 cup prepared hummus for the refried black beans; and 2 to 3 tablespoons diced pimiento, drained, for the salsa. If desired, use chickpea flour (found in health food stores and natural food markets) in lieu of the all-purpose flour. Proceed as otherwise directed in the recipe. Serve in pita bread with Tahini-Yogurt Sauce (page 142).

CHIPOTLE MAYONNAISE

Dairy-free with vegan option
MAKES ABOUT ½ CUP

Use this fiery mayonnaise as a topping for veggie burgers, as well. Chipotle sauce is a spicy, smoky-sweet condiment made from smoked jalapeño chilies. It can be found in specialty stores and some well-stocked supermarkets. To make the recipe vegan, use soy mayonnaise; Nasoya is a reliable brand.

5 tablespoons reduced-fat regular mayonnaise
   or soy mayonnaise
2½ tablespoons chipotle sauce

In a small bowl, stir together the mayonnaise and sauce until well combined. Serve chilled or at room temperature. (Sauce can be stored, covered, in refrigerator up to 3 days.)

PER SERVING (ABOUT 1 TABLESPOON)
Calories 23 ▪ Protein 0g ▪ Total Fat 2g ▪
Sat. Fat 0g ▪ Cholesterol 3mg ▪ Carbohydrate 2g ▪
Dietary Fiber 0g ▪ Sodium 48mg

BLACK BEAN TACOS

Vegan

MAKES 6 SERVINGS

Everyone seems to love tacos, and these super-easy, super-healthy meatless renditions are no exception. If already-shredded iceberg lettuce is not available, substitute with any plain packaged lettuce and tear the leaves into smaller pieces with your fingers. Should you opt to use cheese, I don't recommend using vegan soy cheese substitutes for the tacos as they typically don't melt well.

12 taco shells

1 teaspoon extra-virgin olive oil

1 teaspoon whole cumin seeds

1 (15-ounce) can black beans, rinsed and drained

¾ cup frozen yellow corn

1 (4-ounce) can diced mild green chilies, drained

⅓ cup water, or more as necessary

3 tablespoons ketchup

1 teaspoon chili powder

½ teaspoon garlic powder

½ teaspoon onion powder

½ teaspoon sugar

¼ teaspoon ground cumin

¼ teaspoon salt, or to taste

Freshly ground black pepper, to taste

Toppings: ready-washed already-shredded iceburg lettuce; sour cream or nondairy sour cream; assorted already-shredded cheeses such as Mexican blend, taco-style, Monterey Jack, or cheddar; and taco sauce or salsa

Preheat oven to 350F (175C). Place the taco shells on a large ungreased baking sheet. Bake on the middle shelf until crisp, 3 to 5 minutes. Keep warm in a low oven until needed.

Meanwhile, in a medium deep-sided skillet, heat the oil over medium-low heat. Add the cumin seeds and cook, stirring constantly, 2 to 3 minutes, or until lightly toasted and fragrant. Add the black beans, corn, chilies, water, ketchup, chili powder, garlic powder, onion powder, sugar, ground cumin, salt, and pepper; bring to a brisk simmer over medium-high heat, stirring occasionally. Reduce the heat to low and cook, uncovered, stirring occasionally, until the mixture is thickened, about 5 minutes. If not serving immediately, cover the skillet and keep warm over very low heat up to 1 hour, stirring occasionally and adding additional water as necessary.

To assemble the tacos, place about 2 heaping tablespoons of the bean mixture in each shell. Add the desired toppings, ending with the taco sauce. Serve at once.

PER SERVING (2 TACOS WITHOUT TOPPINGS)
Calories 242 ■ Protein 9g ■ Total Fat 7g ■
Sat. Fat 1g ■ Cholesterol 0mg ■ Carbohydrate 40g ■
Dietary Fiber 9g ■ Sodium 266mg

CAJUN-STYLE VEGGIE-RICE CAKES WITH CREOLE-HONEY MUSTARD MAYONNAISE

Dairy-free with vegan option

MAKES 6 SERVINGS

These spicy rice cakes are ideal for casual and relaxed entertaining, as they can be assembled and refrigerated up to 12 hours before sautéing. Serve them inside kaiser rolls, atop toasted English muffin halves, or on their own, accompanied by Corn on the Cob with Cajun Butter (page 140) and a tossed green salad. Cajun spice or seasoning can be found in the spice aisle of most supermarkets. To make the rice cakes and the Creole-Honey Mustard Mayonnaise completely vegan, replace the regular mayonnaise with soy mayonnaise and the honey with brown sugar. Omit the egg altogether, or substitute with ¼ cup mashed soft tofu.

- **½ cup reduced-fat regular mayonnaise or soy mayonnaise**
- **1 egg (see recipe headnote, above for vegan option)**
- **1 teaspoon Cajun spice**
- **½ teaspoon garlic powder**
- **½ teaspoon onion powder**
- **½ teaspoon salt**
- **¼ teaspoon vegetarian Worcestershire sauce (see Cook's Tip, at right)**
- **2 cups cooked white or brown rice (see Cook's Tip, page 126)**
- **1 cup frozen peas and carrots, cooked according to package directions, drained and cooled**
- **2 tablespoons canned diced mild green chilies, drained**
- **2 tablespoons diced pimientos, drained**
- **About ¾ cup plain bread crumbs**
- **2 tablespoons canola oil**
- **Creole-Honey Mustard Mayonnaise (below)**

In a medium bowl, whisk together the mayonnaise, egg, Cajun spice, garlic powder, onion powder, salt, and Worcestershire sauce until well blended. Add the rice, peas and carrots, chilies, and pimiento; mix until thoroughly combined. Form mixture into 6 patties, about ¾ inch in thickness. Place the bread crumbs in a shallow bowl. Gently dredge each patty in the bread crumbs and place on a tray

(discard unused bread crumbs). Cover with plastic wrap and refrigerate 1 hour, or overnight.

In a large nonstick skillet, heat the oil over medium heat. Add the patties and cook until golden brown, 4 to 5 minutes per side. Top each cake with about 4 teaspoons of the Creole–Honey Mustard Mayonnaise. Serve at once.

PER SERVING (INCLUDES CREOLE–HONEY MUSTARD MAYONNAISE)
Calories 293 ■ Protein 6g ■ Total Fat 12g ■ Sat. Fat 2g ■ Cholesterol 46mg ■ Carbohydrate 40g ■ Dietary Fiber 2g ■ Sodium 516mg

Cook's Tip Worcestershire sauce is traditionally made with anchovies (very tiny, salty fish) to give it flavor. Vegetarian Worcestershire sauce, typically made with miso (a salty fermented soy paste that closely replicates the taste of anchovies) is available in health food stores and natural food markets. If necessary, substitute with teriyaki, soy, or tamari sauce, or omit entirely.

CREOLE-HONEY MUSTARD MAYONNAISE
Dairy-free with vegan options
MAKES ABOUT ½ CUP

Use this tasty mayonnaise as a topping for sandwiches, as well. Creole mustard can be found in specialty stores and the condiment aisle of well-stocked supermarkets. Dijon mustard can be substituted, if necessary. For a vegan recipe, use soy mayonnaise (Nasoya is a reliable brand) and replace the honey with brown sugar.

- **¼ cup reduced-fat regular mayonnaise or soy mayonnaise**

¼ cup Creole mustard

1 tablespoon honey or light brown sugar

In a small bowl, whisk together all ingredients until thoroughly blended. Cover and refrigerate up to 1 week until ready to use.

PER SERVING (ABOUT 1 TABLESPOON)
Calories 31 ▪ Protein 0g ▪ Total Fat 2g ▪
Sat. Fat 0g ▪ Cholesterol 3mg ▪ Carbohydrate 4g ▪
Dietary Fiber 0g ▪ Sodium 131mg

CALIFORNIA-STYLE WHITE TORTILLA PIZZAS

Egg-free

MAKES 4 MAIN-DISH OR 8 TO 16 APPETIZER SERVINGS

Monterey Jack cheese gives this quick and easy pizza its California flair, but any white cheese can be used. Because they don't melt well, vegan cheese substitutes are not recommended here.

2 teaspoons extra-virgin olive oil

1 teaspoon refrigerated bottled garlic

4 (10-inch) flour tortillas, preferably whole wheat

2 cups (8 ounces) already-shredded reduced-fat Monterey Jack cheese, with jalapeño chilies, if desired

¼ cup canned sliced black olives, drained

¼ cup canned diced mild green chilies, drained

Salsa, sour cream or nondairy sour cream, and/or guacamole (optional)

Preheat oven to broil, positioning rack on highest rung. Lightly oil 2 large baking sheets and set aside.

In a small skillet or saucepan, heat the oil over medium heat. Add the garlic and cook, stirring constantly, until just beginning to brown, 1 to 2 minutes. Remove from heat and set briefly aside.

Place the tortillas on prepared baking sheets (some overlapping is okay). Working with 1 baking sheet at a time, broil until just beginning to brown and puff, about 30 seconds. Turn over and repeat. Remove from oven and position rack one rung lower.

Brush one side of each tortilla evenly with the oil and garlic mixture. Sprinkle each with ¼ cup of the cheese. Scatter the olives and chilies evenly over the top, then sprinkle with the remaining cheese. Working with 1 baking sheet at a time, broil until the cheese melts, 1 to 2 minutes, taking care not to burn the tortillas. If using as appetizers, cut into desired number of wedges. Serve at once, with toppings passed separately, if using.

PER SERVING
Calories 246 ▪ Protein 17g ▪ Total Fat 10g ▪
Sat. Fat 3g ▪ Cholesterol 12mg ▪ Carbohydrate 22g ▪
Dietary Fiber 1g ▪ Sodium 588mg

CARIBBEAN BLACK BEAN RELISH ROLL-UPS

Vegan

MAKES 4 SERVINGS

Protein-packed and chock-full of vitamin C, these delicious roll-ups get their kick from jerk seasoning, available in the spice aisle of well-stocked supermarkets. If you don't have any on hand, you can improvise with a mixture of cayenne pepper, cumin, allspice, and turmeric. Should you opt to use cheese, vegan soy substitutes will work here because the dish is not heated.

1 (16-ounce) can black beans, rinsed and drained

1 cup frozen yellow corn, cooked according to package directions

½ cup (2 ounces) already-shredded reduced-fat cheddar cheese or vegan equivalent (optional)

½ cup canned diced tomatoes with jalapeño chilies, drained

¼ cup canned diced pineapple chunks, drained

1 tablespoon extra-virgin olive oil

1 tablespoon bottled lime juice

1 teaspoon Caribbean jerk seasoning, or more to taste

Salt and freshly ground black pepper, to taste

4 (10-inch) flour tortillas, preferably whole wheat

In a medium bowl, stir together the beans, corn, cheese (if using), tomatoes, pineapple, oil, lime juice, jerk seasoning, salt, and pepper until well combined. Spoon equal amounts down the center of each tortilla and roll up, tucking the ends in as you roll. Serve at once.

PER SERVING
Calories 284 ▪ Protein 11g ▪ Total Fat 7g ▪
Sat. Fat 1g ▪ Cholesterol 0mg ▪ Carbohydrate 48g ▪
Dietary Fiber 5g ▪ Sodium 287mg

CHEESE QUESADILLAS

Egg-free

MAKES 4 MAIN-COURSE OR
8 APPETIZER OR SNACK SERVINGS

The ultimate grilled cheese sandwiches for lunch or a casual supper, these quesadillas also make terrific ap-

petizers when you want to serve a little more than chips and salsa. I don't recommend vegan soy cheese substitutes here as they don't melt well.

8 (10-inch) flour tortillas

2 cups (8 ounce) already-shredded reduced-fat cheddar cheese

1 (4-ounce) can diced mild green chilies, drained

½ cup canned diced tomatoes, drained (optional)

Salsa, sour cream or nondairy sour cream, and/or guacamole (optional)

Preheat oven to 170F (75C).

Heat a 12-inch nonstick skillet over medium-high heat. Place 1 tortilla in skillet. Sprinkle with ¼ cup of the cheese and one-fourth each of chilies and tomatoes (if using). Sprinkle with another ¼ cup of the cheese. Top with another tortilla, pressing down lightly. When bottom is lightly browned, 1 to 2 minutes (not long after top tortilla is in place), turn over. Cook 1 to 2 minutes longer or until bottom is lightly browned. Transfer to an ungreased baking sheet and place in the warm oven.

Repeat with remaining ingredients, stacking the quesadillas on top of each other on the baking sheet as they are cooked. Cut each quesadilla into wedges and serve at once, accompanied with the salsa, sour cream, and/or guacamole, if desired.

PER SERVING
Calories 334 ▪ Protein 20g ▪ Total Fat 9g ▪
Sat. Fat 3g ▪ Cholesterol 12mg ▪ Carbohydrate 42g ▪
Dietary Fiber 3g ▪ Sodium 683mg

CLASSIC CHEESELESS PIZZA ALLA MARINARA

Vegan

MAKES 6 SERVINGS

This simplified version of the Neapolitan classic takes advantage of canned pizza dough and canned tomato puree to make easy work of pizza alla marinara, which is never ever prepared with cheese in Italy. When people first try the following recipe, they are invariably surprised by how sweet and flavorful the marinara sauce tastes, unmasked by gobs of gooey cheese. However, if you would really like to add cheese, sprinkle 1½ cups (6 ounces) of already-shredded part-skim mozzarella over the tomato sauce before you drizzle with the remaining oil.

1 (10¾-ounce) can tomato puree

3 tablespoons extra-virgin olive oil

2 teaspoons refrigerated bottled minced garlic

1 teaspoon dried oregano

¼ teaspoon sugar

¼ teaspoon salt, or to taste

Freshly ground black pepper, to taste

1 (10-ounce) can refrigerated pizza dough (see first Cook's Tip at right)

Preheat oven to 350F (175C). Lightly oil a baking sheet and set aside.

In a small saucepan, combine the tomato puree, 1 tablespoon of the oil, garlic, oregano, sugar, salt, and pepper; bring to simmer over medium-high heat, stirring occasionally. Remove from the heat and set aside.

Unroll the pizza dough onto prepared baking sheet and press to fit. Brush 1 tablespoon of the remaining oil evenly over the dough. Spread the tomato mixture evenly on top. Drizzle evenly with the remaining oil.

Bake in the center of the oven 15 minutes. Transfer to bottom rack and bake 5 minutes, or until the edges are nicely browned. Cut into wedges and serve warm.

PER SERVING
Calories 187 ■ Protein 4g ■ Total Fat 8g ■ Sat. Fat 1g ■ Cholesterol 0mg ■ Carbohydrate 26g ■ Dietary Fiber 2g ■ Sodium 293mg

Cook's Tips Refrigerated 10-ounce cans of pizza dough can be found alongside the canned biscuits in the refrigerated section of most supermarkets. Fresh or frozen 16-ounce bags of pizza dough, also available in most stores, can be used as well, but you will need to thaw the dough first, if necessary, and work a bit harder to stretch and fit it into the baking sheet. Also, the pizza will have a thicker crust and may take an extra 5 minutes or so to brown.

Use the marinara sauce in lieu of prepared pizza sauce in any of this book's recipes where pizza sauce is called for, thereby reducing that recipe's sodium content.

ENGLISH MUFFIN PIZZAS

Egg-free

**MAKES 4 MAIN COURSE OR
8 APPETIZER SERVINGS**

This favorite after-school snack can serve as a light supper for the whole family when accompanied by a bowl of soup and salad. I don't recommend vegan soy cheese substitutes here as they don't melt well. Moreover, English muffins typically contain milk products—see the bagel and French bread variations, below.

> 4 English muffins, preferably whole wheat, split
>   and lightly toasted
> ½ cup prepared pizza sauce (see second
>   Cook's Tip, page 70)
> 1 cup (4 ounces) already-shredded part-skim
>   mozzarella cheese
> 2 teaspoons extra-virgin olive oil
> Dried oregano, to taste

Preheat oven to broil. Spread each muffin half evenly with 1 tablespoon of the pizza sauce. Top each half with 2 tablespoons of the cheese. Drizzle each with ¼ teaspoon oil, then sprinkle lightly with oregano. Transfer to an ungreased baking sheet. Broil 6 to 8 inches from heating element until the cheese is melted, 1 to 2 minutes. Serve at once.

PER SERVING

Calories 254 ▪ Protein 13g ▪ Total Fat 9g ▪
Sat. Fat 4g ▪ Cholesterol 15mg ▪ Carbohydrate 30g ▪
Dietary Fiber 0g ▪ Sodium 611mg

Variations

Pizza Bagels: Substitute 2 large plain bagels (about 3½ ounces each), split and lightly toasted, for the English muffins. Proceed as otherwise directed in the recipe, using twice the amount of ingredients for each half (you will have 4, versus 8, halves). Makes 4 servings.

French Bread Pizzas: Preheat oven to 350F (175C). Cut 1 (about 24-inch-long) fresh French baguette (10 ounces) crosswise in half. Slice each baguette half lengthwise in half, not cutting all the way through. Open each half out carefully, leaving the "hinge" intact (this helps them keep their balance on the baking sheet). Assemble as directed for the English muffins, using twice the amount of ingredients for each half (you will have 4, versus 8, halves). Place on an ungreased baking sheet and bake in the center of the oven 10 to 15 minutes, or until the cheese is melted and the bread is lightly toasted. Serve at once. Makes 4 servings.

GARLIC BREAD

Vegan

MAKES 6 SERVINGS

You can use Italian bread here, but because it is thicker, you will need to bake it a bit longer. If you don't have garlic-flavored olive oil, use regular extra-virgin olive oil instead and replace the coarse salt with garlic salt to taste.

> 12-inch length French baguette (about 5
>   ounces), cut lengthwise in half but not all
>   the way through
> 1 tablespoon garlic-flavored olive oil
> ½ teaspoon coarse salt, or to taste

Preheat oven to 400F (205C). Open out bread and brush each side with half of the oil. Sprinkle one half with the coarse salt, then fold the other half over. Wrap tightly in foil and bake 10 to 12 minutes, or until hot through the center. Remove the foil, slice crosswise into 6 equal pieces, and serve hot.

PER SERVING
Calories 85 ▪ Protein 2g ▪ Total Fat 3g ▪
Sat. Fat 1g ▪ Cholesterol 0mg ▪ Carbohydrate 12g ▪
Dietary Fiber 1g ▪ Sodium 301mg

Variation
Pesto Bread: Substitute 2 tablespoons refrigerated prepared pesto for the garlic oil and only brush on one half of the bread. Sprinkle with about half the amount of coarse salt. Proceed as otherwise directed in the recipe.

GARLIC PITA TOASTS

Vegan
MAKES 4 TO 8 SERVINGS

I make these toasts endlessly, varying the topping according to the occasion—dried oregano to accompany spaghetti, dried thyme to complement vegetable soup, sesame seeds to flatter hummus, or just plain garlic salt when I'm in the mood for a quick piece of garlic bread and not a whole loaf. Though often pooh-poohed by purists and gourmets, garlic salt is a convenient blend of garlic, garlic oil, and coarse salt that is indispensable to a busy cook.

  4 (6-inch-diameter) pita breads, preferably
    whole wheat, fresh or slightly stale
  2 teaspoons extra-virgin olive oil

About ½ teaspoon garlic salt, or to taste
Dried oregano, dried thyme, sesame seeds, or
  poppy seeds, to taste (optional)

Preheat oven to 400F (205C). Place pita breads on an ungreased light-colored baking sheet. Brush the top of each pita evenly with ½ teaspoon of the oil. Sprinkle lightly with garlic salt and oregano (if using). Bake 5 to 7 minutes on the middle rack, or until lightly toasted. Cut crosswise in half, if desired, and serve warm.

PER SERVING (PER BREAD)
Calories 191 ▪ Protein 6g ▪ Total Fat 4g ▪
Sat. Fat 1g ▪ Cholesterol 0mg ▪ Carbohydrate 35g ▪
Dietary Fiber 5g ▪ Sodium 597mg

Variation
Parmesan-Garlic Pita Toasts: Omit optional toppings except dried oregano, if desired. After brushing with the oil and sprinkling lightly with garlic salt, top each pita with 2 tablespoons already-shredded Parmesan cheese. Sprinkle lightly with oregano, if using. Bake 5 minutes, or until cheese is melted. Cut crosswise in half and serve at once.

GRILLED PORTOBELLO
MUSHROOM SANDWICHES
WITH PAPRIKA AÏOLI

Dairy-free with vegan option
MAKES 4 SANDWICHES

Thick and juicy grilled portobello mushrooms are fast becoming the healthy alternative to hamburgers among vegetarians and meat-eaters alike, and with good reason—they're simply delicious. For a vegan sandwich, prepare the aïoli, below, with soy mayonnaise.

4 large (about 2 ounces each) packaged
   portobello mushroom caps
2 teaspoons extra-virgin olive oil
Salt and freshly ground black pepper, to taste
4 large (about 2 ounces each) crusty sandwich
   rolls, preferably whole wheat
Paprika Aïoli (below)
Ready-washed romaine lettuce or spinach
   leaves

Heat a nonstick grill pan over medium-high heat. Brush each mushroom on the rounded underside and rim with ½ teaspoon of the oil; season with salt and pepper to taste. Place the mushrooms, gill sides down, in pan and grill 3 minutes. Turn over and grill 3 to 4 more minutes, rotating each mushroom a half turn after 2 minutes, or until bottoms are nicely browned. Place a mushroom, gill sides up, on the bottom half of each roll. Fill each cap with about 2 tablespoons of the aïoli, then top with the romaine. Close each roll and serve at once.

PER SERVING (INCLUDES PAPRIKA AÏOLI)
Calories 236 ▪ Protein 7g ▪ Total Fat 10g ▪
Sat. Fat 2g ▪ Cholesterol 9mg ▪ Carbohydrate 34g ▪
Dietary Fiber 5g ▪ Sodium 432mg

Variation

Grilled Portobello Mushroom Sandwiches with Pesto Mayonnaise: Omit the Paprika Aïoli and substitute with a combination of 6 tablespoons reduced-fat mayonnaise and 2 tablespoons refrigerated prepared pesto.

PAPRIKA AÏOLI

Dairy-free with vegan option
MAKES ABOUT ½ CUP

Use this colorful sauce as a topping for veggie burgers, poached eggs, and steamed vegetables. For a vegan recipe, use soy mayonnaise in lieu of the regular variety.

7 tablespoons reduced-fat regular mayonnaise
   or soy mayonnaise
½ tablespoon lemon juice, preferably prepared
   from frozen concentrate
½ teaspoon garlic powder
½ teaspoon Spanish paprika
Pinch of cayenne pepper (optional)
Salt and freshly ground black pepper, to taste

Place the mayonnaise, lemon juice, garlic powder, paprika, cayenne (if using), salt, and black pepper in a small bowl; whisk until smooth and well combined. Let stand 15 minutes to allow the flavors to blend. Alternatively, cover and refrigerate up to 2 days before using.

PER SERVING (ABOUT 1 TABLESPOON)
Calories 32 ▪ Protein 0g ▪ Total Fat 3g ▪
Sat. Fat 0g ▪ Cholesterol 5mg ▪ Carbohydrate 2g ▪
Dietary Fiber 0g ▪ Sodium 65mg

MEXICAN-STYLE PIZZA

Egg-free

MAKES 6 MAIN-DISH OR

8 TO 12 APPETIZER SERVINGS

Simplicity rules in this virtually assembled pizza. I don't recommend vegan soy cheese here; unfortunately, the only substitutes that melt well contain casein, which is a milk product. For a dairy-free variation, simply omit the cheese; the pizza will still be quite tasty.

> **1 (16-ounce) can vegetarian refried beans**
> **1 (14-ounce) Boboli or similar prebaked pizza shell**
> **1 cup mild or medium salsa, drained well**
> **1 to 1½ cups (4 to 6 ounces) already-shredded reduced-fat cheddar or Mexican-blend cheese**
> **½ tablespoon extra-virgin olive oil**
> **Dried oregano, to taste**
> **Cumin seeds, to taste (optional)**
> **Sour cream or nondairy sour cream (optional)**

Preheat oven to 350F (175C).

Spread the beans evenly on the Boboli shell. Top with the salsa, then sprinkle with the cheese. Drizzle evenly with the oil, then sprinkle lightly with oregano and the cumin seeds (if using). Bake in the center of the oven about 15 minutes, or until the cheese is melted and the shell is lightly browned. Cut into wedges and serve warm, with the sour cream passed separately, if desired.

PER SERVING

Calories 324 ▪ Protein 15g ▪ Total Fat 6g ▪
Sat. Fat 2g ▪ Cholesterol 4mg ▪ Carbohydrate 51g ▪
Dietary Fiber 5g ▪ Sodium 1,030mg

PESTO PIZZA WITH FRESH MOZZARELLA AND CHERRY TOMATOES

Egg-free

MAKES 6 MAIN-DISH OR

8 TO 12 APPETIZER SERVINGS

This gourmet-style pizza is as eye-appealing as it is delicious. Fresh mozzarella is located in the refrigerated section of most well-stocked supermarkets. Six ounces (1½ cups) of already-shredded mozzarella cheese can be substituted, if desired.

> **5 tablespoons refrigerated prepared pesto**
> **1 (14-ounce) Boboli or similar prebaked pizza shell**
> **6 ounces (about 20 pieces) water-packed small fresh mozzarella cheese balls, drained well**
> **1 cup small cherry or grape tomatoes**

Preheat oven to 350F (175C).

Spread the pesto evenly over the pizza shell, reserving about ½ tablespoon. Top evenly with the cheese and tomatoes. Prick each tomato with the prongs of a fork. Dab the cheese and tomatoes evenly with the remaining pesto. Bake in the center of the oven about 15 minutes, or until the cheese is melted and the shell is lightly browned. Cut into wedges and serve warm.

PER SERVING

Calories 352 ▪ Protein 14g ▪ Total Fat 16g ▪
Sat. Fat 7g ▪ Cholesterol 29mg ▪ Carbohydrate 38g ▪
Dietary Fiber 1g ▪ Sodium 688mg

PINEAPPLE PIZZA

Egg-free

**MAKES 6 MAIN-DISH OR
8 TO 12 APPETIZER SERVINGS**

If you've never tried it, the combination of warm pineapple and melted mozzarella is delicious. Serve with a tossed green salad to round out a delightful meal. I don't recommend vegan soy cheese here; the only substitutes that melt well contain casein, which is a milk product.

- ¾ cup pizza sauce (see second Cook's Tip, page 70)
- 1 (14-ounce) Boboli or similar prebaked pizza shell
- 1 (16-ounce) can unsweetened crushed pineapple, well drained
- 1 to 1½ cups (4 to 6 ounces) already-shredded part-skim mozzarella cheese
- ½ tablespoon extra-virgin olive oil
- Dried oregano (optional)

Preheat oven to 350F (175C).

Spread the pizza sauce evenly over the pizza shell. Top with the pineapple, then sprinkle with the cheese. Drizzle evenly with the oil, then sprinkle lightly with oregano (if using). Bake in the center of the oven about 15 minutes, or until the cheese is melted and the shell is lightly browned. Cut into wedges and serve warm.

PER SERVING
Calories 299 ▪ Protein 12g ▪ Total Fat 8g ▪
Sat. Fat 3g ▪ Cholesterol 10mg ▪ Carbohydrate 45g ▪
Dietary Fiber 1g ▪ Sodium 779mg

Variation

Traditional Cheese Pizza: Omit the pineapple and use 1½ to 2 cups (6 to 8 ounces) cheese. Prepare and bake as otherwise directed.

PITA STUFFED WITH CHICKPEAS IN TAHINI SAUCE

Vegan

MAKES 4 SERVINGS

I make these stuffed pocket bread sandwiches often for their healthfulness, convenience, and good taste. Loaded with protein and calcium, tahini is an oily, nut-like paste made entirely from ground sesame seeds. It can be found in Middle Eastern markets and many well-stocked supermarkets. Serve the chickpeas and sauce in lettuce cups or roll up in large romaine or spinach leaves in lieu of the pita bread, if desired.

- 1 (19-ounce) can chickpeas, rinsed and drained
- 2 tablespoons sesame tahini
- 1½ to 2 tablespoons lemon juice, preferably prepared from frozen concentrate
- ½ teaspoon toasted (dark) sesame oil
- ¼ teaspoon garlic salt, or to taste
- Freshly ground black pepper, to taste
- Sweet paprika, to taste (optional)
- 4 (6-inch-diameter) pita breads, preferably whole wheat
- Romaine or other lettuce leaves

In a medium bowl, combine the chickpeas, tahini, lemon juice, oil, garlic salt, pepper, and paprika (if using); toss until well combined. Let stand 10 to 15 minutes to allow the flavors to blend; toss again.

(At this point, the mixture can be covered and re-frigerated up to 2 days before serving.) Stuff each pita bread with equal amounts of the chickpea mixture and lettuce leaves. Serve immediately.

PER SERVING

Calories 356 ▪ Protein 15g ▪ Total Fat 8g ▪
Sat. Fat 1g ▪ Cholesterol 0mg ▪ Carbohydrate 60g ▪
Dietary Fiber 8g ▪ Sodium 475mg

Cook's Tip Lemon juice from frozen concentrate, available in the frozen food section of most major supermarkets, has a much fresher taste than the concentrated lemon juice found in bottles or lemon-shaped plastic containers. Thawed (you do not need to dilute it), it stays fresh for up to 8 weeks in the refrigerator.

POLENTA PIZZA WITH ROASTED RED PEPPERS

Egg-free

MAKES 6 MAIN-DISH OR 8 TO 12 APPETIZER SERVINGS

The use of polenta instead of dough for the crust renders this scrumptious pizza ideal for those with wheat allergies. The quick-cooking variety can be found in most well-stocked supermarkets. If unavailable, use coarse-ground yellow cornmeal or corn grits and cook according to the package directions until tender. I don't recommend vegan soy cheese here; the only substitutes that melt well contain casein, which is a milk product.

1 (14-ounce) can (1¾ cups) low-sodium
   vegetable broth
1¼ cups water

1 cup quick-cooking polenta
1½ tablespoons extra-virgin olive oil
½ teaspoon garlic powder
Salt and freshly ground black pepper, to taste
2 (7.25-ounce) jars roasted red bell peppers,
   drained well
¾ cup prepared pizza sauce (see second
   Cook's Tip, page 70)
½ cup frozen chopped onion, cooked
   according to package directions and
   drained well
1 cup (4 ounces) already-shredded part-skim
   mozzarella cheese
¼ cup (1 ounce) already-shredded Parmesan
   cheese
Dried oregano leaves, to taste

Preheat oven to broil. Lightly oil a 12-inch pizza pan and set aside. In a medium stockpot, bring the broth, water, polenta, 2 teaspoons of the oil, garlic powder, salt, and pepper to a boil over high heat. Immediately reduce the heat to medium and cook, stirring often with a long-handled spoon (polenta will sputter), 5 minutes. Immediately spoon the polenta into the prepared pan, pressing down with the back of a large spoon to form a smooth surface. Let stand about 15 minutes to become firm. (At this point, the crust can be held up to 1 hour at room temperature before continuing with the recipe.)

Meanwhile, arrange the roasted peppers on a couple layers of paper towels. Using your fingers, tear them into thin strips. Pat the tops with paper towels to further dry. Set briefly aside.

Brush the top of the polenta evenly with 1 teaspoon of the remaining oil. Broil 4 to 6 inches from the heating element until lightly browned, 3 to 5 minutes. Remove from the oven and spread evenly with the pizza sauce. Scatter evenly with the onion, then top with the roasted peppers. Sprinkle evenly with the mozzarella cheese, then the Parmesan cheese. Sprinkle with oregano, then drizzle with the remaining oil. Return to the oven and broil until the cheese is melted, 1 to 2 minutes, watching carefully. Cut into wedges and serve at once.

PER SERVING

Calories 258 ▪ Protein 14g ▪ Total Fat 10g ▪
Sat. Fat 4g ▪ Cholesterol 14mg ▪ Carbohydrate 31g ▪
Dietary Fiber 6g ▪ Sodium 529mg

PROVENÇAL-STYLE GOAT CHEESE AND OLIVE FOCACCIA

Egg-free
MAKES 6 SERVINGS

This is a true flatbread focaccia; use the recipe as a blueprint and select your own favorite toppings. If you can't locate the crumbled Provençal-herbed goat cheese (typically a blend of thyme, basil, and sweet red pepper sprinkled over goat cheese) sprinkle the plain variety lightly with the suggested herbs. Crumbled feta can replace the goat cheese, if desired.

- **1 (10-ounce) can refrigerated pizza dough (see first Cook's Tip, page 70)**
- **1 tablespoon garlic-flavored olive oil**
- **1 (2¼-ounce) can sliced black olives, drained**
- **½ cup (2 ounces) already-crumbled goat cheese, preferably the Provençal-herbed variety**
- **Dried thyme, basil, and/or oregano (if not using herbed goat cheese)**

Preheat oven to 350F (175C). Lightly oil a baking sheet and set aside.

Unroll the pizza dough onto prepared baking sheet and press to fit. Brush the oil evenly over the dough. Arrange the olives evenly over the dough, then top evenly with the goat cheese. Sprinkle lightly with the herbs, if necessary. Bake in the center of the oven 15 minutes. Transfer to the bottom rack and bake 5 minutes, or until nicely browned. Cut into wedges and serve warm or at room temperature.

PER SERVING

Calories 178 ▪ Protein 6g ▪ Total Fat 8g ▪
Sat. Fat 3g ▪ Cholesterol 10mg ▪ Carbohydrate 21g ▪
Dietary Fiber 1g ▪ Sodium 127mg

REFRIED BEAN TOSTADAS

Egg-free
MAKES 4 SERVINGS

Tostadas make terrific snacks or appetizers served on their own, but become the stuff of a satisfying lunch or light supper when accompanied by soup and salad. While you do need 2 tablespoons of oil for the recipe, happily, about half of it is absorbed in the paper towels and left behind in the skillet after frying. I don't recommend using vegan cheese substitutes here, because they don't melt well. Instead, I often omit the cheese altogether and find that with the optional salsa or guacamole, these tostadas are more than satisfying.

2 tablespoons canola oil

4 (6-inch) corn tortillas

Salt, preferably the coarse variety, to taste
    (optional)

1 (15-ounce) can vegetarian refried beans

1 cup (4 ounces) already-shredded reduced-fat
    cheddar or Monterey Jack cheese

Sliced pickled jalapeño chilies (optional)

Salsa, sour cream or nondairy sour cream,
    and/or guacamole (optional)

Preheat oven to 225F (105C).

Line a baking sheet with several layers of paper towels and set aside. In a small 7- or 8-inch skillet, heat the oil over medium-high heat. Working with 1 tortilla at a time, fry tortillas 20 to 30 seconds on each side or until light golden. Transfer tortillas to prepared baking sheet and blot between paper towels. Remove paper towels and sprinkle tortillas lightly with salt (if using).

Meanwhile, in a small saucepan, heat the beans over medium heat, stirring occasionally. Spread equal amounts of beans over the tortillas. Sprinkle each with ¼ cup of the cheese, then top with jalapeño chilies (if using). Bake about 5 minutes, or until the cheese is melted. Serve at once, with the optional toppings passed separately, if desired.

PER SERVING

Calories 248 ▪ Protein 15g ▪ Total Fat 7g ▪
Sat. Fat 2g ▪ Cholesterol 6mg ▪ Carbohydrate 32g ▪
Dietary Fiber 7g ▪ Sodium 665mg

RICE AND BEAN EMPANADAS

Vegan
MAKES 4 SERVINGS

Refrigerated piecrusts allow even novice cooks to put these savory Mexican turnovers together with little effort. If you happen to have a cup of rice left over from Chinese takeout, you can really beat the clock. Should you opt to use cheese, I don't recommend using vegan soy cheese substitutes here as they typically don't melt well.

1 cup cooked white or brown rice (see Cook's
    Tip, page 126)

½ cup canned vegetarian refried beans

¼ cup salsa, well drained

¼ cup already-shredded reduced-fat cheddar
    cheese (optional)

½ (15-ounce) package (1 crust) refrigerated
    lard-free piecrusts (see Cook's Tip
    page 79)

Preheat oven to 400F (205C).

In a medium bowl, combine the rice, beans,

salsa, and cheese (if using). Unfold the piecrust; using your fingers or a table knife, divide into fourths, using the folds as a guide. Favoring one side, spoon one-fourth of the rice mixture on each quarter of the piecrust. Fold the crust over the filling. Seal and crimp the edges. Cut 2 small slits in the top of each pastry and transfer to an ungreased baking sheet. Bake about 20 minutes, or until golden brown. Serve warm.

PER SERVING

Calories 340 ▪ Protein 6g ▪ Total Fat 16g ▪ Sat. Fat 5g ▪ Cholesterol 0mg ▪ Carbohydrate 43g ▪ Dietary Fiber 2g ▪ Sodium 483mg

Cook's Tip When purchasing refrigerated or frozen piecrusts, check the label carefully to make sure that the product has been made with vegetable shortening, not lard, which is fat rendered from hogs. While not as convenient as the ready-to-use refrigerated variety, a frozen 9-inch deep-dish piecrust, thawed according to package directions, can be used in this recipe.

SMOKED PROVOLONE AND ROASTED RED PEPPER PANINI

Egg-free
MAKES 4 SANDWICHES

These scrumptious sandwiches get their characteristic grill marks not from an expensive panini press, but from a standard nonstick grill pan topped with a smaller heavy-bottomed skillet for weight. Use this recipe as a model for creating your own signature panini. I don't recommend using vegan soy cheese substitutes for these panini as they typically don't melt well.

> 2 (7.25-ounce) jars roasted red bell peppers, well drained
> 8 large slices presliced Italian, sourdough, or rustic whole grain bread (about 1¼ ounces each)
> Vegetable cooking spray, preferably olive oil variety
> 4 ounces sliced smoked or regular provolone cheese
> 2 teaspoons extra-virgin olive oil
> Dried oregano, to taste
> Freshly ground black pepper, to taste
> Garlic salt, to taste

Arrange the roasted peppers on a couple layers of paper towels. Using your fingers, tear them into 4 equal servings. Pat the tops with paper towels to further dry. Set briefly aside.

Lightly spray one side of each bread slice with vegetable spray. Assemble each sandwich as follows: 1 slice prepared bread, unsprayed side up, one-fourth of the cheese, one-fourth of the reserved roasted peppers, ½ teaspoon of the oil (brushed over peppers), a sprinkle of oregano, a sprinkle of black pepper, and 1 slice prepared bread, sprayed side up. Repeat to make 4 sandwiches. Sprinkle the top of each sandwich lightly with the garlic salt.

Heat a large nonstick grill pan over medium heat. Have ready a slightly smaller heavy-bottomed skillet, preferably cast iron. Place the sandwiches, garlic-salted side down, in the pan. Place the bottom of the smaller skillet on top of the sandwiches and press down lightly for 1 minute. Uncover and cook until golden, another minute or so. Sprinkle lightly with the garlic salt and turn over; cover with the smaller skillet and press down lightly for 1 minute. Uncover and continue cooking until golden, another minute or so. Serve immediately.

Variation

Smoked Provolone and Roasted Red Pepper Subs or Grinders: Preheat oven to 350F (175C). Fill 4 (6-inch-long) sub or hoagie rolls, sliced horizontally in half, with ingredients in the order listed above, omitting the vegetable spray and adding a sprinkling of garlic salt along with the oregano, if desired. Wrap each sandwich tightly in aluminum foil. Place on a baking sheet and bake 15 to 20 minutes, or until the cheese is melted and all is heated through. Serve at once.

SPINACH AND CHEESE STROMBOLI

Egg-free

MAKES 6 SERVINGS

You simply can't beat the convenience of canned pizza dough, found alongside the canned biscuits in the refrigerated section of most supermarkets. Use this recipe as a model to create your own favorite stromboli. I don't recommend using vegan mozzarella cheese substitutes here as they typically don't melt well.

6 large spinach leaves, tough stems removed

1 (10-ounce) can refrigerated pizza dough

1 tablespoon Dijon mustard

Dried oregano, to taste

8 ounces (2 cups) already-shredded part-skim mozzarella cheese

Preheat oven to 400F (205C). Lightly oil a large baking sheet and set aside.

Fill a kettle or pot with about 6 cups water and bring to a boil. Place the spinach in a colander; slowly pour boiling water over the spinach. Drain well, pressing down with the back of a large wooden spoon to extract most of the liquids. Place the spinach between paper towels to blot completely dry.

Unroll the pizza dough on the prepared baking sheet and pat into an 11 × 13 inch rectangle. Spread the mustard over the dough to within ½ inch of the edges. Arrange the spinach leaves down the center of the dough, leaving a 3-inch border on either short edge and a ½-inch border at either long edge. Sprinkle the spinach lightly and evenly with oregano, then with half of the cheese. Sprinkle again with oregano, followed with the remaining cheese. Fold one short side of dough, then the other, over the filling, pressing to seal, then fold in top and bottom, pressing to seal.

Bake in the center of the oven 7 to 10 minutes, or until the top is lightly browned. Remove from the oven and turn over with a wide spatula. Cut 2 small vents in the top and bake 7 to 10 minutes, or until the top is lightly browned. Let stand 15 minutes before slicing. Serve warm.

Cook's Tip Fresh pizza dough, typically sold in 16-ounce balls in most supermarkets, is not recommended for use in this particular recipe. The 10-ounce cans of refrigerated pizza dough, because they roll out into an even thickness, are much easier to shape into stromboli.

SPINACH, TOMATO, AND MOZZARELLA FRENCH BREAD MELTS WITH PESTO

Lacto-ovo with egg-free option
MAKES 4 SERVINGS

I like to use vine-ripened cocktail cherry tomatoes here; piercing them ensures that they won't burst when you bite into these scrumptious sandwiches. Any lettuce can replace the spinach, if desired. For an egg-free sandwich, use soy mayonnaise in lieu of the regular variety. I don't recommend using vegan mozzarella cheese substitutes here as they typically don't melt well.

1 (about 24-inch-long) fresh French baguette
    (10 ounces), cut crosswise into quarters
6 tablespoons nonfat or reduced-fat regular
    mayonnaise or soy mayonnaise
2 tablespoons refrigerated prepared pesto
½ teaspoon lemon pepper seasoning
½ teaspoon dried oregano
2 cups ready-washed baby spinach leaves
About 16 cocktail-size cherry tomatoes,
    preferably vine-ripened, or grape tomatoes
4 (1-ounce) slices part-skim mozzarella cheese

Preheat broiler. Slice each baguette quarter lengthwise in half (you will have 4 bottom halves and 4 top halves.)

In a small bowl, combine the mayonnaise, pesto, lemon pepper seasoning, and oregano. Spread 1 tablespoon of the mayonnaise mixture evenly over each piece of bread. Divide the spinach evenly among the bottom pieces; top each

with about 4 tomatoes. Pierce each tomato twice with the tines of a fork. Top with 1 cheese slice. Transfer the bottom halves to an ungreased baking sheet. Broil 6 to 8 inches from the heating element until the cheese is melted, 1 to 2 minutes. Remove from oven and turn off the broiler.

Cover bottom halves with top halves of rolls, pressing the tops down gently to release some of the tomatoes' juice. Return to bottom rack of oven and shut the oven door. Let sit in the oven 1 minute, or until the tops are hot. Remove from oven and serve at once.

PER SERVING
Calories 348 ■ Protein 16g ■ Total Fat 11g ■
Sat. Fat 5g ■ Cholesterol 17mg ■ Carbohydrate 47g ■
Dietary Fiber 3g ■ Sodium 969mg

TEX-MEX BAKED POTATOES WITH CHILI BEANS

Vegan

MAKES 4 SERVINGS

Despite the hour or so of cooking, baked potatoes are effortless, the ultimate side dish for multitasking cooks in a pinch. Instead of the usual slather of butter, the following recipe uses the heartier—and healthier—topping of chili beans enlivened with salsa to turn them into an easy weekend lunch or casual weeknight supper. Chili beans in mild sauce can be found near the baked beans in most supermarkets. Should you opt to use cheese, I don't recommend using vegan substitutes for this recipe as they typically don't melt well.

4 (8-ounce) russet potatoes, washed and
    scrubbed
1 (16-ounce) can chili beans in mild sauce
6 tablespoons mild or medium salsa
4 tablespoons canned diced mild green chilies
½ teaspoon ground cumin
Already-shredded reduced-fat cheddar cheese
    and/or light sour cream or nondairy sour
    cream, for topping (optional)

Preheat oven to 450F (230C). Prick the potatoes with a fork and bake on the center rack for 1 hour, or until tender.

Meanwhile, combine the chili beans, salsa, green chilies, and cumin in a small saucepan. Bring to a simmer over medium heat, stirring occasionally.

To serve, split the potatoes in half and transfer to 4 plates. Spoon equal amounts of the chili mixture evenly over each potato. Top with the cheese and/or sour cream, if desired. Serve at once.

Variation

Baked Potatoes with Broccoli and Cheese Sauce: Bake the potatoes as directed above. Meanwhile, prepare the Broccoli with Cheese Sauce (page 135), keeping the broccoli spears and the cheese sauce separate. Split the baked potatoes in half and top each half with equal portions of the broccoli spears. Top with equal amounts of the cheese sauce and serve at once.

THAI VEGETABLE STIR-FRY WRAP WITH HOT PEANUT SAUCE

Vegan

MAKES 4 SERVINGS

This hot and spicy wrap is a favorite of mine; you can tone the heat down by adjusting the amount of chili paste in the Hot Peanut Sauce. Lavosh is a round, thin bread that comes in both soft and crisp versions; you can find it in Middle Eastern markets as well as many well-stocked supermarkets. Four 10-inch flour tortillas can be used instead, if desired.

1 tablespoon toasted (dark) sesame oil
1 cup frozen mixed bell pepper strips
¼ cup frozen chopped onion
2 teaspoons curry powder
1 teaspoon ground ginger
1 teaspoon refrigerated bottled minced garlic
1 (16-ounce) bag coleslaw mix
2 tablespoons reduced-sodium soy sauce

2 tablespoons bottled lime juice

Salt and freshly ground black pepper, to taste

1 soft lavosh, slightly warmed, if desired

Hot Peanut Sauce (below)

In a large nonstick skillet, heat the oil over medium heat. Add the bell pepper and onion and cook, stirring, until softened and thawed, about 3 minutes. Add the curry powder, ginger, and garlic and cook, stirring, 2 minutes. Add the coleslaw mix and increase the heat to medium-high; cook, stirring and tossing constantly, until the cabbage is wilted and tender, 4 to 5 minutes. Stir in the soy sauce and lime juice. Remove from the heat and season with salt and pepper.

Unfold the lavosh. Spoon the vegetable mixture evenly along the lower quarter of bread. Pour the peanut sauce evenly over the vegetable mixture. Fold in the bottom and top portions of the bread. Roll up from one side to completely enclose the filling. Cut into 4 equal portions and serve at once.

PER SERVING (INCLUDES PEANUT SAUCE)
Calories 298 ▪ Protein 9g ▪ Total Fat 13g ▪
Sat. Fat 2g ▪ Cholesterol 0mg ▪ Carbohydrate 41g ▪
Dietary Fiber 6g ▪ Sodium 851mg

3 tablespoons creamy peanut butter

2 tablespoons reduced-sodium soy sauce

2 tablespoons light brown sugar

1 tablespoon bottled lime juice

1 tablespoon water

2 teaspoons Chinese chili paste, or to taste

In a small saucepan, combine all ingredients. Bring to a gentle simmer over medium-low heat, stirring occasionally. Remove from heat and let cool to room temperature.

PER SERVING (ABOUT 2 TABLESPOONS)
Calories 103 ▪ Protein 4g ▪ Total Fat 6g ▪
Sat. Fat 1g ▪ Cholesterol 0mg ▪ Carbohydrate 10g ▪
Dietary Fiber 1g ▪ Sodium 361mg

HOT PEANUT SAUCE

Vegan
MAKES ABOUT ½ CUP

This sauce can be used to flavor countless vegetables, stir-fries, and rice or noodle dishes. If you would prefer a moderately hot sauce, use half the amount of Chinese chili paste.

THREE-CHEESE CALZONES

Egg-free

MAKES 4 SERVINGS

These tasty pizza turnovers are a family favorite; feel free to experiment with the cheeses and other fillings of your choice. Vegan soy cheese substitutes are not recommended for the mozzarella and Parmesan because they don't melt well. If you'd like, you can substitute ½ cup crumbled firm tofu for the ricotta to reduce the amount of dairy in the recipe.

1 (10-ounce) can refrigerated pizza dough

1 (15-ounce) can pizza sauce

1 cup (4 ounces) already-shredded part-skim mozzarella cheese

½ cup (4 ounces) nonfat ricotta cheese

¼ cup (1 ounce) already-shredded Parmesan cheese

Preheat oven to 375F (190C). Lightly grease a large baking sheet.

Unroll the pizza dough onto a lightly floured work surface and divide into 4 equal portions. Press out each portion into a 6- or 7-inch circle. Working with one circle at a time, transfer dough to prepared baking sheet. Spread 2 tablespoons of the pizza sauce over each circle to within ½ inch of the edge. Favoring one side of each circle, top each with ¼ cup of the mozzarella cheese, 2 tablespoons of the ricotta cheese, and 1 tablespoon of the Parmesan cheese. Fold over other side, pressing edges tightly to seal.

Bake 12 to 15 minutes, or until the tops are lightly browned. Remove the baking sheet from the oven and, using a wide spatula, turn the calzones over. Cut 4 slits in the dough on top of each. Return to oven and bake 10 to 12 minutes, or until tops are lightly browned.

Meanwhile, place the remaining pizza sauce in a small saucepan and heat over medium-low heat, stirring occasionally. Place the calzones on 4 plates and top with equal portions of sauce. Alternatively, pass sauce separately for dipping.

PER SERVING

Calories 360 ■ Protein 21g ■ Total Fat 12g ■ Sat. Fat 5g ■ Cholesterol 25mg ■ Carbohydrate 43g ■ Dietary Fiber 0g ■ Sodium 1,007mg

Cook's Tip Fresh pizza dough, available in 16-ounce balls in most supermarkets, is not recommended here as it is harder to press out and shape. Also, you will either need to use less of it or make the calzones larger.

VEGGIE-HUMMUS WRAPS

Vegan

MAKES 4 MAIN-DISH OR
8 TO 12 APPETIZER SERVINGS

With no cooking required, these colorful, make-ahead wraps are ideal for relaxed summer outdoor entertaining when it's too hot to heat up the grill. If hummus with roasted red bell peppers is available, omit the pimiento and save even more time.

1 (8-ounce) container hummus

1 (4-ounce) jar chopped pimiento, drained

4 (10-inch) flour tortillas

4 cups ready-washed baby spinach leaves

2 cups already-shredded carrots

In a small bowl, mix together the hummus and pimiento until thoroughly combined. Spread about 4 tablespoons, or one-fourth, of the hummus mixture over each tortilla, leaving a ¾-inch border all around. Layer each tortilla with 1 cup of the spinach, then ½ cup of the carrots, ending about 1½ inches from the top of each tortilla (this makes rolling easier).

Tightly roll up each tortilla from the edge nearest you, tucking in the sides as you roll. Cover tightly with plastic wrap and refrigerate a minimum of 30 minutes, or up to 24 hours. To serve, cut each wrap in half crosswise and serve on individual plates. Alternatively, cut each wrap in half crosswise, then cut each half in thirds, alternating diagonal cuts with straight cuts. Arrange on a serving platter and serve.

PER SERVING (2 HALVES)

Calories 253 ■ Protein 8g ■ Total Fat 8g ■ Sat. Fat 1g ■ Cholesterol 0mg ■ Carbohydrate 40g ■ Dietary Fiber 7g ■ Sodium 373mg

Variation

Veggie-Guacamole Wraps: Substitute 1 (8-ounce) container prepared guacamole for the hummus, and 1 (4-ounce) can sliced black olives, drained, for the pimiento. Proceed as otherwise directed in the recipe.

Oodles of Noodles

Pasta is a busy cook's saving grace. Not only is it quick and easy to prepare, but the whole world seems to love it. Indeed, this chapter could almost have been entitled "Calling All Pasta Lovers!" But it is devoted exclusively to those slippery, squiggly noodles you can either slurp from a fork (linguine, lo mein), coat with thick sauces (fusilli, penne), nestle tiny gems of vegetables inside (shells, wagon wheels), or bake in the oven (lasagna, ziti). Couscous, gnocchi, and orzo, wonderful pastas in their own right that don't quite fit the "noodle" bill, are amply represented in other chapters. On the other hand, pasta "salads," several of which consist of noodles, can be found in "Simply Salads." While most of the following recipes are primarily main dishes, with the exceptions of Fresh Leaf Spinach Lasagna and Cheese-Stuffed Shells, all can be served as side dishes or pasta courses, as well. A few, such as Buttered Noodles with Capers and Lemon, though traditional sides, can easily be treated as the main event. One final note before you dig into this chapter: Please don't worry about overdosing on carbs; most of the main-dish servings are based on a 2- to 2½-ounce portion of pasta, which contains a very reasonable amount of carbohydrates for a healthy adult of average weight. Besides, many supermarkets now regularly stock whole wheat pastas that can be used interchangeably with the refined white varieties in most of the recipes. Although these "brown" pastas generally take a little bit longer to cook, they contain more fiber and are higher in good-for-you complex carbohydrates.

So relax and *mangia!*

BOW TIE PASTA WITH SUN-DRIED TOMATOES AND OLIVES

Vegan

**MAKES 5 TO 6 MAIN-DISH OR
8 TO 10 SIDE-DISH OR PASTA-COURSE SERVINGS**

This is an ideal pasta dish to bring to a picnic or potluck as it holds up well at room temperature. Fusilli or penne can replace the bow tie pasta, if desired. If you don't have garlic-flavored oil, add ¼ teaspoon garlic powder to the broth mixture.

1 cup low-sodium vegetable broth

½ cup pitted black olives, preferably kalamata

2 tablespoons garlic-flavored olive oil

½ teaspoon coarse salt, or to taste

Freshly ground black pepper, to taste

12 ounces bow tie (farfalle) pasta

½ cup frozen pearl onions

3 tablespoons sun-dried tomato bits

2 tablespoons pine nuts, toasted if desired
    (see Cook's Tip, page 71) (optional)

In a small bowl, mix together the broth, olives, oil, salt, and pepper. Set aside.

Meanwhile, bring a large pot of salted water to a boil over high heat. Add the pasta and cook according to package directions until al dente, about 10 minutes, adding the pearl onions and tomato bits the last 3 minutes or so of cooking. Drain well. Return to the stockpot and add the reserved broth mixture. Cook over medium-low heat, stirring and tossing often, until the pasta has absorbed most of the liquids, 3 to 5 minutes. Serve warm or at room temperature, garnished with the pine nuts, if desired.

PER SERVING
Calories 336 ▪ Protein 12g ▪ Total Fat 8g ▪
Sat. Fat 1g ▪ Cholesterol 0mg ▪ Carbohydrate 55g ▪
Dietary Fiber 3g ▪ Sodium 458mg

WHOLE WHEAT FETTUCCINE WITH GOAT CHEESE, PINE NUTS, AND RAISINS

Egg-free

MAKES 6 MAIN-DISH OR

8 TO 10 SIDE-DISH OR PASTA-COURSE SERVINGS

Tangy chèvre, garlicky soft cheese, crunchy pine nuts, and sweet raisins coat whole wheat fettuccine nicely in this rather rustic yet simply superb pasta dish. Breaking the pasta in half before cooking makes it easier to toss and coat with the sauce.

2 tablespoons pine nuts

12 ounces whole wheat fettuccine or linguine, broken in half

6 tablespoons dark raisins

1 cup (4 ounces) crumbled goat cheese

¼ cup reduced-fat garlic-and-herb spreadable cheese

¼ cup skim milk, or more as necessary

Salt and freshly ground black pepper, to taste

Heat a small, heavy-bottomed skillet over medium heat. Add the pine nuts and cook, stirring often, until fragrant and lightly toasted, about 2 minutes. Immediately remove nuts from the skillet and set aside.

In a large stockpot, cook the pasta in boiling salted water according to package directions until al dente, adding the raisins the last 30 seconds or so of cooking. Drain well.

Add the goat cheese, spreadable cheese, and milk to the stockpot; stir over medium-low heat until smooth. Add the fettuccine, reserved pine nuts, salt, and pepper; toss well to combine. For a thinner sauce, add additional skim milk in small amounts until desired consistency is achieved. Transfer to a warm serving bowl and serve at once.

PER SERVING

Calories 366 ▪ Protein 16g ▪ Total Fat 11g ▪ Sat. Fat 6g ▪ Cholesterol 25mg ▪ Carbohydrate 52g ▪ Dietary Fiber 2g ▪ Sodium 129mg

FUSILLI WITH SPICY BABY BROCCOLI AND CAPERS

Vegan

MAKES 4 MAIN-DISH OR 6 TO 8 SIDE-DISH

OR PASTA-COURSE SERVINGS

This is an excellent buffet dish as it holds up well at room temperature. The combination of broccoli, capers, and red pepper flakes is a classic Sicilian touch; in Italy, this spicy dish would never be offered with cheese.

8 ounces fusilli or other twist pasta

2 tablespoons extra-virgin olive oil

2 teaspoons refrigerated bottled minced garlic

¼ teaspoon crushed red pepper flakes, or to taste

1 (16-ounce) package frozen baby broccoli florets or regular-size florets

2 tablespoons capers, drained

½ cup low-sodium vegetable broth

½ teaspoon salt, or to taste

Freshly ground black pepper, or to taste

In a large stockpot filled with boiling salted water, cook the pasta according to package directions until just al dente, about 9 minutes. Drain well.

Meanwhile, in a large deep-sided nonstick skillet with a lid, heat the oil over medium heat. Add the garlic and red pepper flakes and cook, stirring, until fragrant and beginning to sizzle, 1 to 2 minutes. Add the broccoli, capers, broth, salt, and black pepper, stirring well to combine; cover and bring to a brisk simmer over high heat. Reduce the heat to medium-low and cook, covered, until the broccoli is tender but still slightly crunchy, about 3 minutes, shaking the skillet a few times to redistribute the vegetables. Add the drained pasta and cook, tossing and stirring often, until the pasta has absorbed most of the liquid, about 2 minutes. Serve warm or at room temperature.

PER SERVING
Calories 312 ▪ Protein 12g ▪ Total Fat 8g ▪
Sat. Fat 1g ▪ Cholesterol 0mg ▪ Carbohydrate 49g ▪
Dietary Fiber 5g ▪ Sodium 362mg

FRESH LEAF SPINACH LASAGNA

Egg-free

MAKES 8 MAIN-DISH SERVINGS

A favorite in my household, this spinach lasagna is superb prepared with organic tomato-basil pasta sauce, to which I often add a few torn fresh basil leaves for added flavor. The use of ready-washed young spinach leaves, available at most major supermarkets, makes stemming and chopping them unnecessary. To reduce the amount of dairy, 2 cups crumbled firm tofu can replace the ricotta cheese, if desired. However, because vegan soy cheeses typically do not melt well, their substitution for the mozzarella and Parmesan cheeses is not recommended.

1 (9-ounce) bag ready-washed baby spinach

1 (26-ounce) jar pasta sauce, preferably a tomato-basil variety

1 (8-ounce) can no-salt-added tomato sauce

4 to 6 basil leaves, torn in half or in quarters, depending on size (optional)

6 oven-ready lasagna noodles

1 (15-ounce) container nonfat or reduced-fat ricotta cheese

2 cups (8 ounces) already-shredded part-skim mozzarella cheese

4 to 6 tablespoons already-shredded Parmesan cheese

Preheat oven to 375F (190C). In a large stockpot, bring about 4 quarts water to a brisk simmer. Lightly oil a 13 × 9 inch baking dish and set aside. Lightly oil a piece of aluminum foil large enough to tightly cover the dish and set aside.

Place the spinach in a colander. Slowly pour simmering water over the spinach. Press the spinach firmly with the back of a large wooden spoon to extract most of the liquid. Set briefly aside.

In a medium bowl, combine the pasta sauce, tomato sauce, and basil (if using). Spread one-third (about 1⅓ cups) of the sauce in the bottom of the prepared dish. Arrange 3 noodles crosswise over sauce, leaving equal space around the noodles so that they don't overlap or touch the sides of the dish. Arrange half of the spinach over the noodles. Arrange half of the ricotta over the spinach. Pour another one-third of the sauce over the ricotta cheese. Sprinkle 1 cup of the mozzarella cheese over the sauce. Repeat, beginning with the remaining noodles, then spinach, then ricotta cheese, then sauce, then mozzarella cheese, ending with the Parmesan cheese. Cover tightly with the prepared foil, oiled side down.

Bake 35 minutes. Uncover and bake 7 to 10 more minutes, or until the cheese is melted and just beginning to brown. Let stand 10 minutes before cutting and serving. Serve at once.

PER SERVING

Calories 446 ■ Protein 28g ■ Total Fat 10g ■
Sat. Fat 4g ■ Cholesterol 26mg ■ Carbohydrate 64mg
■ Dietary Fiber 3g ■ Sodium 912mg

Cook's Tip You can bake the lasagna in an 11 × 7 inch casserole for a more compact dish, but break off the ends of the noodles so they don't touch the sides of the pan as they expand.

LINGUINE WITH FETA AND MINT

Egg-free

MAKES 5 TO 6 MAIN-DISH OR 8 TO 10 SIDE-DISH OR PASTA-COURSE SERVINGS

This recipe draws its inspiration from the French island of Corsica; try to use French feta, if possible. If you are lucky enough to have some fresh mint growing in the garden, the whole leaves make a lovely garnish.

- 1 tablespoon extra-virgin olive oil
- 1 cup frozen chopped onion
- 1 cup low-sodium vegetable broth
- 1 cup crumbled feta cheese (4 ounces)
- 1 teaspoon dried chopped mint
- Salt and freshly ground black pepper, to taste
- 12 ounces linguine or other similar pasta
- Pitted Niçoise, kalamata, or other good-quality black olives (optional)

In a large nonstick skillet, heat the oil over medium heat. Add the onion and cook, stirring,

until softened and translucent, about 5 minutes. Stir in the broth, feta, and mint. Reduce the heat to low and cook, uncovered, stirring occasionally, until the sauce is just heated through, about 5 minutes. Season with salt and pepper.

Meanwhile, in a large stockpot filled with boiling salted water, cook the pasta according to package directions until al dente. Drain and transfer to a large bowl. Add the feta sauce and toss well to combine. Serve at once, garnished with the olives, if desired.

PER SERVING

Calories 357 ■ Protein 14g ■ Total Fat 9g ■
Sat. Fat 4g ■ Cholesterol 20mg ■ Carbohydrate 55g ■
Dietary Fiber 3g ■ Sodium 366mg

LINGUINE WITH PANTRY MARINARA SAUCE

Vegan

MAKES 4 TO 5 MAIN-DISH OR 6 TO 8 SIDE-DISH OR PASTA-COURSE SERVINGS; ABOUT 2½ CUPS SAUCE

This thick and rich marinara sauce is so flavorful that no one will ever guess it came straight from the pantry—unless, of course, you tell! Though optional, cheese is not typically served with marinara sauce in Italy. If you like artichokes in your marinara, see the tangy variation below.

- 1 (28-ounce) can crushed tomatoes
- 1½ tablespoons extra-virgin olive oil
- 1 teaspoon onion powder
- 1 teaspoon dried oregano
- 1 teaspoon sugar
- ½ teaspoon garlic powder

¼ teaspoon salt, or to taste

Freshly ground black pepper, or to taste

10 ounces linguine

Already-shredded Parmesan cheese (optional)

In a medium deep-sided skillet or wide saucepan, combine all ingredients except the linguine and cheese. Bring to a simmer over medium-high heat, stirring occasionally. Reduce the heat to between low and medium-low; simmer, uncovered, stirring occasionally, until the sauce is thickened, about 20 minutes.

Meanwhile, in a large stockpot filled with boiling salted water, cook the pasta according to package directions until al dente. Drain and transfer to a large bowl. Add the sauce and toss well to combine. Serve at once, with the cheese passed separately, if desired.

PER SERVING

Calories 357 ▪ Protein 11g ▪ Total Fat 7g ▪
Sat. Fat 1g ▪ Cholesterol 0mg ▪ Carbohydrate 64g ▪
Dietary Fiber 4g ▪ Sodium 561mg

Variation

Artichoke-Marinara Sauce: Add 1 (12-ounce) jar marinated quartered artichoke hearts, well-drained, to the sauce the last 10 minutes of simmering, stirring occasionally and breaking up the artichoke quarters with a wooden spoon. Serve as directed in the recipe.

Cook's Tip The completely cooled sauce can be placed in a freezer bag and frozen up to three months. If doubling the amount of marinara sauce, select a medium stockpot in which to simmer it.

LINGUINE WITH TOMATO-BASIL SAUCE

Vegan

MAKES 5 TO 6 MAIN-DISH OR 8 TO 10 SIDE-DISH OR PASTA-COURSE SERVINGS

I make this pasta dish often throughout the summer when basil is plentiful and relatively cheap. The versatile quick-cooking sauce, at once both chunky and light, can also be used to spread over pizza or polenta, but increase the final simmering time by about 10 minutes to further thicken it.

2 tablespoons extra-virgin olive oil

½ cup frozen chopped onion

1½ teaspoons refrigerated bottled minced garlic

1 (28-ounce) can whole peeled tomatoes, juice included

½ teaspoon dried thyme leaves

½ teaspoon sugar

½ teaspoon salt, or to taste

Freshly ground black pepper, to taste

½ cup packed whole fresh basil leaves, torn in half or quarters, depending on size

12 ounces linguine or other pasta

Already-shredded Parmesan cheese (optional)

Heat the oil in a medium saucepan over medium heat. Add the onion and cook, stirring, until just beginning to brown, 4 to 5 minutes. Add the garlic and cook, stirring constantly, 30 seconds. Add the tomatoes with their juice, thyme, sugar, salt, and pepper; bring to a boil over medium-high heat, crushing the tomatoes with the back of a large wooden spoon to break them up. Reduce the heat to medium-low and simmer 10 minutes, stirring occasionally. Add the basil and simmer, uncovered, 2 to 3 minutes, stirring a few times.

Meanwhile, cook the linguine in a large stockpot filled with boiling salted water according to package directions until al dente. Drain and transfer to a large bowl. Add the sauce and toss well to combine. Serve at once, with the cheese passed separately, if desired.

PER SERVING

Calories 344 ■ Protein 11g ■ Total Fat 7g ■
Sat. Fat 1g ■ Cholesterol 0mg ■ Carbohydrate 60g ■
Dietary Fiber 4g ■ Sodium 559mg

SZECHUAN-STYLE LO MEIN STIR-FRY WITH BROCCOLI SLAW AND PEANUTS

Vegan

MAKES 6 MAIN-DISH OR 8 TO 10 SIDE-DISH SERVINGS

Pungent and mildly hot Szechuan pepper adds zest to this easy stir-fry. If you don't have the Szechuan variety, available in Asian markets as well as the spice aisle of many major supermarkets, substitute with regular ground black pepper and add a pinch of cayenne.

12 ounces lo mein noodles or other thin pasta

1 tablespoon peanut or plain sesame oil

½ cup frozen chopped onion

½ tablespoon refrigerated bottled minced garlic

½ teaspoon ground Szechuan pepper, or more to taste

1 (16-ounce) package broccoli slaw mix

⅓ cup water

⅓ cup reduced-sodium soy sauce

1 tablespoon bottled chopped ginger or ½ teaspoon ground ginger

½ tablespoon sugar

2 tablespoons chunky peanut butter

1 tablespoon toasted (dark) sesame oil

¼ cup unsalted chopped peanuts

In a large stockpot filled with boiling salted water, cook the noodles according to package directions until just al dente. Drain in a colander and rinse briefly under running cold water. Set aside until needed.

Meanwhile, in a large nonstick skillet or wok, heat the peanut oil over medium heat. Add the onion and cook, stirring, until softened and thawed, about 3 minutes. Add the garlic and Szechuan pepper and cook, stirring, 1 minute. Increase the heat to medium-high and add half of the broccoli slaw. Cook, stirring and tossing constantly, until just wilted, about 3 minutes. Stir in the water, soy sauce, ginger, and sugar; let come to a simmer. Reduce the heat to low and add the peanut butter and toasted sesame oil, stirring until well incorporated. Fold in the reserved noodles and remaining broccoli slaw; cook, stirring, until heated through. Serve at once, with each serving garnished with some chopped peanuts.

PER SERVING

Calories 349 ■ Protein 13g ■ Total Fat 11g ■
Sat. Fat 2g ■ Cholesterol 0mg ■ Carbohydrate 51g ■
Dietary Fiber 3g ■ Sodium 578mg

"ENLIGHTENED" MACARONI AND CHEESE

Egg-free

**MAKES 6 TO 8 MAIN-DISH OR
10 TO 12 SIDE-DISH SERVINGS**

The ultimate comfort food for many children, this popular casserole is often avoided by health-conscious adults because of its typically heavy fat content. Yet with just a little tweaking, the following rendition weighs in at a respectable 12 grams of fat per serving, a mere 3 of those saturated. While you can use rice milk in lieu of the skim milk to reduce the total amount of dairy in the recipe, vegan substitutes are not recommended for the cheddar cheese as they do not melt well.

16 ounces elbow macaroni

3 tablespoons canola oil

3 tablespoons all-purpose flour

1½ cups skim milk or rice milk

3 cups (12 ounces) already-shredded reduced-fat cheddar cheese

¼ teaspoon ground nutmeg

Pinch cayenne pepper, or to taste (optional)

Salt and freshly ground black pepper, to taste

Preheat oven to 350F (175C). Lightly oil a 13 × 9 inch baking dish or similar casserole and set aside.

Cook the macaroni in a large stockpot of boiling salted water according to package directions until just al dente. Drain well and return to pot.

Meanwhile, in a medium saucepan, heat the oil over medium heat. Add the flour and cook, stirring constantly, 2 minutes. Slowly whisk in the milk and bring to a gentle boil, whisking frequently. Boil, stirring constantly, 1 minute. Reduce the heat to low and stir in 2 cups of the cheese, 1 cup at a time. When the cheese is completely incorporated, add the nutmeg, cayenne (if using), salt, and black pepper; stir well to combine. Add the cheese sauce to the macaroni and toss well to combine.

Transfer the macaroni mixture to the prepared baking dish. Bake 20 minutes, or until the top is just beginning to brown. Sprinkle evenly with the remaining cheese and bake until melted, about 5 minutes. Serve immediately.

PER SERVING

Calories 475 ▪ Protein 26g ▪ Total Fat 12g ▪
Sat. Fat 3g ▪ Cholesterol 13mg ▪ Carbohydrate 64g ▪
Dietary Fiber 2g ▪ Sodium 384mg

Variation

Macaroni and Cheese with Tomato: Add 1 (14-ounce) can diced tomatoes, preferably the petite-cut variety, well drained, when you combine the macaroni and cheese sauce.

SKILLET MACARONI AND CHEESE WITH BROCCOLI

Egg-free

MAKES 4 MAIN-DISH OR 6 TO 8 SIDE-DISH OR
PASTA-COURSE SERVINGS

This spicy variation on the classic pasta casserole is popular with adult taste buds. The heat can be reduced or omitted entirely, if desired. If you don't own a flame-proof skillet, assemble the casserole in a lightly oiled 2½-quart gratin or similar-size shallow flameproof baking dish before broiling. Vegan cheese substitutes are not recommended here, as they don't melt well.

8 ounces elbow macaroni

½ tablespoon extra-virgin olive oil

1 teaspoon refrigerated bottled minced garlic

¼ teaspoon crushed red pepper flakes,
     or to taste

1 (16-ounce) package frozen broccoli cuts

½ cup low-sodium vegetable broth

¼ teaspoon salt, or to taste

¼ teaspoon freshly ground black pepper,
     or to taste

1 cup (4 ounces) already-shredded part-skim
     mozzarella cheese

¼ cup (1 ounce) freshly grated Parmesan
     cheese

1 tablespoon Italian-seasoned bread crumbs

In a large stockpot of boiling salted water, cook the macaroni according to package directions until just al dente, about 9 minutes. Drain well.

Meanwhile, preheat the oven to broil.

In a large deep-sided flameproof skillet with a lid, heat the oil over medium-high heat. Add the garlic and red pepper flakes and cook, stirring constantly, 30 seconds. Add the broccoli, broth, salt, and black pepper; cover and let come to a brisk simmer over high heat. Reduce the heat to medium-low and cook, covered, until broccoli is crisp-tender, about 3 minutes, shaking the pan occasionally. Uncover and increase the heat to high; cook, stirring occasionally, until all the liquid has evaporated, about 3 minutes.

Remove from the heat and add the macaroni, tossing well to combine. Add the mozzarella cheese, tossing quickly to combine (otherwise, the cheese will become stringy). Sprinkle evenly with the Parmesan cheese, then the bread crumbs.

Broil 4 to 6 inches from the heating element until the Parmesan cheese is melted and top is lightly browned, 1 to 2 minutes. Serve at once.

PER SERVING

Calories 385 ▪ Protein 23g ▪ Total Fat 10g ▪ Sat. Fat 5g ▪ Cholesterol 21mg ▪ Carbohydrate 52g ▪ Dietary Fiber 5g ▪ Sodium 553mg

BUTTERED NOODLES WITH CAPERS AND LEMON

Lacto-ovo with vegan options

MAKES 6 SIDE-DISH OR
3 TO 4 MAIN-DISH SERVINGS

This is one of my favorite ways to eat broad noodles. Though the clarified butter is optional, I've included a recipe for it as many people who otherwise avoid dairy for health reasons will consume butter when the milk solids have been removed. However, because it contains more fat per serving than regular butter, you typically need to use less. For a vegan dish, use egg-free noodles and a vegan butter substitute; Earth Balance makes an excellent brand that contains no harmful trans fats.

- **8 ounces wide egg noodles or egg-free broad noodles**
- **2 tablespoons butter or vegan substitute or 1½ tablespoons clarified butter (see recipe below)**
- **2 tablespoons drained capers**
- **1 tablespoon lemon juice, preferably prepared from frozen concentrate**
- **½ teaspoon salt, preferably the coarse variety, or to taste**
- **¼ teaspoon freshly ground black pepper, or to taste**

Cook the noodles in a large stockpot of boiling salted water according to package directions until al dente. Drain and return to pot. Add the butter, capers, lemon juice, salt, and pepper, tossing until noodles are thoroughly coated. Serve at once.

PER SERVING (BASED ON REGULAR BUTTER)
Calories 179 ■ Protein 5g ■ Total Fat 5g ■
Sat. Fat 3g ■ Cholesterol 46mg ■ Carbohydrate 27g ■
Dietary Fiber 1g ■ Sodium 229mg

CLARIFIED BUTTER

Egg-free

MAKES ABOUT ¾ CUP OR 12 TABLESPOONS

Also known as ghee, clarified butter is essentially butter from which the milk solids, as well as much of the water and salt, have been removed. Clarified butter has a higher smoking point, and is frequently used in French cuisine for sautéing. In Indian cuisine, it is often used as a dipping sauce for fresh vegetables.

- **2 sticks (8 ounces) unsalted butter, cut into 16 pieces**

In a small heavy-bottomed saucepan, melt the butter over low heat, swirling the pan occasionally. Remove the pan from the heat and let stand 5 minutes. Carefully skim the foam from the top. Slowly pour into a container, discarding the milky solids in the bottom of the pan. If not using immediately, cover and store in the refrigerator up to 1 month.

PER SERVING (1 TABLESPOON)
Calories 119 ■ Protein 0g ■ Total Fat 14g ■
Sat. Fat 8g ■ Cholesterol 35mg ■ Carbohydrate 0g ■
Dietary Fiber 0g ■ Sodium 0mg

STIR-FRIED CELLOPHANE NOODLES WITH BABY BROCCOLI AND CHINESE FIVE-SPICE

Vegan

**MAKES 4 MAIN-DISH OR
6 TO 8 SIDE-DISH SERVINGS**

This tasty dish, made with wheat-free cellophane noodles, or bean threads, is ideal for those with wheat allergies. In that instance, use tamari in the recipe; unlike regular soy sauce, it contains no wheat. Any thin Asian noodle or pasta (broken in half and cooked according to the package directions until almost al dente) can replace the cellophane noodles, if desired. Chinese hot oil, a fiery combination of soybean oil and chili extract, can be found in Asian markets and the international aisle of most well-stocked supermarkets.

2 (3.75-ounce) packages cellophane noodles (bean threads) (see Cook's Tip, page 61)

1 tablespoon peanut oil

½ cup frozen chopped onion

1 teaspoon refrigerated bottled minced garlic

1¼ cups low-sodium vegetable broth

2 tablespoons reduced-sodium soy sauce or tamari

1 teaspoon ground ginger

½ teaspoon Chinese five-spice powder (see Cook's Tip, at right)

Salt and freshly ground black pepper, to taste

1 (16-ounce) bag baby or petite broccoli florets

1 tablespoon mango chutney or ginger jelly

2 teaspoons toasted (dark) sesame oil

1 teaspoon Chinese hot oil or Chinese chili paste

In a large stockpot of boiling salted water, cook the cellophane noodles 30 seconds. Drain and rinse briefly under cold running water. Set aside.

Meanwhile, in a large nonstick skillet or wok, heat the peanut oil over medium heat. Add the onion and cook, stirring, until softened and thawed, about 3 minutes. Add the garlic and cook, stirring, 1 minute. Stir in the broth, soy sauce, ginger, five-spice powder, salt, and pepper; add the broccoli and bring to a brisk simmer over high heat. Reduce the heat to medium-low, cover, and cook until the broccoli is tender but still crunchy, about 3 minutes. Stir in the chutney, sesame oil, and hot oil. Add the cellophane noodles, pulling them into long bunches and tearing into 2-inch clumps with your fingers as you go. Cook, tossing and stirring often, until the noodles are soft and have absorbed all the liquid, about 3 minutes. Serve at once.

PER SERVING

Calories 322 ▪ Protein 8g ▪ Total Fat 8g ▪
Sat. Fat 1g ▪ Cholesterol 0mg ▪ Carbohydrate 58g ▪
Dietary Fiber 7g ▪ Sodium 489mg

Cook's Tip Chinese five-spice powder, an aromatic blend typically of anise, ginger, star anise, cinnamon, and cloves, can be located in the spice aisle of most well-stocked supermarkets.

NOODLES WITH TOASTED ALMONDS AND POPPY SEEDS

Vegan

**MAKES 6 SIDE-DISH OR
3 TO 4 MAIN-DISH SERVINGS**

These noodles are a terrific accompaniment to any variety of vegetables. Toss with 2 cups cooked broccoli florets and 3 to 4 tablespoons plumped raisins for a quick and easy dinner serving three or four.

1½ **tablespoons extra-virgin olive oil**

¼ **cup slivered almonds**

½ **teaspoon refrigerated bottled minced garlic**

8 **ounces egg-free broad noodles, preferably whole wheat**

1 **tablespoon poppy seeds**

½ **teaspoon salt, preferably the coarse variety, or to taste**

¼ **teaspoon freshly ground black pepper, or to taste**

In a large nonstick skillet, heat the oil over medium-low heat. Add the almonds and cook, stirring often, 2 minutes. Add the garlic and cook, stirring often, until garlic is fragrant and almonds are lightly browned, about 2 minutes. Remove the skillet from the heat.

Meanwhile, in a large stockpot of boiling salted water, cook the noodles according to package directions until al dente, about 6 minutes. Drain well. Add the noodles, poppy seeds, salt, and pepper to the skillet, tossing well to combine. Serve warm.

ASIAN GINGER-PEANUT NOODLES

Vegan

**MAKES 6 SIDE-DISH OR
3 TO 4 MAIN-DISH SERVINGS**

This mildly spiced noodle dish is delicious served with lightly steamed or blanched vegetables. Soba noodles, or Japanese buckwheat pasta, can be found in Asian markets as well as gourmet and health food stores. Any thin pasta—such as vermicelli—can be substituted.

8 **ounces soba or somen noodles, broken in half (see Cook's Tip, page 101)**

2 **tablespoons reduced-sodium soy sauce**

1 **tablespoon rice vinegar**

1 **tablespoon toasted (dark) sesame oil**

½ **tablespoon peanut oil**

½ **tablespoon freeze-dried chives**

1 **teaspoon ground ginger**

1 **teaspoon sugar**

½ **teaspoon onion powder**

Salt and freshly ground black pepper, to taste

¼ **cup unsalted chopped peanuts**

In a large stockpot, cook the noodles according to package directions until al dente. (Or see Chilled Somen Noodles with Spicy Peanut Sauce, page 100, for method.) Drain and rinse under running cold water until completely cooled. Drain well.

In a large bowl, whisk together the soy sauce,

vinegar, sesame oil, peanut oil, chives, ginger, sugar, onion powder, salt, and pepper. Let stand 5 minutes to allow the flavors to blend, then whisk again. Add the noodles and peanuts; toss to thoroughly combine. Serve at room temperature, or cover and refrigerate up to 2 days and serve chilled.

STIR-FRIED RICE NOODLES WITH CABBAGE

Vegan

MAKES 5 TO 6 MAIN-DISH OR 8 TO 10 SIDE-DISH SERVINGS

Rice noodles, available in Asian markets and many well-stocked supermarkets, are a delicious pasta alternative for those with wheat allergies, as is tamari, which, unlike regular soy sauce, is wheat-free.

- 12 ounces rice noodles or rice vermicelli (thin rice noodles)
- 1½ tablespoons peanut or plain sesame oil
- ½ cup frozen chopped onion
- 1 teaspoon refrigerated bottled minced garlic
- 1 (14-ounce) can (1¾ cups) low-sodium vegetable broth
- 3 tablespoons reduced-sodium soy sauce, or tamari, plus additional to taste, if desired
- 1 tablespoon toasted (dark) sesame oil
- 1 (16-ounce) package shredded coleslaw mix, preferably green cabbage, red cabbage, and carrots

Salt, if necessary, and freshly ground black pepper, to taste

In a large stockpot, soak the noodles according to package directions until almost al dente. (Or see Cook's Tip, below, for soaking methods.) Drain well and rinse with cold water for 30 seconds. Set aside.

Meanwhile, in a large deep-sided nonstick skillet or wok, heat the peanut oil over medium-high heat. Add the onion and cook, stirring, until thawed and softened, 2 to 3 minutes. Add the garlic and cook, stirring constantly, 1 minute. Add the broth, soy sauce, sesame oil, and coleslaw mix; let come to a brisk simmer, stirring occasionally. Reduce the heat to medium-low and cook, stirring occasionally, until the vegetables are crisp-tender, 3 to 5 minutes. Fold in the rice noodles and cook, stirring and turning often, until the noodles have absorbed most of the liquid and are soft yet firm to the bite, about 5 minutes. Season with salt if necessary, pepper, and additional soy sauce, if desired. Serve at once.

Cook's Tip There are at least two ways to soak rice noodles in preparation for further cooking in stir-fries or soups. For the quicker hot-soak method, using 12 ounces of rice noodles or rice vermicelli (thin rice noodles), bring 6 to 8 cups water to a boil in a large stockpot. Remove from heat and add the rice noodles. Let stand, stirring occasionally, until the noodles are soft yet still quite chewy, 4 to 6 minutes for the vermicelli noodles, 6 to 8 minutes for regular noodles. Drain well and rinse under running cold water for 30 seconds. Noodles are now ready for further cooking. For a longer cold-soak method, soak noodles about 30 minutes in like amount of cold water. Drain well and proceed to cook as directed in the recipe.

CHILLED SESAME NOODLES WITH CASHEWS

Vegan

**MAKES 4 MAIN-DISH OR
6 TO 8 SIDE-DISH SERVINGS**

The combination of toasted sesame oil, soy sauce, and maple syrup lends this crunchy noodle dish a smoky-sweet nuance. Serve on a bed of spinach leaves or other greens for an unusual main-dish salad. Sliced or slivered almonds can replace the cashews, if desired.

- 8 ounces somen or soba noodles, broken in half (see Cook's Tip, page 101)
- 2 tablespoons soy sauce
- 2 tablespoons pure maple syrup or honey
- 1½ tablespoons toasted (dark) sesame oil
- 1 tablespoon freeze-dried chives
- 2 teaspoons sesame seeds, toasted if desired (see Cook's Tip, page 44)
- ½ teaspoon onion powder
- Salt and freshly ground black pepper, to taste
- ¼ cup cashew pieces, toasted if desired (see Cook's Tip, page 71)
- ½ cup bean sprouts
- ¼ cup already-shredded carrots

In a large stockpot, cook the noodles according to package directions until al dente. (Or see Chilled Somen Noodles with Spicy Peanut Sauce, page 100, for method.) Drain and rinse under running cold water until completely cooled. Drain well.

In a large bowl, whisk together the soy sauce, maple syrup, sesame oil, chives, sesame seeds, onion powder, salt, and pepper. Let stand 5 minutes to allow the flavors to blend, then whisk again. Add the noodles, cashews, sprouts, and carrots; toss to thoroughly combine. Serve at room temperature, or cover and refrigerate up to 12 hours and serve chilled.

PER SERVING
Calories 330 ▪ Protein 11g ▪ Total Fat 10g ▪ Sat. Fat 2g ▪ Cholesterol 0mg ▪ Carbohydrate 54g ▪ Dietary Fiber 2g ▪ Sodium 754mg

COLD SOBA NOODLES

Vegan

MAKES 4 TO 6 SIDE-DISH OR

3 MAIN-DISH SERVINGS

Soba, a thin brownish-gray buckwheat pasta, is commonly used in cold dishes or hot soups in Japanese cuisine. This recipe is as basic as it gets; feel free to toss with your favorite vegetables. Or consider serving these noodles as part of a totally vegan Asian-style buffet, accompanied by Chilled Sugar Snap Peas in Sesame-Mustard Vinaigrette (page 152), Orange-Glazed Chinese-Style Beets (page 134), and Asian-Style Coleslaw (page 44), with Coconut Sticky Rice Pudding (page 185) for dessert.

> 8 ounces soba or somen noodles (see Cook's
>   Tip, page 101)
> 1 tablespoon toasted (dark) sesame oil
> 1 tablespoon reduced-sodium soy sauce
> ¼ teaspoon onion powder
> Salt and freshly ground black pepper, to taste

In a large stockpot, cook the noodles according to package directions until al dente. (Or see Chilled Somen Noodles with Spicy Peanut Sauce, at right, for method.) Drain and rinse under running cold water until completely cooled. Drain well. Transfer to a large serving bowl.

In a small bowl, stir together the sesame oil, soy sauce, and onion powder. Add to the noodles, tossing well to combine. Season with salt and pepper and serve at room temperature. Alternatively, cover and refrigerate up to 2 days and serve chilled.

Variation

Cold Soba Noodles with Black Bean Sauce: Substitute 1 tablespoon Asian black bean sauce for the soy sauce. Black bean sauce, made with fermented black soybeans and garlic, can be found in the international aisle of most well-stocked supermarkets.

CHILLED SOMEN NOODLES WITH SPICY PEANUT SAUCE

Vegan

MAKES 6 SIDE-DISH OR

3 TO 4 MAIN-DISH SERVINGS

The heat of this spicy noodle dish can be adjusted according to taste, or omitted entirely, if desired. Somen noodles, the favorite pasta of Japan, are located in Asian markets as well as many well-stocked supermarkets. If unavailable, vermicelli, spaghettini, or capellini, broken in half, makes a fine substitute. For a main dish for four, add 2 cups cooked frozen broccoli pieces to the recipe before chilling, and garnish with chopped peanuts just before serving.

> 8 ounces somen or soba noodles (see Cook's
>   Tip, below)
> ¼ cup chunky peanut butter
> ¼ cup warm water
> 2 tablespoons reduced-sodium soy sauce
> 1 tablespoon rice vinegar
> 1 teaspoon plain sesame oil or peanut oil

1 teaspoon toasted (dark) sesame oil

½ teaspoon Chinese chili paste or crushed red
   pepper flakes, to taste

Bring a large stockpot filled with salted water to a boil. Add the noodles, reducing the heat to medium-high once the water returns to a boil. Cook, stirring occasionally, until the noodles are just firm to the bite, about 3 minutes. Drain in a colander and rinse under running cold water until cool; drain well.

In a large bowl, whisk the peanut butter, water, soy sauce, vinegar, oils, and chili paste until thoroughly blended. Add the noodles and toss well to thoroughly combine. Cover and refrigerate a minimum of 30 minutes, or up to 3 days. Serve chilled.

PER SERVING
Calories 215 ▪ Protein 7g ▪ Total Fat 7g ▪
Sat. Fat 1g ▪ Cholesterol 0mg ▪ Carbohydrate 31g ▪
Dietary Fiber 2g ▪ Sodium 948mg

Variation

Cold Chinese Noodles with Spicy Peanut Sauce: Substitute 8 ounces fine Chinese noodles for the somen noodles and substitute 1 teaspoon Chinese hot oil, located in the international aisle of most major supermarkets, for the Chinese chili paste. Proceed as otherwise directed in the recipe.

Cook's Tip If using soba noodles (Japanese buckwheat pasta), cook 1 to 2 minutes longer than the somen noodles.

MUSHROOM STROGANOFF NOODLES

Lacto-ovo with vegan options

MAKES 6 SIDE-DISH OR
3 TO 4 MAIN-DISH SERVINGS

Primarily a side dish, these noodles are so delicious, you might want to toss 1½ cups cooked frozen baby peas and pearl onions into the completed recipe and serve as an entrée for three or four. For a vegan dish, use nondairy sour cream (Tofutti Better than Sour Cream is an excellent brand) and egg-free noodles.

1 tablespoon canola oil

1 (8-ounce) package presliced fresh white
   mushrooms

¼ cup low-sodium vegetable broth

1 teaspoon dried parsley

½ teaspoon onion powder

¼ teaspoon garlic powder

¾ cup light sour cream or nondairy sour cream

1½ teaspoons vegetarian Worcestershire
   sauce (see Cook's Tip, page 67)

Salt and freshly ground black pepper, to taste

8 ounces wide egg noodles or egg-free broad
   noodles

In a large nonstick skillet, heat the oil over medium heat. Add the mushrooms and cook, stirring often, until the mushrooms have released most of their liquid, about 5 minutes. Stir in the broth, parsley, onion powder, and garlic powder; bring to a boil over medium-high heat. Cook, stirring occasionally, until the liquid is mostly reduced, 3 to 5 minutes. Remove from heat and stir in the sour cream, Worcestershire sauce, salt, and pepper, stirring well to combine.

Meanwhile, in a large stockpot of boiling salted water, cook the noodles according to package directions until al dente, about 6 minutes. Drain and add to the mushroom mixture, tossing well to combine. Serve at once.

PER SERVING

Calories 188 ▪ Protein 7g ▪ Total Fat 5g ▪
Sat. Fat 1g ▪ Cholesterol 38mg ▪ Carbohydrate 30g ▪
Dietary Fiber 2g ▪ Sodium 51mg

ONE-SKILLET PASTA AND MUSHROOMS WITH MARSALA

Vegan

MAKES 4 MAIN-DISH OR 6 TO 8 SIDE-DISH OR PASTA-COURSE SERVINGS

The classic combination of fresh mushrooms and Marsala adds a sophisticated touch to this otherwise simple one-skillet pasta dish. Marsala is a relatively inexpensive fortified wine with a nutty taste; do not use the watered-down marsala cooking wine found in most supermarkets. Cheese would not be offered with this dish in Italy.

2 tablespoons extra-virgin olive oil

1 (8-ounce) package presliced fresh white mushrooms

¼ cup dry Marsala wine, dry sherry, or dry Madiera

1 (14-ounce) can (1¾ cups) low-sodium vegetable broth

½ cup water, plus additional, as necessary

1 tablespoon instant minced onion

½ tablespoon dried parsley flakes

½ teaspoon dried oregano leaves

½ teaspoon dried thyme leaves

½ teaspoon garlic powder

Salt and freshly ground black pepper, to taste

8 ounces rotelle, rotini, or other twist pasta

In a large nonstick skillet with a lid, heat the oil over medium heat. Add the mushrooms and cook, stirring, until softened, about 2 minutes. Add the Marsala and increase the heat to medium-high; cook, stirring often, until the mushrooms have released all their liquid and the Marsala is greatly reduced, about 5 minutes. Add the broth, water, onion, parsley, oregano, thyme, garlic powder, salt, and pepper; bring to a boil over high heat. Stir in the pasta and let return to a boil. Reduce the heat to medium and simmer, covered, about 12 minutes, stirring occasionally, or until the pasta is tender and has absorbed most of the liquid. (If pasta is not done by the time most of the liquid has been absorbed, add water by ¼ cup at a time until the pasta is cooked to desired doneness.) Serve at once.

PER SERVING

Calories 322 ▪ Protein 14g ▪ Total Fat 8g ▪
Sat. Fat 1g ▪ Cholesterol 0mg ▪ Carbohydrate 47g ▪
Dietary Fiber 4g ▪ Sodium 234mg

PENNE WITH RED PEPPER CREAM AND PINE NUTS

Egg-free

MAKES 4 TO 5 MAIN-DISH OR 6 TO 8 SIDE-DISH OR PASTA-COURSE SERVINGS

If lack of time or limited kitchen skills is what typically holds you back from entertaining, this easy yet elegant recipe is for you. Sweet red pepper spread can be found among the olives and pimientos in most well-stocked supermarkets. While you can reduce the dairy by replacing the half-and-half with a soy creamer or other nondairy coffee creamer, the use of a vegan soy cheese substitute for the Parmesan cheese is definitely not recommended here.

- 10 ounces penne or other short tubular pasta
- 1 (6-ounce) jar sweet red pepper spread
- ½ cup half-and-half, soy creamer, or other nondairy coffee creamer
- ¼ cup (1 ounce) already-shredded Parmesan cheese
- Salt and freshly ground black pepper, to taste
- 2 to 3 tablespoons pine nuts

In a large stockpot of boiling salted water, cook the pasta according to package directions until al dente. Drain well.

While the pasta is draining, add the red pepper spread, half-and-half, and cheese to the stockpot. Cook, stirring constantly, over medium-low heat, until the cheese is melted and the mixture is smooth. Season with salt and pepper and add the drained pasta and pine nuts, tossing well to thoroughly combine. Serve at once.

PER SERVING

Calories 360 ▪ Protein 13g ▪ Total Fat 9g ▪
Sat. Fat 4g ▪ Cholesterol 15mg ▪ Carbohydrate 58g ▪
Dietary Fiber 3g ▪ Sodium 103mg

Variation

Penne with Gorgonzola and Red Pepper Cream: Substitute 3 to 4 tablespoons crumbled Gorgonzola or other mild blue cheese for the Parmesan cheese, and ¼ cup walnut pieces for the pine nuts, if desired.

RIGATONI AL FORNO

Egg-free

MAKES 8 TO 10 MAIN-DISH OR
12 TO 16 SIDE-DISH OR
PASTA-COURSE SERVINGS

This classic casserole is an excellent choice to feed a crowd as it can be assembled 24 hours in advance of baking. If made ahead, add about 10 minutes to the final cooking time. To reduce the total amount of dairy in the recipe, 2 cups crumbled firm tofu can replace the ricotta cheese, if desired. However, because vegan soy cheeses typically do not melt well, their substitution for the mozzarella and Parmesan cheeses is not recommended.

- 16 ounces rigatoni
- 1 (26-ounce) jar favorite pasta sauce
- 1 (14-ounce) can diced tomatoes, preferably petite-cut, well drained
- 1 (15-ounce) container nonfat ricotta cheese (see headnote above for nondairy alternative)
- 2 cups (8 ounces) already-shredded part-skim mozzarella cheese
- ½ cup (2 ounces) already-shredded Parmesan cheese
- 1 egg (optional)
- 1 teaspoon dried oregano leaves
- Salt and freshly ground black pepper, to taste

Preheat oven to 425F (220C). Lightly oil a 13 × 9 inch baking dish and set aside.

Cook the pasta in boiling salted water according to package directions until just al dente, about 14 minutes. Drain. Return to stockpot and add the pasta sauce and tomatoes, stirring well to combine. Set aside.

Meanwhile, in a large bowl, mix together the ricotta, 1½ cups of the mozzarella, half of the Parmesan, the egg (if using), oregano, salt, and pepper until thoroughly combined.

Arrange half of the pasta mixture in the prepared baking dish, then spread evenly with the ricotta mixture. Arrange remaining pasta mixture over top. Cover with foil and bake 30 minutes, or until hot through the center. Sprinkle with remaining cheeses and bake 5 minutes, uncovered, or until the cheeses are melted. Serve at once.

PER SERVING

Calories 461 ▪ Protein 27g ▪ Total Fat 12g ▪
Sat. Fat 5g ▪ Cholesterol 27mg ▪ Carbohydrate 63g ▪
Dietary Fiber 5g ▪ Sodium 910mg

SHELLS WITH BLACK BEAN SALSA

Vegan

MAKES 5 TO 6 MAIN-DISH OR
8 TO 10 SIDE-DISH SERVINGS

Black beans team up with durum wheat to provide complete protein in this Mexican-inspired entrée, a nice change of pace from rice and beans. If you opt for cheese as a topping, vegan soy substitutes are not recommended here as they don't melt well.

2 tablespoons extra-virgin olive oil

1½ teaspoons whole cumin seeds

1 (15-ounce) can black beans, rinsed and drained

1 (14.5-ounce) can diced tomatoes with jalapeño chilies or green chilies, juice included

1 teaspoon onion powder

½ teaspoon garlic powder

½ teaspoon ground cumin

½ teaspoon dried oregano

½ teaspoon sugar

Salt and freshly ground black pepper, to taste

Dash Tabasco sauce, or to taste (optional)

¼ cup fresh whole cilantro leaves (optional)

1 tablespoon bottled lime juice, or more to taste

12 ounces medium shells, elbows, bow ties, or other similar pasta

Already-shredded reduced-fat cheddar, Monterey Jack, or Mexican cheese blend and/or sour cream or nondairy sour cream, for topping (optional)

In a medium saucepan, heat 1 tablespoon of the oil over medium heat. Add the cumin seeds and cook, stirring often, until fragrant, 1 to 2 minutes. Add the beans, tomatoes with their juice, remaining oil, onion powder, garlic powder, ground cumin, oregano, sugar, salt, pepper, and Tabasco sauce (if using); bring to a brisk simmer over medium-high heat, stirring occasionally. Reduce the heat and simmer, stirring occasionally, until slightly thickened, about 5 minutes. Remove from the heat and stir in the cilantro (if using) and lime juice.

Meanwhile, bring a large pot of salted water to a boil over high heat. Add the pasta and cook according to package directions until al dente. Drain and transfer to a large serving bowl or return to stockpot. Add the black bean mixture and toss well to combine. Serve at once, garnished with the toppings, if desired.

PER SERVING

Calories 394 ▪ Protein 14g ▪ Total Fat 7g ▪
Sat. Fat 1g ▪ Cholesterol 0mg ▪ Carbohydrate 69g ▪
Dietary Fiber 5g ▪ Sodium 182mg

CHEESE-STUFFED SHELLS

Egg-free

MAKES 5 TO 6 MAIN-DISH SERVINGS

You can make this convenient Italian classic in two stages for easy entertaining. If baking straight from the refrigerator, add about 10 minutes to the final cooking time. To reduce the total amount of dairy in the recipe, 2 cups crumbled firm tofu can replace the ricotta cheese, if desired. However, because vegan soy cheeses typically do not melt well, their substitution for the mozzarella and Parmesan cheeses is not recommended.

6 to 7 ounces (24 shells) jumbo pasta shells

1 (15-ounce) container nonfat ricotta cheese (see headnote above for dairy-free alternative)

1 cup (4 ounces) already-shredded part-skim mozzarella cheese

½ cup (2 ounces) already-shredded Parmesan cheese

½ teaspoon dried oregano leaves

¼ teaspoon salt, or to taste

Freshly ground black pepper, to taste

1½ cups prepared pasta sauce, preferably the tomato-basil variety

Preheat oven to 425F (220C). Lightly oil a 9 × 13-inch baking dish and set aside.

Cook the shells in boiling salted water according to package directions until just al dente, about 10 minutes.

Drain well. Let cool in a single layer on wax paper to prevent sticking.

In a medium bowl, stir together the ricotta cheese, mozzarella cheese, ¼ cup of the Parmesan cheese, the oregano, salt, and pepper until well combined.

Spread about half of the pasta sauce over the bottom of the prepared baking dish. Fill each shell with about 2 tablespoons of the cheese mixture and place them, seam side up, in the prepared dish. Top with remaining sauce and sprinkle with the remaining Parmesan cheese. Cover tightly with foil. (At this point, the dish can be refrigerated up to 24 hours before baking.) Bake 20 to 25 minutes, or until the shells are hot through the center and the Parmesan cheese is melted. Serve at once.

PER SERVING

Calories 380 ▪ Protein 29g ▪ Total Fat 11g ▪ Sat. Fat 5g ▪ Cholesterol 34mg ▪ Carbohydrate 42g ▪ Dietary Fiber 3g ▪ Sodium 956mg

SPAGHETTI WITH RED SAUCE

Vegan

MAKES 6 TO 8 MAIN-DISH OR 10 TO 12 SIDE-DISH OR PASTA-COURSE SERVINGS

Born from a couple cans of tomato paste—an excellent source of cancer-fighting lycopene—this fragrant and flavorful red sauce dresses your spaghetti or other favorite pasta in fine style in just about 20 minutes. Its success rests upon sautéing the garlic until golden, not burnt, so take care with this step.

> 2 tablespoons extra-virgin olive oil
> 1 tablespoon refrigerated bottled minced garlic
> 4 cups water
> 2 (6-ounce) cans tomato paste
> 1 teaspoon dried parsley
> 1 teaspoon dried oregano
> 1 teaspoon dried basil
> 1 teaspoon sugar
> ¼ teaspoon salt, preferably the coarse variety, or to taste
> ¼ teaspoon freshly ground black pepper, or to taste
> 16 ounces spaghetti or other pasta
> Already-shredded Parmesan cheese (optional)

In a medium stockpot, heat the oil over medium heat. Add the garlic and cook, stirring constantly, until sizzling and golden, 1 to 2 minutes. Add the water, tomato paste, parsley, oregano, basil, sugar, salt, and pepper, stirring until well combined. Increase the heat to medium-high and cook, stirring often, until the mixture comes to a gentle boil. Reduce the heat and simmer, partially covered, stir-

ring occasionally, until the sauce is thickened, about 20 minutes.

Meanwhile, cook the pasta in a large stockpot of boiling salted water according to package directions until al dente. Drain and transfer to a large bowl. Add the sauce and toss well to thoroughly combine. Serve at once, sprinkled with Parmesan cheese, if desired.

PER SERVING

Calories 375 ▪ Protein 12g ▪ Total Fat 6g ▪ Sat. Fat 1g ▪ Cholesterol 0mg ▪ Carbohydrate 69g ▪ Dietary Fiber 4g ▪ Sodium 532mg

Cook's Tip If you only need three or four main-dish servings, cook 8 ounces pasta but prepare all the sauce. Refrigerate half of the sauce for up to 3 days and use in other pasta recipes or as a topping for pizza or polenta. The sauce can also be placed in a freezer bag and frozen for up to 3 months.

CURRIED VERMICELLI WITH CHICKPEAS

Vegan

MAKES 5 TO 6 MAIN-DISH OR 8 TO 10 SIDE-DISH OR PASTA-COURSE SERVINGS

This spicy, curry-scented pasta dish is nice for parties or buffets as it can be served at room temperature. While the chickpeas provide additional protein and fiber, they can be omitted, if desired. The pimiento, though optional, lends pretty flecks of color. For a milder flavor, use the lesser amount of curry powder and halve the amount of chili paste.

> 3 tablespoons reduced-sodium soy sauce
> 1 tablespoon peanut oil or plain sesame oil

1 tablespoon toasted (dark) sesame oil

2 teaspoons mild curry powder, or to taste

½ teaspoon onion powder

½ teaspoon Chinese chili paste, or crushed
   red pepper flakes, to taste

½ teaspoon sugar

½ teaspoon garlic powder

12 ounces vermicelli or other thin pasta,
   broken in half

1 (15-ounce) can chickpeas

1 (4-ounce) jar diced pimiento, drained
   (optional)

Salt and freshly ground black pepper, to taste,
   if necessary

In a small bowl, whisk together the soy sauce, peanut oil, toasted sesame oil, curry powder, onion powder, chili paste, sugar, and garlic powder. Set aside to let the flavors blend.

Meanwhile, in a large stockpot of boiling salted water, cook the pasta according to package directions until al dente. While the pasta is cooking, drain the chickpeas in a large colander and rinse with running cold water. Carefully pour the cooked pasta over the chickpeas and drain. Return the hot pasta mixture to the stockpot. Add the soy mixture and pimiento (if using); toss well to thoroughly combine. Season with salt and pepper, if necessary. Serve warm or at room temperature.

PER SERVING
Calories 397 ■ Protein 14g ■ Total Fat 8g ■
Sat. Fat 1g ■ Cholesterol 0mg ■ Carbohydrate 68g ■
Dietary Fiber 4g ■ Sodium 369mg

JAPANESE VERMICELLI IN PEANUT SAUCE

Vegan

MAKES 5 TO 6 MAIN-DISH OR 8 TO 10 SIDE-DISH OR PASTA-COURSE SERVINGS

All the ingredients for this tasty pasta dish come straight from the pantry. If time permits, you can make your own teriyaki sauce (see page 138) for use in the peanut sauce, which is a pleasant change of pace from the usual tomato-based pasta sauce or basil pesto.

½ cup low-sodium vegetable broth, warmed

6 tablespoons creamy peanut butter

2½ to 3 tablespoons teriyaki sauce

½ teaspoon garlic powder

½ teaspoon onion powder

Freshly ground black pepper, to taste

Pinch cayenne pepper, or to taste (optional)

12 ounces vermicelli or thin spaghetti

5 to 6 tablespoons unsalted chopped peanuts
   (optional)

In a small bowl, combine the broth, peanut butter, teriyaki sauce, garlic powder, onion powder, black pepper, and cayenne (if using). Set aside.

In a large stockpot of boiling salted water, cook the vermicelli according to package directions until al dente. Drain and return to stockpot. Immediately add the peanut butter mixture. Toss well to thoroughly coat the vermicelli. Serve at once, garnished with the chopped peanuts, if desired.

PER SERVING
Calories 370 ■ Protein 12g ■ Total Fat 10g ■
Sat. Fat 2g ■ Cholesterol 0mg ■ Carbohydrate 59g ■
Dietary Fiber 2g ■ Sodium 489mg

CAULIFLOWER AND WAGON WHEELS WITH GREEN OLIVE-CAPER SAUCE

Vegan

MAKES 5 TO 6 MAIN-DISH OR 8 TO 10 SIDE-DISH OR PASTA-COURSE SERVINGS

One of my favorite pasta recipes in this book, this tangy dish is perfect for a party or buffet as it can be served at room temperature. Mild green chilies lend it a spirited punch, which, in Italy, would never be compromised by the addition of Parmesan cheese. If you don't have garlic-flavored olive oil, add ¼ teaspoon garlic powder to the broth mixture.

- 1 cup low-sodium vegetable broth
- ½ cup green olives, drained
- 1 (4-ounce) can diced mild green chilies, briefly drained
- 3 tablespoons diced pimiento, drained
- 3 tablespoons capers, drained
- 2 tablespoons garlic-flavored olive oil
- ¼ teaspoon coarse salt, or to taste
- Freshly ground black pepper, to taste
- 12 ounces wagon wheels, bow ties, shells, or other similar pasta
- 8 ounces frozen cauliflower pieces
- Slivered almonds or pine nuts, toasted if desired (see Cook's Tip, page 7) (optional)

In a small bowl, mix together the broth, olives, chilies, pimiento, capers, oil, salt, and pepper. Set aside.

Meanwhile, bring a large pot of salted water to a boil over high heat. Add the pasta and cook according to package directions until just al dente, adding the cauliflower the last 3 or 4 minutes of cooking. Drain well. Return to the stockpot and add the reserved broth mixture. Cook over medium-low heat, stirring and tossing often, until the pasta has absorbed most of the liquid, 3 to 5 minutes. Serve warm or at room temperature, garnished with the nuts, if desired.

PER SERVING
Calories 346 ▪ Protein 12g ▪ Total Fat 8g ▪
Sat. Fat 1g ▪ Cholesterol 0mg ▪ Carbohydrate 56g ▪
Dietary Fiber 4g ▪ Sodium 380mg

BAKED ZITI WITH CAPONATA AND THREE CHEESES

Egg-free

MAKES 5 TO 6 MAIN-DISH OR 8 TO 10 SIDE-DISH OR PASTA-COURSE SERVINGS

This rustic casserole is excellent served with a mixed green salad and crusty Italian bread. Caponata is an Italian sweet-and-sour eggplant relish that can be found near the olives and pimiento in most major supermarkets. To reduce the total amount of dairy in the recipe, 1 cup crumbled firm tofu can replace the ricotta cheese, if desired. However, because vegan soy cheeses typically do not melt well, their substitution for the mozzarella and Parmesan cheeses is not recommended.

- 10 ounces ziti
- 1 cup nonfat ricotta cheese (see headnote above for dairy-free alternative)
- 1 (14-ounce) can diced tomatoes, preferably petite-cut, well drained

½ teaspoon dried oregano

Salt and freshly ground black pepper, to taste

1 (7½-ounce) jar caponata

¾ cup (3 ounces) already-shredded part-skim mozzarella cheese

¼ cup (1 ounce) already-shredded Parmesan cheese

Sliced canned or pitted whole black olives, for garnish (optional)

Preheat oven to 425F (220C). Lightly oil an 11 × 7-inch baking dish and set aside.

In a large stockpot of boiling salted water, cook the pasta according to package directions until just al dente, about 8 minutes. Drain and return to stockpot. Add the ricotta cheese, tomatoes, oregano, salt, and pepper; toss well to combine. Transfer to the prepared baking dish. Spread evenly with the caponata. Sprinkle evenly with the mozzarella cheese, then top with the Parmesan cheese. Garnish with the olives, if desired. Cover with foil and bake 20 to 25 minutes, or until the cheeses are melted and the casserole is hot through the center. Serve at once.

PER SERVING

Calories 376 ■ Protein 22g ■ Total Fat 9g ■
Sat. Fat 4g ■ Cholesterol 21mg ■ Carbohydrate 51g ■
Dietary Fiber 3g ■ Sodium 863mg

Hearty Vegetable, Grain, and Legume Combos

Of all the chapters in this book, here is where you will find the greatest concentration of streamlined stand-alone suppers, from hearty stuffed cabbage rolls to exotic Asian-style stir-fries. Most are perfect for quick weeknight meals; a week hardly goes by where I don't serve Asian Barley Pilaf with Mixed Vegetables or Easy Risotto with Peas and Basil for my family. Others are ideal for casual gatherings; Taco Casserole with Refried Beans and Corn is popular with children as well as adults. For a more elegant dinner, consider Couscous-Stuffed Portobello Mushroom Caps with Pesto, which can be prepared in two stages for stress-free entertaining. Whatever the occasion, the following recipes are sure to help you beat the kitchen clock in record time!

BARLEY-FILLED CABBAGE ROLLS WITH TANGY TOMATO-MUSTARD SAUCE

Dairy-free with vegan option

MAKES 4 MAIN-DISH SERVINGS

Enjoying a comeback as a nutritious pasta and rice alternative, old-fashioned barley is a good source of niacin, phosphorus, and iron. While any type of barley can be used, the quick-cooking variety allows the busy cook to pull this wholesome meal together in well under an hour. Although the egg helps to bind the barley together, you can prepare the filling without it, or substitute with ¼ cup mashed soft tofu, if desired. A leftover cabbage roll, with a little smear of mustard, makes a terrific midnight snack straight from the refrigerator!

2 cups water

¼ teaspoon salt, plus additional to taste

1 cup quick-cooking barley

8 large, whole, outside cabbage leaves

½ cup already-shredded carrots

1 egg (see headnote above for vegan options)

3 tablespoons ketchup

1 tablespoon extra-virgin olive oil

1 teaspoon onion powder

¼ teaspoon garlic powder

¼ teaspoon dried oregano

¼ teaspoon ground black pepper

1 cup low-sodium vegetable broth

Tangy Tomato-Mustard Sauce (page 112)

Preheat oven to 425F (220C). Lightly oil a 13 × 9-inch baking dish and set aside.

In a medium saucepan, bring the water and salt to a boil over high heat. Stir in the barley and reduce the heat to low. Cover and simmer until the barley is tender and most of the liquid has been absorbed, 12 to 15 minutes. Transfer to a medium mixing bowl and let cool slightly.

Meanwhile, partly fill a large stockpot with water and bring to a boil over high heat. Add the cabbage leaves and boil until slightly tender, 1 minute. Remove with tongs and drain well.

Add the carrots, egg, ketchup, oil, onion powder, garlic powder, oregano, pepper, and salt (if necessary) to the barley; mix until thoroughly combined. Place one-eighth of the barley mixture on the stem end of each cabbage leaf and roll up, tucking the sides in as you go. Transfer, seam side down, to the prepared baking dish.

Pour the broth over the cabbage rolls. Cover tightly with foil and bake 20 to 25 minutes, or until the cabbage is tender and the filling is hot through the center. Transfer the rolls to a serving platter or individual plates and drizzle evenly with the Tomato-Mustard Sauce. Serve at once.

PER SERVING

Calories 314 ▪ Protein 13g ▪ Total Fat 6g ▪
Sat. Fat 1g ▪ Cholesterol 53mg ▪ Carbohydrate 55g ▪
Dietary Fiber 11g ▪ Sodium 546mg

TANGY TOMATO-MUSTARD SAUCE

Vegan

MAKE ABOUT 1⅓ CUPS; 4 SERVINGS

This tangy tomato sauce also goes well with stuffed peppers and veggie burgers.

1 (8-ounce) can no-salt-added tomato sauce

2 tablespoons prepared yellow mustard

2 tablespoons light brown sugar

1 tablespoon cider vinegar

¼ teaspoon dried oregano

Combine all the ingredients in a small saucepan. Bring to a simmer over medium heat, stirring occasionally. Cover and keep warm over low heat until needed. (Sauce can be cooled and stored, covered, in refrigerator up to 5 days. Reheat over low heat.)

PER SERVING (ABOUT ⅓ CUP)

Calories 55 ▪ Protein 1g ▪ Total Fat 0g ▪
Sat. Fat 0g ▪ Cholesterol 0mg ▪ Carbohydrate 12g ▪
Dietary Fiber 1g ▪ Sodium 113mg

ASIAN BARLEY PILAF WITH MIXED VEGETABLES

Vegan

MAKES 3 TO 4 MAIN-DISH OR
5 TO 6 SIDE-DISH SERVINGS

A nice change of pace from ordinary rice pilaf, this tasty dish cooks up in about 20 minutes with the help of quick-cooking barley. If possible, select an Asian blend of frozen mixed vegetables containing petite peas, baby whole carrots, snow peas, and baby cob corn. Just about any frozen vegetable, however, will work well here.

1 tablespoon peanut oil or other vegetable oil

1 cup quick-cooking barley

1 teaspoon refrigerated bottled minced garlic

1¾ cups water

1½ cups frozen Asian-style mixed vegetables

½ cup frozen pearl onions

2 tablespoons reduced-sodium soy sauce

½ tablespoon toasted (dark) sesame oil

1 teaspoon sugar

½ teaspoon onion powder

Salt and freshly ground black pepper, to taste

In a large deep-sided nonstick skillet with a lid, heat the peanut oil over medium heat. Add the barley and cook, stirring, 2 minutes. Add the garlic and cook, stirring, 1 more minute. Add the water, mixed vegetables, pearl onions, soy sauce, sesame oil, sugar, onion powder, salt, and pepper; bring to a brisk simmer over medium-high heat. Reduce the heat, cover, and simmer until barley is tender and has absorbed most of the liquid, 12 to 15 minutes.

Stir to evenly distribute the ingredients and serve at once.

PER SERVING

Calories 357 ▪ Protein 12g ▪ Total Fat 9g ▪
Sat. Fat 2g ▪ Cholesterol 0mg ▪ Carbohydrate 62g ▪
Dietary Fiber 12g ▪ Sodium 453mg

TOASTED BARLEY AND ORZO WITH BLACK-EYED PEAS

Vegan

**MAKES 4 MAIN-DISH OR
6 TO 8 SIDE-DISH SERVINGS**

This healthful grain combination looks particularly festive flecked with green basil and red tomatoes. If you don't have any fresh basil on hand, you can omit it and the dish will still be delicious. Also, plain diced canned tomatoes can be used in lieu of the Italian-seasoned variety, but add some garlic powder, dried basil, and dried oregano, to taste.

1½ tablespoons extra-virgin olive oil

1 cup quick-cooking barley

1 (14-ounce) can (1¾ cups) low-sodium
    vegetable broth

¾ cup water

½ cup orzo

1 (15.5-ounce) can black-eyed peas, rinsed
    and drained

1 cup canned diced Italian-seasoned
    tomatoes, preferably the basil, garlic, and
    oregano variety, drained

¼ cup whole basil leaves, torn in half or in
    quarters, depending on size

Salt, preferably the coarse variety, and pepper,
    to taste

In a medium deep-sided skillet with a lid, heat 1 tablespoon of the oil over medium heat. Add the barley and cook, stirring constantly, until golden and toasted, about 5 minutes. Add the broth and water; bring to a boil over medium-high heat. Add the orzo, black-eyed peas, and tomatoes, stirring to combine. Return to a boil, reduce the heat to low, cover, and simmer 10 minutes. Remove from the heat and let stand, covered, 5 minutes, or until all the liquid is absorbed. Uncover and add the basil, remaining oil, salt, and pepper, stirring to combine. Serve warm.

PER SERVING
Calories 355 ▪ Protein 18g ▪ Total Fat 7g ▪
Sat. Fat 1g ▪ Cholesterol 0mg ▪ Carbohydrate 58g ▪
Dietary Fiber 16g ▪ Sodium 240mg

BULGUR PILAF WITH CHICKPEAS

Vegan

**MAKES 4 MAIN-DISH OR
6 TO 8 SIDE-DISH SERVINGS**

In this hearty pilaf, the chickpeas can be replaced with other legumes or vegetables (black-eyed peas or frozen green peas and carrots are other good choices), or they can be omitted entirely (in that case, use less cumin, if desired). I like to prepare it with chickpeas and serve it with Roasted Eggplant and Zucchini with Tahini-Yogurt Sauce (page 141) for an exotic Middle Eastern medley. Bulgur, a precooked wheat product, is available in fine- and medium-grain forms in most major supermarkets. The fine-grain variety is preferred here, as it requires less cooking time.

1 cup fancy (fine-grain) bulgur wheat

1 cup boiling water

1 tablespoon extra-virgin olive oil

½ tablespoon toasted (dark) sesame oil

½ cup frozen chopped onion

1 teaspoon refrigerated bottled minced garlic

1 (19-ounce) can chickpeas, rinsed and
    drained

1 cup low-sodium vegetable broth

2 tablespoons diced pimiento, drained
    (optional)

1 teaspoon ground cumin

Salt and freshly ground black pepper, to taste

In a medium bowl, combine the bulgur and boiling water. Let stand 10 minutes to soften.

Meanwhile, in a medium deep-sided skillet with a lid, heat the olive oil and sesame oil over medium heat. Add the onion and cook, stirring, until softened and thawed, about 3 minutes. Add the garlic and cook, stirring constantly, 1 minute. Add the chickpeas, broth, reserved bulgur (and any accumulated water at bottom of bowl), pimiento (if using), cumin, salt, and pepper, stirring well to combine; bring to a boil over high heat. Reduce the heat to low, cover, and simmer until the bulgur has absorbed all the liquid, about 15 minutes. If the bulgur seems too wet (it should be moist, not soggy), increase the heat to medium and cook, uncovered, stirring often, until fairly dry. Fluff with a fork and serve warm.

PER SERVING
Calories 304 ▪ Protein 14g ▪ Total Fat 8g ▪
Sat. Fat 1g ▪ Cholesterol 0mg ▪ Carbohydrate 49g ▪
Dietary Fiber 12g ▪ Sodium 143mg

CHILI-BEAN AND CHEESE CASSEROLE

Egg-free

MAKES 4 MAIN-DISH SERVINGS

This cheesy bean dish is wonderful accompanied by tortilla chips and a tossed green salad. While you can reduce the dairy by using rice milk, I don't recommend using vegan cheese substitutes here; not only are the shredded varieties limited, but also I find that they don't melt properly.

2 tablespoons canola oil

2 tablespoons all-purpose flour

1 cup skim milk or rice milk

¼ teaspoon onion powder

Salt and freshly ground black pepper, to taste

Dash Tabasco sauce (optional)

1 (7-ounce) can diced mild green chilies,
   drained
1 (16-ounce) can kidney beans, rinsed and
   drained
1½ cups (6 ounces) already-shredded
   reduced-fat Monterey Jack cheese with
   jalapeño chilies or Mexican blend cheese
Salsa, sour cream or nondairy sour cream,
   and/or guacamole (optional)

Preheat oven to 375F (190C). Lightly oil an 8-inch-square baking dish and set aside.

In a small saucepan, heat the oil over medium-low heat. Add the flour and cook, stirring constantly, until smooth and beginning to bubble, 3 to 5 minutes. Remove from the heat and gradually stir in the milk. Add the onion powder, salt, and pepper. Return to heat and bring to a boil over medium heat, stirring constantly. Boil, stirring constantly, 1 minute. Remove from the heat and stir in the Tabasco sauce (if using).

Arrange half of the chilies in the prepared baking dish. Top with half of the beans, followed by half of the cheese. Layer with the remaining chilies, then beans. Pour the sauce over the beans, and then sprinkle with the remaining cheese. Bake, uncovered, about 20 minutes, or until puffed and brown. Let cool slightly before serving warm, with the optional toppings passed separately, if desired.

PER SERVING

Calories 269 ▪ Protein 19g ▪ Total Fat 10g ▪
Sat. Fat 3g ▪ Cholesterol 10mg ▪ Carbohydrate 25g ▪
Dietary Fiber 4g ▪ Sodium 296mg

COUSCOUS-STUFFED PORTOBELLO MUSHROOM CAPS WITH PESTO

Egg-free

MAKES 4 MAIN-DISH OR
8 FIRST-COURSE OR APPETIZER SERVINGS

Stuffed mushrooms always seem elegant. You can prepare this easy recipe in two stages for carefree entertaining.

1 (14-ounce) can (1¾ cups) low-sodium
   vegetable broth
½ teaspoon onion powder
¼ teaspoon garlic powder
Salt and freshly ground black pepper, to taste
1 cup instant couscous, preferably whole
   wheat
2 tablespoons sun-dried tomato bits (if using
   regular pesto)
½ cup refrigerated prepared regular pesto or
   sun-dried tomato pesto
2 tablespoons pine nuts (optional)
8 large (about 2 ounces each) packaged
   portobello mushroom caps

Preheat oven to 400F (205C). Lightly grease a shallow casserole large enough to hold the mushrooms in a single layer and set aside.

In a medium saucepan, bring 1½ cups of the broth, the onion powder, garlic powder, salt, and pepper to a boil over high heat. Stir in the couscous and sun-dried tomato bits (if using); cover and remove from the heat. Let stand until all the liquid has been absorbed, about 7 minutes. Uncover and stir in the pesto and pine nuts (if using), stirring well to combine. (At this point, the mixture can be cooled and stored, covered, in refrigerator 24 hours before continuing with recipe.)

Fill each mushroom cap with about ½ cup of the couscous mixture. Transfer to the prepared casserole. Spoon ½ tablespoon of the remaining broth over each mushroom cap. Cover tightly with foil and bake 45 minutes. Uncover and bake 5 minutes, or until the tops are lightly browned and crusty. Serve warm.

PER SERVING

Calories 365 ▪ Protein 18g ▪ Total Fat 15g ▪
Sat. Fat 4g ▪ Cholesterol 9mg ▪ Carbohydrate 42g ▪
Dietary Fiber 5g ▪ Sodium 442mg

Variation

Couscous with Pesto and Cherry Tomatoes: Omit the mushrooms and the sun-dried tomatoes; use regular pesto and proceed as otherwise directed in the recipe, adding 1 to 1½ cups cherry or grape tomatoes to the cooked couscous. Serve warm or at room temperature. Makes 4 main-dish or 6 side-dish servings.

CURRIED ISRAELI COUSCOUS WITH RAISINS AND COCONUT

Vegan

MAKES 4 MAIN-DISH OR
6 TO 8 SIDE-DISH SERVINGS

This aromatic dish is one of my favorite ways to eat Israeli couscous, a larger-grained version of the tiny beadlike Moroccan pasta. Sometimes called toasted or Middle Eastern couscous, Israeli couscous is available in Middle Eastern and health food markets, as well as many well-stocked grocery stores. Dark raisins can be substituted for the golden variety, if desired.

- 1 cup water
- ¾ cup orange juice from frozen concentrate
- ¼ cup golden raisins
- 1 tablespoon extra-virgin olive oil
- 2 teaspoons mild curry powder
- ½ teaspoon onion powder
- ½ teaspoon salt
- 1⅓ cups Israeli couscous
- ¼ cup unsweetened shredded coconut
- ¼ cup slivered almonds (optional)

In a medium saucepan, combine the water, juice, raisins, oil, curry powder, onion powder, and salt. Bring to a boil over medium-high heat. Stir in the couscous, reduce the heat to medium-low, and cover. Simmer until all the liquids have been absorbed, 12 to 15 minutes.

Transfer the couscous mixture to a medium serving bowl. Add the coconut and almonds (if using), tossing thoroughly to combine. Serve warm or at room temperature.

PER SERVING

Calories 321 ▪ Protein 8g ▪ Total Fat 6g ▪
Sat. Fat 2g ▪ Cholesterol 0mg ▪ Carbohydrate 59g ▪
Dietary Fiber 4g ▪ Sodium 276mg

TOASTED ISRAELI COUSCOUS WITH CHICKPEAS AND TAHINI

Vegan

**MAKES 5 MAIN-DISH OR
8 TO 10 SIDE-DISH SERVINGS**

Unlike the much finer grains of traditional Moroccan couscous, the giant pearl-shaped grains of the Israeli variety stand up well to a substantive tahini sauce. Tahini is a protein-packed, calcium-rich paste made from ground sesame seeds that has a consistency similar to natural peanut butter. Both Israeli couscous and tahini are available in Middle Eastern and health food markets, as well as many well-stocked supermarkets.

½ tablespoon extra-virgin olive oil

1⅓ cups Israeli couscous

1 (14-ounce) can (1¾ cups) low-sodium
    vegetable broth

½ teaspoon garlic powder

1 (15-ounce) can chickpeas, rinsed and
    drained

2 tablespoons chopped pimiento, drained
    (optional)

3 tablespoons sesame tahini

1½ tablespoons lemon juice, preferably
    prepared from frozen concentrate

Salt, preferably the coarse variety, and freshly
    ground black pepper, to taste

In a medium deep-sided skillet with a lid, heat the oil over medium heat. Add the couscous and cook, stirring often, until lightly browned, about 3 minutes.

Meanwhile, in a small saucepan, bring the broth to a boil. Slowly add to the couscous and bring to a boil over high heat. Reduce the heat to medium-low, stir in the garlic powder, and cover. Simmer until all the liquid is absorbed, 12 to 15 minutes.

Remove from the heat and add the chickpeas, pimiento (if using), tahini, lemon juice, salt, and pepper; toss well to combine. Cover and let stand 5 minutes. Uncover and toss again. Serve warm or at room temperature.

PER SERVING

Calories 339 ▪ Protein 16g ▪ Total Fat 8g ▪
Sat. Fat 1g ▪ Cholesterol 0mg ▪ Carbohydrate 53g ▪
Dietary Fiber 6g ▪ Sodium 190mg

WHOLE WHEAT COUSCOUS WITH PEAS, PEARL ONIONS, AND ARTICHOKES

Vegan

**MAKES 3 TO 4 MAIN-DISH OR
6 SIDE-DISH SERVINGS**

Ready in just about 10 minutes, this healthful entrée will quickly become a part of your quick-food repertoire for busy weeknights.

1½ cups water

¼ teaspoon dried grated lemon peel

1 cup instant whole wheat couscous

1½ cups frozen peas and pearl onions, unthawed

1 (6-ounce) jar marinated quartered artichoke hearts, drained, 1 tablespoon marinade reserved

1 tablespoon extra-virgin olive oil

Salt and freshly ground black pepper, to taste

In a medium saucepan, bring the water and lemon peel to a boil over high heat. Stir in the couscous, peas and pearl onions, artichokes and reserved marinade, olive oil, salt, and pepper. Return to a boil, cover, and remove from the heat. Let stand until all the liquids have been absorbed, 7 minutes. Uncover and fluff with a fork. Season with additional salt and pepper as necessary. Serve warm or at room temperature.

PER SERVING

Calories 344 ▪ Protein 12g ▪ Total Fat 7g ▪
Sat. Fat 1g ▪ Cholesterol 0mg ▪ Carbohydrate 60g ▪
Dietary Fiber 9g ▪ Sodium 119mg

LENTILS WITH SPINACH AND BASIL OVER RICE

Vegan

MAKES 4 MAIN-DISH SERVINGS

I like to serve this iron-rich, protein-packed dish with Garlic Pita Toasts (page 72) and Marinated Baby Bella Mushroom and Grape Tomato Salad (page 48) for a complete meal. The optional curried-yogurt sauce will lend it a distinctive East Indian taste. Couscous can replace the rice, if desired.

1 cup dried lentils, rinsed

4 cups water

1 tablespoon extra-virgin olive oil or canola oil

1 teaspoon refrigerated bottled minced garlic

½ cup low-sodium vegetable broth

2 tablespoons lemon juice, preferably prepared from frozen concentrate

½ teaspoon salt, preferably the coarse variety, or to taste

¼ teaspoon freshly ground black pepper, or to taste

4 cups ready-washed spinach, coarsely torn

1 cup fresh basil leaves, coarsely torn

3 cups hot cooked white or brown rice (see Cook's Tip, page 126)

Curried Yogurt Sauce (page 139; optional)

In a medium saucepan, bring the lentils and water to a boil over high heat. Reduce the heat, partially cover, and simmer until tender, about 40 minutes, stirring occasionally. Drain.

In a large nonstick skillet, heat the oil over medium heat. Add the garlic and cook, stirring, until softened and fragrant, 1 to 2 minutes. Add the broth, lemon juice, lentils, salt, and pepper. Bring to a simmer over medium-high heat. Add the spinach and basil and cook, tossing and stirring constantly, until just wilted. Immediately remove from heat. Spoon ¾ cup rice onto each of 4 plates. Top with equal amounts of lentil-spinach mixture. Serve at once, with the curried-yogurt sauce passed separately, if desired.

PER SERVING

Calories 404 ▪ Protein 21g ▪ Total Fat 5g ▪
Sat. Fat 1g ▪ Cholesterol 0mg ▪ Carbohydrate 71g ▪
Dietary Fiber 17g ▪ Sodium 353mg

Cook's Tip You can use either baby or mature spinach in this recipe, but if using the latter, remove any thick stems and ribs before cooking.

HERBED POLENTA PIE WITH CAPONATA AND PINE NUTS

Vegan

**MAKES 4 TO 6 MAIN-DISH OR
8 TO 12 SIDE-DISH OR APPETIZER SERVINGS**

Polenta, coarse-ground yellow cornmeal, is a staple in many homes throughout northern Italy. Bland on its own, it is the perfect foil for the sweet-and-sour eggplant caponata. Serve this rustic pie with a simple tossed green salad for a low-key Italian-style meal. Smaller portions make wonderful appetizer, side-dish, or first-course servings. Vegan soy cheese substitutes for the optional Parmesan cheese are not recommended here.

1 (14-ounce) can (1¾ cups) low-sodium
    vegetable broth

1¼ cups water

1 cup instant polenta

2 teaspoons extra-virgin olive oil

1 teaspoon refrigerated bottled minced garlic

1 teaspoon dried thyme leaves

½ teaspoon dried rosemary leaves

Salt and freshly ground black pepper, to taste

2 (4.75-ounce) cans caponata

¼ cup already-shredded Parmesan cheese
    (optional)

2 tablespoons pine nuts, toasted if desired
    (see Cook's Tip, page 7)

Lightly oil an 8½- or 9-inch pie plate and set aside.

In a medium stockpot, bring the broth, water, polenta, oil, garlic, thyme, rosemary, salt, and pepper to a boil over high heat. Immediately reduce the heat to medium; cook, stirring often with a long-handled spoon, 5 minutes. Immediately spoon the polenta into the prepared pie plate, pressing down with the back of a large spoon to form a smooth surface. Cover with foil and let stand about 15 minutes to become firm.

Meanwhile, in a small saucepan, bring the caponata to a simmer over medium heat, stirring occasionally. Spread evenly over the polenta. Sprinkle with the cheese (if using), followed by the pine nuts. (If not serving immediately, polenta pie can be held, loosely covered, in a warm oven up to 1 hour before serving.) Cut into wedges and serve warm.

PER SERVING

Calories 383 ▪ Protein 13g ▪ Total Fat 10g ▪
Sat. Fat 1g ▪ Cholesterol 0mg ▪ Carbohydrate 61g ▪
Dietary Fiber 10g ▪ Sodium 811mg

BASMATI RICE WITH SPICED CASHEWS, MIXED VEGETABLES, AND CHUTNEY

Vegan

**MAKES 4 MAIN-DISH OR
6 TO 8 SIDE-DISH SERVINGS**

Redolent of curry and turmeric, cashews lend a spice and crunch to basmati rice in this exotic main dish or side dish. Available in well-stocked supermarkets, basmati is a fragrant, nutty rice grown in India and Pakistan. Long-grain white rice can be substituted, if desired.

1 (14-ounce) can (1¾ cups) low-sodium
    vegetable broth
1 cup basmati rice
½ teaspoon onion powder
¼ teaspoon salt, plus additional to taste
Freshly ground black pepper, to taste
¼ cup mango chutney
1 teaspoon canola oil
½ cup whole unsalted roasted cashews
¼ teaspoon curry powder
¼ teaspoon turmeric
Pinch cayenne pepper
2 cups frozen mixed Asian-style vegetables,
    cooked according to package directions
    and drained

In a medium saucepan with a tight-fitting lid, bring the broth, rice, onion powder, salt, and black pepper to a boil over high heat, stirring once. Reduce the heat to low, cover, and cook until the rice is tender and all the water is absorbed, 17 to 20 minutes. Uncover and stir in the chutney. Re-cover and let stand 5 minutes.

Meanwhile, in a small skillet or sauté pan, heat the oil over medium heat. Add the cashews and cook, tossing constantly, until fragrant and just beginning to brown, 1 to 2 minutes. Add the curry powder, turmeric, cayenne, and additional salt and black pepper as needed; cook, tossing constantly, 1 minute. Remove from the heat and let stand a few minutes to further crisp.

In a warm serving bowl, toss the rice, cashews, and vegetables until combined. Serve at once.

PER SERVING

Calories 343 ▪ Protein 12g ▪ Total Fat 10g ▪
Sat. Fat 2g ▪ Cholesterol 0mg ▪ Carbohydrate 52g ▪
Dietary Fiber 4g ▪ Sodium 405mg

Cook's Tips To enable you to toss the nuts so they don't burn while you add the spices, measure out the spices and other seasonings beforehand and place in a single container for easy addition.

Other nuts that work well here are whole almonds and macadamia nuts. The nuts, alone, make a terrific party snack. To make seasoned nuts, add ½ teaspoon sugar along with the curry powder and other seasonings, if desired. Store completely cooled nuts in an airtight container up to 1 week for optimal freshness.

CARIBBEAN-STYLE RICE AND GREEN PIGEON PEAS

Vegan

**MAKES 4 MAIN-DISH OR
6 TO 8 SIDE-DISH SERVINGS**

The speckled green pigeon pea is the Caribbean's best-loved bean; not surprisingly, arroz con gandules is one of the Caribbean's best-loved rice dishes. Canned pigeon peas can be found in Jamaican and Latin markets as well as the specialty aisle of many well-stocked supermarkets. Black-eyed peas can be substituted, if desired.

1 tablespoon canola oil

¼ cup frozen chopped onion

¼ cup frozen chopped green bell pepper

½ teaspoon refrigerated bottled minced garlic

1 (14-ounce) can (1¾ cups) low-sodium
   vegetable broth

¼ cup water

¼ teaspoon ground coriander

¼ teaspoon ground cumin

¼ teaspoon ground thyme

1 large bay leaf

Salt and freshly ground black pepper, to taste

1 cup long-grain white rice

1 (15-ounce) can green pigeon peas, rinsed
   and drained

In a medium deep-sided skillet with a lid, heat the oil over medium heat. Add the onion and bell pepper and cook, stirring, until softened and thawed, 2 to 3 minutes. Add the garlic and cook, stirring, 1 minute. Add the broth, water, coriander, cumin, thyme, bay leaf, salt, and pepper; bring to a boil over high heat. Stir in the rice and peas and let come to a brisk simmer. Reduce the heat to low, cover, and simmer until all the liquid is absorbed, 17 to 20 minutes. Remove from the heat and let stand, covered, 5 minutes. Remove the bay leaf, fluff the rice with a fork, and serve at once.

PER SERVING
Calories 305 ▪ Protein 13g ▪ Total Fat 4g ▪
Sat. Fat 0g ▪ Cholesterol 0mg ▪ Carbohydrate 54g ▪
Dietary Fiber 2g ▪ Sodium 233mg

Variation

Caribbean-Style Rice and Red Beans: Substitute 1 (15-ounce) can red kidney beans for the pigeon peas. Omit the green bell pepper and increase the amount of onion to ½ cup. Replace the coriander, cumin, and thyme with 1 teaspoon Caribbean jerk seasoning, if desired. Proceed as otherwise directed in the recipe.

CUBAN-STYLE BLACK BEANS AND RICE

Vegan

**MAKES 4 MAIN-DISH OR
6 TO 8 SIDE-DISH SERVINGS**

This classic bean dish is traditionally served over white rice, but brown rice is an equally delicious, and more nutritious, alternative. The beans are also wonderful over couscous or tossed with small shells or elbow macaroni.

2 tablespoons extra-virgin olive oil
½ cup frozen chopped onion
¼ cup frozen chopped green bell pepper
1 teaspoon refrigerated bottled minced garlic
1 (16-ounce) can black beans, rinsed and
    drained
½ cup low-sodium vegetable broth or water
1 tablespoon cider vinegar
1 teaspoon dried oregano
½ teaspoon ground cumin
1 bay leaf
Pinch cayenne pepper, or to taste (optional)
Salt and freshly ground black pepper, to taste
3 cups hot cooked rice (see Cook's Tip, page
    126)

In a large nonstick skillet, heat the oil over medium heat. Add the onion and bell pepper, and cook, stirring often, until thawed and softened, about 3 minutes. Add the garlic and cook, stirring often, 2 minutes. Add the beans, broth, vinegar, oregano, cumin, bay leaf, cayenne (if using), salt, and pepper; bring to a brisk simmer over medium-high heat. Reduce the heat to low and simmer, un-

covered, stirring occasionally, until the liquid is mostly reduced, about 10 minutes.

To serve, divide the rice evenly among 4 dinner plates. Top with equal amounts of the bean mixture and serve at once.

PER SERVING
Calories 343 ▪ Protein 11g ▪ Total Fat 8g ▪
Sat. Fat 1g ▪ Cholesterol 0mg ▪ Carbohydrate 57g ▪
Dietary Fiber 4g ▪ Sodium 70mg

CURRIED PEAS IN COCONUT SAUCE OVER BASMATI RICE

Vegan

MAKES 5 TO 6 MAIN-DISH SERVINGS

While regular long-grain white rice can be used with success in this Thai-inspired recipe, I prefer the nutty flavor of the fragrant basmati variety. All golden or all dark raisins can be used, or omitted entirely, if desired.

2½ cups water
1½ cups basmati rice
¼ cup golden raisins
¼ cup dark raisins
½ teaspoon salt, plus additional to taste
Freshly ground black pepper, to taste
2 tablespoons canola oil
2 tablespoons all-purpose flour
1 to 1½ teaspoons mild curry powder
¾ cup canned coconut milk, preferably light
¾ cup low-sodium vegetable broth
2 cups frozen peas and pearl onions, quickly
    rinsed under running cold water to thaw
    slightly, drained

Sliced almonds, unsalted chopped peanuts, or unsalted cashew pieces, for garnish (optional)

In a medium saucepan with a tight-fitting lid, bring the water, rice, golden and dark raisins, salt, and pepper to a boil over high heat, stirring once. Reduce the heat to low, cover, and cook until the rice is tender and all the water is absorbed, 17 to 20 minutes. Uncover and fluff with a fork.

Meanwhile, in a medium deep-sided skillet, heat the oil over medium-low heat. Add the flour and curry powder and cook, stirring constantly, until smooth and beginning to bubble, about 5 minutes. Remove from heat and gradually stir in the coconut milk and broth. Return to the heat and bring to a boil over medium heat, stirring constantly. Boil, stirring, 1 minute. Add the peas and pearl onions, salt, and pepper; let come to a simmer, stirring often. Reduce the heat to low and cook, stirring occasionally, until the peas and pearl onions are tender and heated through, about 3 minutes.

To serve, divide the rice evenly among 5 or 6 plates. Spoon equal portions of the pea mixture over top and garnish with the nuts, if desired. Serve at once.

PER SERVING

Calories 398 ▪ Protein 11g ▪ Total Fat 13g ▪ Sat. Fat 6g ▪ Cholesterol 0mg ▪ Carbohydrate 62g ▪ Dietary Fiber 4g ▪ Sodium 389mg

DIXIE GREEN RICE WITH BLACK-EYED PEAS

Vegan

MAKES 4 MAIN-DISH OR 6 TO 8 SIDE-DISH SERVINGS

Collard greens are a staple in American southern cooking; adding them to rice is an easy way of incorporating this iron- and calcium-rich food into a healthy diet. Spinach can be used in their place, if desired. Though optional, the addition of yellow corn and red pimiento lend this delicious dish eye-catching appeal.

1 tablespoon canola oil

¼ cup frozen chopped onion

1 cup long-grain white rice

½ teaspoon refrigerated bottled minced garlic

1 (14-ounce) can (1¾ cups) low-sodium vegetable broth

½ cup water

1 (10-ounce) package frozen chopped collard greens, cooked according to package directions, well drained, or 1 (15-ounce) can chopped collard greens, rinsed and drained well

1 (15-ounce) can black-eyed peas, with or without jalapeño chilies, rinsed and drained

1 cup frozen yellow corn (optional)

2 tablespoons diced pimiento, drained (optional)

½ teaspoon salt

¼ teaspoon freshly ground black pepper

Pinch cayenne pepper (optional)

In a medium deep-sided skillet with a lid, heat the oil over medium heat. Add the onion and cook, stirring, until softened and thawed, 2 to 3 minutes. Add the rice and garlic and increase the heat to medium-high; cook, stirring constantly, until just beginning to brown, 2 to 3 minutes. Add the broth, water, greens, peas, and the corn and pimiento (if using). Add the salt, pepper, and cayenne (if using); bring to a boil over high heat. Reduce the heat to low, cover, and simmer until all the liquid has been absorbed, about 20 minutes. Stir to evenly redistribute the ingredients. Serve hot.

PER SERVING

Calories 323 ■ Protein 15g ■ Total Fat 4g ■
Sat. Fat 0g ■ Cholesterol 0mg ■ Carbohydrate 57g ■
Dietary Fiber 8g ■ Sodium 533mg

ITALIAN-STYLE BROWN RICE WITH ARTICHOKES AND PEAS

Vegan

MAKES 3 TO 4 MAIN-DISH OR
6 SIDE-DISH SERVINGS

Brown rice is a rarity in Italian cooking, yet in the Piedmont area of Italy, where rice is even more popular than pasta, the natural kernel is frequently paired with artichokes. The following recipe includes green peas, an immature legume, for added protein.

1 (14-ounce) can (1¾ cups) low-sodium
    vegetable broth
¼ cup water
1 cup brown rice
1 (6-ounce) jar marinated quartered artichoke
    hearts, drained, 1 tablespoon marinade
    reserved

½ tablespoon extra-virgin olive oil
½ teaspoon onion powder
½ teaspoon dried oregano
½ teaspoon salt, or to taste
¼ teaspoon dried thyme
¼ teaspoon garlic powder
¼ teaspoon lemon pepper seasoning
1½ cups frozen green peas or peas and pearl
    onions, thawed under running cold water
    and drained

In a medium saucepan, combine the broth, water, rice, reserved marinade, oil, onion powder, oregano, salt, thyme, garlic powder, and lemon pepper seasoning; bring to a boil over high heat. Reduce the heat to low, cover, and cook until the rice has absorbed most of the liquid, about 30 minutes. Remove from heat and add the artichoke hearts and peas, tossing gently to combine. Return to heat and cook, covered, until all the liquid has been absorbed, 5 to 10 minutes. Fluff rice with a fork and serve at once.

PER SERVING

Calories 379 ■ Protein 17g ■ Total Fat 6g ■
Sat. Fat 1g ■ Cholesterol 0mg ■ Carbohydrate 66g ■
Dietary Fiber 10g ■ Sodium 823mg

MEXICAN RICE AND BEAN CASSEROLE

Lacto-ovo with egg-free option
MAKES 4 MAIN-DISH SERVINGS

This is a kid-friendly casserole I look forward to making it with leftover rice from Chinese takeout. Its heat can be controlled according to the spiciness of the salsa used. One egg may be omitted, if desired, to reduce the amount of cholesterol in the recipe. For an egg-free dish, ½ cup mashed soft tofu can be used in lieu of the 2 eggs. Because vegan cheese does not cook well, I don't recommend its substitution here.

- **2 cups cooked white or brown rice (see Cook's Tip, page 126)**
- **2 eggs (see headnote above for other options)**
- **1½ cups mild or medium salsa**
- **1 cup (4 ounces) already-shredded reduced-fat cheddar cheese**
- **1 (15-ounce) can red kidney beans, drained**
- **¼ teaspoon chili powder**

Preheat oven to 400F (205C). Grease an 8-inch-square baking dish and set aside.

In a medium bowl, mix together the rice, eggs, ½ cup of the salsa, and half of the cheese until well combined. Spoon into the bottom of the prepared dish, pressing down with the back of the spoon.

In a small bowl, mix together the beans and remaining salsa. Spoon over the rice mixture, then sprinkle evenly with the remaining cheese. Dust the cheese evenly with the chili powder. Cover tightly with foil and bake 25 minutes. Uncover and bake 2 to 3 minutes, or until the cheese is melted and the mixture is bubbly. Let stand a few minutes before serving warm.

PER SERVING

Calories 312 ■ Protein 19g ■ Total Fat 5g ■
Sat. Fat 2g ■ Cholesterol 112mg ■ Carbohydrate 47g
■ Dietary Fiber 6g ■ Sodium 461mg

Variation

Mexican Rice and Chipotle-Bean Casserole: Replace 2 to 3 tablespoons of the salsa with chipotle sauce.

STIR-FRIED CINNAMON-CURRIED RICE WITH PEAS, DRIED FRUIT, AND COCONUT

Vegan

MAKES 4 MAIN-DISH OR
6 TO 8 SIDE-DISH SERVINGS

This eye-catching, delightfully spiced rice dish will perfume your home for hours with the exotic scents of the Orient.

- **2 cups water**
- **2 cinnamon sticks**
- **½ teaspoon salt**
- **¼ teaspoon onion powder**
- **¼ teaspoon garlic powder**
- **Freshly ground black pepper, to taste**
- **1 cup long-grain white rice**
- **1 tablespoon canola oil**
- **2 teaspoons mild curry powder, or to taste**
- **¼ cup water**
- **1½ cups frozen peas and pearl onions, thawed under cold-running water and drained**
- **½ cup dried apricots, soaked in warm water to cover for 15 minutes and drained**
- **¼ cup zante currants or dark raisins, soaked in warm water to cover for 15 minutes and drained**
- **¼ cup shredded unsweetened coconut**
- **¼ cup slivered almonds, toasted if desired (see Cook's Tip, page 7), for garnish (optional)**

In a medium saucepan, bring the water, cinnamon sticks, salt, onion powder, garlic powder, and pepper to a boil over high heat. Stir in the rice, reduce the heat to low, and cover. Simmer 17 to 20 minutes, or until the rice has absorbed all the liquid. Remove from the heat and discard the cinnamon sticks. Stir the rice and let stand, covered, 5 minutes. Uncover and spread the rice out on a baking sheet to cool completely.

In a large nonstick skillet or wok, heat oil over medium-high heat. Add the curry powder and cook, stirring constantly, 10 seconds, or until fragrant. Add the water and cooked rice, and cook, tossing and breaking up the rice with a spatula, until the rice is lightly browned, about 3 minutes. Add the peas and pearl onions, apricots, and currants, tossing and stirring until heated through, 2 to 3 minutes. Remove from heat and stir in the coconut. Serve at once, garnished with the almonds, if desired.

PER SERVING
Calories 337 ▪ Protein 7g ▪ Total Fat 6g ▪
Sat. Fat 2g ▪ Cholesterol 0mg ▪ Carbohydrate 67g ▪
Dietary Fiber 9g ▪ Sodium 317mg

STIR-FRIED ASIAN VEGETABLES OVER RICE WITH THAI CURRY SAUCE

Vegan

MAKES 4 MAIN-DISH SERVINGS

This is a great way to dress up those frozen bags of mixed stir-fry vegetables without actually stir-frying them. I think they taste much better steamed or microwaved anyway. Just make sure to get a variety that doesn't already contain a sauce. Thai curry sauces are notoriously hot; you can prepare the one below with-

out the curry paste and enliven it with a pinch or two of cayenne, if desired.

> **4 cups hot cooked white or brown rice (see Cook's Tip below)**
> **1 (16-ounce) bag mixed Asian vegetables for stir-fry, steamed or microwaved according to package directions and drained**
> **½ recipe Thai Curry Sauce (page 127)**

Divide the rice evenly among 4 plates or shallow bowls. Top with equal amounts of vegetables, then sauce (about ¼ cup per serving). Serve at once.

PER SERVING
Calories 368 ▪ Protein 9g ▪ Total Fat 9g ▪
Sat. Fat 7g ▪ Cholesterol 0mg ▪ Carbohydrate 64g ▪
Dietary Fiber 5g ▪ Sodium 395mg

Cook's Tip One-third cup uncooked regular long-grain white rice, basmati rice, or jasmine rice will yield about 1 cup cooked. One-quarter cup of raw brown rice will yield about 1 cup cooked. To make 4 cups cooked long-grain white rice, combine 1⅓ cups white rice and 2⅔ cups salted water in a medium saucepan; bring to a boil over high heat. Reduce heat to low, cover, and simmer until all the water has been absorbed, 17 to 20 minutes. Fluff with a fork and serve. To make 4 cups cooked brown rice, combine 1 cup brown rice and 2¼ cups salted water in a medium saucepan. Cook as directed for white rice, increasing cooking time to 35 to 40 minutes.

THAI CURRY SAUCE

Vegan

MAKES ABOUT 2 CUPS

Spoon this fiery curry sauce over rice, noodles, and steamed or stir-fried vegetables. Thai curry paste—a blend of chili peppers, garlic, and spices—is available in Asian grocery stores as well as many well-stocked supermarkets. You can omit it entirely if a mild coconut sauce is desired, or substitute with a pinch or two of cayenne for a touch of liveliness.

- **1 tablespoon soy sauce**
- **1 tablespoon cornstarch**
- **1 (14-ounce) can light coconut milk**
- **⅓ cup low-sodium vegetable broth**
- **1½ to 2 teaspoons Thai curry paste (red or green)**
- **½ teaspoon dried basil**
- **½ teaspoon onion powder**

In a small container, combine the soy sauce and cornstarch until smooth. Set aside.

In a small saucepan, bring the coconut milk, broth, curry paste, basil, and onion powder to a gentle simmer over medium heat, stirring occasionally. Add the cornstarch mixture and cook, stirring constantly, 1 to 2 minutes, or until the sauce is thickened. Serve warm. (The cooled sauce can be stored, covered, in the refrigerator up to 3 days before reheating over low heat.)

PER SERVING (ABOUT ¼ CUP)
Calories 88 ■ Protein 2g ■ Total Fat 8g ■
Sat. Fat 6g ■ Cholesterol 0mg ■ Carbohydrate 4g ■
Dietary Fiber 0g ■ Sodium 142mg

SZECHUAN SALAD BAR STIR-FRY WITH BROWN RICE

Vegan

MAKES 4 MAIN-DISH SERVINGS

Imagine, all the makings for a fabulous fresh vegetable stir-fry prepped and ready to go at your local supermarket salad bar. The following recipe is meant to be a model, so feel free to improvise with your favorite veggies. If you don't have Szechuan pepper—a mildly hot reddish-brown pepper located in Asian markets as well as the spice aisle of most major supermarkets—substitute with ground black pepper and add a pinch of cayenne. Cooking the rice pasta-style makes for fluffier grains and cuts off about 15 minutes of the standard cooking time. For directions using the traditional method, see the Cook's Tip on page 126.

- **1 cup brown rice**
- **½ cup low-sodium vegetable broth**
- **¼ cup reduced-sodium soy sauce**
- **1 tablespoon cornstarch**
- **½ tablespoon sugar**
- **1 teaspoon toasted (dark) sesame oil**
- **1½ tablespoons peanut or plain sesame oil**
- **½ teaspoon ground Szechuan pepper**
- **1 cup sliced onion**
- **1 cup sliced green bell pepper**
- **1 teaspoon refrigerated bottled minced garlic**
- **2 cups sliced mushrooms**
- **1 cup broccoli florets**
- **1 cup pre-shredded carrots**
- **1 cup snow peas**
- **½ cup unsalted sunflower seeds (optional)**

Bring a large stockpot of boiling salted water to a boil over high heat. Add the rice and cook pasta-style, stirring a few times, until the rice is tender yet firm to the bite, testing a grain after about 20 minutes. Drain well.

Meanwhile, in a small bowl, whisk together the broth, soy sauce, cornstarch, sugar, and toasted sesame oil until smooth. Set briefly aside.

In a large deep-sided nonstick skillet or wok, heat the peanut oil over medium-high heat. Add the Szechuan pepper and cook, stirring, 15 seconds. Add the onion, bell pepper, and garlic and stir-fry 1 minute. Add the mushrooms, broccoli, and carrots and stir-fry 2 minutes. Add the snow peas and cook 1 minute. Whisk the reserved soy sauce mixture and add to the vegetable mixture. Reduce the heat to medium and cook, stirring, until the liquid thickens slightly, about 3 minutes.

Divide the rice evenly among 4 dinner plates and spoon the vegetable mixture over the rice. Sprinkle each serving with 2 tablespoons sunflower seeds, if desired. Serve at once.

PER SERVING

Calories 316 ▪ Protein 9g ▪ Total Fat 8g ▪
Sat. Fat 1g ▪ Cholesterol 0mg ▪ Carbohydrate 54g ▪
Dietary Fiber 5g ▪ Sodium 684mg

SUMMER SUCCOTASH AND RICE

Vegan

MAKES 4 TO 5 MAIN-DISH OR
6 TO 8 SIDE-DISH SERVINGS

The use of frozen and canned vegetables makes this tangy summertime version of corn and lima beans, the quintessential complete protein combo, available any time of the year. Over rice, it's a satisfying meal.

1 tablespoon canola oil
1 teaspoon refrigerated bottled minced garlic
2 cups frozen yellow corn
1 (15-ounce) can lima beans, rinsed and drained
1 (14-ounce) can diced tomatoes, juice included
1 tablespoon red wine vinegar
½ tablespoon sugar
1 teaspoon ground sage
Salt and freshly ground black pepper, to taste
3 to 4 cups hot cooked rice (see Cook's Tip, page 126)

In a large nonstick skillet, heat the oil over medium heat. Add the garlic and cook, stirring, 1 minute. Add the corn, lima beans, tomatoes with their juice, vinegar, sugar, sage, salt, and pepper; bring to a brisk simmer over medium-high heat, stirring occasionally. Reduce the heat to medium-low and simmer, uncovered, stirring occasionally, until the liquid is reduced by half, about 5 minutes. To serve, divide the rice evenly among 4 or 5 plates. Top with equal amounts of the lima bean mixture and serve at once.

PER SERVING

Calories 391 ▪ Protein 13g ▪ Total Fat 5g ▪
Sat. Fat 1g ▪ Cholesterol 0mg ▪ Carbohydrate 77g ▪
Dietary Fiber 9g ▪ Sodium 218mg

TEX-MEX RICE AND TWO-BEAN PILAF

Vegan

**MAKES 4 MAIN-DISH SERVINGS
OR 6 TO 8 SIDE-DISH SERVINGS**

The lentils in this spirited two-bean pilaf are slightly undercooked, lending it a nice crunch. Kidney beans or black-eyed peas can replace the pinto beans, if desired.

- 1½ tablespoons extra-virgin olive oil
- ½ cup frozen chopped onion
- 1 cup long-grain white rice
- 1 teaspoon refrigerated bottled minced garlic
- 1¼ cups water
- ¼ cup dried lentils
- 1 (15-ounce) can pinto beans, rinsed and drained
- 1 cup frozen yellow corn
- 1 cup medium salsa
- 1 teaspoon chili powder, or to taste
- ½ teaspoon ground cumin
- ½ teaspoon salt, or to taste
- Freshly ground black pepper, to taste

In a medium deep-sided skillet with a lid, heat the oil over medium heat. Add the onion and cook, stirring, until softened and thawed, about 3 minutes. Add the rice and garlic and cook, stirring, 2 minutes. Add the water, lentils, pinto beans, corn, salsa, chili powder, cumin, salt, and pepper; bring to a boil over medium-high heat, stirring occasionally. Reduce the heat, cover, and simmer until the rice has absorbed most of the liquid, about 20 minutes. Serve at once.

PER SERVING
Calories 389 ■ Protein 14g ■ Total Fat 7g ■
Sat. Fat 1g ■ Cholesterol 0mg ■ Carbohydrate 71g ■
Dietary Fiber 11g ■ Sodium 450mg

EASY RISOTTO WITH PEAS AND BASIL

Vegan

**MAKES 3 TO 4 MAIN-DISH OR
6 SIDE-DISH SERVINGS**

This super-easy recipe eliminates the constant stirring of a traditional risotto while maintaining the dish's creamy texture. Feel free to substitute your favorite vegetables for the peas and pearl onions.

- 1 (14-ounce) can (1¾ cups) low-sodium vegetable broth
- ¼ cup water
- 1 tablespoon extra-virgin olive oil
- ¼ teaspoon garlic powder
- 1 cup arborio rice
- 1½ cups frozen peas and pearl onions, thawed under running cold water and drained
- 1 tablespoon diced pimiento, drained
- ½ cup fresh basil leaves, torn into small pieces
- Salt and freshly ground black pepper, to taste

In a medium deep-sided skillet with a lid, bring the broth, water, oil, and garlic powder to a boil over high heat. Stir in the rice, reduce the heat to low, and cover; simmer, without stirring, 10 minutes. Uncover and stir in the peas and pearl onions and pimiento. Cover and simmer 8 to 10 minutes, without stirring, or until the rice is tender and creamy, but not runny. Remove from the heat and let stand, covered, 5 minutes. Uncover and stir in the basil. Season with salt and pepper and serve at once.

PER SERVING

Calories 345 ▪ Protein 14g ▪ Total Fat 5g ▪ Sat. Fat 1g ▪ Cholesterol 0mg ▪ Carbohydrate 60g ▪ Dietary Fiber 5g ▪ Sodium 371mg

TACO CASSEROLE WITH REFRIED BEANS AND CORN

Egg-free

MAKES 5 TO 6 MAIN-DISH SERVINGS

This is a great way to use up any broken or unused taco shells—simply break them up into bite-size pieces with your fingers. I don't recommend using vegan cheese in this recipe because it does not melt well.

2½ cups broken-up taco shells in bite-size pieces (about 6 whole shells)

1 (16-ounce) can vegetarian refried beans

2 cups frozen yellow corn, cooked according to package directions and drained

1 cup medium picante sauce or salsa

2 cups (8 ounces) already-shredded reduced-fat cheddar or Monterey Jack cheese

Light sour cream or nondairy sour cream and/or guacamole (optional)

Preheat oven to 425F (220C). Lightly oil an 8-inch-square baking dish. Layer 1 cup crushed taco shells, half of the refried beans, half of the corn, half of the picante sauce, and half of the cheese in prepared dish. Repeat, ending with the remaining ½ cup crushed taco shells. Cover tightly with foil

and bake 20 minutes; uncover and bake 5 minutes, or until lightly brown. Serve at once, with the optional sour cream and/or guacamole, if desired.

PER SERVING

Calories 306 ▪ Protein 20g ▪ Total Fat 8g ▪ Sat. Fat 3g ▪ Cholesterol 9mg ▪ Carbohydrate 42g ▪ Dietary Fiber 8g ▪ Sodium 846mg

Super Sides

Featuring thirty-eight tasty recipes, from a Mediterranean-style artichoke sauté to an all-American sweet potato gratin, this chapter touts the endless possibilities of side dishes. Vegetarian cooks who frequently focus meals around meat substitutes and are always searching for faster-than-fast side dishes to accompany them will flip through these pages often. It's also a boon for anyone who has ever tried to round out a store-bought main dish, such as "tofurky" at Thanksgiving, only to wish hours later that they'd brought home the entire feast instead. Traditional supporting roles aside, most of the vegetable recipes easily become the main event when served over rice, pasta, or other grains. Most of the grain side dishes, on the other hand, become entrées when teamed up with vegetables. So if you are a simple, no-fuss cook like me, you will think nothing of pairing up the Thai-Style Curried Golden Rice with the Sugar Snap Peas with Almonds and Garlic, or of tossing the Baby Broccoli with Honey-Lemon Peanut Sauce with some quick-cooking Japanese soba noodles, and calling it a fine dinner at the end of a long day.

SAUTÉED ARTICHOKES WITH GARLIC AND THYME

Vegan

MAKES 4 SERVINGS

Fresh artichokes are arguably the most labor-intensive of vegetables when it comes to preparation, so it's not surprising that frozen quartered artichoke hearts are a bit on the expensive side. But one bite of this delicious sauté, and you'll be convinced that every now and again the splurge is worth it. Serve over rice for a complete meal.

- 1 tablespoon extra-virgin olive oil
- ½ cup frozen chopped onion
- 1 teaspoon refrigerated bottled minced garlic
- 1 (9-ounce) package frozen quartered artichoke hearts
- ½ cup low-sodium vegetable broth
- ½ teaspoon dried thyme leaves
- ½ teaspoon salt, preferably the coarse variety, or to taste
- ¼ teaspoon lemon pepper seasoning

In a large nonstick skillet with a lid, heat the oil over medium heat. Add onion and cook, stirring, until softened and thawed, 2 to 3 minutes. Add the garlic and cook, stirring, 1 minute. Add the artichokes, broth, thyme, salt, and lemon pepper seasoning. Bring to a boil over medium-high heat, separating the artichokes with a large wooden spoon, if necessary. Reduce the heat, cover, and simmer, stirring a few times, until the artichokes are fork tender, 10 to 15 minutes. Uncover, increase the heat to medium-high, and cook, stirring often, until most of the liquid has evaporated, about 3 minutes. Serve warm.

PER SERVING

Calories 69 ■ Protein 3g ■ Total Fat 4g ■ Sat. Fat 1g ■ Cholesterol 0mg ■ Carbohydrate 7g ■ Dietary Fiber 3g ■ Sodium 353mg

Cook's Tip: "Refrigerated bottled minced garlic" refers to the fresh bottled minced garlic found in the spice aisle that requires refrigeration after opening, as distinguished from the dehydrated bottled minced garlic that can be stored as a dried herb or spice. Use ½ teaspoon refrigerated bottled minced garlic to replace 1 minced medium clove of garlic.

ASPARAGUS IN LEMON-THYME SAUCE

Vegan

MAKES 4 SERVINGS

Pencil-thin asparagus in a delicate lemon-thyme sauce is a lovely celebration of spring. You can enjoy this dish any time of year using frozen asparagus cooked according to the package directions. It is also delicious prepared with fresh green beans; simply snap off the tough end of each bean, leaving the tender end intact. Enjoy over rice for a complete meal.

- 1¼ pounds fresh asparagus, preferably pencil-thin, tough ends snapped off (see Cook's Tip below)
- ½ cup dry white wine
- ½ cup low-sodium vegetable broth
- ½ tablespoon lemon juice, preferably prepared from frozen concentrate
- ¼ teaspoon dried thyme leaves
- ½ tablespoon extra-virgin olive oil
- Salt and freshly ground black pepper, to taste

Bring a large pot of salted water to a boil; add the asparagus and cook until just tender, 3 to 5 minutes, depending on thickness. Drain into a colander and immediately refresh under cold running water; drain and return to pot.

Meanwhile, in a small saucepan, bring the wine, broth, lemon juice, and thyme to a boil over medium heat. Boil until reduced to about ¼ cup. Remove from the heat and whisk in the oil. Pour over the asparagus, tossing well to coat. Heat over low heat, turning occasionally, until the asparagus is just heated through. Season with salt and pepper and serve warm or slightly above room temperature.

PER SERVING

Calories 59 ▪ Protein 3g ▪ Total Fat 2g ▪
Sat. Fat 0g ▪ Cholesterol 0mg ▪ Carbohydrate 4g ▪
Dietary Fiber 2g ▪ Sodium 68mg

Cook's Tip: To snap the ends off fresh asparagus, hold each stalk in both hands and bend; the tough end will break off at the appropriate point.

ROASTED ASPARAGUS WITH SHERRY-SHALLOT DRESSING

Vegan

MAKES 4 SERVINGS

This sophisticated side dish is ideal for entertaining as it can be served warm or at room temperature. Dehydrated minced shallots can be found in specialty stores and gourmet markets; dehydrated minced onion can replace them, if desired. Serve on a bed of rice and treat yourself to a delicious dinner.

3 tablespoons low-sodium vegetable broth

1½ tablespoons extra-virgin olive oil

1 tablespoon sherry vinegar or balsamic vinegar

2 teaspoons dehydrated minced shallots

½ tablespoon Dijon mustard

1 to 1¼ pounds medium asparagus, tough ends snapped off (see Cook's Tip, at left)

Salt, preferably the coarse variety, and freshly ground black pepper, to taste

Preheat oven to 425F (220C). Lightly oil a baking sheet with sides and set aside.

In a small bowl, whisk together the broth, oil, vinegar, shallots, and mustard. Let stand a few minutes to allow the shallots to rehydrate. Whisk again.

Place the asparagus on the baking sheet and toss with the dressing until thoroughly coated. Spread the asparagus in a single layer. Roast for 10 to 15 minutes, or until the stalks are tender and browned, turning once or twice. Remove from the oven and immediately season with salt and pepper. Toss and serve warm or at room temperature.

PER SERVING

Calories 65 ▪ Protein 2g ▪ Total Fat 5g ▪
Sat. Fat 1g ▪ Cholesterol 0mg ▪ Carbohydrate 4g ▪
Dietary Fiber 1g ▪ Sodium 28mg

Variation

Roasted Green Beans with Sherry-Shallot Dressing: Substitute fresh green beans, tough ends snapped off (see Cook's Tip, page 143), for the asparagus. Cook as otherwise directed, noting that the finished green beans will appear somewhat shriveled as well as browned.

BEETS DIJON

Vegan

MAKES 4 SERVINGS

The tanginess of the dressing contrasts nicely with the inherent sweetness of the beets in the following recipe. As a first course, serve the beets at room temperature over mixed bitter salad greens.

1½ tablespoons extra-virgin olive oil

1½ tablespoons red wine vinegar

½ tablespoon Dijon mustard

½ tablespoon freeze-dried chives

½ teaspoon sugar

Salt and freshly ground black pepper, to taste

1 (15-ounce) can sliced beets

In a medium bowl, whisk together the oil, vinegar, mustard, chives, sugar, salt, and pepper. Let stand at room temperature about 5 minutes to allow the chives to rehydrate and the flavors to blend. Whisk again.

Meanwhile, heat the beets according to label directions; drain and add to the bowl. Toss gently to thoroughly coat. Serve warm or at room temperature.

PER SERVING

Calories 80 ▪ Protein 1g ▪ Total Fat 5g ▪
Sat. Fat 1g ▪ Cholesterol 0mg ▪ Carbohydrate 8g ▪
Dietary Fiber 1g ▪ Sodium 303mg

ORANGE-GLAZED CHINESE-STYLE BEETS

Vegan

MAKES 5 TO 6 SERVINGS

This virtually fat-free dish is ideal for buffets as it can be served cold, warm, or at room temperature. It also makes a delicious dinner served over rice or couscous. Chinese mustard, considerably hotter than most, is available in Asian markets and many well-stocked supermarkets. For a milder taste, Dijon mustard can be substituted, if desired.

¼ cup orange marmalade, preferably the bitter Seville variety

2 teaspoons reduced-sodium soy sauce

½ teaspoon extra-hot Chinese mustard, or to taste

2 (15-ounce) cans whole beets, drained

Salt and freshly ground black pepper, to taste

In a medium saucepan, bring the marmalade, soy sauce, and mustard to a simmer over medium heat, stirring occasionally. Add the beets, tossing and stirring to combine. Reduce the heat to medium-low and cook, stirring and tossing occasionally, until the beets are heated through, about 5 minutes. Season with salt and pepper and serve warm or at room temperature. Alternatively, cover and refrigerate a minimum of 3 hours, or up to 2 days, and serve chilled.

PER SERVING

Calories 90 ▪ Protein 2g ▪ Total Fat 0g ▪
Sat. Fat 0g ▪ Cholesterol 0mg ▪ Carbohydrate 22g ▪
Dietary Fiber 3g ▪ Sodium 543mg

BROCCOLI WITH CHEESE SAUCE

Egg-free
MAKES 6 SERVINGS

This classic side dish is delicious on its own or served over rice or atop split baked potatoes (see variation, page 82). Frozen asparagus spears can be substituted for the broccoli, if desired. Vegetarian Worcestershire sauce, made without anchovies, is available in health food stores and natural foods markets. While you can reduce the amount of dairy by using rice milk in lieu of the whole milk, vegan cheddar cheese substitutes are not recommended, as they don't cook well.

⅓ cup whole or 2% milk or rice milk
¼ teaspoon vegetarian Worcestershire sauce
    (see Cook's Tip, page 67)
¼ teaspoon onion powder
Pinch sweet paprika
Salt and freshly ground black pepper, to taste
1½ cups (6 ounces) already-shredded
    reduced-fat cheddar cheese
1 (16-ounce) package frozen broccoli spears,
    cooked according to package directions
    and kept warm

In a medium saucepan, combine the milk, Worcestershire sauce, onion powder, paprika, salt, and pepper. Add the cheese and cook over medium heat, stirring frequently, until the cheese is melted and the mixture is smooth, about 5 minutes. (At this point, the mixture can be covered and held in the top of a double boiler over very hot, but not simmering, water up to 1 hour, stirring occasionally.)

To serve, divide broccoli among 6 plates. Top with equal amounts of cheese sauce and serve at once.

PER SERVING
Calories 80 ■ Protein 10g ■ Total Fat 3g ■
Sat. Fat 2g ■ Cholesterol 8mg ■ Carbohydrate 5g ■
Dietary Fiber 2g ■ Sodium 195mg

Variation
Broccoli with Cheese Sauce in Puff Pastry Shells: Bake 1 (10-ounce) package frozen puff pastry shells (6 shells) according to package directions. Meanwhile, prepare the cheese sauce as directed. Substitute 1 (10-ounce) package frozen broccoli cuts or baby broccoli florets, cooked according to package directions, for the broccoli spears. To serve, fill the shells with equal amounts of the broccoli, and then top with equal amounts of the cheese sauce. Serve at once.

BABY BROCCOLI WITH HONEY-LEMON PEANUT SAUCE

Egg-free and dairy-free, with vegan option
MAKES 4 SERVINGS

This recipe is a great way to get children, as well as adults, to eat their broccoli. Serve on a bed of brown rice or toss with thin Japanese soba noodles, garnished with chopped peanuts, for a delicious and nutritious high-fiber meal. Use frozen broccoli cuts in lieu of the baby broccoli florets, if desired. For a vegan recipe, replace the honey, a bee product, with brown sugar.

1 (14-ounce) bag frozen baby broccoli florets

2 tablespoons reduced-sodium soy sauce

2 tablespoons warm water

1 tablespoon lemon juice, preferably prepared from frozen concentrate

1 tablespoon creamy peanut butter

1 tablespoon honey or brown sugar

¼ teaspoon ground ginger

Freshly ground black pepper, to taste

Cook the broccoli according to package directions; drain and keep warm.

Meanwhile, in a large bowl, whisk together the soy sauce, water, lemon juice, peanut butter, honey, ginger, and pepper until thoroughly blended. Add the drained broccoli and toss well to thoroughly combine. Serve warm.

PER SERVING
Calories 75 ■ Protein 5g ■ Total Fat 2g ■
Sat. Fat 0g ■ Cholesterol 0mg ■ Carbohydrate 12g ■
Dietary Fiber 3g ■ Sodium 336mg

ROASTED BRUSSELS SPROUTS WITH OLIVE OIL AND COARSE SALT

Vegan
MAKES 4 SERVINGS

Brussels sprouts, like all cruciferous vegetables, have long been classified as an anticancer food, rich in vitamin C, other nutrients, and fiber. Even confirmed Brussels sprouts naysayers often succumb to this dish, my favorite way to eat the tiny cabbagelike vegetable.

1 (16-ounce) package frozen Brussels sprouts, partially thawed under cold running water and drained

1½ tablespoons extra-virgin olive oil

1 teaspoon sugar

½ teaspoon coarse salt

¼ teaspoon freshly ground black pepper

Preheat oven to 400F (205C). Lightly oil a baking sheet with sides and set aside.

In a medium bowl, combine the Brussels sprouts, oil, sugar, salt, and pepper. Transfer to prepared baking sheet. Roast 20 to 30 minutes, or until lightly browned and tender, stirring and turning a few times. Serve warm.

PER SERVING
Calories 96 ■ Protein 4g ■ Total Fat 6g ■
Sat. Fat 1g ■ Cholesterol 0mg ■ Carbohydrate 10g ■
Dietary Fiber 4g ■ Sodium 246mg

Cook's Tip Coarse salt, sometimes called coarse sea salt or kosher salt, can be located in the specialty or spice aisle of many well-stocked super-markets. While it contains the same amount of sodium as regular table salt, coarse salt is generally distinguished from the latter by the fact that its larger, coarser grains have not been treated with additives such as calcium silicate (an anticaking agent) and dextrose. As a result, the grains have a cleaner, sharper, "saltier" taste that is highly prized by many professional and home cooks.

GINGER-GLAZED BABY CARROTS

Vegan

MAKES 4 TO 6 SERVINGS

Ginger jelly is available in gourmet markets and the specialty food section of many major supermarkets. If desired, ready-sliced crinkle-cut carrots can be used in lieu of baby carrots. For a wonderful meal for four, pair these with Thai-Style Curried Golden Rice (page 152).

    1 (16-ounce) bag ready-washed baby carrots
    3 tablespoons ginger jelly
    1 tablespoon toasted (dark) sesame oil
    Salt and freshly ground black pepper, to taste

Place the carrots and enough water to cover in a large deep-sided skillet with a lid. Bring to a boil over high heat. Reduce the heat to medium, cover, and simmer briskly until just crisp-tender, about 5 minutes, depending on thickness of carrots. Drain in a colander and set briefly aside.

Add the jelly and oil to the skillet. Cook over medium heat, stirring, until melted and bubbly. Reduce the heat to medium-low and add the carrots, salt, and pepper. Cook, stirring and turning frequently, until carrots are glazed and hot, about 5 minutes. Serve hot or warm.

PER SERVING
Calories 112 ▪ Protein 1g ▪ Total Fat 4g ▪
Sat. Fat 1g ▪ Cholesterol 0mg ▪ Carbohydrate 19g ▪
Dietary Fiber 3g ▪ Sodium 45mg

Variation

Orange-Glazed Carrots: Substitute 3 tablespoons orange marmalade, preferably the bitter Seville variety, for the ginger jelly.

ROASTED CARROTS WITH CHUTNEY

Vegan

MAKES 4 TO 6 SERVINGS

These carrots are a family favorite for Thanksgiving. Mango chutney, a spicy-sweet condiment, can be found in the specialty food aisle of well-stocked su-permarkets.

    ¼ cup mango chutney (do not include any
        large chunks of fruit)
    1 tablespoon canola oil
    ½ teaspoon curry powder
    ¼ teaspoon ground cumin
    Salt and freshly ground black pepper, to taste
    1 (16-ounce) bag ready-washed baby carrots

Preheat oven to 400F (205C). Lightly grease a bak-ing sheet with sides and set aside.

In a medium bowl, stir together the chutney, oil, curry powder, cumin, salt, and pepper until well combined. Add the carrots and toss to thor-oughly coat. Arrange in a single layer on the prepared baking sheet. Roast 20 to 30 minutes, or until lightly browned and tender, stirring and turning a few times. Serve warm.

SHREDDED CARROTS TERIYAKI

Vegan
MAKES 4 TO 5 SERVINGS

Homemade teriyaki sauce brings out the inherent sweetness of carrots beautifully in the following recipe, delicious served over rice or tossed with thin Asian noodles. If really pressed for time, use store-bought teriyaki sauce. Shredded cabbage or broccoli slaw works nicely here, as well.

- ½ tablespoon toasted (dark) sesame oil
- ½ tablespoon peanut oil
- ½ teaspoon refrigerated bottled minced garlic
- 1 (10-ounce) bag shredded carrots
- ¼ cup Teriyaki Sauce (below) or store-bought teriyaki sauce
- 1 tablespoon sesame seeds (optional)

In a large nonstick skillet, heat the two oils over medium-high heat. Add the garlic and cook, stirring constantly, 30 seconds. Add the carrots and teriyaki sauce. Cook, tossing and stirring constantly, until the carrots are crisp-tender, about 3 minutes. Serve immediately, sprinkled with the sesame seeds, if desired.

TERIYAKI SAUCE

Vegan
MAKES ABOUT ¾ CUP

Homemade teriyaki sauce is incredibly easy to make; the secret to the following recipe's tastiness is the brown sugar.

- ½ cup reduced-sodium soy sauce
- 2 tablespoons sherry wine
- 2 tablespoons light brown sugar
- 1 tablespoon rice vinegar
- 2 teaspoons toasted (dark) sesame oil

In a small nonreactive saucepan, bring all the ingredients to a gentle simmer over medium heat, stirring a few times. Remove from the heat and let cool to room temperature. If not using immediately, cover and store in the refrigerator up to 5 days.

CAULIFLOWER WITH CURRIED YOGURT SAUCE

Egg-free with vegan option

MAKES 4 SERVINGS

This is one of my favorite ways to enjoy cauliflower— and steamed whole okra, as well! For a vegan dish, prepare the sauce using plain soy yogurt or nondairy sour cream.

Curried Yogurt Sauce (below)
1 (16-ounce) package frozen cauliflower florets
Salt and freshly ground black pepper, to taste

Prepare the sauce.

Cook the cauliflower according to package directions; drain well. While still quite hot, transfer the cauliflower to a warm serving bowl. Add the sauce and toss well to combine. Season with salt and pepper and serve at once.

PER SERVING
Calories 50 ▪ Protein 4g ▪ Total Fat 1g ▪
Sat. Fat 0g ▪ Cholesterol 2mg ▪ Carbohydrate 8g ▪
Dietary Fiber 3g ▪ Sodium 49mg

CURRIED YOGURT SAUCE

Egg-free with vegan option

MAKES ABOUT ½ CUP

Use this versatile sauce with a wide variety of steamed or blanched vegetables, including potatoes.

It is also fabulous stirred into cooked lentils or lentil soup. For a vegan sauce, use plain soy yogurt, available in health food stores and many well-stocked supermarkets.

½ cup plain low-fat yogurt or soy yogurt
1 teaspoon mild curry powder
½ teaspoon ground turmeric
¼ teaspoon ground cumin
Pinch sugar (optional)
Salt and freshly ground black pepper, to taste

In a small bowl, stir together the yogurt, curry powder, turmeric, cumin, sugar (if using), salt, and pepper until well combined. Set briefly aside to let the flavors blend before using. (Sauce can be stored, covered, in the refrigerator up to 2 days.)

PER SERVING (ABOUT 1 TABLESPOON)
Calories 11 ▪ Protein 1g ▪ Total Fat 0g ▪
Sat. Fat 0g ▪ Cholesterol 1mg ▪ Carbohydrate 1g ▪
Dietary Fiber 0g ▪ Sodium 10mg

CHILI-LIME CORN

Vegan

MAKES 6 SERVINGS

This is a great way to enliven plain frozen corn, particularly if you're serving a Mexican or Southwestern-style meal. To make an outstanding succotash, see the variation below.

3 cups frozen yellow corn

2 tablespoons canola oil

1½ tablespoons bottled lime juice

½ teaspoon chili powder, or to taste

¼ teaspoon garlic salt, or to taste

Freshly ground black pepper, to taste

Cook the corn according to package directions; drain and transfer to a medium bowl. Add the oil, lime juice, chili powder, garlic salt, and pepper; toss well to combine. Serve warm or at room temperature.

PER SERVING
Calories 114 ■ Protein 3g ■ Total Fat 5g ■ Sat. Fat 0g ■ Cholesterol 0mg ■ Carbohydrate 18g ■ Dietary Fiber 2g ■ Sodium 90mg

Variation

Chili-Lime Succotash: Use only 1 cup corn. Heat 1 (15-ounce) can baby lima beans according to label directions. Drain well and add to the bowl with the cooked corn. Proceed as otherwise directed in the recipe. Makes 6 side-dish servings or 4 main-dish servings over rice.

CORN ON THE COB WITH CAJUN BUTTER

Egg-free with vegan option

MAKES 4 SERVINGS

There's nothing like fresh corn on the cob in the summertime. To enjoy this tasty side dish any time of year, add the Cajun butter to cooked frozen corn. For a vegan alternative, prepare the Cajun butter using vegan margarine as directed below.

4 ears fresh corn, husked

½ recipe Cajun Butter (below)

Bring a large stockpot of salted water to a boil over high heat. Carefully add the corn and return to a boil; cover and remove from the heat. Let stand until tender, 15 to 20 minutes. Using tongs, transfer the corn to corn holders or serving plates and rub each ear with about ½ tablespoon of the Cajun butter. Serve at once.

PER SERVING
Calories 129 ■ Protein 3g ■ Total Fat 7g ■ Sat. Fat 4g ■ Cholesterol 15mg ■ Carbohydrate 18g ■ Dietary Fiber 3g ■ Sodium 226mg

Variation

Oven-Roasted Corn on the Cob with Cajun Butter: Do not husk the corn. Preheat oven to 350F (175C). Place corn directly on center oven rack. Roast until the corn is soft, about 30 minutes. Remove husks and serve as directed above.

CAJUN BUTTER

Egg-free with vegan option
MAKES ABOUT ¼ CUP

Toss this versatile butter with your favorite vegetables and add to baked or mashed potatoes. Cajun spice or seasoning can be found in the spice aisle of most well-stocked supermarkets. Vegan margarine (Earth Balance makes an excellent brand) can replace the butter, if desired.

**4 tablespoons butter or vegan margarine,
    softened**
1 teaspoon Cajun spice
½ teaspoon garlic salt
Generous pinch onion powder
Freshly ground black pepper, to taste

In a small crock or container, mash all ingredients with a fork until well combined. Cover and refrigerate up to 1 week.

PER SERVING (ABOUT 1 TABLESPOON)
Calories 103 ▪ Protein 0g ▪ Total Fat 11g ▪
Sat. Fat 7g ▪ Cholesterol 31mg ▪ Carbohydrate 1g ▪
Dietary Fiber 0g ▪ Sodium 426mg

ROASTED EGGPLANT AND ZUCCHINI WITH TAHINI-YOGURT SAUCE

Egg-free with vegan option
MAKES 6 SERVINGS

Tiny Italian or Japanese eggplants can be found in the produce section of well-stocked supermarkets throughout the year. If you can't locate them, use all zucchini. For a vegan recipe, prepare the sauce with plain soy yogurt.

**3 (4-ounce) Italian or Japanese
    eggplants**
3 (4-ounce) zucchini squash
1½ teaspoons extra-virgin olive oil
**½ recipe (about ⅔ cup) Tahini-Yogurt
    Sauce (page 142)**

Preheat oven to 350F (175C).

Prick eggplant and zucchini with the tines of a fork in several places. Rub each with about ¼ teaspoon of the oil and place on an ungreased baking sheet. Bake 35 to 40 minutes for eggplant and 30 to 35 minutes for zucchini, turning halfway through cooking time, or until eggplants are slightly collapsed and zucchini are soft through the center.

Cool slightly. Carefully remove stems and cut lengthwise into halves. Turn the eggplant halves over and drain briefly on paper towels. Transfer the vegetables to a serving tray or divide among 6 plates, using one of each vegetable half per plate. Spoon 2 to 3 teaspoons of the sauce over each vegetable half and serve at once.

Cook's Tip Tahini is an oily, nutlike paste made from ground sesame seeds. It is available in Middle Eastern markets, specialty stores, and many well-stocked supermarkets. Be sure to stir it well before using as the oil and solids tend to separate in the container.

TAHINI-YOGURT SAUCE

Egg-free with vegan option

MAKES ABOUT 1⅓ CUPS

Use this versatile sauce at room temperature as a topping for cooked vegetables and falafel, or as a dressing for salads. It also makes a superb dip for raw vegetables or an appetizing filling for canned whole artichokes or artichoke bottoms. For a vegan alternative, use plain soy yogurt, such as Silk soy yogurt, in lieu of the regular yogurt.

½ cup sesame tahini
½ cup plain low-fat yogurt, buttermilk,
   or soy yogurt
3 to 4 tablespoons lemon juice, preferably
   prepared from frozen concentrate
2 tablespoons water
½ teaspoon toasted (dark) sesame oil
½ teaspoon onion powder
½ teaspoon garlic powder
½ teaspoon ground cumin
Pinch sweet paprika
Pinch cayenne, or to taste (optional)
Salt and freshly ground black pepper,
   to taste

In a small bowl, whisk together all the ingredients until thoroughly combined. Serve chilled or at room temperature. (The sauce can be stored, covered, in the refrigerator up to 3 days.)

GREEN BEANS WITH HORSERADISH CREAM SAUCE

Lacto-ovo with vegan options

MAKES 4 SERVINGS

This is a terrific way to jazz up green beans—particularly the frozen variety—for company. The trick is to add the sauce while the beans are still quite hot to "cook" the sauce. Because fresh green beans require little preparation, I've given directions using them, as well. The horseradish cream, below, easily converts to a vegan sauce.

Horseradish Cream Sauce (below)
1 to 1¼ pounds fresh green beans,
   tough ends snapped off (see Cook's Tip
   below), or 1 (16-ounce) bag frozen green
   beans

Prepare the sauce.

If using fresh beans: Bring a large pot of salted water to a boil; add the beans and cook until just tender, 3 to 5 minutes, depending on thickness. Drain well.

If using frozen green beans: Prepare the beans according to package directions. Drain well.

Transfer the hot beans to a serving bowl. Immediately add the sauce; toss well to combine. Serve at once.

PER SERVING
Calories 80 ■ Protein 3g ■ Total Fat 3g ■
Sat. Fat 1g ■ Cholesterol 7mg ■ Carbohydrate 12g ■
Dietary Fiber 3g ■ Sodium 85mg

Variation

Pesto Green Beans: Omit the Horseradish Cream Sauce and substitute with 3 tablespoons refrigerated prepared pesto.

Cook's Tip When preparing fresh green beans, it is only necessary to snap off the tough stem end of each bean, thereby leaving the tender end intact.

HORSERADISH CREAM SAUCE

Lacto-ovo with vegan options
MAKES ABOUT ½ CUP

This tangy sauce can enliven any variety of vegetables and potatoes. If a vegan recipe is desired, soy mayonnaise and nondairy sour cream can easily replace the respective regular mayonnaise and dairy sour cream.

- ¼ cup reduced-fat regular mayonnaise or soy mayonnaise
- ¼ cup light sour cream or nondairy sour cream
- 1 tablespoon prepared horseradish
- 1 teaspoon refrigerated bottled minced garlic
- Salt and freshly ground black pepper, to taste

In a small bowl, stir together all the ingredients until well blended. Let stand a few minutes at room temperature to allow the flavors to blend before using. (The sauce may be stored, covered, in the refrigerator up to 3 days.)

PER SERVING (ABOUT 1 TABLESPOON)
Calories 21 ■ Protein 0g ■ Total Fat 2g ■
Sat. Fat 0g ■ Cholesterol 3mg ■ Carbohydrate 2g ■
Dietary Fiber 0g ■ Sodium 41mg

CREAMY POLENTA WITH PARMESAN

Egg-free
MAKES 6 SERVINGS

Depending on its consistency, this rustic, porridgelike dish can be served as a side dish in lieu of mashed potatoes or as an unusual first-course soup. Either way, it's delicious. Vegan soy Parmesan cheese substitutes are definitely not recommended here.

- 1 (14-ounce) can (1¾ cups) low-sodium vegetable broth
- 1¼ cups water
- ¾ cup quick-cooking polenta
- 1 tablespoon extra-virgin olive oil
- Salt and freshly ground black pepper, to taste
- ¾ cup (3 ounces) already-shredded Parmesan cheese

In a medium stockpot, bring the broth and water to a boil over high heat, preferably on a back burner as the polenta sputters. Slowly add the polenta, stirring constantly with a long-handled wooden spoon. Reduce the heat to medium and add the oil, salt, and pepper; cook, stirring constantly, until the mixture is the consistency of cream of wheat, about 5 minutes. Remove from the heat and immediately add the cheese, stirring until thoroughly combined.

If serving as a first-course soup, ladle equal portions into soup bowls and serve at once. If serving as a side dish, let stand, uncovered, about 5 minutes, stirring occasionally, until mixture is the consistency of mashed potatoes. Transfer to a warm serving bowl and serve at once.

PER SERVING

Calories 201 ■ Protein 10g ■ Total Fat 5g ■
Sat. Fat 2g ■ Cholesterol 7mg ■ Carbohydrate 28g ■
Dietary Fiber 4g ■ Sodium 321mg

EASY POTATOES AU GRATIN

Egg-free

MAKES 5 TO 6 SERVINGS

This classic side dish is wonderful with steamed broccoli or asparagus. If you add a tossed green salad and some whole-grain dinner rolls, why not serve it for supper? Cheddar cheese can replace the Swiss variety, if desired. While you can reduce the amount of dairy in the recipe by using rice milk in lieu of the skim milk, vegan cheese substitutes are not recommended, as they typically don't melt well.

2 tablespoons canola oil
2 tablespoons all-purpose flour
½ teaspoon onion powder
⅛ teaspoon garlic powder
1 cup skim milk or rice milk
1 cup (4 ounces) already-shredded reduced-fat Swiss cheese
Salt and freshly ground black pepper, to taste

2 (15-ounce) cans sliced potatoes, rinsed and drained

Preheat oven to 375F (190C). Lightly oil an 8-inch-square baking dish and set aside.

In a medium saucepan, heat the oil over medium-low heat. Stir in the flour, onion powder, and garlic powder. Cook, stirring constantly, until the mixture is smooth and bubbly. Remove from the heat and gradually stir in the milk. Return to the heat and bring to a boil over medium heat, stirring constantly. Boil, stirring vigorously from the bottom to prevent sticking, 1 minute. Reduce the heat to low and stir in half of the cheese, salt, and pepper. Cook, stirring constantly, until the cheese is melted. Add the potatoes and toss well to combine.

Transfer the potato mixture to prepared dish. Bake 20 minutes, uncovered, or until lightly browned. Sprinkle with the remaining cheese and bake 5 minutes, or until the cheese is melted. Serve at once.

PER SERVING

Calories 186 ■ Protein 11g ■ Total Fat 7g ■
Sat. Fat 1g ■ Cholesterol 9mg ■ Carbohydrate 21g ■
Dietary Fiber 3g ■ Sodium 596mg

PAN-ROASTED BABY YUKON GOLD POTATOES WITH GARLIC AND PAPRIKA

Vegan

MAKES 6 SERVINGS

This is a terrific method for roasting potatoes when it's too hot to turn on the oven, or when you need the oven free for cooking other things. Any small potato can be used successfully here.

24 ounces (1½ pounds) baby Yukon Gold
  potatoes, scrubbed and left whole
¼ cup water
2 tablespoons extra-virgin olive oil
1 teaspoon coarse salt, or to taste
½ teaspoon refrigerated bottled minced garlic
¼ teaspoon sweet paprika
Freshly ground black pepper, to taste

In a large nonstick skillet with a lid, combine the potatoes, water, oil, salt, and garlic; bring to a brisk simmer over medium-high heat. Cover, reduce the heat to medium-low, and cook until the potatoes are just tender through the center, 25 to 30 minutes, shaking the pan occasionally to turn the potatoes. Uncover and increase the heat to medium-high. Cook, stirring and turning constantly, until most of the water has evaporated, about 5 minutes. Add the paprika and cook until all the water has evaporated, about 1 minute, stirring and turning constantly. Season with pepper and serve warm.

PER SERVING
Calories 108 ▪ Protein 2g ▪ Total Fat 5g ▪
Sat. Fat 1g ▪ Cholesterol 0mg ▪ Carbohydrate 15g ▪
Dietary Fiber 1g ▪ Sodium 319mg

OVEN-ROASTED POTATOES WITH CUMIN

Vegan
MAKES 6 SERVINGS

These yummy potatoes pair up nicely with Mexican-style dishes; try serving them with Breakfast Burritos (page 161) or Black Bean Tacos (page 66) in lieu of rice or refried beans. If you don't have garlic-flavored olive oil, use plain extra-virgin olive oil and use garlic salt instead of the coarse salt.

24 ounces (1½ pounds) small new red
  potatoes, scrubbed and left whole
1½ tablespoons garlic-flavored olive oil
2 to 3 teaspoons whole cumin seeds
½ teaspoon coarse salt, or to taste
Freshly ground black pepper, to taste

Preheat the oven to 400F (205C). Place the potatoes in a shallow baking dish large enough to comfortably hold them in a single layer. Drizzle with the oil and toss well to evenly coat. Sprinkle with the cumin seeds, salt, and pepper. Toss again.

Roast for 40 to 50 minutes, depending on size, turning halfway through cooking time, or until the potatoes are nicely browned and tender through the center. Serve hot.

PER SERVING
Calories 100 ▪ Protein 2g ▪ Total Fat 4g ▪
Sat. Fat 1g ▪ Cholesterol 0mg ▪ Carbohydrate 16g ▪
Dietary Fiber 1g ▪ Sodium 163mg

Variation
Oven-Roasted Rosemary Potatoes: Substitute 2 to 3 teaspoons dried whole rosemary leaves for the cumin seeds. Bake as directed.

STEAMED CONFETTI POTATOES WITH FRESH HERBS

Vegan

MAKES 6 SERVINGS

I look forward to preparing this dish for the simple pleasure of picking herbs straight from my garden that will bypass the chopping board! Confetti potatoes are typically an assortment of red, purple, and yellow-skinned potatoes, yet any tiny new potato can be used.

3 cups water

24 ounces (1½ pounds) baby confetti potatoes or tiny new potatoes, scrubbed and left whole

1 teaspoon refrigerated bottled minced garlic

½ teaspoon coarse salt, plus additional to taste

2 tablespoons extra-virgin olive oil

1 tablespoon fresh whole rosemary, tarragon, and/or thyme leaves

Freshly ground black pepper, to taste

Place a steaming basket in a large deep-sided skillet with a lid; add the water. Arrange the potatoes in the steaming basket; sprinkle evenly with the garlic and salt. Bring to a boil over high heat. Cover, reduce the heat to medium-high, and cook until potatoes are fork-tender but not mushy, about 15 minutes, depending on size.

Transfer the hot potatoes to a serving bowl and immediately add the oil, herbs, pepper, and additional salt, as necessary. Toss gently yet thoroughly to combine. Serve warm or at room temperature.

PER SERVING

Calories 108 ▪ Protein 2g ▪ Total Fat 5g ▪
Sat. Fat 1g ▪ Cholesterol 0mg ▪ Carbohydrate 15g ▪
Dietary Fiber 2g ▪ Sodium 162mg

CURRIED GOLDEN NEW POTATOES

Vegan

MAKES 6 SERVINGS

These potatoes are fine accompaniments to many Indian-style curry dishes; try serving them with Curried Lentils with Indian Flatbread (page 10) and turn a delicious appetizer or lunch into a complete meal. Select tiny new potatoes that are about 1½ inches in diameter for the best results.

24 ounces (1½ pounds) baby Yukon Gold potatoes, scrubbed and left whole

1 tablespoon canola oil

1 teaspoon mild curry powder

1 teaspoon ground turmeric

¼ teaspoon ground cumin

½ tablespoon lemon juice, preferably from frozen concentrate

½ teaspoon coarse salt, or to taste

Freshly ground black pepper, to taste

Place the potatoes in a large saucepan or medium stockpot with salted water to cover; bring to a boil over high heat. Reduce the heat to a gentle boil and cook until the potatoes are just tender, 10 to 15 minutes, depending upon size. Drain and set aside to cool slightly.

In a large nonstick skillet, heat the oil over medium-high heat. Add the curry powder, turmeric, and cumin; cook, stirring constantly, until fragrant, about 10 seconds. Add the potatoes, lemon juice, and salt, tossing and stirring well to coat. Cook, tossing and stirring, until the potatoes are heated through, 1 to 2 minutes. Season with pepper to taste. Serve at once.

PER SERVING

Calories 91 ■ Protein 2g ■ Total Fat 3g ■
Sat. Fat 0mg ■ Cholesterol 0mg ■ Carbohydrate 16g
■ Dietary Fiber 2g ■ Sodium 476mg

BOILED NEW POTATOES WITH LEMON-CAPER AÏOLI

Dairy-free with vegan option
MAKES 6 SERVINGS

Aïoli is a garlic mayonnaise popular in French and Spanish cuisine. Though typically served with fish, it is superb with many vegetables, particularly potatoes. The aïoli easily converts to a vegan sauce, as suggested below.

24 ounces (1½ pounds) tiny whole new potatoes, scrubbed and left whole
Lemon-Caper Aïoli (below)

Place the potatoes in a large saucepan or medium stockpot with enough salted water to cover; bring to a boil over high heat. Reduce the heat to a gentle boil and cook until the potatoes are just tender, 10 to 15 minutes, depending upon size. Drain.

Transfer the hot potatoes to a serving bowl and immediately add the aïoli. Toss gently yet thoroughly to combine. Serve at once.

PER SERVING

Calories 104 ■ Protein 2g ■ Total Fat 3g ■
Sat. Fat 1g ■ Cholesterol 5mg ■ Carbohydrate 18g ■
Dietary Fiber 1g ■ Sodium 108mg

LEMON-CAPER AÏOLI

Dairy-free with vegan option
YIELDS ABOUT ½ CUP

This sauce is also delicious tossed with artichokes, asparagus, cauliflower, and green beans. Substitute soy mayonnaise, such as Nasoya, to create a vegan recipe.

6 tablespoons reduced-fat regular mayonnaise or soy mayonnaise
1 tablespoon capers, drained
½ tablespoon lemon juice, preferably prepared from frozen concentrate
½ tablespoon Dijon mustard
½ teaspoon refrigerated bottled minced garlic
Salt and freshly ground black pepper, to taste

In a small bowl, whisk together all the ingredients until well combined. Set briefly aside to let the flavors blend before using. (The sauce can be stored, covered, in the refrigerator up to 3 days.)

PER SERVING (ABOUT 1 TABLESPOON)

Calories 27 ■ Protein 0g ■ Total Fat 2g ■
Sat. Fat 0g ■ Cholesterol 4mg ■ Carbohydrate 2g ■
Dietary Fiber 0g ■ Sodium 77mg

MAKE-AHEAD BAKED MASHED POTATOES

Egg-free with vegan options

MAKES 8 SERVINGS

This is a great recipe to bookmark for easy holiday entertaining, because it can be made ahead. Leaving on the skins of the potatoes adds not only fiber, but attractive flecks of red to the dish. Rice milk or soy milk, nondairy cream cheese, and nondairy sour cream can replace the respective skim milk, cream cheese, and sour cream, but add ½ teaspoon onion powder to the mashed potatoes. The butter can be omitted altogether, or replaced with vegan margarine; Earth Balance makes an excellent brand.

2½ pounds small red-skin potatoes, scrubbed and left whole

½ cup skim milk, rice milk, or soy milk

4 ounces (½ cup) light cream cheese with chives or nondairy cream cheese, softened, cut into 4 pieces

¼ cup light sour cream or nondairy sour cream

1 tablespoon butter or soy margarine, plus 1 tablespoon cut into small pieces (optional)

1 teaspoon garlic salt

¼ teaspoon freshly ground black pepper

Preheat oven to 425F (220C). Lightly oil a shallow 2½-quart baking dish and set aside.

Place the potatoes on a large ungreased baking sheet and prick with a fork. Bake 45 to 60 minutes, depending on their size, until tender through the center. If completing recipe right away, reduce oven temperature to 350F (175C). Otherwise, turn off oven.

Transfer half of the potatoes to a large mixing bowl and mash into large chunks with a potato masher. Add the remaining potatoes and mash again. Add the milk, cream cheese, sour cream, the 1 tablespoon butter, garlic salt, and pepper. Mash into small coarse pieces, then stir well with a wooden spoon to thoroughly combine.

Transfer the potatoes to the prepared dish, spreading evenly with a spatula. Dot the top with pieces of butter, if desired.

If completing the recipe right away: Bake, uncovered, 45 to 60 minutes, or until the top is lightly browned.

If preparing the recipe in advance: Cover tightly with foil and refrigerate overnight, or up to 24 hours. Preheat the oven to 350F (175C). Bake the refrigerated potatoes, covered, 30 minutes. Uncover and bake 45 to 60 more minutes, or until the top is lightly browned. Serve hot.

PER SERVING

Calories 138 ▪ Protein 4g ▪ Total Fat 4g ▪ Sat. Fat 3g ▪ Cholesterol 13mg ▪ Carbohydrate 21g ▪ Dietary Fiber 2g ▪ Sodium 367mg

SCALLOPED POTATOES DIJONNAISE WITH TARRAGON

Dairy-free with vegan option

MAKES 6 SERVINGS

Here is a dish that is easy enough to accompany a quick weeknight supper, yet elegant enough to serve to company. Rinsing the potatoes removes much of the salt used in the canning process. For a vegan recipe, replace the regular mayonnaise with a soy variety; Nasoya is a reliable brand.

½ cup reduced-fat regular mayonnaise or soy mayonnaise

2 tablespoons Dijon mustard

½ teaspoon dried tarragon leaves

Salt and freshly ground black pepper, to taste

2 (15-ounce) cans sliced potatoes, rinsed and drained

Preheat oven to 425F (220C). Lightly grease a 10-inch pie plate or quiche dish and set aside.

In a small bowl, combine the mayonnaise, mustard, tarragon, salt, and pepper. Set briefly aside.

Starting from the outside and working toward the middle, arrange the potatoes in overlapping concentric circles in the prepared pie plate. Using a rubber spatula, spread the mayonnaise mixture evenly over the top.

Bake 20 minutes, or until the top is lightly browned. Cut into wedges and serve at once.

PER SERVING

Calories 107 ▪ Protein 2g ▪ Total Fat 4g ▪
Sat. Fat 1g ▪ Cholesterol 7mg ▪ Carbohydrate 16g ▪
Dietary Fiber 2g ▪ Sodium 589mg

TWICE-BAKED STUFFED POTATOES WITH HUMMUS

Vegan

MAKES 4 GENEROUS OR 8 STANDARD SIDE-DISH SERVINGS

The notion of hummus as a topping for baked potatoes never occurred to me until I started writing this book—yum! The following twice-baked version is ideal for company as the potatoes can be made up to 12 hours ahead of the final baking. If you're really pressed for time, serve the potatoes immediately after the initial baking and use the hummus as a topping, omitting the optional chives and the paprika.

4 (8-ounce) russet potatoes, washed and scrubbed

¾ cup prepared hummus

1 tablespoon freeze-dried chopped chives (optional)

Salt and freshly ground black pepper, to taste

Sweet paprika, to taste

Preheat oven to 450F (230C). Prick the potatoes with a fork and bake on the center rack for 1 hour, or until tender. Reduce the heat to 375F (190C) and let the potatoes cool at room temperature about 15 minutes before handling.

Meanwhile, in a small bowl, combine the hummus, chives (if using), salt, and pepper. Set briefly aside.

When the potatoes are cool enough to handle, cut in half lengthwise and scoop out the potato, leaving a shell about ¼ inch thick. Add the warm scooped-out potato to the hummus mixture and mash well to thoroughly blend. Stuff the mixture back into the potato halves and smooth the surface with the tines of a fork. Sprinkle lightly with the paprika. (At this point, the potatoes can be covered with plastic wrap and refrigerated up to 12 hours before continuing with the recipe.)

Transfer the stuffed potatoes to an ungreased baking sheet and bake on the center rack until heated through, about 15 minutes (about 25 minutes if they've been refrigerated). Serve at once.

PER SERVING

Calories 213 ▪ Protein 6g ▪ Total Fat 4g ▪
Sat. Fat 1g ▪ Cholesterol 0mg ▪ Carbohydrate 40g ▪
Dietary Fiber 5g ▪ Sodium 123mg

Variations

Twice-Baked Stuffed Potatoes with Chives: Substitute ¾ cup light cream cheese with chives for the hummus. Omit the optional chives and the paprika.

Twice-Baked Stuffed Potatoes with Garden Vegetables: Substitute ¾ cup light cream cheese with garden vegetables for the hummus. Omit the optional chives and the paprika.

Twice-Baked Stuffed Potatoes with Herbs: Substitute ¾ cup reduced-fat garlic-and-herb spreadable cheese for the hummus. Omit the optional chives, as well as the paprika, if desired.

COCONUT JASMINE RICE WITH GINGER

Vegan

MAKES 4 TO 5 SERVINGS

Jasmine rice is a fragrant, delicate variety popular in Thai cuisine. It can be found in Asian markets as well as the international aisle of most well-stocked supermarkets. For a complete meal for four, try pairing this tasty rice dish with Sugar Snap Peas with Almonds and Garlic (page 154) or simply tossing with 1½ cups microwaved frozen green peas.

- 1 cup water
- ¾ cup canned light coconut milk
- ½ teaspoon ground ginger
- ½ teaspoon salt, or to taste
- ¼ teaspoon freshly ground black pepper, or to taste
- 1 cup jasmine rice, rinsed

In a medium saucepan, combine the water, coconut milk, ginger, salt, and pepper; bring to a boil over medium-high heat. Stir in the rice, cover, reduce the heat to low, and simmer until all the liquids have been absorbed, 17 to 20 minutes. Remove from heat and let stand, covered, 10 minutes. Fluff with a fork and serve at once.

PER SERVING
Calories 244 ■ Protein 5g ■ Total Fat 8g ■ Sat. Fat 6g ■ Cholesterol 0mg ■ Carbohydrate 40g ■ Dietary Fiber 1g ■ Sodium 281mg

LEMON-HERB RICE WITH MUSHROOMS

Vegan

MAKES 4 TO 6 SERVINGS

I often rely on this recipe when I need something quick and easy to accompany a special entrée; indeed, my kids used to call it "company rice." Toss in about 1½ cups cooked frozen peas and pearl onions to the finished dish and voilà—a simple yet elegant main course.

- 1 (14-ounce) can (1¾ cups) low-sodium vegetable broth
- 1 tablespoon lemon juice, preferably prepared from frozen concentrate
- 1 tablespoon extra-virgin olive oil
- 2 teaspoons dried parsley flakes
- ¼ teaspoon dried thyme leaves
- ¼ teaspoon dried grated lemon peel
- 1 cup long-grain white rice
- 1 (3- or 4-ounce) can sliced mushrooms with garlic, with or without butter, all the liquid included

Salt and freshly ground black pepper, to taste

Fresh whole thyme leaves, for garnish (optional)

In a medium saucepan, bring the broth, lemon juice, oil, parsley, thyme, and lemon peel to a boil over high heat. Stir in the rice and mushrooms with their liquid. Cover, reduce the heat to low, and simmer until all the liquid is absorbed, 17 to 20 minutes.

Remove the pan from the heat. Season the rice with salt and pepper and stir to evenly distribute the ingredients. Let stand, uncovered, 1 minute, then fluff with a fork. Serve at once, garnished with the fresh thyme leaves, if desired.

PER SERVING

Calories 227 ■ Protein 9g ■ Total Fat 4g ■ Sat. Fat 1g ■ Cholesterol 0mg ■ Carbohydrate 39g ■ Dietary Fiber 3g ■ Sodium 320mg

SPANISH RICE

Vegan

MAKES 4 TO 5 SERVINGS

This is a perfect side dish to serve with Black Bean Tacos (page 66) or Bean Enchiladas with Green Sauce (page 63). Although I usually make it with a standard tomato salsa, feel free to experiment with any variety that strikes your fancy.

1¾ cups water

½ cup mild or medium salsa

½ tablespoon extra-virgin olive oil

¼ teaspoon salt

1 cup long-grain white rice

In a medium saucepan, bring the water, salsa, oil, and salt to a boil over medium-high heat. Stir in the rice, cover, and reduce the heat to low. Simmer until all the liquid is absorbed, 17 to 20 minutes.

Remove the pan from the heat. Stir the rice to evenly distribute the ingredients. Re-cover and let stand 5 minutes. Fluff with a fork and serve at once.

PER SERVING

Calories 191 ■ Protein 4g ■ Total Fat 2g ■ Sat. Fat 0g ■ Cholesterol 0mg ■ Carbohydrate 39g ■ Dietary Fiber 1g ■ Sodium 219mg

THAI-STYLE CURRIED GOLDEN RICE

Vegan

MAKES 4 TO 6 SERVINGS

A touch of coconut milk lends this curried rice dish a nutty nuance that's simply irresistible. Though optional, flecks of red pimiento are a pretty contrast with its distinctively golden grains. Serve with Sugar Snap Peas with Almonds and Garlic (page 154) or Ginger-Glazed Baby Carrots (page 137) for a memorable meal for four.

1 tablespoon canola oil

¼ cup frozen chopped onion

½ teaspoon refrigerated bottled minced garlic

1¾ cups water

¼ cup canned light coconut milk

1 cup long-grain white rice

2 tablespoons diced pimiento, drained (optional)

1 teaspoon curry powder

½ teaspoon ground turmeric

Salt and freshly ground black pepper, to taste

In a medium deep-sided skillet with a lid, heat the oil over medium heat. Add the onion and cook, stirring, until softened and thawed, 2 to 3 minutes. Add the garlic and cook, stirring, 1 minute. Stir in the water, coconut milk, rice, pimiento (if using), curry powder, turmeric, salt, and pepper; bring to a brisk simmer over medium-high heat. Reduce the heat to low, cover, and simmer until all the liquid is absorbed, 17 to 20 minutes. Remove from the heat and let stand, covered, 5 minutes. Fluff the rice with a fork and serve at once.

PER SERVING

Calories 233 ■ Protein 4g ■ Total Fat 7g ■ Sat. Fat 3g ■ Cholesterol 0mg ■ Carbohydrate 39g ■ Dietary Fiber 1g ■ Sodium 7mg

CHILLED SUGAR SNAP PEAS IN SESAME-MUSTARD VINAIGRETTE

Vegan

MAKES 4 SERVINGS

Quickly blanching fresh snap peas cooks them just enough to release their inherent sweetness while preserving their natural crunch. If stringless snap peas are unavailable, pinch the ends off the regular ones and remove the strings. You can use fresh snow peas, but blanch for half the amount of time.

12 ounces ready-washed fresh stringless sugar snap peas

1 tablespoon peanut or plain sesame oil

½ tablespoon toasted (dark) sesame oil

1 tablespoon rice vinegar

½ tablespoon Dijon mustard

Salt and freshly ground black pepper, to taste

Bring a large stockpot of salted water to a boil over high heat. Prepare a large bowl of ice water. Add the peas to the boiling water and cook 1 minute. Drain and immediately place in the ice water to cool and refresh. Drain well.

In a medium bowl, whisk together the peanut oil, toasted sesame oil, vinegar, mustard, salt, and pepper. Add the peas, tossing to thoroughly coat. Let stand about 10 minutes to allow the flavors to blend. Toss again and serve. Alternatively, cover and refrigerate a minimum of 1 hour, or overnight, and serve chilled or return to room temperature.

PER SERVING

Calories 83 ▪ Protein 3g ▪ Total Fat 5g ▪
Sat. Fat 1g ▪ Cholesterol 0mg ▪ Carbohydrate 7g ▪
Dietary Fiber 2g ▪ Sodium 27mg

SESAME SNAP PEAS

Vegan

MAKES 4 SERVINGS

Sugar snap peas never tasted better than in this quick and easy recipe, a perfect accompaniment to many of this book's Asian-style noodle or rice dishes. As fresh snap peas are increasingly available in major supermarkets, I've given directions for using both fresh and frozen.

> 2 teaspoons plain sesame oil or peanut oil
>
> 1 teaspoon toasted (dark) sesame oil
>
> 14 ounces ready-washed fresh stringless sugar snap peas or 1 (14-ounce) package frozen sugar snap peas
>
> 1 tablespoon sesame seeds
>
> 1 tablespoon reduced-sodium soy sauce
>
> Salt and freshly ground black pepper, to taste

In a large nonstick skillet, heat the two oils over medium-high heat.

If using fresh peas: Add the peas and sesame seeds to the skillet and cook, stirring and tossing often, until the peas are just beginning to brown and the sesame seeds are toasted, about 3 minutes. Remove the skillet from the heat and add the soy sauce, tossing well to combine. Season with salt and pepper.

If using frozen peas: Add the peas and sesame seeds to the skillet and cook, stirring and tossing often, until peas are thawed, 2 to 3 minutes. Increase the heat to high and cook, stirring and tossing constantly, until the peas are just beginning to brown and the sesame seeds are toasted, 2 to 3 minutes. Remove the skillet from the heat and add the soy sauce, tossing well to combine. Season with salt and pepper.

Serve warm.

PER SERVING

Calories 87 ▪ Protein 3g ▪ Total Fat 5g ▪
Sat. Fat 1g ▪ Cholesterol 0mg ▪ Carbohydrate 8g ▪
Dietary Fiber 3g ▪ Sodium 154mg

SUGAR SNAP PEAS WITH ALMONDS AND GARLIC

Vegan
MAKES 4 SERVINGS

Adding toasted almonds makes snap peas even snappier. For a decidedly Asian flavor, use the combination of peanut oil and toasted sesame oil and the optional soy sauce, if desired. Try teaming this recipe up with Coconut Jasmine Rice with Ginger (page 150) or Thai-Style Curried Golden Rice (page 152) for a memorable meal for four. If fresh stringless snap peas are unavailable, pinch the ends off the regular ones and remove the strings, or see the Cook's Tip below. You can use fresh snow peas instead, but reduce the initial cooking time by about 1 minute.

- 16 ounces ready-washed fresh stringless sugar snap peas
- ½ cup water
- 1 tablespoon peanut oil *or* 2 teaspoons peanut oil plus 1 teaspoon toasted (dark) sesame oil
- 2 tablespoons slivered or sliced almonds
- 1 teaspoon refrigerated bottled minced garlic
- 1 tablespoon low-sodium soy sauce (optional)
- Salt and freshly ground black pepper, to taste

In a large nonstick skillet with a lid, bring the peas and water to a boil over high heat. Cover, reduce the heat to medium, and cook until the peas are barely tender, about 3 minutes, shaking the pan a few times to redistribute the peas. Drain the water from the skillet. Return to the heat and add the oil and almonds. Increase the heat to medium-high and cook, tossing and stirring constantly, 1 minute.

Add the garlic and cook, tossing and stirring constantly, 1 minute, or until the garlic is fragrant but not colored and the almonds are lightly browned. Remove from the heat and add the soy sauce (if using), tossing well to combine. Season with salt and pepper. Serve at once.

PER SERVING
Calories 99 ▪ Protein 4g ▪ Total Fat 6g ▪ Sat. Fat 1g ▪ Cholesterol 0mg ▪ Carbohydrate 9g ▪ Dietary Fiber 3g ▪ Sodium 5mg

Cook's Tip An equal amount of frozen sugar snap peas can be used in lieu of fresh ones. Increase the initial cooking time to about 5 minutes.

MARINATED SNOW PEAS AND CARROTS

Vegan
MAKES 4 SERVINGS

This colorful and refreshing side dish is great for picnics or party buffets as it holds up well at room temperature. Ready-washed fresh sugar snap peas can be substituted for the snow peas, if desired, but blanch them as long as the carrots. For a tasty and unusual pasta salad serving four as a main dish or up to eight as a side, toss with 8 ounces somen or soba noodles that have been cooked and rinsed under running cold water, then drained well.

- 4 ounces shredded carrots
- 1 (8-ounce) bag ready-washed fresh snow peas
- 2 tablespoons orange juice
- 2 tablespoons rice vinegar
- 1 tablespoon peanut or plain sesame oil

- 1 tablespoon toasted (dark) sesame oil
- 1 tablespoon refrigerated bottled minced ginger
- 1 teaspoon sugar
- ½ teaspoon salt, or to taste
- ¼ teaspoon freshly ground black pepper, or to taste
- 2 tablespoons toasted sesame seeds (see Cook's Tip, page 44; optional)

Bring a large stockpot of salted water to a boil over high heat. Prepare a large bowl of ice water. Add the carrots and boil 30 seconds. Add the peas and boil 30 seconds. Drain and immediately place in ice water to cool and refresh. Drain well.

In a large bowl, whisk together the orange juice, vinegar, peanut oil, toasted sesame oil, ginger, sugar, salt, and pepper. Add the vegetables and toss gently yet thoroughly to combine. Let stand about 10 minutes at room temperature to allow the flavors to blend. Toss again and serve, sprinkled with the sesame seeds, if desired. Alternatively, cover and refrigerate a minimum of 1 hour, or up to 1 day, and serve chilled or return to room temperature.

PER SERVING

Calories 105 ▪ Protein 2g ▪ Total Fat 7g ▪
Sat. Fat 1g ▪ Cholesterol 0mg ▪ Carbohydrate 10g ▪
Dietary Fiber 2g ▪ Sodium 278mg

CREAMED SPINACH

Egg-free with vegan option

MAKES 4 TO 6 SERVINGS

A little of this rich and creamy dish goes a long way; even those who typically shun spinach usually enjoy it.

For a vegan recipe, replace the half-and-half with a soy creamer; Silk is a reliable brand. If you use other nondairy coffee creamers, note that most of the leading brands contain a casein derivative, which is a milk product.

- ½ cup plus 2 tablespoons water
- 1 tablespoon cornstarch
- 2 (10-ounce) bags ready-washed spinach
- ⅔ cup half-and-half or soy creamer
- ⅛ teaspoon ground nutmeg, or more to taste
- Salt and freshly ground black pepper, to taste

In a small container, stir together the 2 tablespoons water and cornstarch until smooth. Set aside.

In a large nonstick skillet, bring half the spinach and the ½ cup water to a boil over medium-high heat. Reduce the heat, cover, and simmer until all the spinach is beginning to wilt, stirring and tossing a few times, about 2 minutes. Add the remaining spinach, cover, and simmer until all the spinach is wilted, stirring and tossing a few times, 2 to 3 minutes. Uncover and increase the heat to medium-high; cook, stirring and breaking up the spinach with the edge of a spatula, until most of the liquid has evaporated and the spinach is greatly reduced in volume. Reduce the heat to medium and add the half-and-half, nutmeg, and cornstarch mixture. Cook, stirring, until thickened and bubbly, about 3 minutes. Season with salt and pepper and serve at once.

PER SERVING

Calories 91 ▪ Protein 5g ▪ Total Fat 5g ▪
Sat. Fat 3g ▪ Cholesterol 15mg ▪ Carbohydrate 9g ▪
Dietary Fiber 4g ▪ Sodium 129mg

Variations

Creamed Spinach in Puff Pastry Shells: Bake 1 (10-ounce) package frozen puff pastry shells (6 shells) according to package directions. Prepare the creamed spinach as directed above. To serve, fill the shells with equal amounts of the creamed spinach. Serve at once.

Eggs Florentine: Poach 4 eggs as directed on page 165. Prepare the creamed spinach as directed above and divide equally among 4 plates. Top each with a poached egg and serve at once.

WILTED SPINACH WITH GARLIC

Vegan

MAKES 3 SERVINGS

This classic Mediterranean dish is delicious served over rice, noodles, or couscous. You can use mature spinach, but remove any thick stems and ribs before cooking.

1 tablespoon extra-virgin olive oil

1 teaspoon refrigerated bottled minced garlic

1 (9-ounce) bag ready-washed baby spinach

2 tablespoons water

Pinch ground nutmeg (optional)

Salt and freshly ground black pepper,
   to taste

In a large nonstick skillet, heat the oil over medium heat. Add the garlic and cook, stirring constantly, until softened but not browned, about 2 minutes. Add half the spinach and 1 tablespoon of the water; toss and turn until the leaves are just beginning to wilt, about 30 seconds. Add the remaining spinach and water to the skillet; cook, tossing and turning constantly, until the spinach is

wilted but not shriveled, 1 to 2 minutes. Remove from the heat and add nutmeg (if using), salt, and pepper, tossing well to combine. Serve at once.

PER SERVING
Calories 60 ▪ Protein 3g ▪ Total Fat 5g ▪
Sat. Fat 1g ▪ Cholesterol 0mg ▪ Carbohydrate 3g ▪
Dietary Fiber 2g ▪ Sodium 67mg

Variation

Wilted Spinach with Pine Nuts and Raisins: Add ¼ cup raisins (plumped in warm water to cover for 15 minutes, then drained) when you add the last half of the spinach to the skillet. Sprinkle the finished dish with 2 tablespoons pine nuts, toasted if desired (see Cook's Tip, page 7).

Cook's Tip While you can double the recipe, you will need to cook the spinach in two separate batches.

SWEET POTATO GRATIN

Egg-free with vegan options
MAKES 6 SERVINGS

A good source of fiber and rich in vitamins A and C, the B vitamins, potassium, and iron, the sweet potato is an important vegetable to be enjoyed year-round, and not just at Thanksgiving. That said, this is a perfect gratin to accompany that tofu turkey as it can be assembled a day ahead of the final baking. Vegan soy margarine (Earth Balance brand contains no trans fats) can replace the butter, and maple syrup or brown sugar can replace the honey for a completely vegan dish.

3 (8-ounce) sweet potatoes, scrubbed

2 tablespoons butter or vegan soy margarine

¼ cup low-sodium vegetable broth

2 tablespoons honey, pure maple syrup, or brown sugar

1 tablespoon bottled lime juice

Salt and freshly ground black pepper, to taste

Preheat the oven to 350F (175C). Lightly grease an 8½-or 9-inch pie plate and set aside.

Prick the potatoes with the tines of a fork and place on an ungreased baking sheet. Roast until the potatoes are tender through the center, 50 minutes to 1 hour. Remove from the oven and let cool slightly. Do not turn off oven.

When the potatoes are cool enough to handle, peel off the skins with the help of a fork and place the flesh in a large bowl. Mash into large chunks with a potato masher. Add 1½ tablespoons of the butter. When the butter is mostly melted, add the broth, honey, lime juice, salt, and pepper; mash into a coarse puree.

Transfer the mixture to the prepared pie plate and dot with the remaining butter. (At this point, the mixture can be cooled completely and refrigerated, covered, up to 24 hours before proceeding with recipe.) Bake 30 to 40 minutes, or until the top is lightly browned and the casserole is warmed through. Serve warm.

PER SERVING
Calories 177 ▪ Protein 2g ▪ Total Fat 4g ▪ Total Fat 2g ▪ Cholesterol 10mg ▪ Carbohydrate 34g ▪ Dietary Fiber 4g ▪ Sodium 75mg

SWEET-AND-SOUR ASIAN VEGETABLES

Vegan
MAKES 4 SERVINGS

Here is a quick and easy way to dress up any number of vegetables; the frozen Asian mix is especially tasty prepared this way. To make dinner for four, toss the vegetables with approximately twice the amount of sauce ingredients and serve over 3 to 4 cups hot cooked rice (see Cook's Tip, page 126) or about 8 ounces thin Asian-style noodles, cooked, rinsed, and drained.

3 tablespoons Asian sweet-and-sour sauce

1 tablespoon reduced-sodium soy sauce

2 teaspoons toasted (dark) sesame oil

½ teaspoon onion powder

¼ teaspoon extra-hot Chinese mustard, or to taste (optional)

1 (16-ounce) package frozen mixed Asian-style vegetables

Salt and freshly ground black pepper, to taste

In a small bowl, stir together the sweet-and-sour sauce, soy sauce, oil, onion powder, and mustard (if using). Set briefly aside.

Cook the vegetables according to package directions; drain well and transfer to a serving bowl. Immediately add the sauce mixture, tossing well to combine. Season with salt and pepper and serve at once.

PER SERVING
Calories 57 ▪ Protein 3g ▪ Total Fat 3g ▪
Sat. Fat 0mg ▪ Cholesterol 0mg ▪ Carbohydrate 7g ▪
Dietary Fiber 3g ▪ Sodium 177mg

Variation
Curried Asian Vegetables with Chutney: Replace the sweet-and-sour sauce with mango chutney. Omit the soy sauce and optional Chinese mustard. Add ½ tablespoon water and ½ to 1 teaspoon mild curry powder and proceed as otherwise directed in the recipe.

Brunch and Egg Dishes

Brunch is my favorite forum for entertaining, not only because it's informal (no one expects to be handed a martini or served a four-course meal from anyone still padding around in slippers), but also because most breakfast foods are quick and require little, if any, preparation. That's exactly why the following recipes, from simple shirred eggs to a more substantial Spanish Tortilla, are perfect for busy weeknight suppers. You will even find two delicious sides—Skillet Breakfast Potatoes and Cherry Tomato Gratin—to accompany them. So as you sit down to eat Breakfast Burritos or Breakfast Pizza, enjoy your breakfast for dinner, or dinner for breakfast, or whatever!

Eggs

While eggs contain relatively high amounts of cholesterol (about 213 milligrams per large egg), one large egg contains about 75 calories, 6 grams of protein, 5 grams of total fat, and 2 grams of saturated fat, which, as of this writing, is just a little more than 10 percent of the FDA's recommended Daily Value (DV) based on a 2,000-calorie-per-day diet. Furthermore, while limiting cholesterol intake is important, many health experts now agree that a diet low in saturated fats is even more essential in the prevention of heart disease and other related illnesses. Finally, I am pleased to report that all of the recipes in this chapter were tested using certified organic eggs from free-roaming hens in Lancaster, Pennsylvania.

BAKED EGGS

Dairy-free
MAKES 6 SERVINGS

Baking, or shirring, eggs may not be the quickest method of preparing eggs, but it is definitely the easiest. During the 15 minutes or so that your eggs are baking, you have time to prepare Skillet Breakfast Potatoes (page 166) and Broccoli with Cheese Sauce (page 135) and voilà, an instant brunch or quick weeknight supper. If you don't own a 6-cup muffin pan, use a 12-cup muffin tin and fill the empty cups halfway with water to promote even cooking. Individual 6-ounce custard molds may also be used.

6 large eggs
Salt and freshly ground black pepper, to taste

Preheat oven to 350F (175C). Lightly oil a 6-cup muffin pan.

Carefully break an egg into each muffin cup.

Season with salt and pepper. Bake in the center of the oven to desired doneness, about 15 minutes for medium-set yolks. Loosen the eggs with the tip of a knife, transfer to plates, and serve at once.

PER SERVING
Calories 75 ■ Protein 6g ■ Total Fat 5g ■
Sat. Fat 2g ■ Cholesterol 213mg ■ Carbohydrate 1g ■
Dietary Fiber 0g ■ Sodium 63mg

BASIL, ARUGULA, AND MUSHROOM FRITTATA

Dairy-free
MAKES 4 SERVINGS

I love the combination of pungent basil and peppery arugula here, nicely counterbalanced with the richness of sautéed mushrooms. Feel free to experiment with other fresh greens or herbs, such as fresh spinach and oregano. Cherry Tomato Gratin (page 168) makes a delicious and colorful accompaniment.

8 large eggs
¼ cup water
2 teaspoons quick-mixing all-purpose flour (see Cook's Tip below)
½ teaspoon salt, preferably the coarse variety, plus additional to taste
¼ teaspoon freshly ground black pepper
3 tablespoons chopped pimiento, drained
1½ tablespoons extra-virgin olive oil
1 (8-ounce) package presliced fresh white mushrooms
1 cup arugula leaves, torn into bite-size pieces
½ cup fresh whole basil leaves, torn in half or in quarters, depending on size

Adjust the oven rack 6 to 8 inches from the broiler. Preheat the oven to broil.

In a medium bowl, whisk together the eggs, water, flour, salt, and pepper until smooth. Stir in the pimiento and set aside.

In a 10-inch nonstick ovenproof skillet, heat the oil over medium heat. Add the mushrooms and cook, stirring occasionally, until they release their liquid, 4 to 5 minutes. Add the arugula and basil and cook, stirring often, until wilted, about 2 minutes.

Quickly stir the egg mixture to recombine and pour into the skillet. Cook, stirring gently with a wooden spoon in an east-west-north-south pattern, for 2 minutes. Reduce the heat to low and cook, without stirring, until only the top of the egg mixture is runny, about 5 minutes. Immediately place the skillet under the broiler.

Broil, watching carefully and turning the skillet to promote even cooking, until puffed and lightly browned, 2 to 4 minutes. Loosen the sides of the frittata with a knife and the bottom with a spatula, then slide onto a platter. Sprinkle with additional coarse salt, if desired. Cut into 4 wedges and serve warm.

PER SERVING
Calories 221 ▪ Protein 15g ▪ Total Fat 16g ▪
Sat. Fat 4g ▪ Cholesterol 431mg ▪ Carbohydrate 6g ▪
Dietary Fiber 1g ▪ Sodium 367mg

Cook's Tip If you don't have any quick-mixing flour on hand, combine 2 teaspoons all-purpose flour with 1 tablespoon of the water in a small covered container and shake until well blended before whisking with the eggs.

BREAKFAST BURRITOS
Lacto-ovo with dairy-free option
MAKES 6 SERVINGS

This is an excellent brunch recipe as the burritos can be assembled up to one hour before baking. Oven-Roasted Potatoes with Cumin (page 145) are delicious accompaniments. Vegan soy cheese substitutes are not recommended here; unfortunately, they don't melt well. For a dairy-free alternative, use nondairy sour cream in lieu of the regular variety and omit the cheese altogether—the burritos will still be quite delicious!

1 cup salsa, preferably medium
1 tablespoon canola or other mild vegetable oil
½ cup frozen chopped onion
½ cup frozen chopped green bell pepper
10 eggs, whisked together until blended
Salt and freshly ground black pepper, to taste
6 tablespoons nonfat or light sour cream or nondairy sour cream
6 (10-inch) flour tortillas
¾ cup (3 ounces) already-shredded reduced-fat cheddar, Monterey Jack, or Mexican-blend cheese

Preheat oven to 350F (175C). Briefly drain ¼ cup of the salsa of most of its liquid and set aside.

In a large nonstick skillet, heat the oil over medium heat. Add the onion and bell pepper and cook, stirring, until softened and thawed, 3 to 5 minutes. Add the eggs, the ¼ cup drained salsa, salt, and black pepper, stirring well with a balloon whisk to combine. Cook, whisking often, until the mixture has thickened into small, soft curds but is still moist, 4 to 5 minutes. Remove the skillet from the heat and add the sour cream, whisking to incorporate. Let cool slightly.

Place equal amounts of the egg mixture along the center of each tortilla. Top each with 2 tablespoons of the remaining salsa, then sprinkle with 2 tablespoons of the cheese. Roll up, tucking ends inside as you go. Place each burrito, seam side down, on an ungreased baking sheet. Cover with foil. (At this point, the burritos can be held at room temperature up to 1 hour before baking.) Bake until heated through, 15 to 20 minutes. Serve warm.

PER SERVING

Calories 308 ▪ Protein 19g ▪ Total Fat 14g ▪ Sat. Fat 4g ▪ Cholesterol 359mg ▪ Carbohydrate 26g ▪ Dietary Fiber 2g ▪ Sodium 483mg

Variation

Tex-Mex Scrambled Eggs: Use a large nonstick skillet with a lid, and omit the tortillas or serve them, heated, on the side. Cook the eggs as directed. After removing the skillet from the heat and whisking in the sour cream, sprinkle evenly with the cheese. Cover and return to low heat without stirring until the cheese is melted and eggs are set to a medium degree of softness, about 2 minutes. Divide evenly among 6 plates and serve at once, with the remaining salsa passed separately.

BREAKFAST PIZZA

Lacto-ovo with dairy-free option
MAKES 4 SERVINGS

This is an easy-to-make, fun-to-eat brunch recipe that's ideal for teens to pop in the oven themselves after a sleepover. Vegan soy cheese substitutes are not recommended here; for a dairy-free pizza, simply omit the cheese and top with extra pizza sauce or ketchup after baking.

> ¼ cup prepared pizza sauce (see second Cook's Tip, page 70) or tomato ketchup, plus additional, if desired
> 4 (6-inch-diameter) Boboli or other small prebaked pizza shells
> 4 large eggs
> 1 cup (4 ounces) already-shredded part-skim mozzarella or Italian-blend cheese
> Dried oregano (optional)

Preheat oven to 350F (175C).

Thinly spread 1 tablespoon of the pizza sauce over each pizza shell. Transfer the shells to a large ungreased baking sheet without sides. Crack an egg into a small container and, from that, carefully slide onto pizza shell. Repeat with remaining eggs and pizza shells.

Bake in the center of the oven about 15 minutes, or until the egg whites are set but the yolks are still soft. Remove the baking sheet from oven. Sprinkle each pizza with ¼ cup of the cheese, then sprinkle lightly with oregano, if using. Bake about 5 minutes, or until the cheese is melted and yolks are medium-soft or desired doneness. Serve at once, with additional pizza sauce passed separately, if desired.

PER SERVING

Calories 409 ▪ Protein 22g ▪ Total Fat 14g ▪ Sat. Fat 5g ▪ Cholesterol 228mg ▪ Carbohydrate 47g ▪ Dietary Fiber 0g ▪ Sodium 930mg

Variation

Mexican-Style Breakfast Pizza: Substitute Mexican-blend, cheddar, or Monterey Jack cheese for the mozzarella. Garnish with sour cream and/or salsa, if desired.

BROCCOLI AND CHEESE OMELET

Lacto-ovo with dairy-free option

MAKES 2 SERVINGS

A nonstick skillet is essential for a failproof omelet. Using the 10-inch size produces a thin, quick-cooking omelet that looks generous enough to serve two. I selected broccoli and cheddar cheese for this recipe, but asparagus and Swiss is another good combination. Vegan soy cheese substitutes are not recommended here; for a dairy-free dish, simply omit the cheese.

3 large eggs

1 tablespoon water

Salt and freshly ground black pepper, to taste

½ tablespoon extra-virgin olive oil

1 cup frozen chopped broccoli cuts or florets, cooked according to package directions and well drained

½ cup (2 ounces) already-shredded cheddar cheese

In a medium bowl, whisk together the eggs, water, salt, and pepper until frothy.

In a 10-inch nonstick skillet with a lid, heat the oil over medium-low heat. Add the eggs and cook without stirring until the edges are set and the middle is slightly runny, 5 to 7 minutes. Scatter the broccoli on one half of the egg mixture, then evenly sprinkle the cheese over the broccoli. Season lightly with salt and pepper. Using a wide spatula, fold the plain half of the omelet over the filled half. Reduce the heat to low, cover, and cook until the cheese melts, 1 to 2 minutes. Slide onto a plate, cut in half, and serve at once.

PER SERVING

Calories 215 ▪ Protein 19g ▪ Total Fat 13g ▪ Sat. Fat 4g ▪ Cholesterol 325mg ▪ Carbohydrate 6g ▪ Dietary Fiber 3g ▪ Sodium 290mg

FRIED EGGS AND SALSA ON CORN TORTILLAS

Lacto-ovo with dairy-free option

MAKES 4 SERVINGS

This festive egg dish is perfect for brunch or carefree weeknight suppers. If you use a nonstick skillet and let the excess oil drip back into the skillet before transferring the cooked tortillas to the baking sheet, you should not need to use the extra ½ tablespoon of oil for frying the eggs. For a dairy-free dish, omit the cheese altogether; unfortunately, the soy cheese substitutes that melt well contain casein, which is a milk product.

4 large eggs

2 to 2½ tablespoons canola oil

4 (6-inch) corn tortillas

¾ cup (3 ounces) already-shredded reduced-fat cheddar cheese

Salt and freshly ground black pepper, to taste

½ cup mild to medium salsa

4 tablespoons light sour cream or nondairy sour cream (optional)

Preheat oven to 225F (105C). Line a baking sheet with several layers of paper towels and set aside.

Gently crack each egg into its own small cup and set briefly aside. In a large nonstick skillet with a lid, heat 2 tablespoons of the oil over medium-high heat. Working with 1 tortilla at a time, fry tortillas until light golden, 20 to 30 seconds on each side. Transfer the tortillas to prepared baking sheet and blot between paper towels. When the last tortilla is cooked, remove the skillet from the heat but do not clean. Remove the paper towels from the baking sheet and sprinkle each tortilla with 3 tablespoons of the cheese. Place the tortillas in the oven about 10 minutes, or until the cheese is melted.

Meanwhile, add the remaining oil to skillet, if necessary; heat over medium-low heat. Carefully pour each egg into the skillet; cook, covered, about 5 minutes for moderately soft-cooked eggs, or to desired doneness. Remove from the heat and season with salt and pepper.

To serve, place a tortilla on each of 4 plates. Top each tortilla with an egg. Spoon 2 tablespoons of the salsa over each egg, then top with 1 tablespoon of sour cream, if desired. Serve at once.

PER SERVING
Calories 234 ■ Protein 13g ■ Total Fat 14g ■
Sat. Fat 3g ■ Cholesterol 217mg ■ Carbohydrate 14g
■ Dietary Fiber 2g ■ Sodium 317mg

OVEN-BAKED CINNAMON FRENCH TOAST

Lacto-ovo with dairy-free options

MAKES 4 SERVINGS

I prefer to make French toast this way because the whole batch cooks at the same time, rather than in two stages. Best of all, it frees all of my stovetop burners for other things. If I'm preparing it for a crowd, I can double the recipe and pop two baking sheets in the oven at the same time. For a dairy-free alternative, use soy or rice milk in lieu of the skim milk and vegan

soy margarine in lieu of the butter; Earth Balance is a good brand. Just be sure to check the cinnamon bread's list of ingredients; a leading brand contains dairy.

> **3 eggs**
> **¾ cup skim milk, soymilk, or rice milk**
> **1 tablespoon sugar**
> **2 tablespoons butter or vegan soy margarine**
> **8 slices cinnamon bread, with or without raisins**
> **Pure maple syrup or confectioners' sugar, to serve**

Preheat oven to 450F (230C). In a medium bowl, whisk together the eggs, milk, and sugar. Set briefly aside.

Smear the butter evenly on a standard-size baking sheet. Place the baking sheet in the oven 1 minute, or until hot. Quickly dip the bread slices in the egg mixture and arrange on the hot baking sheet. Drizzle half of the remaining egg mixture over the bread. Bake in the upper third of the oven 5 minutes, or until the tops are golden and puffy. Remove from oven and, using a spatula, turn the bread over. Drizzle evenly with the remaining egg mixture. Bake 3 to 4 minutes, or until the tops are golden and puffy. Serve at once, with maple syrup passed separately.

PER SERVING (2 PIECES OF TOAST)
Calories 268 ■ Protein 10g ■ Total Fat 11g ■
Sat. Fat 5g ■ Cholesterol 176mg ■ Carbohydrate 31g
■ Dietary Fiber 1g ■ Sodium 398mg

Variation

Skillet French Toast: Preheat oven to 170F (75C). Melt 1 tablespoon of the butter in a large nonstick skillet over medium heat. Quickly dip 4 slices of the bread in the egg mixture and place in the skillet. Cook until golden brown, 3 to 4 minutes on each side. Transfer to a baking sheet and place in the oven to keep warm. Repeat with the remaining ingredients and serve at once.

POACHED EGGS ON ENGLISH MUFFINS WITH WELSH RAREBIT SAUCE

Lacto-ovo

MAKES 4 SERVINGS

Known as a "golden buck" in England, a poached egg atop Welsh rarebit is a delightful, and less fussy, alternative to eggs Benedict. Four slices of toast, preferably rye, can replace the English muffins. Traditionally, a serving consists of two eggs, one on top of each muffin half, but I've found that one egg and one muffin half served with steamed asparagus or broccoli and a potato dish, such as Skillet Breakfast Potatoes (page 166), is more than sufficient. For heartier appetites, simply double the recipe.

- **4 eggs**
- **2 English muffins, split in half, lightly toasted, buttered or plain**
- **½ recipe Welsh Rarebit Sauce (at right)**

Lightly oil a baking dish large enough to hold the cooked eggs in a single layer. In a medium deep-sided skillet, pour enough water to measure 1 inch. Bring the water to a gentle simmer over medium-high heat.

Meanwhile, crack each egg into its own small custard cup or similar container. When the water has reached a gentle simmer, quickly yet carefully slide each egg from its cup into the water. After about 30 seconds, using a slotted spoon and beginning with the first immersed egg, quickly yet gently push each egg white back toward the yolk to form a circular shape, taking care that the eggs do not touch one another. Lower the heat as necessary to maintain a gentle simmer. As the eggs begin to firm, use the slotted spoon to gently lift each egg so that it does not stick to the bottom. Poach until the egg whites are firm and the yolks are still soft, about 3 minutes. Using the slotted spoon, remove the eggs from the water and carefully transfer them to the prepared baking dish. If not using immediately, cover and keep warm in a very low oven up to 1 hour.

To assemble the dish, top each muffin half with 1 egg and spoon about 5 tablespoons of the Welsh rarebit sauce over the top. Alternatively, spoon equal amounts of sauce over each muffin half and top with an egg.

PER SERVING (½ MUFFIN WITH EGG AND SAUCE)
Calories 285 ■ Protein 17g ■ Total Fat 15g ■ Sat. Fat 6g ■ Cholesterol 230mg ■ Carbohydrate 19g ■ Dietary Fiber 0g ■ Sodium 548mg

WELSH RAREBIT SAUCE

Egg-free

MAKES ABOUT 2½ CUPS

Other recipes for rarebit sauce are more or less fondues, which must be served immediately; otherwise, the cheese has a tendency to separate and become stringy. The following recipe, using a standard white sauce as the base, will retain its smoothness indefinitely so long as it is held over low heat once the cheese has been added. It can also be refrigerated up to 2 days and reheated gently, stirring occasionally. Vegetarian Worcestershire sauce, made without anchovies, is available in health food stores and natural food markets. While you can reduce the amount of dairy and cholesterol in the recipe by using all canola oil in lieu of the butter and substituting rice milk or soy creamer for the whole milk, I'm afraid that using vegan soy cheddar cheese substitutes would result in a disappointing sauce.

2 tablespoons butter or 2 tablespoons canola oil

2 tablespoons canola oil

¼ cup all-purpose flour

½ teaspoon salt

¼ teaspoon freshly ground black pepper

¼ teaspoon dried mustard

¼ teaspoon vegetarian Worcestershire sauce

1 cup whole or 2% milk, rice milk, or soy creamer

½ to ⅔ cup beer

2 cups (8 ounces) already-shredded reduced-fat cheddar cheese

1 to 2 pinches sweet paprika (optional)

In a medium saucepan, heat the butter and oil over medium-low heat until the butter is melted. Blend in the flour, salt, pepper, mustard, and Worcestershire sauce. Cook, stirring constantly, until the mixture is smooth and bubbly. Remove from the heat and gradually stir in the milk. Return to medium heat and bring to a boil, stirring constantly. Boil 1 minute, stirring vigorously from the bottom to prevent sticking. Gradually stir in the beer. Reduce the heat to low and stir in the cheese and paprika (if using). Cook, stirring constantly, until the cheese is melted. If not using immediately, cover and keep warm on the top of a double boiler over very hot, but not simmering, water up to 1 hour, stirring occasionally.

SKILLET BREAKFAST POTATOES

Vegan

MAKES 4 TO 5 SERVINGS

This quick and easy potato dish goes well with many of this cookbook's egg or brunch-style dishes. While you can make them in a regular nonstick skillet, I'm always looking for excuses to pull out my seasoned cast-iron skillet, which browns them so nicely. They are delicious on their own or topped with ketchup, salsa, or sour cream.

2 tablespoons canola oil

1 cup frozen chopped onion

2 (15-ounce) cans sliced potatoes, rinsed and drained

Salt and freshly ground black pepper, to taste

Adjust the oven rack 6 to 8 inches from the broiler. Preheat the oven to broil.

In a 10-inch ovenproof nonstick skillet (preferably cast-iron), heat the oil over medium heat. Add the onion and cook, stirring, until softened and lightly browned, 3 to 5 minutes. Add the potatoes, salt, and pepper; toss well to combine. Pack the potatoes down lightly in the skillet. Cook, without stirring, until the bottom is lightly browned, 5 to 8 minutes. Remove from the heat and place the skillet under the broiler.

Broil until the top is lightly browned, turning

the skillet to promote even cooking, 3 to 5 minutes. Serve warm.

PER SERVING

Calories 158 ▪ Protein 3g ▪ Total Fat 7g ▪
Sat. Fat 1g ▪ Cholesterol 0mg ▪ Carbohydrate 22g ▪
Dietary Fiber 4g ▪ Sodium 644mg

SOUTHWESTERN-STYLE BAKED POLENTA AND EGG CASSEROLE

Lacto-ovo

MAKES 6 SERVINGS

Polenta makes a perfect nest for baked eggs in this yummy make-ahead southwestern-style casserole, ideal for carefree entertaining. Vegan soy cheese substitutes are not recommended for this recipe, as they typically do not melt well.

1 (14-ounce) can (1¾ cups) low-sodium
   vegetable broth
1¼ cups water
1 cup quick-cooking polenta
1 tablespoon extra-virgin olive oil
Salt and freshly ground black pepper, to taste
1 cup (4 ounces) already-shredded reduced-fat
   Monterey Jack or Mexican-blend cheese
1 (4-ounce) can diced mild green chilies,
   drained
6 large eggs
Salsa and/or sour cream, for topping

Preheat oven to 350F (175C). Lightly oil a 13 × 9-inch baking dish and set aside.

In a medium stockpot, bring the broth and water to a boil over high heat, preferably on a back burner, as the polenta sputters. Slowly add the polenta, stirring constantly with a long-handled wooden spoon. Reduce the heat to medium and add the oil, salt, and pepper; cook, stirring constantly, until mixture is the consistency of cream of wheat, about 5 minutes. Remove from heat and immediately add ¾ cup of the cheese and the chilies, stirring until thoroughly combined.

Transfer to prepared baking dish. Let stand a few minutes to allow the polenta mixture to cool slightly and begin to set. With your fingers, make 6 shallow circular indentations in the polenta mixture, building up the sides slightly to form a rim. (At this point, the polenta can be held at room temperature up to 1 hour before proceeding with the recipe. Alternatively, it can be cooled completely and stored, covered, in the refrigerator up to 24 hours.)

Break an egg into each indentation. Bake uncovered 20 to 25 minutes, or until the whites are set and the yolks are fairly hard. Sprinkle with the remaining cheese and bake 2 minutes, or until the cheese is melted. Serve at once, with the toppings passed separately.

PER SERVING

Calories 313 ▪ Protein 18g ▪ Total Fat 9g ▪
Sat. Fat 3g ▪ Cholesterol 216mg ▪ Carbohydrate 39g
▪ Dietary Fiber 6g ▪ Sodium 330mg

SPANISH TORTILLA

Dairy-free

MAKES 4 SERVINGS

In Spain, when you ask for a tortilla, the following recipe is a quick-cooking version of what you'll get. Similar to an Italian frittata, a tortilla is more substantial than a French omelet and can actually be held in a warm oven about 20 minutes without any noticeable change in texture or appearance. Serve with Cherry Tomato Gratin (at right) for a memorable brunch menu.

6 large eggs

Salt and freshly ground black pepper, to taste

2 tablespoons chopped pimiento, drained

4 teaspoons extra-virgin olive oil

½ cup frozen chopped onion

½ cup frozen chopped green bell pepper

1 teaspoon refrigerated bottled minced garlic

1 (15-ounce) can sliced potatoes, rinsed and
    well drained

Adjust the oven rack 6 to 8 inches from the broiler. Preheat the oven to broil.

In a large bowl, whisk together the eggs, salt, and pepper until frothy. Stir in the pimiento and set aside.

In a 10-inch ovenproof nonstick skillet, heat the oil over medium heat. Add the onion and bell pepper and cook, stirring, until softened and thawed, about 3 minutes. Add the garlic and cook, stirring, 1 minute. Add the potatoes and stir gently to combine. Quickly stir the egg mixture to recombine, then pour over the potato mixture. Reduce the heat to medium-low and cook without stirring until the edges are set and the middle is slightly runny, about 5 minutes. Immediately place the skillet under the broiler.

Broil, watching carefully and turning the skillet to promote even cooking, until puffed and nicely browned, 2 to 3 minutes. Loosen the sides of the tortilla with a knife and the bottom with a spatula, then slide onto a platter. Cut into 4 wedges and serve warm.

PER SERVING

Calories 206 ■ Protein 11g ■ Total Fat 12g ■
Sat. Fat 3g ■ Cholesterol 319mg ■ Carbohydrate 13g
■ Dietary Fiber 2g ■ Sodium 418mg

CHERRY TOMATO GRATIN

Vegan

MAKES 5 TO 6 SERVINGS

This colorful and unusual side dish is a terrific accompaniment to various brunch and egg dishes. While I prefer plain dry bread crumbs, you can use Italian-seasoned bread crumbs instead, but omit the dried oregano and garlic powder from the recipe.

2½ to 3 cups cherry or grape tomatoes

2 tablespoons extra-virgin olive oil

½ teaspoon dried oregano

½ teaspoon salt, preferably the coarse variety,
    or to taste

¼ teaspoon freshly ground black pepper

3 tablespoons plain dry bread crumbs

2 tablespoons freshly grated Parmesan cheese
    (optional)

½ teaspoon garlic powder

Fresh whole oregano or marjoram leaves, for
    garnish (optional)

Preheat oven to 425F (220C).

Select enough cherry tomatoes to cover the bottom of an 8½- or 9-inch pie dish in a single, compact layer. Transfer selected tomatoes to a medium bowl and add half the oil, the oregano, salt, and pepper; toss well to combine. Lightly oil the pie dish and return the tomatoes in a single layer.

In a small bowl, combine the bread crumbs, cheese (if using), and garlic powder. Sprinkle the bread crumb mixture evenly over the tomatoes. Drizzle evenly with the remaining oil.

Bake 15 minutes, or until the tomato skins have just begun to split and the top is lightly browned. Let cool slightly before serving. Serve warm or slightly above room temperature, garnished with the fresh oregano leaves, if desired.

PER SERVING
Calories 111 ■ Protein 2g ■ Total Fat 8g ■
Sat. Fat 1g ■ Cholesterol 0mg ■ Carbohydrate 10g ■
Dietary Fiber 2g ■ Sodium 314mg

Sweet Endings

A sweet tooth needs to be satisfied every now and again, if only for the sake of our mental well-being, and maybe, just maybe, our waistlines. Indeed, research has shown that it isn't the occasional food that keeps us from achieving or maintaining a healthy weight; rather, it's what we eat on a daily basis. Limiting desserts to one or two a week could actually be more effective than forbidding them, which often makes sweets downright irresistible. Even so, the majority of this chapter's recipes contain 10 grams or less of fat per serving. Five of them—Maple-Glazed Bananas with Pecans, Fresh Melon Kebobs with Honey-Yogurt Sauce, Baked Pears with Caramel and Amaretti, Mexican Rice Pudding, and Strawberry-Orange Parfaits—contain a mere 5 grams or less of fat. Three others—Blueberries in Cassis over Lemon Sorbet, Mediterranean Dried Fruit Compote, and Fruited Tapioca Pudding—are veritably fat-free.

Ahhhhh . . . sweet endings!

TWO-INGREDIENT APPLE STRUDEL

Vegan
MAKES 6 SERVINGS

We can never get enough of this strudel in my house. It is excellent made with peach pie filling, as well. While recipes for homemade puff pastry invariably use butter, the leading commercial frozen brand is dairy-free.

1 egg (for optional egg wash)

1 tablespoon water (for optional egg wash)

1 sheet (½ [17.3-ounce] package) frozen puff pastry, thawed according to package directions

2 cups (all but ¼ cup from a 21-ounce can) prepared apple pie filling

Preheat oven to 375F (190C). If using the optional egg wash, mix egg and water with a fork and set aside.

Unfold pastry onto an ungreased baking sheet. Using your fingers, line half the apple slices along the middle third of the pastry, then spoon over some of the liquid filling. Fold the third of the pastry to your left over the apples; line with remaining slices, spooning over any remaining liquids. Fold the third of the pastry to your right as far over to the other side as it will comfortably stretch, pressing the dough together where it meets to seal. (Do not seal the ends.) Brush with egg wash (if using).

Cut about 6 (1-inch long) slits across the top. Bake in the center of the oven about 25 minutes, or until golden. Cool on the baking sheet on a wire rack 30 minutes. Cut into 6 slices and serve warm or at room temperature.

PER SERVING
Calories 291 ▪ Protein 3g ▪ Total Fat 11g ▪
Sat. Fat 3g ▪ Cholesterol 0mg ▪ Carbohydrate 47g ▪
Dietary Fiber 4g ▪ Sodium 175mg

Variation

Apple-Filled Puff Pastry Shells: Bake 1 (10-ounce) package puff pastry shells (6 shells) according to package directions. In a small saucepan over medium-low heat, heat the entire can of apple pie filling until hot, stirring occasionally. Arrange pastry shells on 6 dessert plates and fill with equal amounts of the pie filling. Serve warm, garnished with granola or whipped cream, if desired.

Cook's Tip Though optional, an egg wash is traditionally brushed over puff pastry just before baking for added sheen. For a vegan alternative, try brushing the pastry with a few tablespoons of soy creamer instead.

BANANAS WITH CHOCOLATE-COCONUT SAUCE

Vegan

MAKES 4 SERVINGS

This dairy-free tropical dessert is a fine conclusion to any special meal. You can prepare the desserts and let them stand at room temperature up to 1 hour before serving, for easy entertaining.

4 medium bananas, peeled

Chocolate-Coconut Sauce (below)

Chopped peanuts (optional)

Unsweetened shredded coconut (optional)

Arrange the bananas on each of 4 dessert plates. Spoon about ¼ cup of the sauce along the length of each banana to coat. Sprinkle with the peanuts and/or shredded coconut, if desired. Serve.

PER SERVING

Calories 242 ■ Protein 3g ■ Total Fat 8g ■ Sat. Fat 7g ■ Cholesterol 0mg ■ Carbohydrate 45g ■ Dietary Fiber 4g ■ Sodium 15mg

Variations

Bananas with Chocolate-Hazelnut Sauce: Prepare Easy Chocolate-Hazelnut Fondue (page 176) and serve the bananas as otherwise directed, using chopped hazelnuts instead of peanuts, if desired, and omitting the optional coconut. Just before serving, garnish with whipped cream, if desired.

Chocolate-Coconut or Chocolate-Hazelnut Banana Splits: Prepare desired sauce (page 172 or page 176). Cut the bananas in half lengthwise and arrange 2 halves on each of 4 dessert plates. Place 2 (¼-cup) scoops vanilla ice cream, frozen yogurt, or nondairy frozen dessert in the center of each banana split and top with sauce. Garnish the chocolate-coconut banana splits with peanuts or the chocolate-hazelnut banana splits with hazelnuts. Top with whipped cream and a maraschino cherry, if desired, and serve at once.

CHOCOLATE-COCONUT SAUCE

Vegan

MAKES ABOUT 1 CUP

Spoon this thick, rich, dairy-free sauce over any variety of fruits, pound cake, ice cream, frozen yogurt, or nondairy frozen dessert. It can also be used as a dip for fresh or dried fruit.

1 tablespoon water

½ tablespoon cornstarch

¾ cup canned light coconut milk

¼ cup sugar

3 tablespoons unsweetened cocoa powder, preferably Dutch process

½ teaspoon vanilla extract

In a small container, mix together the water and cornstarch until smooth. Set aside.

In a small saucepan, combine the coconut milk, sugar, and cocoa powder; bring to a gentle simmer over medium-high heat, whisking often. Reduce the heat to medium and whisk in the cornstarch mixture and vanilla. Cook, whisking constantly, until slightly thickened, about 2 minutes. Remove from the heat and let cool to slightly warm or room temperature. (The cooled sauce can be stored, covered, in the refrigerator up to 3 days. Reheat over low heat or let come to room temperature before using.)

PER SERVING (1 TABLESPOON)
Calories 34 ▪ Protein 1g ▪ Total Fat 2g ▪
Sat. Fat 2g ▪ Cholesterol 0mg ▪ Carbohydrate 5g ▪
Dietary Fiber 0g ▪ Sodium 3mg

MAPLE-GLAZED BANANAS WITH PECANS

Vegan

MAKES 4 SERVINGS

This is a dessert for all seasons that is simple enough to make on a busy weeknight, yet elegant enough to serve at a weekend brunch or dinner party. Yum!

- ¾ cup pure maple syrup
- ¼ teaspoon ground cinnamon
- ⅛ teaspoon ground nutmeg
- 4 bananas, peeled
- ¼ cup pecan chips
- Ready-whipped cream (optional)

In a skillet large enough to hold the bananas comfortably in a single layer, bring the maple syrup, cinnamon, and nutmeg to a boil over medium heat, stirring occasionally. Boil until reduced to ½ cup. Reduce the heat to low and add the bananas, turning gently to coat evenly with the syrup mixture.

Transfer a banana to each of 4 dessert plates, drizzling equally with any remaining syrup mixture. Sprinkle the pecans evenly over each banana. Serve at once, garnished with whipped cream, if desired.

PER SERVING
Calories 305 ▪ Protein 2g ▪ Total Fat 5g ▪
Sat. Fat 1g ▪ Cholesterol 0mg ▪ Carbohydrate 68g ▪
Dietary Fiber 3g ▪ Sodium 7mg

SUMMER BERRIES WITH SPICED CRÈME FRAÎCHE

Egg-free with vegan options

MAKES 4 SERVINGS

These luscious berries are also delicious served over tiny sponge tarts or in puff pastry shells. For a vegan dessert, omit the ladyfingers and use nondairy sour cream or plain soy yogurt in lieu of the crème fraîche. But in that instance, you might want to add a bit more confectioners' sugar to the recipe.

- 2 cups (1 pint) fresh raspberries, blackberries, and/or blueberries, washed and drained
- 2 tablespoons granulated sugar
- ½ cup crème fraîche, sour cream, nondairy sour cream, or plain soy yogurt
- 2 tablespoons confectioners' sugar
- ¼ teaspoon ground cinnamon
- ⅛ teaspoon ground nutmeg
- Pinch ground ginger
- 24 ladyfingers (3 ounces)

Sprinkle the berries with the granulated sugar; stir gently. Cover and refrigerate 2 hours or overnight.

In a small bowl, whisk together the crème fraîche, confectioners' sugar, cinnamon, nutmeg, and ginger. (If not using immediately, cover and refrigerate up to 2 days.) Place 2 stacks of 3 ladyfingers each on 4 dessert plates. Arrange ½ cup of the berries over the ladyfingers, then drizzle evenly with the accumulated berry juices. Top each serving with 2 tablespoons of the crème fraîche mixture. Serve immediately.

PER SERVING

Calories 230 ▪ Protein 4g ▪ Total Fat 11g ▪ Sat. Fat 6g ▪ Cholesterol 104mg ▪ Carbohydrate 31g ▪ Dietary Fiber 3g ▪ Sodium 45mg

BLUEBERRIES IN CASSIS OVER LEMON SORBET

Vegan
MAKES 6 SERVINGS

Simplicity reigns in this superb summertime dessert. The versatile blueberry sauce can be spooned over vanilla ice cream, frozen yogurt, or nondairy frozen dessert, as well as pound or sponge cake. While any berry or sorbet can be used, I prefer the sweetness of blueberries contrasted with the tartness of lemon sorbet.

2 cups (1 pint) blueberries or other berries
3 tablespoons sugar
1 tablespoon water
3 to 4 tablespoons crème de cassis,
    Chambord, or other berry-flavored liqueur
3 cups lemon or other fruit sorbet

In a small nonreactive saucepan, combine the berries, sugar, and water. Bring to a simmer over medium-low heat, stirring gently until the sugar dissolves. Add the liqueur and cook, stirring occasionally, 3 minutes. Remove from the heat and let cool until just warm to the touch, or to room temperature, if desired. (At this point, the mixture can be stored, covered, in the refrigerator up to 3 days before serving chilled or returning to room tem-

perature.) Divide the sorbet evenly among 6 dessert dishes. Top each serving with 3 to 4 tablespoons of the sauce. Serve at once.

PER SERVING

Calories 192 ▪ Protein 1g ▪ Total Fat 0g ▪ Sat. Fat 0g ▪ Cholesterol 0mg ▪ Carbohydrate 50g ▪ Dietary Fiber 2g ▪ Sodium 4mg

BLUEBERRY GRANOLA COBBLER

Vegan
MAKES 6 SERVINGS

This fiber-rich and crunchy cobbler can be made with any berry. For a lower-fat dessert, select a low-fat granola.

2 cups (1 pint) fresh blueberries
1¾ cups favorite granola
2 tablespoons light brown sugar
2 tablespoons granulated sugar
Vanilla ice cream, frozen yogurt, or nondairy
    frozen dessert, or ready-whipped cream, for
    topping (optional)

Preheat oven to 425F (220C). Lightly oil an 8½- or 9-inch pie dish and set aside.

In a medium bowl, toss the blueberries, granola, and brown sugar until well combined. Transfer to prepared pie dish and sprinkle evenly with the granulated sugar. Cover tightly with foil and bake 25 minutes. Uncover and bake 5 more minutes, or until lightly browned and bubbly. Serve warm or at room temperature with the toppings, if desired.

CHERRY-CRANBERRY COMPOTE IN PUFF PASTRY CUPS

Vegan

MAKES 6 SERVINGS

Decorated with the optional candied green cherries, this becomes a festive holiday dessert that can be made ahead in two stages and assembled just before serving. The compote is also delicious served over ice cream, frozen yogurt, nondairy frozen dessert, or pound cake. While recipes for homemade puff pastry invariably use butter, the leading brand of frozen puff pastry shells is dairy-free.

> 1 (10-ounce) package frozen puff pastry shells (6 shells)
> ½ tablespoon cornstarch
> ⅓ cup water
> 1 (15-ounce) can pitted tart cherries in water, drained
> ¼ cup sweetened dried cranberries
> ⅓ cup sugar
> ½ teaspoon dried chopped orange peel
> Candied green cherries, for garnish (optional)
> Ready-whipped cream, for garnish (optional)

Bake the pastry according to package directions. (If not serving immediately, let cool completely and store in an airtight container at room temperature up to 24 hours. Reheat in a low oven to crisp just before serving.)

Meanwhile, in a small container, stir the cornstarch in 1 tablespoon of the water until smooth; set briefly aside. In a small saucepan, bring the cherries, cranberries, remaining water, sugar, and orange peel to a gentle simmer over medium heat, stirring occasionally. Add the cornstarch mixture and let come to a boil, stirring gently and constantly. Reduce the heat to low and cook, stirring gently and constantly, 1 minute. Remove from the heat and let cool about 15 minutes. (At this point, the mixture can be completely cooled and refrigerated, covered, up to 3 days before reheating over low heat.) Place a pastry shell on each of 6 dessert plates and fill with equal amounts of compote (some will overflow). Serve warm, garnished with the candied cherries and whipped cream, if desired.

EASY CHOCOLATE-HAZELNUT FONDUE

Egg-free
MAKES 1 CUP (4 SERVINGS)

Nutella is a chocolate-hazelnut spread that is enormously popular in Europe, where it is smeared on just about everything—fresh and dried fruits, crepes, croissants, cookies, bread sticks, pretzels, toast—with abandonment. It can be found alongside the peanut butter in most well-stocked supermarkets. I love to serve the following fondue as a dip for pretzels or vanilla wafers, but it's delicious with fresh and dried fruit, as well. It also makes a great topping for ice cream, frozen yogurt, or nondairy frozen dessert. To reduce the amount of dairy in the recipe, use soy creamer or canned coconut milk in lieu of the half-and-half.

¼ cup half-and-half
¾ cup Nutella
Pretzels, plain cookies, and/or assorted fresh
    and dried fruit, for dipping.

In a small saucepan, heat the half-and-half over medium-low heat until just warm. Add the Nutella and cook, stirring, until thoroughly incorporated and hot. Transfer to a serving bowl and serve warm or just above room temperature, accompanied by pretzels. (The sauce can be stored, covered, in the refrigerator up to 3 days. Reheat over low heat before using.)

PER SERVING (1 TABLESPOON)
Calories 76 ■ Protein 4g ■ Total Fat 5g ■
Sat. Fat 1g ■ Cholesterol 1mg ■ Carbohydrate 5g ■
Dietary Fiber 0g ■ Sodium 77mg

Variations

To make a lower-fat fondue or sauce with a less-pronounced hazelnut flavor, omit the half-and-half and combine ¾ cup nonfat chocolate syrup and ¼ cup Nutella in a small pan. Heat as otherwise directed. Serve warm or at room temperature. (The sauce can be stored, covered, in the refrigerator up to 1 week.)

Neapolitan Ice Cream Sundaes with Chocolate-Hazelnut Sauce: Divide 3 cups Neapolitan ice cream (or plain vanilla, chocolate, or strawberry ice cream, frozen yogurt, or nondairy frozen dessert) among 6 dessert dishes and top with about 2½ tablespoons of the Chocolate-Hazelnut Fondue, slightly warm or at room temperature. Serve at once, garnished with ready-whipped cream and a maraschino cherry, if desired. This is a delightful ending to any Italian-style meal.

CHOCOLATE-GRANOLA REFRIGERATOR COOKIES

Vegan
MAKES ABOUT 24 COOKIES

If you use bittersweet chocolate, these no-bake refrigerator cookies are dairy-free as well as delicious. For directions on toasting coconut, refer to the Crunchy Toasted Coconut Ice Cream Balls (page 178).

4 ounces bittersweet or semisweet baking
    chocolate
1 cup granola, preferably low-fat
¼ cup chopped walnuts or pecans
¼ cup zante currants or raisins
½ cup sweetened shredded coconut, toasted
    if desired

Line 1 large or 2 medium baking sheets with parchment or waxed paper and set aside.

Place the chocolate in the top of a double boiler over barely simmering water. Heat, stirring occasionally, until completely melted. Add the granola, nuts, currants, and half of the coconut; stir until well combined. Drop by heaping tablespoons onto the prepared baking sheet. Sprinkle with the remaining coconut. Refrigerate 30 minutes, or until set. (At this point, the cookies can be transferred to a covered container, layered between sheets of waxed paper, and refrigerated up to 3 days.) Serve chilled.

PER COOKIE

Calories 68 ▪ Protein 2g ▪ Total Fat 5g ▪
Sat. Fat 2g ▪ Cholesterol 0mg ▪ Carbohydrate 6g ▪
Dietary Fiber 2g ▪ Sodium 2mg

GERMAN CHOCOLATE CAKE SUNDAES

Lacto-ovo with dairy-free options

MAKES 6 SERVINGS

This sinfully simple sundae has all the decadence of German chocolate cake—chocolate, coconut, and pecans—without the baking. If desired, soy creamer can replace the evaporated skim milk to make a vegan sauce. For a totally vegan dessert, omit the cookies and use chocolate or vanilla nondairy frozen dessert in lieu of the regular ice cream.

½ cup sugar

¼ cup water

½ cup evaporated skim milk or soy creamer

¼ cup unsweetened shredded coconut

3 tablespoons pecan pieces

6 large (3-inch-diameter) soft Dutch cocoa sugar cookies

3 cups (1½ pints) reduced-fat chocolate or vanilla ice cream, frozen yogurt, or nondairy frozen dessert

In a small saucepan, combine the sugar and water. Bring to a boil over medium heat, stirring only until the sugar is dissolved. Boil without stirring until the mixture turns a light amber color, 5 to 8 minutes, taking care not to burn it. Remove from heat and let cool a minute or so.

Add the milk; the sugar mixture will harden. Return to medium heat and bring to a boil, stirring constantly until the sugar mixture is incorporated into the milk. Boil, stirring often, until the mixture darkens and thickens to the consistency of heavy cream, 4 to 5 minutes, lifting the pan briefly off the heat whenever the mixture threatens to boil over. Remove from the heat and stir in the coconut and pecans. Set aside to cool slightly.

Place a cookie on each of 6 dessert plates and top with ½ cup ice cream. Spoon about 2 to 3 tablespoons of the sauce evenly over each serving. Serve at once.

PER SERVING

Calories 283 ▪ Protein 6g ▪ Total Fat 10g ▪
Sat. Fat 5g ▪ Cholesterol 31mg ▪ Carbohydrate 44g ▪
Dietary Fiber 1g ▪ Sodium 86mg

Cook's Tip Use the sauce, without the coconut and pecans, as a basic caramel topping for sundaes, brownies à la mode, and any variety of canned fruits or bananas. Makes about ½ cup sauce.

CRUNCHY TOASTED COCONUT ICE CREAM BALLS

Lacto-ovo with vegan options
MAKES 4 SERVINGS

Simply sprinkle this yummy topping over the ice cream if you don't have time to form it into balls. It is also delicious over warmed canned peaches or apricots. For a vegan alternative, frosted corn flakes can replace the honey oat cereal, and you can use nondairy frozen dessert.

½ cup sweetened shredded coconut
½ cup honey oat cereal, with or without almonds
1 pint (2 cups) reduced-fat vanilla ice cream, frozen yogurt, or nondairy frozen dessert

Preheat the oven to 300F (150C). Arrange the coconut in a single layer on an ungreased light-colored baking sheet. Bake 5 to 8 minutes, or until lightly toasted, stirring once.

Meanwhile, place the cereal in a self-sealing plastic sandwich bag and crush into small bits with your fingers and palms. Transfer to a small bowl. Add the toasted coconut, tossing well to combine.

To serve, place about 3 tablespoons of the coconut mixture in each of 4 dessert dishes. Scoop ½ cup ice cream and form into a ball while still in the container. Transfer it to a dessert dish and quickly turn it in the coconut mixture to coat. Repeat with remaining ice cream and coconut mixture. Serve at once.

PER SERVING
Calories 178 ■ Protein 5g ■ Total Fat 8g ■ Sat. Fat 6g ■ Cholesterol 25mg ■ Carbohydrate 23g ■ Dietary Fiber 1g ■ Sodium 70mg

COCONUT SORBET WITH PINEAPPLE-GINGER SAUCE

Vegan
MAKES 4 SERVINGS

Bottled chopped ginger lends this simple pineapple topping a hint of the exotic; spooned over coconut sorbet, it becomes a refreshing conclusion to any tropical or Asian-style meal. Coconut sorbet can be found in gourmet stores and, increasingly, in many well-stocked supermarkets. Vanilla ice cream, frozen yogurt, or nondairy frozen dessert can be substituted for the sorbet, if desired.

¼ cup sugar
2 tablespoons water
1 (8-ounce) can juice-packed crushed pineapple, juice included
1 tablespoon bottled chopped ginger or 1 teaspoon ground ginger
1 tablespoon rum (optional)
2 cups coconut sorbet
Maraschino cherries, for garnish (optional)

In a small saucepan, combine the sugar and water. Bring to a boil over medium heat, stirring only until the sugar is dissolved. Boil without stirring until the mixture turns a pale brown, about 5 minutes, taking care not to burn it. Remove from the heat and let cool a minute or so.

Stir in the pineapple with its juice and ginger;

the sugar mixture will harden. Return to medium heat and bring to a brisk simmer, stirring constantly until the sugar mixture is melted and incorporated. Cook, stirring occasionally, until the mixture is reduced to about ¾ cup, about 2 minutes. Remove from the heat and stir in the rum (if using). Let cool to room temperature. (At this point, the mixture can be stored, covered, in the refrigerator up to 3 days before serving chilled or returning to room temperature.)

Divide the sorbet evenly among 4 dessert bowls. Top each serving with about 3 tablespoons of the pineapple sauce. Garnish with a cherry, if desired, and serve at once.

PER SERVING

Calories 223 ▪ Protein 3g ▪ Total Fat 8g ▪
Sat. Fat 5g ▪ Cholesterol 0mg ▪ Carbohydrate 38g ▪
Dietary Fiber 1g ▪ Sodium 59mg

HAWAIIAN COCONUT PUDDING PIE

Vegan

MAKES 10 TO 12 SERVINGS

A coconut lover's delight, this tropical pie's richness is apparent in the first scrumptious bite. If you can't locate light coconut milk (Trader Joe's is the brand I use); I recommend using all full-fat coconut milk, rather than substituting with dairy, soy, or rice milk, for the best flavor.

½ cup cornstarch

1½ cups canned light coconut milk

1½ cups canned full-fat coconut milk

2 tablespoons vanilla extract

½ cup sugar

1 (9-inch) prepared graham cracker crust (6 ounces)

½ cup unsweetened shredded coconut

In a glass measuring cup, combine the cornstarch and ½ cup of the light coconut milk, stirring until smooth; set aside.

In a medium heavy-bottomed saucepan over medium heat, bring the remaining light coconut milk, regular coconut milk, and vanilla to a gentle simmer, stirring often. Reduce the heat to low and cook, stirring, 3 minutes. Whisk in the reserved cornstarch mixture, then the sugar. Cook, stirring constantly, until thickened, 3 to 5 minutes. Remove the pan from the heat and immediately pour the pudding mixture into the graham cracker crust. Let cool 20 minutes.

Cover the pie loosely and refrigerate until firm, a minimum of 3 hours, or up to 2 days (cover securely after 12 hours). Sprinkle evenly with the shredded coconut. Cut into wedges and serve chilled.

PER SERVING

Calories 302 ▪ Protein 3g ▪ Total Fat 16g ▪
Sat. Fat 10g ▪ Cholesterol 0mg ▪ Carbohydrate 37g ▪
Dietary Fiber 1g ▪ Sodium 162mg

MEDITERRANEAN DRIED FRUIT COMPOTE

Vegan
MAKES 4 SERVINGS

This is a wonderful dessert to make during the winter months when many fresh fruits aren't in season. Served cold, leftovers are delicious stirred into cereal or yogurt, or spooned over vanilla ice cream or nondairy frozen dessert.

½ pound unsweetened pitted dried prunes, apricots, and/or figs

¼ cup raisins

1½ cups water

¼ cup sugar

1 (2-inch) stick cinnamon

¼ teaspoon chopped dried orange peel

1 tablespoon Grand Marnier, Cointreau, or other orange liqueur (optional)

Ready-whipped cream, for topping (optional)

In a medium saucepan, bring the fruit, water, sugar, cinnamon stick, and orange peel to a boil over medium-high heat, stirring occasionally. Reduce the heat to medium-low, partially cover, and simmer, stirring occasionally, until the fruit is tender, 15 to 20 minutes. Uncover and increase the heat to medium; cook, stirring occasionally, until the liquid is reduced and syrupy, about 5 minutes. Remove from the heat and discard the cinnamon stick. Stir in the liqueur (if using). Serve warm or at room temperature, topped with whipped cream, if desired.

PER SERVING
Calories 223 ▪ Protein 2g ▪ Total Fat 0g ▪
Sat. Fat 0g ▪ Cholesterol 0mg ▪ Carbohydrate 59g ▪
Dietary Fiber 7g ▪ Sodium 12mg

TOASTED HAZELNUT ICE CREAM WITH FRANGELICO

Lacto-ovo with vegan option
MAKES 4 SERVINGS

If you are searching for a stress-free grand finale to a special meal, this is it. See the variations below for kid-friendly recipes. For a vegan alternative, use nondairy frozen dessert.

¼ cup hazelnuts

2 cups reduced-fat vanilla ice cream or nondairy frozen dessert

½ cup Frangelico or other hazelnut liqueur

Preheat oven to 350F (175C). Spread the nuts in a single layer on an ungreased baking sheet. Bake about 5 minutes, or until lightly toasted. Remove from the baking sheet and let cool a few minutes. Rub in a cotton dishcloth to remove the skins.

Divide the ice cream evenly among 4 dessert bowls or ice cream goblets. Spoon 2 tablespoons of liqueur over each serving, then top with 1 tablespoon of the nuts. Serve at once.

PER SERVING
Calories 255 ▪ Protein 4g ▪ Total Fat 9g ▪
Sat. Fat 3g ▪ Cholesterol 25mg ▪ Carbohydrate 27g ▪
Dietary Fiber 1g ▪ Sodium 40mg

Variations

Toasted Almond Ice Cream with Amaretto: Substitute ¼ cup slivered almonds for the hazelnuts and ½ cup amaretto liqueur for the Frangelico.

Mexican Ice Cream with Kahlua: Substitute ½ cup Kahlua for the Frangelico. Sprinkle each serving with a few roasted coffee beans, if desired.

Toasted Almond Ice Cream with Honey: Substitute ¼ cup slivered almonds for the hazelnuts and ½ cup honey (at room temperature) for the Frangelico.

Toasted Maple-Walnut Ice Cream: Substitute ¼ cup walnut pieces for the hazelnuts and ½ cup pure maple syrup (at room temperature) for the Frangelico.

LEMON TARTS

Lacto-ovo with dairy-free option

MAKES 6 TARTS

These tangy little no-cook lemon pies are ideal for stress-free entertaining, as they can be prepared a day ahead of serving. Jars of lemon curd (a tart, sweet, creamy filling made with eggs) can be found among the jams and jellies in most well-stocked supermarkets. Lime curd can be substituted for the lemon variety, if desired. For a dairy-free dessert, use plain soy yogurt instead of the regular variety.

1 cup prepared lemon curd, at room temperature
1 cup plain nonfat yogurt or plain soy yogurt
1 (6-crust) package ready-made graham cracker piecrusts
Ready-whipped light cream, for garnish (optional)

In a small bowl, whisk together the lemon curd and yogurt until thoroughly blended. Spoon ⅓ cup into each crust. Place on a tray, cover with plastic wrap, and refrigerate a minimum of 1 hour, or up to 1 day. Serve chilled, garnished with whipped cream, if desired.

PER SERVING
Calories 390 ■ Protein 6g ■ Total Fat 13g ■ Sat. Fat 3g ■ Cholesterol 66mg ■ Carbohydrate 63g ■ Dietary Fiber 0g ■ Sodium 297mg

Variations

Lemon Pie: Double the amounts of lemon curd and yogurt and substitute 1 (9-inch) prepared graham cracker piecrust (6 ounces) for the 6 individual crusts. Fill and serve chilled. Serves 10 to 12.

Lemon-Filled Puff Pastry Shells: Bake 1 (10-ounce) package frozen puff pastry shells (6 shells) according to package directions. When shells are completely cooled, fill. Serve chilled.

Cook's Tip In order for the lemon curd to blend easily with the yogurt, it should be at room temperature. If the lemon curd is refrigerated, immerse the tightly closed jar in a bowl of hot water a few minutes to soften.

FRESH MELON KEBOBS WITH HONEY-YOGURT SAUCE

Egg-free with vegan options
MAKES 4 TO 6 SERVINGS

This is always a light, refreshing, elegant treat during the summer months. Any fresh fruit (pineapple chunks and whole strawberries are other good choices) can replace part of the melon, if desired. For a vegan dessert, use plain soy yogurt or nondairy sour cream, and substitute light brown sugar or pure maple syrup for the honey.

1 cup plain nonfat yogurt, plain soy yogurt,
    light sour cream, or nondairy sour cream
3 tablespoons honey, light brown sugar, or
    pure maple syrup
1 tablespoon bottled lime juice
Pinch ground cinnamon
Pinch ground nutmeg
1½ pounds (about 4 cups) ready-cut fresh
    cantaloupe and/or honeydew melon
Whole mint leaves, for garnish (optional)
Unsweetened shredded coconut, for garnish
    (optional)

In a small bowl, mix together the yogurt, honey, lime juice, cinnamon, and nutmeg. (At this point, the mixture can be stored, covered, in the refrigerator up to 2 days before using.) Skewer the fruit evenly on each of 12 bamboo skewers. To serve, place the yogurt sauce in the center of a large serving platter and garnish with mint leaves, if desired. Arrange the fruit kebobs around the sauce and garnish with coconut, if desired. Serve at once.

CRUNCHY GRANOLA PEACH GRATIN

Vegan
MAKES 6 SERVINGS

This is a great dessert for casual, relaxed entertaining as it can be assembled a few hours before serving, then popped under the broiler while you brew the coffee or tea. To reduce the fat in the recipe, use low-fat granola.

⅔ cup granola
¼ cup packed light brown sugar
2 tablespoons vegetable shortening or
    butter
2 tablespoons chopped nuts (optional)
1 (29-ounce) can peach halves in light syrup,
    briefly drained
Ready-whipped cream or vanilla ice cream,
    frozen yogurt, or nondairy frozen dessert,
    for topping (optional)

Set oven to broil. Lightly grease an 8-inch-square baking dish and set aside.

In a small bowl, using your fingers or a small spoon, combine the granola, sugar, shortening, and nuts (if using). Arrange the peaches in prepared dish, cut sides up; top evenly with the granola mixture.

Broil 6 to 8 inches from heat source until lightly brown, 2 to 3 minutes, rotating a few times to evenly brown. Transfer to the bottom oven rack and turn off the oven. After a few seconds, close the oven door and leave for about 10 minutes, or until heated through. Serve warm with the toppings, if desired.

PER SERVING

Calories 240 ■ Protein 2g ■ Total Fat 8g ■
Sat. Fat 2g ■ Cholesterol 0mg ■ Carbohydrate 44g ■
Dietary Fiber 3g ■ Sodium 13mg

BAKED PEARS WITH CARAMEL AND AMARETTI

Lacto-ovo with egg-free and vegan options

MAKES 6 SERVINGS

Pears for dessert always seem special; baked in caramel, then sprinkled with crumbled amaretti, they are the perfect conclusion to an elegant meal. Amaretti, tiny biscuitlike cookies from Saronno, Italy, can be found at gourmet and Italian markets. Though their name implies otherwise, they are made from sugar, apricot kernels, and egg whites. Crumbled vanilla wafers or gingersnaps can be substituted. For an egg-free alternative, omit the cookies altogether; the dish will still be delicious. For a vegan option, see the Cook's Tip, below.

> 2 (29-ounce) cans pear halves in juice, drained (12 halves)
> ½ cup prepared caramel ice cream topping
> 6 amaretti cookies (1 ounce), crumbled

Preheat oven to 350F (175C). Lightly oil a shallow baking dish just large enough to hold the pears in a single layer. Place the pear halves, cut sides down, in prepared dish. Drizzle with the topping.

Cover with foil and bake 15 minutes, or until the pears and caramel are heated through.

Divide evenly among 6 dessert plates. Sprinkle evenly with the crumbled amaretti and serve warm.

PER SERVING

Calories 228 ■ Protein 2g ■ Total Fat 1g ■
Sat. Fat 0g ■ Cholesterol 3mg ■ Carbohydrate 57g ■
Dietary Fiber 6g ■ Sodium 121mg

Cook's Tip To make homemade caramel topping, see the recipe for German Chocolate Cake Sundaes (page 177), and prepare the topping without the coconut or pecans. You should have approximately ½ cup caramel sauce. For a vegan sauce, use soy creamer in lieu of the evaporated skim milk.

PINEAPPLE CRISP

Vegan
MAKES 6 TO 8 SERVINGS

Use this versatile crunchy topping to dress up any variety of canned fruits. Peaches are especially delicious, as are fresh berries.

- 2 (20-ounce) cans juice-packed pineapple chunks, drained, ½ cup juice reserved
- 2 tablespoons granulated sugar
- ½ cup rolled oats (do not use instant variety)
- ½ cup unbleached all-purpose flour
- ½ cup packed light brown sugar
- ¾ teaspoon ground cinnamon
- ¼ teaspoon ground nutmeg
- 5 tablespoons vegetable shortening or butter, softened, in 5 pieces

Preheat oven to 375F (190C). Lightly oil an 8-inch-square baking dish.

Arrange the pineapple in the prepared dish and add the reserved juice. Sprinkle evenly with the granulated sugar and set aside.

In a medium bowl, combine the oats, flour, brown sugar, cinnamon, and nutmeg. With a fork or your fingers, work the shortening into the dry ingredients until the mixture resembles coarse meal. Sprinkle the topping evenly over the pineapple. Bake 20 to 25 minutes, or until the topping is lightly browned.

Let cool slightly. Serve warm or at room temperature.

PER SERVING
Calories 360 ■ Protein 3g ■ Total Fat 11g ■ Sat. Fat 4g ■ Cholesterol 0mg ■ Carbohydrate 64g ■ Dietary Fiber 2g ■ Sodium 10mg

RASPBERRIES WITH AMARETTO CREAM

Lacto-ovo with vegan options
MAKES 4 SERVINGS

This is a truly divine dessert, ideal for elegant summertime entertaining. For an exotic vegan variation, use coconut milk in lieu of the heavy cream and omit the sponge tarts.

- ½ tablespoon cornstarch
- 2 tablespoons amaretto liqueur
- ¾ cup heavy cream or canned coconut milk
- 2 tablespoons sugar
- 4 packaged small sponge tarts
- 1⅓ cups fresh raspberries or blackberries

In a small bowl, dissolve the cornstarch in the amaretto and whisk until smooth.

In a small saucepan, bring the cream to a simmer over medium heat. Add the amaretto mixture and cook, whisking constantly, 1 minute. Reduce the heat to low and cook, whisking constantly, until slightly thickened, 1 minute. Remove from the heat and add the sugar. Whisk until the sugar is dissolved. Let cool to room temperature. (At this point, the mixture may be stored, covered, in the refrigerator up to 2 days before using. Serve chilled or return to room temperature.)

To serve, place a sponge tart on each of 4 dessert plates. Top each tart with ⅓ cup of the berries. Spoon about ¼ cup of sauce over each serving. Serve at once.

MINI RASPBERRY PHYLLO TARTS

Egg-free with vegan option
MAKES 15 MINI TARTS

This virtually assembled dessert is a light and lovely addition to any summertime buffet when fresh raspberries are in season. Any berry preserve and corresponding whole fruit can be substituted for the raspberry. Create vegan tarts by using nondairy cream cheese; Tofutti makes an excellent brand.

1 (2.1-ounce) package frozen mini phyllo dough shells (15 shells)
5 tablespoons light cream cheese or nondairy cream cheese
2½ tablespoons all-fruit raspberry preserves
15 fresh raspberries
15 small fresh mint leaves, preferably spearmint, for garnish (optional)

Bake the phyllo shells according to package directions. Cool completely.

Fill each shell with 1 teaspoon of the cream cheese. Top with ½ teaspoon of the preserves. (At this point, the phyllo shells may be stored, covered, in the refrigerator up to 3 hours before serving.) Just before serving, top each tart with a raspberry. Garnish each with a small whole mint leaf, if desired.

COCONUT STICKY RICE PUDDING

Vegan
MAKES 6 TO 8 SERVINGS

Versions of this rich and creamy dessert appear in one form or another in several Asian cultures. Sticky, or glutinous, rice is available in Asian markets and many well-stocked supermarkets.

1 cup sticky (glutinous) rice
2 cups water
1½ cups canned light coconut milk
½ cup sugar
¼ teaspoon salt
Canned mandarin orange segments or pineapple chunks, drained (optional)

Rinse the rice in cold water twice; drain. Transfer the rice to a medium saucepan and add the water. Bring to a boil over high heat. Reduce the heat to medium and cook, stirring occasionally, until thick and soupy, 8 to 10 minutes. Add the coconut milk, sugar, and salt. Bring to a gentle simmer over medium-high heat. Reduce the heat to low and cook, stirring constantly, 3 minutes. Remove from the heat and let cool slightly. Serve warm or at room temperature, garnished with the mandarin orange segments, if desired. Alternatively, cover and refrigerate up to 3 days and serve chilled.

PER SERVING
Calories 278 ■ Protein 4g ■ Total Fat 10g ■
Sat. Fat 9g ■ Cholesterol 0mg ■ Carbohydrate 45g ■
Dietary Fiber 1g ■ Sodium 108mg

MEXICAN RICE PUDDING

Egg-free with vegan option
MAKES 6 SERVINGS

This fragrant and ultra-creamy pudding is an ideal way to cap off a Mexican-style meal. While any cooked rice works well, I prefer the chewy texture and nutty nuance of the brown variety. For a delicious vegan option, use rice milk or equal parts rice milk and light coconut milk in lieu of the low-fat milk.

- 1¾ cups low-fat milk or rice milk and/or canned light coconut milk
- ¼ cup orange juice
- 2 cups cooked rice, preferably the brown variety (see Cook's Tip, page 126, on cooking rice)
- ½ cup sugar
- ⅓ cup dark raisins
- ¼ cup unsweetened shredded coconut (optional)
- ½ teaspoon vanilla extract
- ½ teaspoon grated dried orange peel
- 1 whole cinnamon stick

In a medium saucepan, combine the milk, orange juice, rice, sugar, raisins, coconut (if using), vanilla, orange peel, and cinnamon stick. Bring to a gentle simmer over medium heat, stirring often.

Reduce the heat to medium-low and cook, stirring often, until thickened and creamy, 20 to 30 minutes, or until desired consistency. Remove from the heat and let cool 1 hour. Remove the cinnamon stick and stir well. Serve just warm or at room temperature.

Alternatively, cover and refrigerate a minimum of 2 hours and serve chilled.

PER SERVING
Calories 197 ■ Protein 4g ■ Total Fat 1g ■
Sat. Fat 1g ■ Cholesterol 3mg ■ Carbohydrate 43g ■
Dietary Fiber 2g ■ Sodium 38mg

Variation

Old-Fashioned Rice Pudding: Omit the orange juice, optional coconut, vanilla extract, orange peel, and cinnamon stick. Add ½ teaspoon ground cinnamon and ⅛ teaspoon ground nutmeg when you combine the milk, rice, sugar, and raisins. Proceed as otherwise directed in the recipe.

CHOCOLATE-DIPPED STRAWBERRIES

Egg-free
MAKES 12 STRAWBERRIES

The long-stemmed roses of the food world, chocolate-dipped strawberries are the quintessence of elegance.

- ½ cup semisweet chocolate chips
- 6 tablespoons heavy cream
- 12 large long-stemmed strawberries

Line a flat surface or tray with parchment or waxed paper and set aside.

Place the chocolate and cream in the top of a

double boiler set over barely simmering water. When the chocolate is melted, stir until well combined and remove from the heat. Dip each strawberry in the chocolate, coating about three-fourths of the flesh, and set aside on the paper to dry. Serve at once or refrigerate, covered, up to 24 hours.

PER STRAWBERRY
Calories 113 ▪ Protein 1g ▪ Total Fat 6g ▪
Sat. Fat 3g ▪ Cholesterol 10mg ▪ Carbohydrate 16g ▪
Dietary Fiber 4g ▪ Sodium 5mg

In a small bowl, stir together the preserves and liqueur until well combined. Gently stir in the orange segments. To serve, spoon alternating layers of ¼ cup of the ice cream, 1½ tablespoons of the sauce, ¼ cup of the ice cream, then 1½ tablespoons of the sauce into 6 parfait or wine glasses. Garnish with whipped cream and/or a decorative wafer, if desired. Serve at once.

PER SERVING
Calories 239 ▪ Protein 3g ▪ Total Fat 4g ▪
Sat. Fat 3g ▪ Cholesterol 25mg ▪ Carbohydrate 45g ▪
Dietary Fiber 1g ▪ Sodium 56mg

STRAWBERRY-ORANGE PARFAITS

Lacto-ovo with vegan option
MAKES 6 SERVINGS

Top-notch strawberry preserves make quick work of this pretty ice cream dessert. For a vegan alternative, use nondairy frozen dessert.

- ¾ cup good-quality strawberry preserves, such as Bonne Maman, at room temperature
- 2 tablespoons Grand Marnier, Cointreau, or other orange-flavored liqueur, or 2 tablespoons orange juice
- ¼ cup canned mandarin orange segments, drained
- 3 cups (1½ pints) reduced-fat vanilla ice cream, frozen yogurt, or nondairy frozen dessert
- Ready-whipped cream (optional)
- Decorative wafers or thin fluted cookies (optional)

FRUITED TAPIOCA PUDDING

Vegan

MAKES 6 SERVINGS

This refreshing pudding is a splendid ending to a spicy meal. You can omit all or part of the fruit, if you prefer.

½ cup sugar
¼ cup quick-cooking tapioca
2½ cups orange juice
½ cup canned mandarin orange segments, drained
½ cup canned diced pineapple, drained
¼ cup chopped pitted dates or raisins

In a medium saucepan, stir together the sugar, tapioca, and orange juice. Let stand 5 minutes. Bring to a boil over medium heat, stirring constantly. Remove from the heat and let cool slightly. Add the orange segments, pineapple, and dates; stir gently yet thoroughly to combine. Transfer to a dessert bowl or 6 individual dessert dishes. Cover and refrigerate a minimum of 3 hours, or overnight. Serve chilled.

PER SERVING
Calories 173 ■ Protein 1g ■ Total Fat 0g ■
Sat. Fat 0g ■ Cholesterol 0mg ■ Carbohydrate 44g ■
Dietary Fiber 1g ■ Sodium 2mg

Index